HUMAN RESOURCE MANAGEMENT AND
ORGANIZATION BEHAVIOR

Human Resource Management and Organization Behavior

Selected perspectives

AHARON TZINER
School of Business Administration
Netanya University College, Israel

Ashgate

Published by
Ashgate Publishing Limited
Gower House
Croft Road
Aldershot
Hampshire GU11 3HR
England

Ashgate Publishing Company
131 Main Street
Burlington, VT 05401-5600 USA

Ashgate website: http://www.ashgate.com

British Library Cataloguing in Publication Data
Tziner, Aharon
    Human resource management and organization
    behavior : selected perspectives
    1.Personnel management 2.Organizational
    behavior
    I.Title
    658.3

Library of Congress Control Number: 2001094286

ISBN 0 7546 1897 8

Printed and bound in Great Britain by Antony Rowe Ltd.,
Chippenham, Wiltshire.

Contents

List of Figures

List of Tables

Preface

In an increasingly changing and competitive economic market, most corporate managers and human resource personnel would agree that their most precious asset is the human component of the organization. Indeed, there is considerable evidence that the effective handling of human resources and attentive management of human organizational behavior are critical means for achieving a 'firm sustainable advantage'. For example, in an investigation of over 2,000 workplaces in the United Kingdom, it was reported that human resources practices substantially impacted on the economic performance of the companies. In fact, it has been claimed that in the twenty-first century companies will attain sustainable economic viability and thrive solely on the basis of the employment of highly competent human resources personnel and the careful monitoring of effective employee organizational behavior.

The rationale behind this premise is that the resources needed to operate an organization, such as financial capital, technology, raw materials, and information, are readily replicated. That is to say, there is no singular correspondence between them and a particular company. In contrast, human resources are unique to each organization.

Two disciplines target the human aspect of organizational endeavor: Human Resource Management (HRM) and Organizational Behavior Management (OBM). HRM develops theoretical knowledge and methodologies regarding the creation, fostering, and embellishing of human assets. OBM attempts to understand human behavior in organizations and its effects on productivity, investigating areas such as motivation, leadership, the evolution of work attitudes, and interpersonal relations in work teams.

The goals of this book are thus twofold:

1   to present an integrative review of the leading trends and findings in selected and salient aspects of these disciplines;
2   to connect these aspects into a unified comprehensive framework.

The book consists of seven chapters covering topics which, in the judgment of the author, represent areas of intense research that has yielded the most highly applicative results. Moreover, these subject areas appear to lend themselves to the goal of integrating the disciplines of HRM and OBM.

Chapter 1 – Job Evaluation

This chapter expands on the tools and procedures used for assessing the functional capabilities of an individual to meet an organization's requirements. The instruments, which are compared and contrasted in terms of their suitability and effectiveness, include: (1) biodata; (2) reference checks; (3) interviews; (4) psychological tests; (5) graphological tests; (6) situational tests; (7) peer evaluation; and (8) assessment centers. Special attention is given to an evaluation of the contribution of the last of these instruments.

Chapter 2 – Work Interests

This relatively unexplored field is treated in depth as an example of the significance of both intrinsic and extrinsic rewards as a key motivating factor and source of adjustment for employees at work. The chapter incorporates a conceptual framework for understanding the nature of interests, how they evolve, how they are clustered, and how they are best measured.

Chapter 3 – Work Adjustment: Essence and Outcomes

This chapter discusses factors involved in an employee's successful adaptation to both the job and the organization, including: (1) the degree to which the work environment suits the employee; and (2) the extent to which individuals meet job requirements and organizational expectations, and experience the fulfillment of work-related needs, as antecedents to work adjustment. Particular attention is paid here to some of the affective and behavioral concomitants of maladjustment. The two major theories describing the various attitudinal and behavioral outcomes of fit/misfit are then reviewed and incorporated into a single theoretical framework.

Chapter 4 – Perspectives on Groups and Work Teams in the Workplace

Various models of group functioning have been adapted for analyzing the growing phenomenon of teamwork in organizations. This chapter highlights both classical and contemporary research on groups, especially small instrumental teams operating in real time situations, focusing on: (1) the relationship between group members' traits, interests, and competencies on the one hand, and work requirements and rewards on the other; and (2) the relationship between work team processes, group adjustment, and performance. An attempt is then made to consolidate the various areas of research on teamwork into an integrative, comprehensive program of theoretical and empirical endeavor.

Chapter 5 – Organization Staffing Methods and Instruments

The purpose of job evaluation is to rank all jobs in a given organization and arrange them according to their contribution to organizational goals. Thus job evaluation is essentially about jobs, rather than employees. However, a fair, systematic evaluation leads to a clear and judicious allocation of human and economic resources, reduces sources of conflict, enhances administration, and promotes efficiency. This chapter presents a critical review of the various tools available for the analysis and systematic comparison of the tasks and requirements involved in the different jobs in an organization.

Chapter 6 – Performance Appraisal

Successful performance is not only gratifying in terms of productivity; it is also an objective indicant of the success of an individual employee's adjustment to the workplace. The results of performance appraisals may thus also be used to foster modifications of work behavior. This chapter discusses the virtues of different methods of appraisal, in terms of their internal qualities and reliability, rater bias and error, rater and ratee satisfaction with the system, and employee outcomes such as level of motivation and commitment, and goal identification. Special attention is paid to the contextual and perceived political ramifications of the appraisal process, and to methods for identifying and measuring political beliefs in the workplace.

Chapter 7 – Assessing the Financial Value of Worker Organizational Behaviors and Human Resource Management Programs and Interventions

Is it financially worthwhile to embark on programs that use a battery of tools to screen suitable potential employees? To what extent and in which circumstances should organizations initiate procedures such as downsizing that are aimed at rationalizing the organization's functioning and improving long-term productivity? What are the financial concomitants of maladjustment? This chapter explores the ramifications of such questions and outlines the use of innovative and empirically tested mathematical tools that enable HRM practitioners to assist in executive decisions and contribute to the cost benefit analyses in their organizations.

In each of the following chapters, the reader will find both useful state-of-the-art research findings, and judicious advice regarding the possible applications of this knowledge. It is hoped that the book will therefore be of benefit to students of HRM, OBM, and I/O Psychology, as well as to managers and human resource practitioners. Through a careful study of the different areas of human resources in the workplace, the reader will be better prepared to understand and cope with obstacles to the effective utilization of human resources. Moreover, he or she will also be equipped with a rich store of conceptual tools and practical skills with which to enhance the productivity and goals of their organizations.

Acknowledgments

Very special thanks are due to Menahem Persoff for his help in preparing this book, and to Sara Kitai for her excellent editorial work.

I would also like to extend my appreciation to Valerie Kedem, who patiently typed the manuscript.

Finally, I am grateful to the Israel Science Foundation for having awarded me a research grant which has been used in part to support the writing of this book.

1 Job Evaluation

AHARON TZINER AND ELISABETH BARANOVSKY

Definition

Job evaluation is a procedure which enables an organization to implement a systematic pay scale by positioning each of its jobs in relation to the others on the basis of differences in the importance of assigned tasks (Campion and Berger, 1990). The resulting pay scale should be considered fair by all members of the organization, and should guarantee equal compensation for work of equal value (or comparable worth). The methodology is based on analyzing and comparing the tasks and requirements intrinsic to each job. In order to ensure a systematic comparison, individual abilities and performances must be completely disregarded: job evaluation is about jobs, not employees.

Objectives

The principle objectives of job evaluation are as follows:

1 to establish a job hierarchy aimed primarily at enabling an organization to allocate its budget for salaries in as equitable a manner as possible;
2 to ensure that all members of the organization share the same view of the relative value of each job.

   Job evaluation is generally undertaken when organizations become aware of one or more of the following situations:

1 identical tasks are not being equally compensated, perhaps resulting in conflicts in the work place;
2 reorganization of some sort (such as a merger) has rendered it necessary to put into place a more coherent pay scale;
3 technological innovation (such as the introduction of new equipment) has changed the nature of certain jobs, hence requiring their re-evaluation;
4 a situation of gender-based salary discrimination must be redressed (one of the most common motives of job evaluation at this time).

Employing a method of job evaluation that is both systematic and perceived as fair by all parties affected is in the best interests of an organization. Not only does the implementation of an appropriate method enhance salary administration, but job analysis and job description, two stages in the job evaluation process, also promote a more rational allocation of budgets, as well as a more judicious organization of work.

Job Analysis

The first phase in any method of job evaluation is to examine and analyze the tasks and activities associated with each job. This is known as job analysis, and its aim is to identify the essential characteristics of a job. Once job requirements are defined, the employee is better able to discharge his or her duties satisfactorily. Certain precise and indispensable information must be gathered. As a rule, this includes:

1   the objectives of each of the various tasks associated with the job;
2   the frequency of each task;
3   the tools and equipment to be used;
4   the nature and degree of responsibility entrusted to the employee;
5   the environment and other working conditions.

The next step is to determine the prerequisite skills, qualifications, and personal attitudes of the individual chosen to carry out the duties associated with each job. This information can be obtained through observation or by means of interviews conducted by a supervisor. It may then be used to establish precise, unambiguous job descriptions. In order to maximize accuracy, a standardized format can be employed to record these descriptions. The choice of a particular method of evaluation is generally made on the basis of considerations such as the number and type of jobs in the organization, the cost of the project, the resources available, and the degree of precision sought.

Methods

Job evaluation techniques fall into two major categories: global methods and factor specific methods. The first involves evaluating a job in its entirety and comparing it to others so as to establish its rank in a job hierarchy. The second consists of breaking down the basic characteristics of a job into different factors and performing a factor-by-factor comparison.

Global Methods

Global methods of job evaluation may employ one of two main techniques: ranking or classification.

Ranking method Using this technique, the sole criteria for positioning jobs in the hierarchy are their relative complexity and value as defined by the organization. It is thus the function of the job, rather than its distinctive aspects, which is taken into consideration.

This method has the advantages of being simple, fast, and inexpensive. However, although it is easy both to introduce and maintain, it is not very exact, since it fails to clearly indicate the differences between jobs. As a result, the method is of little value when there are a large number of jobs to be evaluated. Moreover, criteria may be imprecise, ambiguous, or, quite simply, unspecified. And last but not least, the evaluators may find themselves influenced by elements which are unrelated to the job in question.

Classification method This procedure differs from the ranking method in that the order of the steps is reversed: it begins by defining the classes into which the various jobs are to be grouped. These classes, which take the form of a graduated scale, reflect levels of complexity, responsibility, qualifications, and skills. The CREPID Scale (Appendix 1.1) illustrates such a definition.

This method is more standardized than the ranking technique, since the criteria used to evaluate the job descriptions are specified. However, the most significant, and most difficult, procedure here is to decide on the number, structure, and definition of classes, or the criteria to be employed in evaluating the importance of each job. The U.S. Federal Classification System, for example, employs the following eight factors:

1   Difficulty and Variety of Work;
2   Supervision Received;
3   Judgment;
4   Resourcefulness;
5   Nature and Goal of Professional Relations;
6   Responsibility;
7   Experience;
8   Knowledge.

Classification is relatively simple and inexpensive to implement, and can be applied to a large number of jobs. It is also superior to the ranking method in terms of precision and objectivity, as well as being more adaptable, since new or modified jobs may be readily arranged according to the predetermined classes. Its chief drawback, however, is that subjective judgment enters the job evaluation process at the very start, due to the difficulty of formulating clear definitions of classes.

Factor Specific Methods

The same simplicity mentioned above as one of the chief advantages of global methods may have a negative impact on their justifiability. Indeed, it is often very hard to explain why an organization attributes greater importance to one job than to another. As a result, the use of global methods for job evaluation may trigger conflicts in the work place. Furthermore, since global methods assume that the evaluators are totally familiar with each and every job, they are often of little use when there is a large variety of jobs requiring classification. In order to overcome these deficiencies, it may be preferable to employ one of the techniques based on the examination of specific factors. With this kind of method, the various job functions are broken down into factors common to all jobs, each factor is assigned a point value, and the total number of points ascribed to each job indicates its relative value to the organization. Factor specific methods are both more rigorous and more precise than global methods, and, in addition, yield job and wage hierarchies that score highly with regard to perceived validity. The two principal factor specific techniques are factor comparison and the point method.

Factor comparison This technique consists of classifying the various jobs according to factors, each of which is assigned a monetary value. Pay levels are thus directly determined by job classification. The procedure entails the following steps:

1 selection of a set of 'key' jobs;
2 classification of the key jobs (in relation to each other) according to a series of factors;
3 assignment of a monetary value to the factors based upon the salaries allotted to the key jobs;
4 classification of other jobs and calculation of their salaries accordingly.

In order to illustrate this method, let us assume that an organization has selected four key jobs and the evaluation committee has ranked them on five evaluation factors as follows:

FACTOR⟍ JOB	Overall salary	Mental require-ments	Skill require-ments	Responsi-bility for human perfor-mance	Physical require-ments	Responsi-bility for material assets
Line Manager	$ 1,600	3	3	4	2	4
Quality Control Technician	$ 1,400	4	4	3	4	1
Secretary	$ 1,000	1	1	1	3	2
Personnel Clerk	$ 2,000	2	2	2	1	3

Table 1.1 Illustration of the monotonic relationship of two facets

The committee then assigns a monetary value to each factor by dividing the overall salary of each key job by the sum of its ranks across factors. Thus in this example, the line manager's overall salary is $1,600 per month which is to be divided by the total score for this job, 16, making the monetary value of one rank $100.

$$\frac{1,600}{(3+3+4+2+4)} = \frac{1,600}{16} = 100$$

Consequently, $300 is allocated to mental requirements, $300 to skill requirements, $400 to responsibility for human performance, $200 to physical requirements, and $400 to responsibility for material assets.

These figures then become the standards for evaluating other jobs in the organization. For example, the job of Salesperson might be judged similar to Line Manager in respect to mental requirements, to Quality Control Technician in respect to skill requirements, to Secretary in respect to responsibility for human performance and physical requirements, and to Personnel Clerk in respect to responsibility for material assets. The salary for this job would then be calculated as follows:

$$300 + 350 + 500 + 600 = \$1,750$$

The job comparisons generated by this technique are both more objective and more systematic than those which emerge from global methods. However, the choice of key jobs is an arbitrary one, and assigned monetary values may be difficult to justify.

Point method This job evaluation procedure is the most widely implemented internationally. Using this approach, the position of each job within the organizational hierarchy is determined by assigning points to a series of distinct factors. Each point is equivalent to a fixed monetary value, so that the total number of points obtained by a job, multiplied by the monetary value of one point, yields the job's salary. The same formula is applied to each job to generate the entire pay scale. However, there are no fixed rules as to the factors which should be selected or the relative weights which should be assigned to them. Surprisingly enough, job evaluation programs are often modeled, albeit with certain modifications, after a scheme designed in the U.S. in the 1930s for the National Metal Trades Association. Some of the factors most frequently employed include: knowledge, experience, initiative, directives, effort, interpersonal relations, and working conditions.

In order to ensure a reasonable level of accuracy, it is vital that a very rigorous step-by-step procedure be followed, namely:

1 *Selecting factors*: The factors must be defined with the utmost precision. Thus, for example, 'knowledge' might place a value on the degree of formally acquired knowledge and specialized training needed to perform or learn the tasks associated with a particular job. Only that knowledge specifically applicable to the job should be considered.
2 *Determining degrees*: Degrees must also be strictly defined so as to enable evaluators to assign them in the most objective manner possible. In the case of 'knowledge', for instance, the scale for a specific job might be:
    - Degree 1: training equivalent to a general or professional high school diploma
    - Degree 2: one or two years of post-secondary education
    - Degree 3: an education equivalent to a bachelor's degree in science, administration, industrial relations, economics, social sciences, etc.
    - Degree 4: an education equivalent to a master's degree in science, administration, industrial relations, economics, social sciences, etc.
3 *Weighting the factors*: The objective of weighting the different factors is to establish their relative importance in performing the tasks associated with a specific job. This is determined by means of an evaluation committee,

whose role it is to classify the factors in order of importance and allocate each a percentage of the total worth of the job.

4   *Assigning point values to the degrees*: Once the percentage of each factor has been established, a certain number of points must be allotted to each degree. One of three approaches can be used:
   –   arithmetic progression (5, 10, 15, 20, …)
   –   geometric progression (5, 10, 20, 40, …)
   –   variable progression (5, 10, 25, 35, …).

An illustration of the point method (prepared by E. Baranovsky) appears in Appendix 1.2.

The point method offers several advantages. Above all, it is systematic and gives the impression of being highly objective, thus producing job structures that are both precise and justifiable. Moreover, it can be applied to different kinds of jobs, and is relatively simple to introduce and maintain. Finally, when job value is measured by points, it is a simple matter to convert job classes into salaries.

These advantages notwithstanding, it must be remembered that the selection and weighting of factors, their subdivision into degrees, and the assignment of point values to the degrees and monetary values to the points, are not scientific processes; on the contrary, they are based on the assessments of evaluation committees. In other words, they rely entirely on the pragmatic judgment of individuals who must draw on their knowledge of the operations of the organization, which may be imperfect. As such, although the point method might appear more objective than global procedures, arbitrariness, subjectivity, and human error are nevertheless present at every stage of its application.

Other Factor Specific Methods of Job Evaluation

Two other methods based on the examination of factors are also in use: the Hay Method and the Facets Method.

The Hay Method   The Hay procedure is similar to the point method, but makes use of a collection of data which is richer and more concrete. This design employs only three factors, problem-solving, know-how and accountability, which are then divided into eight sub-factors.

The first factor, problem-solving, refers to the degree to which the employee is required to analyze, evaluate, reason and draw conclusions in order to successfully discharge the responsibilities of a particular job. It is composed of two sub-factors:

1   the degree of discretion called for in the performance of a specific job;
2   the degree of complex reasoning necessary to successfully carry out the responsibilities of the job.

The second factor, know-how, consists of three sub-factors:

1   the abilities and skills essential to accomplish the tasks associated with a job;
2   the proficiency required to coordinate and integrate the work of other employees;
3   the need to motivate others.

The third factor, accountability, also contains three sub-factors:

1   the autonomy of action intrinsic to the job;
2   the nature of the contribution the job to the end results of the organization;
3   the economic value of the unit(s) affected by the job.

After the job descriptions have been completed, the procedure essentially follows that of the point method, with the exception that evaluation of the eight sub-factors relies on the assessments of a number of different evaluators whose conceptual premises do not necessarily coincide. As a result, there may not be a high level of agreement between evaluators, a situation that may eventually result in opposition to the final product of the job ranking procedure.

The Guttman Facet Method The factors employed here, referred to as 'facets', must meet certain criteria. First, they must be monotonically related; that is, as the values of one factor increase, the values of the others may not decrease. The following diagram illustrates how two factors, Professional Work Knowledge and Work Experience, might meet these criteria.

The Guttman method also requires stability, that is, the factors must facilitate a job differentiation which is reliable enough to generate the same job hierarchy regardless of which evaluators are responsible for the evaluation. The final exigency of this technique is universality. In other words, the factors/facets must be applicable to all jobs and not merely to specific ones.

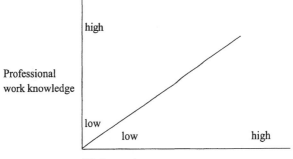

Figure 1.1   **The geographical representation of the monotonic
relationship between two facets**

According to Guttman, the following four factors/facets meet all these criteria:

1   the type of instructions given the employee for fulfilling her or his duties, whether detailed instructions, general instructions, general guidelines, or no instructions at all (i.e., freedom to determine procedures);
2   the level of supervision, i.e., the degree to which supervision is strict during the course of the execution of tasks. More specifically, this facet relates to the restriction of freedom of action imposed through the intensity of supervision exercised during the process of work execution. The possibilities here are: work performance involves following instructions, work performance involves taking advice, or the employee enjoys the freedom to choose his or her advisor;
3   the frequency of control to which the employee is subject, whether throughout the entire work process (direct and permanent), when the work is completed (unrelated to task performance), or periodically;
4   the freedom to effect changes, ranging from the obligation to operate entirely according to standard job procedures (i.e., no discretion to introduce changes), the possibility of changing or interpreting material, information/ data, or the opportunity to devise (create) new elements.

The four facets and their degrees are illustrated in Appendix 1.3. As can be seen there, the various degrees of each facet form a Guttman scale, as their arrangement is both hierarchical and cumulative.

The permutations of degrees contained in the four facets combine to generate a job hierarchy which is determined by the level of restriction of the freedom of action placed on the job. For example, the holder of the job corresponding to 'profile 4333' receives no instructions (enjoys the freedom to determine his/her own procedures), is subject to only periodic control, is free to create new elements within the framework of the job, and is independent of supervision. This job occupies a superior position in the hierarchy than that which fits 'profile 1111', in which the employee must follow detailed directions while performing his/her work, discharges all duties according to precise instructions, is under constant control throughout the entire work process, and always operates in conformity with standard work procedures. A more detailed exposition of this method can be found in Elizur's (1987) excellent book.

Reservations and Recommendations

The primary goal of the various evaluation techniques is to produce an instrument that can be used to evaluate jobs objectively. However, since they all rely on the assessments of evaluation committees or experts, none of them succeed entirely in achieving this goal, as evaluation implies judgment, and judgment unavoidably involves subjectivity. Certain methods attempt to circumscribe the element of arbitrariness by providing precise definitions of factors, and these may be said to come closer than others in achieving the goal of objective evaluation. Nonetheless, arbitrary and subjective measures will always be present, and one can only attempt to reduce their impact at various stages of the process. The following recommendations may be helpful in achieving this end.

Training

It is essential that the individuals assigned the task of analyzing, writing descriptions of, and evaluating jobs receive adequate prior training. Such preparation both familiarizes them with the cognitive processes which are at work in the course of evaluation, and provides them with a set of tools that may enable them to eliminate, or at least reduce, the effects of the biases that spring from these processes.

Harvey and Lozada-Larsen (1980) show that the quantity of descriptive data significantly influences the precision of job analysis and, indirectly, job description. Similarly, Smith, Benson and Hornsby (1990) clearly demonstrate the effect of priority in the integration of the information contained in descriptions. In their research, the order in which information was presented had a significant impact on evaluation, with jobs whose descriptions first listed positive information receiving higher evaluations than those whose descriptions began negatively. In addition, they reported that during the evaluation process, individuals displayed a tendency to utilize a model of information integration that computed the 'algebraic mean' of received information in the same manner as one which calculated its sum. Mount and Ellis (1987) found that knowledge of the pay level of a job had a bearing on its evaluation: the greater the remuneration, the higher the evaluation. Two other studies, by Schwab and Grams (1985) and Grams and Schwab (1985), reached the same conclusion. In examining the effect of gender, Mount and Ellis (1987) discovered that job evaluation had a significantly favorable effect on female-predominant jobs, although Grams and Schwab (1985) entertain the possibility of an indirect bias stemming from a knowledge of the pay scales of female-predominant and male-predominant jobs. Finally, according to Hahn and Dipboye (1988), individuals who received prior training were able to provide job evaluations that were significantly superior in terms of reliability and accuracy.

Materials

In order to maximize objectivity, standardized forms should be used to collect data regarding jobs and their descriptions. If indeed, as indicated by the studies cited above, the structure of job descriptions has a significant impact on evaluation, then standardizing the order of data presentation may represent a means of controlling this effect.

Evaluators

In order to counteract the influence of differences in values, evaluation committees should be composed of an equal number of men and women.

Factors

The factors and their different degrees should be clearly defined.

Job Information Checklist

In view of all the considerations presented above, we offer the following guidelines for preparing a job-evaluation instrument:

1 employ a non-sexist method of data collection for female-predominant jobs;
2 ensure that those responsible for interviews and for the design of questionnaires are conscious of the problems attributable to sexism;
3 maintain an awareness of the distinctive features of both female-predominant and male-predominant jobs;
4 make sure that the descriptions of both female-predominant and male-predominant jobs are uniformly precise;
5 guarantee the objectivity and fairness of the content of questionnaires, job descriptions, and job information summaries;
6 avoid ambiguous statements (e.g., 'perform other required tasks') which add no information of use to the evaluation procedure;
7 compile a detailed list of all equipment used in both female-predominant and male-predominant jobs;
8 verify that all job titles are both correct and non-sexist;
9 enumerate the functions intrinsic to each job. Describe the job, not the employee.

Conclusion

Despite the fact that job evaluation is inevitably based on subjective judgments and thus cannot pretend to universal objectivity (Collins and Muchinsky, 1993), it clearly has considerable advantages.

1 It is a logical methodology which facilitates the hierarchical classification of jobs.
2 It minimizes arbitrary decision-making in respect to wage determination, thereby reducing the element of unfairness which may be inherent in a salary scale.
3 It leads to a reduction in the number of grievances.
4 It provides a basis for dealing with potential complaints.
5 It enables new jobs to be positioned within the hierarchy of an organization.
6 It creates, in the form of the information collected during the job analysis

and job description stages, a foundation for all aspects of personnel management (recruiting, training, etc.).

Thus, despite its weaknesses and the added expense to the organization, job evaluation remains the only device presently available for maximizing the equitableness of a payroll policy. In other words, it should be part of any method designed to ensure equal compensation for work of equal value.

References

Campion, M.A. and Berger, C.J. (1990). 'Conceptual integration and empirical test of job design and compensation relationships'. *Personnel Psychology*, 43, pp. 525–54.

Collins, J.M. and Muchinsky, P.M. (1993). 'An assessment of the construct validity of three job evaluation methods: A field experiment'. *Academy of Management Journal*, 36, pp. 895–904.

Elizur, D. (1987). *Systematic Job Evaluation and Comparable Worth*. Aldershot, Hampshire: Gower.

Grams, R. and Schwab, D.P. (1985). 'An investigation of systematic gender-related error in job evaluation'. *Academy of Management Journal*, 28, pp. 279–90.

Hahn, D.C. and Dipboye, R.L. (1988). 'Effects of training and information in the accuracy and reliability of job evaluations'. *Journal of Applied Psychology*, 73, pp. 146–53.

Harvey, R.J. and Lozada-Larsen, S.R. (1980). 'Influence of amount of job descriptive information on job analysis rating accuracy'. *Journal of Applied Psychology*, 40, pp. 85–95.

Mount, M.K. and Ellis, R.A. (1987). 'Investigation of bias in job evaluation ratings of comparable worth study participants'. *Personnel Psychology*, 40, pp. 85–95.

Rynes, S.L, Weber, C.L. and Milkovich, G.T. (1989). 'Effects of market survey rates, job evaluation, and job gender on job pay'. *Journal of Applied Psychology*, 74, pp. 96–104.

Schitt, N. and Cohen, S.A. (1989). 'Internal analyses of task ratings by job incumbents'. *Journal of Applied Psychology*, 74, pp. 96–104.

Schwab, D.P. and Grams, P. (1985). 'Sex-related errors in job evaluation: A real-world test'. *Journal of Applied Psychology*, 75, pp. 301–9.

Smith, B.N., Benson, P.G. and Hornsby, J.S. (1990). 'The effects of job description content on job evaluation judgments'. *Journal of Applied Psychology*, 75, pp. 301–9.

APPENDIX 1.1

CREPID SCALE: LEVEL OF DIFFICULTY
(management jobs)

Level Definition

0   The inputs, outputs, tools, equipment and procedures are specified. The totality of skills required by the employee is included in the description of tasks. The employee is responsible for a specific quantity of work or a given number of units per hour or per day.

1   The inputs, outputs, tools and equipment are specified but the employee retains a certain leeway with regard to the procedures and methods to be used in the performance of tasks. All the required information is found in the description of tasks. The level of production is measured on a daily or weekly basis.

2   The inputs and outputs are specified, but the employee has a large degree of latitude with regard to procedures and management of time, including the utilization of tools and equipment. She or he must refer to certain information sources (manuals, catalogs, charts). The time required to realize a quantity of work is stipulated, with an allowance of a few hours.

3   The output is specified in the task description, which itself may be in the form of either of a memo or a diagram (a sketch or operational plan). The employee is responsible for devising the means of fulfilling the task, including the selection of tools and equipment, the determination of procedures and the acquisition of the necessary information (manuals, etc.). She or he may either undertake to perform the work personally, or may determine the criteria and procedure to be followed by others.

4   The same definition applies as for the previous level but it is also expected that the employee will be familiar with and will make use of certain theories in order to understand the attributes of the different options for solving a particular problem. It is furthermore assumed that she or he will be capable of choosing from among those options. The employee may be called upon to do some reading (professional or commercial literature) in order to acquire this knowledge.

5 Several outputs are capable of responding to particular technical or administrative needs. The employee must analyze and evaluate them, taking into account the performance specification of a theory which is more creative than mere reference to general information sources. Neither the output, nor the method, procedures, or sources of information are indicated.

6 The nature of a requirement or problem is to be identified, or the course of action to be followed in order to find solutions is to be determined. The employee must therefore consult (non-specific) sources of information, undertake research, make inquiries, or carry out analytic studies for the purpose of defining the problem. She or he must examine and study the relevant variables and formulate the possible outputs and their consequent features.

7 The information or orientations are presented to the employee in the form of tactical, organizational, strategic, or financial requirements. She or he must obtain the reports and recommendations concerning the methods which might be employed to fulfill these requirements. Furthermore, the employee must coordinate both the organizational and technical data for the purpose of making decisions and determining a course of action (outputs) for the principle branches (departments or units) of the organization.

APPENDIX 1.2

ILLUSTRATION OF THE POINT METHOD
(conceived by Elizabeth Baranovsky)

Evaluator factors

Factors	Weight as %
1 Knowledge	13
2 Experience	13
3 Complexity of functions	17
4 Supervision exercised	10
5 Autonomy of action	12
6 Consequences of errors	10
7 Effort or concentration	6
8 Confidential information	7
9 Interpersonal relations	7
10 Manual dexterity	5
	100%

1 KNOWLEDGE

Measures the minimum knowledge and education required to discharge the duties intrinsic to the job in a satisfactory manner. The prerequisites may be obtained by means of formal or informal training.

Degree		Points
1	The job requires a knowledge of mathematics, spelling, grammar, typing, and some of the general high school curriculum. Some high school education is necessary.	13
2	The job requires a knowledge of word processing or the ability to use office equipment such as adding machines, calculators, or tabulators. In addition to a high school education, certain advanced courses are usually necessary.	26
3	The job requires a knowledge of a particular field, such as bookkeeping, data processing, or programming. In addition to a high school education, two or three years of college are necessary.	39

2 EXPERIENCE

Measures the experience the employee must have in order to satisfactorily execute the assigned tasks while working under normal supervision. It includes prior experience obtained when working in other, similar jobs either for the current or other employers.

Degree		Points
1	The job requires zero to three months' experience either in this or similar jobs, working either for the current or other employers.	13
2	The job requires three to six months' experience in this or similar jobs, working either for the current or other employers.	22
3	The job requires six months to a years' experience in this or similar jobs, working either for the current or other employers.	31
4	The job requires one to two years' experience in this or similar jobs, working either for the current or other employers.	40
5	The job requires two to three years' experience in this or similar jobs, working either for the current or other employers.	49
6	The job requires three to four years' experience in this or similar jobs, working either for the current or other employers.	58
7	The job requires four or more years' experience in this or similar jobs, working either for the current or other employers.	67

3 COMPLEXITY OF FUNCTIONS

Indicates the degree to which tasks are complex, as determined by the nature of the work, the multiplicity of the operations and problems, and the number of variable elements calling for analysis, judgment, initiative, and ingenuity.

Degree		Points
1	Tasks are standard and simple, entailing the application of instructions or procedures. They are limited in number and very well defined. There is little choice in terms of course of action.	17
2	Tasks are simple but varied, leaving the employee with very few elements requiring analysis. He or she is occasionally called upon to exercise judgment in order to fulfill work-related duties.	34
3	Tasks are more complex but in a certain sense repetitive, requiring the analysis of a limited number of elements. The field of activity is specialized or semi-specialized, the specialty providing the framework for the analysis and subsequent task fulfillment.	51
4	Tasks are more complex and more varied. The field of activity is specialized. It is frequently necessary to analyze new or varied elements or techniques in order to determine the course of action to be followed. This action must take place within limits that are normally well-defined by practice, function, specialty, or instructions or rules.	68
5	Tasks are diversified and complex. The field of activity is specialized. It is repeatedly necessary to analyze elements and specialized techniques in order to adequately implement more intricate work procedures or to determine, in accordance with established norms, what operation to effect or what action to take. The problems and situations encountered do not always fall within the limits of practice and precedent; it is therefore frequently necessary to adapt or modify the methods and specialized techniques designed for performance of the duties in this field.	49

4 SUPERVISION EXERCISED

Measures the degree of supervision exercised with the aim of controlling the manner in which job functions are carried out. It includes the division of tasks, the choice of operational procedures, and the inspection of work which has been done. The supervisor normally works with other employees, giving them direction in a effort to complete their training.

Degree		Points
1	The employee does not supervise other employees, but occasionally explains how to execute a task.	10
2	The employee assists the immediate superior in the hiring of new employees, may be called upon to guide others in the performance of their tasks, and may occasionally have an assistant who helps discharge duties.	23
3	The employee regularly directs a subordinate and is responsible for the fulfillment of certain tasks. Responsibilities include the division of labor, the issuing of directives, and the inspection of completed work.	36
4	The employee regularly directs two or more subordinates and is responsible for the fulfillment of certain tasks. Responsibilities include the division of labor, the issuing of directives, and the inspection of completed work.	49

5 AUTONOMY OF ACTION

Measures the degree of autonomy intrinsic to the job.

Degree		Points
1	Responsibilities are carried out according to precise instructions or familiar procedures. The most minute details of work to be performed are specified.	12
2	Responsibilities are carried out according to procedures which are more loosely defined. Decisions are of a routine nature.	28

3   Responsibilities allow for a certain freedom of action in   44
the choice of methods, techniques, and procedures.
Decisions are made, however, within prescribed limits.

4   Responsibilities allow for a certain freedom of action in   60
the planning and organization of work, as well as in the
elaboration of methods and procedures. Decisions are
based on management policies and directives.

6 CONSEQUENCES OF ERRORS

Measures the severity of the consequences when errors in judgment or action
are made in the course of task performance. It is also necessary to take into
consideration the seriousness of a mistake, as defined by:
1 the person who discovers it;
2 the time required to correct it;
3 the impact of the error on the individual committing it, on the work of
others in the same or different departments, or on individuals outside the
organization;
4 the resulting damages;
5 the ensuing financial loss;
6 the damage to the reputation of the organization.
The consideration of unlikely errors should be avoided here.

Degree   Points
1   Errors are easy to detect, are of limited consequence and   10
take little time to correct. Work is normally subject to
close inspection.

2   Errors may cause some damage or difficulty, but are easy   24
to correct. Work is regularly checked.

3   Errors may cause considerable damage, such as delays   38
in discovering the mistake, which can only be detected
by inspection at subsequent stages of the process.

4   Errors are considered serious. They may be difficult to   52
discover and may adversely affect the efficiency of the
department or cause financial loss. They may impact
upon the internal or external relations of the organization.

7   EFFORT OR CONCENTRATION

Measures the degree of concentration required to perform the various tasks of the job and its most minute details, as well as measuring the rapidity with which duties must be discharged. Is the employee responsible for processing a considerable amount of work within a specific time frame? Must she or he frequently transfer attention from one job detail to another? Are interruptions, distractions, and outside influences liable to cause confusion?

Degree		Points
1	The volume of work and the nature of the job functions vary little and only intermittently require sustained attention.	6
2	The volume of work and the nature of job functions require sustained concentration during periods of intense activity.	14
3	The volume of work and the nature of job functions require sustained concentration most of the time, although on occasion the pressure is reduced.	22
4	The volume of work and the nature of job functions require sustained effort in order to carry out a considerable number of responsibilities within a limited period of time.	30

8   CONFIDENTIAL INFORMATION

Measures the integrity and discretion required in the handling of confidential information. What is to be examined is the nature of the information and the consequences its disclosure would have on the internal or external relations of the organization. The only information to be considered here is that of which the employee becomes aware on the job and which is either confidential or of limited circulation.

Degree		Points
1	The employee has access to little or no confidential information.	7

2   The employee regularly has access to confidential   14
     information, but not to information which is of restricted
     circulation.

3   The employee regularly has access to information the   21
     circulation of which is limited to management personnel.
     Discretion and integrity are recognized as essential for
     this job. Examples of this category of information are
     departmental policies, salaries, employee files, etc.

4   The employee has access both to information which is   28
     strictly confidential and to information of limited
     circulation relating to the policies and actions of labor
     unions and the federations with which the latter are
     affiliated. The utmost in discretion and integrity are
     requirements of this job.

9   INTERPERSONAL RELATIONS

Evaluates the degree to which the employee must display cooperation, tact, diplomacy, and courtesy in the course of her or his relations with persons inside or outside the organization, whether by oral communication, by telephone, or in correspondence. Communications must be analyzed in terms of the manner in which they are carried out, their goals, and their frequency.

Degree   Points
1   The employee conducts minimal communications   7
     requiring courtesy and tact with other employees or with
     people outside the organization. Interpersonal relations
     are for the most part limited to contacts with coworkers
     and do not constitute an important part of the job.

2   The employee maintains regular contact with other   21
     departments or with individuals outside the organization
     for the purpose of obtaining or supplying information.
     Tact must be used so as to avoid discord. There is no
     particular difficulty involved in obtaining the required
     authorization or cooperation for these communications.

3   The employee conducts frequent communications by   35
        means of telephone, written correspondence, or meetings
        with individuals from other departments and/or from
        outside the organization for the purpose of obtaining or
        providing information. It is necessary to use tact when
        discussing problems or transmitting data.

10 MANUAL DEXTERITY

Measures the degree of coordination required in order to perform a repetitive manual operation, such as operating the various types of office machines and equipment.

Degree		Points
1	Tasks require little or no coordination.	5
2	Tasks require the limited degree of manual dexterity necessary for operating a typewriter or adding machine.	12
3	The repetition of manual tasks, at great speed and for long durations, is a major aspect of the job. Examples of such tasks are operating a computer, data processing, or working on an assembly line.	19
4	Tasks require a high degree of coordination for performance of repetitive manual operations. A certain level of judgment is sometimes essential, as, for example, in the case of the responsibilities typically carried out by a receptionist.	26

APPENDIX 1.3

JOB STRUCTURE
Profiles based on four facets

Facets				Structuple	Rank position
A Instructions	B Supervision	C Control	D Freedom to change		
Determine instructions a_4	Independent b_3	Periodic c_3	Create D_3	4333	13 X
General guidelines a_3		At completion of performance c_2		3333	12 IX
				3323	11 VIII
	Consult b_2			3223	10 VII
				2223	9 VI
General instructions a_2			Change d_2	2222	8 V
				2122	7 IV
	Instructions b_1			1122	6 III
Detailed instructions a_1		Direct and permanent c_1		1112	5 II
			Transfer unchanged d_1	1111	4I

Source: Elizur, D. (1987). *Systematic Job Evaluation and Comparable Worth.*

2   Work Interests

AHARON TZINER AND ELCHANAN MEIR

Definition of Interests

Job performance is affected by many factors, the most important ones being abilities and interests. Strictly speaking, a discussion of interests should come under the heading of psychological testing, but since the treatment of interests has been relatively neglected in testing literature, we have chosen here to present a somewhat more detailed account of the meaning and measurement of interests and their role in predicting occupational choice, level of occupation, degree of achievement, satisfaction, stability on the job, and other measures of well-being.

We use the terms 'occupational interests' and 'vocational interests' interchangeably, and suggest the following definition: 'vocational interests are the expression of the level of attractiveness or inclination towards all occupations'. Replacing the term 'interest' with 'attraction' or 'inclination' may not, at first glance, appear to be of any practical use. However, the focus of this definition is that the interest does not just represent an individual's attitude towards a single occupation; rather, it consists of the level of attraction towards all occupations (or, for practical purposes, towards a representative sample of all occupations). Although the definition relates to attractiveness without any reference to the reason for it, the motives generating attraction are likely to emerge from two fairly independent sources, namely: (1) level of aspiration and (2) level of interest.

Level of aspiration refers to the degree of motivation to identify with or proceed with a particular task or occupation, based on the individual's personal achievement drives and predisposition to exploit personal skills, express authority, and exercise leadership, often in demanding work situations. Execution of these skills is generally associated with higher salary and reputation on the one hand, and with the impingement of work responsibilities on family and leisure time, on the other.

A high level of aspiration in the field of business management, for example, might reflect the drive to manage other people's activities, to achieve the status and income of a high level job, or to seek out opportunities to come into contact with other high status individuals. All these manifestations of aspiration could, of course, be fulfilled by any number of high level occupations, such as hospital administration, political leadership, or an advanced academic position. Conversely, a low level of aspiration is manifested when an individual prefers not to enjoy the above gratifications, possibly in order to avoid the responsibility and stress involved in management activities.

The second source of attraction, level of interest, consists of two facets, personal drives and content. From the perspective of drive, a high level of occupational interest, which generally requires ambition and an elevated degree of perfectionism, is associated with the inclination to control other people's activities so that they will perform according to one's ideas of how things should be done. This high level of interest, however, often carries with it a strong individual drive for continued success, along with the associated anxiety that even a single failure may damage a long-established reputation.

The other aspect of level of interest has to do with the attraction to, or preference for, the specific type of activities (content) that are associated with the task or job at hand. Since people differ in their propensities, we can expect the prospect of a given assignment to appeal to different people in different ways. Thus, the organization of a school outing, for example, may prove appealing because of the adventure, the administrative challenge, the physical exercise, the appreciation of nature, or any number of other inviting elements. Moreover, different occupations have various levels of appeal for different people. For instance, while some people enjoy playing musical instruments, others prefer to evaluate the quality of the performance; while there are those who enjoy executing major engineering projects, others may be more inclined to conduct research on their efficacy.

The term level of interest thus refers to the drawing power of the activity in question, indicated by level of aspiration and type of preference. Positive interest in any given occupation might stem from either one of these sources, or from both. Similarly, negative interest or indifference might be the result of the perceived low status of the occupation or its content, or the result of both these factors.

It should be noted that interests may also be affected by the state of the labor market and job opportunities. Alternatively, they might develop without any regard for job opportunities *per se*, but rather out of continuous frustrations associated with one's current job. Hence current preferences may be replaced by more attractive alternatives.

As we have seen, the degree of attraction of an occupation, current or potential, is a factor of the intrinsic motivations that affect the level and persistence of interest in the job. Yet interest levels are also influenced by *external* gratification, giving rise to the question of the extent to which the rewards associated with any activity should be included in the definition and measurement of interest. Should interest be defined and measured on the assumption that rewards are equal for the various activities, which may seem unrealistic, or should it include some aspect of the external gratification, which may distort the measurement of the fundamental, or real, interest? Perhaps the level of external gratification should be left to the individual's own imagination. On the other hand, it could be argued that any discussion of interests, viewed from the 'non-professional' perspective of the individual counselee, would be unfeasible if it disregarded the level of gratification involved (e.g., salary, status). These are not purely semantic questions; as we shall see, they have serious empirical implications for the measurement of interests.

Origins of Occupational Interests

From where do interests emanate in the first place? Unlike abilities, which appear to be largely inherited (see: Hunter, 1986; Jensen, 1986; Plomin, Pedersen, Lichtenstein, and McClearn 1994), genetic factors were shown by Gati (1991) to contribute 'less than 5% of the interest variance' (p. 312). Studies of twins, however, indicate a more dominant hereditary influence on interests (Lykken, Bouchard, McGue, and Tellegen, 1993; Waller, Lykken, and Tellegen, 1995), while Bouchard (1997) reports that for well-measured vocational interests, the heritability factor reaches levels as high as the 0.40 to 0.50 range (p. 382).

There would appear, therefore, to be methodological issues that hinder a better understanding of the impact of heredity on interests. One example concerns the problem of explaining the fact that in recent centuries the percentage of people employed in rural occupations (e.g., agriculture, animal husbandry) has decreased from some 75 per cent to around 4 per cent in the West, but not in some Far-Eastern cultures. An explanation offered at the Conference of Vocational Interests (May, 1997) was that the hereditary factor is related to *level* of occupations rather than to their field. Level includes a variety of factors such as type of abilities (e.g., verbal, artistic, manual), the need for achievement, and interest in dominance, innovation, and efficiency, some of which are known to be inherited qualities. On the other hand, we can not ignore the fact that in the case of certain specially talented individuals, people with remarkable musical aptitudes for example, their vocational interests appear to be more genetic, and seem to carry over to their offspring.

Congruence Between Interests and Occupation

It follows from basic notions about congruency (Holland, 1973, 1985) that interests congruent with occupation should predict a higher level of job satisfaction, work stability, and achievement on the job. This, in effect, is the essence of the 'congruence hypothesis'. [Considerable support for the congruence hypothesis can be found in Holland and Gottfredson's (1990) annotated bibliography, in published reviews of congruence studies (Spokane, 1985; Edwards, 1991), and in meta-analyses of 53 and 17 studies, respectively, on the relation between congruence and satisfaction, or congruence and other dependent variables (Assouline and Meir, 1987; Tranberg, Slane, and Ekeberg, 1993).]

Congruence between vocational interests and occupational choice is frequently the result of the logical processes of exercising preferences and making adequate decisions. Congruence might also result from a random match – an available job for an undecided person who develops preferences through activities on the job, or a fortuitous match between an available job and the suitable person. Life being what it is, however, many people do not have the good fortune to happen upon such opportunities. In some cases, a job may be offered to a potential employee who does not possess sufficient vocational interest in the position, yet may adapt to the new vocation in response to various defense mechanisms. In other cases, due to misinformation or the lack of adequate knowledge concerning the job or the individual's suitability for it, wrong and frustrating choices can be made.

Beyond the lack of job opportunities, many other sources of frustration associated with occupational interests may be manifested, especially in the workplace itself. For example, consider the high degree of frustration associated with a manager's inability to cope with responsibilities, obligations, skills, or content beyond his or her abilities. Given the expected frustrations resulting from unfulfilled aspirations, we may also assume that incongruence between field of interest and actual occupational field would be a source of frustration similar to that of incongruence between one's aptitudes and the requirements of one's occupation.

Sometimes the lack of occupational satisfaction can be 'compensated' for by the match between interests and the avocational (social and leisure) activities available in a work environment. Moreover, when occupation and interests are in accord, the additional congruence of avocational activities may enhance the existing occupational congruence to produce an even higher level of satisfaction, persistence and achievements (Meir and Melamed, 1986; Meir,

Melamed, and Abu-Freha, 1990; Meir, Melamed, and Dinur, 1995; Melamed, Meir, and Samson, 1995).

The research cited above was carried out in various cultures, using different tools (inventories) and measures. It seems clear, therefore, that however small, a positive relation between congruence and satisfaction does exist across cultures. In Holland's (1985) terms, people who are 'congruent' feel more satisfied with their occupational choice and career, produce more and better, and are more stable in their respective jobs. The opposite obviously also applies to dysfunctional behavior in the workplace: where career is incongruent with interests, people will suffer more from burnout and manifest higher levels of unproductive behaviors, such as disobedience and absenteeism.

Meir (1989) suggests a convenient way of integrating these disparate areas as they reflect on the relationship between interests, aspiration levels, and skills in specific environmental contexts, and work satisfaction, proposing the mapping sentence: 'Level of congruence ———> Well-Being'. This means that every measure of congruence between variables, such as interests, abilities and values, on the one hand, and environment, expectations, requirements and norms, on the other, will correlate positively with variables that reflect well-being in the workplace (e.g., satisfaction, performance, and stability), and negatively with variables that reflect lack of well-being (e.g., burnout, anxiety, accidents).

On the surface, then, it would appear that congruence between interests and occupation is a predictor of satisfaction and, perhaps, also of stability and achievements. In point of fact, however, the efficiency of the prediction, as reflected in the correlations between congruence and indicants of success at work, is generally low. The mean correlations between congruence and satisfaction found in the meta-analyses on the relation between congruence and satisfaction (Assouline and Meir, 1987), or congruence and other dependent variables (Tranberg et al., 1993) were .21 and .20, respectively. The breakdown of these correlations indicates that for certain measures of congruence and types, the mean correlations reached the .40 to .50 level, while for congruence and stability, and congruence and achievements, they were much lower, specifically, .15 and .06, respectively (Assouline and Meir, 1987). This analysis seems to suggest that when within-occupational congruence is measured, or when better indices for assigning congruence scores are employed, higher correlations between congruence and well-being measures are obtained.

Measurement of Vocational Interests

Measurement of vocational interests might intuitively appear very simple: perhaps all that has to be done is to present the question, 'What is your occupational choice?' However, this is clearly not the case. First, as we have defined it, the term vocational interests includes the level of preference towards all (or a representative sample of) occupations.

Moreover, a simple answer such as 'pilot' does not indicate whether this is an expression of aspiration level, incorporating some or all outcomes (e.g., responsibility, skill utilization, salary, status), and/or an expression of level of interest in the substantial aspects of the job (e.g., a combination of intellectual challenge and motor dexterity, the operation of highly sophisticated electronic equipment, travel). In other words, the measurement of interests requires an initial decision on the part of the tester as to whether it will relate to the need for extrinsic gratification or intrinsic needs, or both.

It follows that instructions in the measuring instruments vary according to which preference of the respondent (extrinsic or intrinsic interest) is to be measured. If interests are measured with reference to external gratification, the instructions in the empirical instrument instruction might read:

'How much are you willing to invest (in money, time, etc.), in order to enroll in each of the following academic courses ...?'

or:

'What is your interest in ...?'

without specifying the 'price' of any choice.

However, if interests are to be measured without reference to external gratification, the instructions might be phrased as follows:

'Indicate to what extent you would choose each of these academic subjects as one of three additional courses required for your degree.'

or:

'Assuming the salary is the same, indicate whether or not you would like to be engaged in each of the following occupations.'

In a somewhat separate endeavor, Super and Crites (1962, p. 377) and Crites (1997) have specified five major measuring tools that reflect different aspects of a respondent's interests in a particular occupation:

1 *Expressed Interests* – The tester takes note of what respondents declare they like or dislike about certain occupations.
2 *Manifest Interests* – The tester observes the level of respondents' participation in an activity or occupation.
3 *Tested Interests* – By means of an objective test, the tester accumulates relevant information mastered by the respondents.
4 *Inventoried Interests* – The tester examines respondents' expressions of preference for each item on a list. Here, the answers 'are added in order to yield a score which represents, not a single subjective estimate, as in the case of expressed interests, but a pattern of interests which research has shown to be rather stable' (Super and Crites, 1962, p. 380).
5 *Machine Experimental Measure* – The tester measures how long respondents are willing to view a picture of a certain content that relates in some way to the occupation being studied (Crites, 1997).

The most popular method for measuring interests is the use of an inventory, because it can not only be subjected to item analysis, reliability and validity examination, but is also cheaper to produce, administer, and score. Inventories have the added advantage of better fitting our definition of interests, since they make it possible to measure the level of interest towards an adequate sample of alternatives, rather than relying on a very limited list of options. Consequently, we shall limit our discussion here to inventoried interests.

Inventories differ, among other things, in the content of the items (e.g., occupational titles, self-evaluation of competencies, leisure activities, school subjects), the scale on which responses are given (e.g., 'Yes' or 'No', with or without interim categories, paired comparisons of two or three alternatives, scale of several categories), length, free or forced choice, and grouping by headings or random arrangement of items. Germane to our discussion, however, is the content of the items, rather than their form. Below are several of the more popular inventories in use:

Strong Vocational Interest Blank One of the leading devices in the field of interest measurement is the Strong Vocational Interest Blank, containing no less than 400 indirect questions on the testee's preferences for specific activities in various areas, such as hobbies and reading. The answers are scored according to the degree of the respondent's interests for up to 30 or 40 different occupations.

Strong-Campbell Interest Inventory A revised version of the Strong test, the Strong-Campbell Interest Inventory, which was devised in the seventies, provides a computerized, highly complex profile of professional interests arranged according to broad categories of interest. This method was developed to preclude the possibility that direct questions might induce testees to distort their responses, knowingly or otherwise, because they were either guided by social stereotypes of certain occupations or were not adequately acquainted with all professions.

Minnesota Importance Questionnaire (MIQ) The Minnesota Importance Questionnaire (MIQ), developed by Minnesota researchers, directly investigates work-related needs and expectations of occupational rewards such as recognition, variety, creativity, and achievement (Gay et al., 1971). The respondents are asked to list the order of importance they assign to the fulfillment of 20 occupational needs, using a multiple-comparison format. In addition to its being based on work adjustment theory, this questionnaire's superior psychometric merits have made it one of the highest valued tools in the field.

The efficacy of this instrument was confirmed in Tziner's (1983) study on social workers, which found an average test-retest reliability of 0.87 using the MIQ. It must be stressed that if tests of abilities, intelligence, and personality attributes are designed to assess Congruency I among applicants for a specific job, then inventories of interests, needs, and professional aspirations are administered in order to determine the degree of Congruency II. All these inventories tap areas of interest and activity preferences that are germane to the occupational context.

Kuder Occupational Interest Survey Another inventory, the Kuder Occupational Interest Survey consists of items arranged in 100 groups of three forced-choice triads of alternative activities. The respondent must mark the most preferred and least preferred activity in each triad. The inventory allows scores to be obtained for more than 100 occupations. By way of illustration, one triad might consist of: 'collects autographs' – 'collects coins' – 'collects butterflies'. This inventory makes it possible to check for inconsistency and social desirability in the responses to the items. Reliability and validity attributes are satisfactory.

Ramak Interest Inventory The Ramak Interest Inventory (Meir, 1975) is based on Roe's (1956) occupational classification. It consists of 72 occupational items selected so that for each of Roe's eight occupational fields there are three items for each of the professional-managerial, semi-professional and skilled workers' levels, respectively. Thus, the scores indicate both level of aspiration and the attraction of each of the fields for the respondent. In a seven-year follow-up study on the Hebrew version (Barak and Meir, 1974), correlations of .40 and .28 were found for males and females, respectively, between interest scores at age 17 and satisfaction at age 25. The reliability of the English version (Meir, Rubin, Temple, and Osipow, 1997) was shown to be .83.

Self-Directed Search Interest Inventory (SDS) The Self-Directed Search Interest Inventory was designed by Holland (1973, 1985) for either self-rating or for use in the counseling process. It consists of five sections (activities, competencies, occupational titles, self estimates of abilities, and skills). Hundreds of studies have verified the reliability and validity of the SDS, and it has been translated and adapted for use in various cultures. On the whole, it is a very versatile tool, and has proved to be particularly useful for testing hypotheses relating to the connection between occupational and environmental congruence emerging from Holland's theory of congruence (Holland and Gottfredson, 1990).

The Use of Occupational Titles in Inventories

As we have seen, the differences between interest inventories relate mainly to specific content or scale. Most of the inventories, however, either consist entirely of occupational titles or include a section of them. Indeed, one of the problems associated with inventories centers round the use of occupational titles as items (Kuder, 1970).

Kuder (1970) suggests that if an individual is knowledgeable enough about the meaning of occupational titles, the interest inventory as such might be redundant. Conversely, a person unfamiliar with an occupation may misunderstand the inventory item or have a distorted image of its content; thus, responses may be based on different images of the same item/occupational title. Tziner and Meir (1997) note various sources of the misperceptions of inventory items that employ occupational titles. These include situations in which:

1   testees confuse interest in an occupation with what people actually do at work when engaged in that occupation;
2   testees' responses are influenced by subjective contextual factors;
3   responses of unsophisticated testees are bound to current images of an item that has, over time and with technological development, changed in terms of content, tasks, hierarchical status, norms and values, required training, certification and/or instrumentation;
4   ignorant testees are forced to make decisions and assign preferences to items that have no meaning for them.

In spite of these limitations, studies have clearly demonstrated the reliability and validity (of all kinds) of the common interest inventories. Evidently, the core of real interest emerges from the combination of the many responses that the testee is asked to give. The length of interest inventories, sometimes several hundred items long, is a result of the need to partial out the subjective misconception of items.

Scoring and Norms

According to our definition of interests, the measurement of occupational interests requires measuring the attraction toward all occupations, or an adequate sample of them, in order to produce a profile of scores that reflects the interest level of the respondent toward the various occupations or groups of occupations. The sum of all interest scores toward all occupations is of no significance. Rather, for purposes such as career counseling, interest levels are determined according to the within-individual distribution of scores. The only meaningful references are to the profile and the within-respondent variance among the scores in that profile.

While some interest inventories employ intra-personal comparisons, whereby each score is compared with other scores of the same testee (e.g., Holland, 1973, 1985), others are based on the norms of comparison groups of the same gender and peer group in the relevant culture (e.g., Strong, 1943; Kuder, 1988). Meir and Tziner (1997) note that the measurement of interests is essentially different from that of abilities. In measuring mental abilities, the testees' success in responding to items is always matched against comparison groups. If the majority of the group succeeds in solving the same series of items as the respondent, the respondent's ability is considered moderate or less. Here the similarity or difference between the individual's scores and those of the comparison group are significant, rather than the variance among the scores of the same individual on the various scales of the test battery. Thus, in mental ability measurement a score is considered high only if that or higher scores are very rare in the comparison group.

In contrast, in interest measurement a score will be considered high if it is sufficiently higher than the other scores of the *same individual* on the other items or scales. A very popular occupation is defined as such by the many respondents who express interest in it; a particular respondent's interest can remain high, however, independently of the others. Paradoxically, while the popularity of the occupation may actually serve to increase the individual's level of interest, competition for it may make the pursuit of that occupation impossible. Nevertheless, this situation does not necessarily detract from the content or level of interest expressed by the individual.

Interest inventories based on norms may be subject either to obsolescence of the items (see above) or to changing shifts in popularity in various comparison groups. Consequently, inventories such as Strong's (1943) SVIB have been revised several times for the same culture for which they were originally designed (Walsh and Osipow, 1986). On the other hand, interest inventories based on intra-personal comparisons can be more easily updated and adapted to other cultures. As far as career counseling is concerned, what generally count are the within-individual differences in the counselee's profile, rather than the differences between his or her preferences and those of the norm group.

With regard to updating a norm-based inventory, Meir and Tziner (1997) point out that this process requires examining the applicability of both items and norms; for a non-norm based inventory, only the items need to be examined. This means introducing an adequate representation of new items and deleting those that have become obsolete or that have changed their characteristics to such an extent that they no longer represent the categories they once did.

Updating norms, in contrast, involves collecting current data on the distribution of responses in the relevant comparison group to both versions of the inventory. The basis for interpreting scores on the SVIB and similar inventories is how 'eminent people' of the same gender in the relevant occupation (scale) differ from 'Men in General' or 'Women in General'. However, targeting adequate comparison groups to interpret interest inventories is not a simple task, as illustrated by the following example. One of the authors, an Orthodox Jewish male, found 'minister' to be the seventh suggestion in his Report Form based on his responses to the KOIS (Kuder, 1988) inventory in comparison to his gender, but the first suggestion in comparison to females.

The Structure of Occupations

Understanding the structure of occupations is of both theoretical and practical significance. In theoretical terms, the structure serves as a means of examining the construct validity of the typology and instruments. In practical terms, it allows counselors to interest their clients in alternatives that are closer to their vocational preferences in psychological content and overall configuration.

The structure of occupations has been the subject of repeated study. In two distinctive meta-analyses, Tracey and Rounds (1993) examined this structure according to Holland's (1985) typology, and Tracey and Rounds (1994) did so employing Roe's (1956) occupational classification. Moreover, several cross-cultural studies of vocational interests have investigated the extent to which the underlying structure of occupations is universal.

In Holland's (1973, 1985) model, there are six personality types, R (Realistic), I (Investigative), A (Artistic), S (Social), E (Enterprising), and C (Conventional), and six equivalent environmental types, which together form a hexagonal configuration, abbreviated RIASEC. Meir and Tziner (1997) note that several intercorrelation matrices (e.g., Holland, 1972) support Holland's notion of the circular configuration of RIASEC, albeit with some deviations. In addition, Rounds and Tracey (1993) reviewed 77 U.S. RIASEC correlation matrices based on a variety of samples, and concluded that the six types are equidistant from each other, and that 'the circumplex structure itself is the crucial distinguishing feature' (p. 875). Although this arrangement is also supported by further studies, including Fouad, Cudeck, and Hansen (1984), Fouad and Dancer (1992), and Khan et al. (1990), it has not been universally found or accepted (see, for example: Holland and Gottfredson, 1992; Rounds and Tracey, 1996).

In other studies, Meir (e.g., 1973, 1975) analyzed the responses of 22 Israeli samples (one consisting of Arab respondents: Meir, Sohlberg, and Barak, 1973) to either the Ramak or the Courses interest inventories (in Hebrew). Both instruments were based on Roe's (1956) occupational classification. Smallest Space Analysis (SSA) of these responses demonstrated that they similarly form a circular configuration consisting of the categories of: Business – Organization – General Culture – Service – Arts and Entertainment – Outdoor – Science – Technology. A further investigation using Israeli soldiers as respondents (Meir, Bar, Lahav, and Shalhevet, 1975) employed a variation of the Ramak and Courses for counselees that incorporates a negative response attitude (response scales being Reject, Doubtful, Agree rather than Yes, Doubtful, No). This study also revealed a circular configuration.

The consistency and universal nature of the circular arrangement clearly emerge from Meir and Tziner's (1997) review: the same configuration of occupational fields was found when a combination of the Hebrew adaptation of Holland's Self-Directed Search (SDS) and the Ramak was administered to Israeli participants (Meir and Ben-Yehuda, 1976). This result was replicated in a study of American students (Meir, Rubin, Temple, and Osipow, 1997) using a combination of the VPI, Ramak, and Courses (the latter two translated into English). A translated version of the Ramak into Spanish (Peiser and Meir, 1976) for immigrants to Israel from Latin American countries revealed a similar, though not entirely circular, arrangement. Finally, a translated version of the Ramak into German, with the necessary modifications (Meir and Stauffer, 1980), was administered to Swiss participants twice, at a gap of about one-year. The SSA of the 2 x 8 = 16 fields also yielded a close to circular arrangement of the fields.

Meir and Tziner come out strongly in favor of the circular arrangement, which emerges from Holland's (1973, 1985) typology into six personality types, and from responses on either the VPI or the SDS interest inventories. It has been found using any adaptation of these interest inventories into other languages, as well as when Roe's (1956) classification into eight occupational fields is employed, with responses on either the Ramak or Courses interest inventories. Moreover, the same arrangement emerges whether the data analysis method employed is principal component analysis, SSA, randomization test, or confirmatory factor analysis.

It is worth noting that since occupations in Peiser and Meir's study were classified into eight fields according to Roe's (1956) classification – and not only into six as in Holland's (1985) typology – the number of order predictions was higher by far, incorporating 288 predictions, or statements, of order on the circular arrangement of the eight occupational fields out of 378 possible comparisons (Tracey and Rounds, 1994). Indeed, in a previous meta-analysis by Tracey and Rounds (1994) on 24 correlation matrices, the circular arrangement was found to be the best fit for the configuration of Roe' s (1956) eight occupational fields.

It should also be noted that studies of occupational interests appear to be particularly sensitive to faulty design, which may account for the incongruence of findings. Thus in Fouad and Dancer's (1992) Smallest Space Analysis of Holland's six types, the researchers found that R was somewhat outside the conservative circle. Meir and Tziner (1997), among others (Holland and Gottfredson, 1992; Subich, 1992), attribute the results to the fact that the subjects were engineers for whom the salient distinction among occupations is whether or not they are close to R. In this context, we might do well to remember Holland and Gottfredson's (1992) caveat that mis-shaped polygons rather than perfect hexagons may often be obtained as a result of defects in theory, assessment, or samples.

In response to dissenting claims concerning the circular arrangement, Meir and Tziner argue that the only necessary and sufficient condition for an interest inventory is its predictive validity in respect to a relevant external criterion in a follow-up study. This is illustrated by means of a seven-year follow-up study by Barak and Meir (1974) on responses to the Ramak. The researchers found correlations of .40 and .26 for 158 males and 202 females, respectively, between the interest scores on the chosen occupational field and satisfaction with that choice seven years later. In a further analysis of the same data, Peiser and Meir (1978) found that the greater the proximity on the circular arrangement between the chosen occupational field and the respondent's highest field score seven years earlier, the higher the satisfaction with the occupational choice.

Practical Guidelines

From the previous discussion, it is clear that there is more to the measure of interests than a 'single response'. Despite some of the methodological difficulties outlined above, significant and consistent correlations have been found between measures derived from interest inventories and external criteria. In contrast to the pessimism displayed by Hansen (1987), it is now possible, on the basis of the authors' accumulated empirical experience and theoretical strategy, to offer practical suggestions on how to develop and test interest inventories that will produce reasonable levels of reliability and validity.

In view of the complex nature of the problems involved, the following *requirements* for constructing and employing interest inventories are indicated:

1 Items in an interest inventory should be carefully chosen to avoid misunderstanding.
2 Since any item might be ambiguous to certain respondents, counselors can and should rely on groups of items rather than on single responses.
3 Forms can be structured in a number of ways, including: random or organized with or without headings, on scales of 'Y ? N",L I D' or 'Y N', as paired comparisons or free choice, and with or without a restriction on the number of items to which the participant is allowed to respond positively. Since conclusions are based on within-respondent differences,

it is assumed that the form of presentation will not affect the respondent's attitudes.

4 Appropriate methods of testing (e.g., item analysis) should be used to aid in selecting items that are free of cultural bias.

5 'The proof of the pudding is in the eating' – the quality of items, sums of scores, profiles, and inventories should be subjected to appropriate reliability and validity tests.

Steps in Developing an Interest Inventory

The first step in developing an interest inventory is to decide on the number of levels and fields to include. Although Roe (1956) refers to six occupational levels, in Israel, for example, only four were reliably differentiated (Meir, 1968): professional and managerial, semi-professional, skilled workers, and semi- and unskilled workers. We therefore believe that the number of levels should not exceed four, since it may be difficult to discriminate reliably between any more than that. We would recommend starting with the four levels suggested above.

The decision as to the number of fields is more difficult. Holland (1973, 1985) began with six fields, and seems to have had impressive success to judge by the large number of studies that have adopted his method. However, his typology suffers from low differentiation, especially among females (with Social emerging as the first letter code for about 50 per cent, and as the second letter code for another 30 per cent). Roe (1956) suggests eight occupational fields, using a separate field for Outdoor and making a distinction between Service and General-Cultural, with the former being more person-to-person oriented and the latter more individual-to-group or community oriented.

The combination of four levels (the horizontal dimension) and eight fields (the vertical dimension) means a starting point of 12 definitions and 32 possible clusters of occupations. This has the clear advantages of economy and simplicity. Since the structure of fields appears to be hierarchical in its vertical dimension and circular in its horizontal dimension, theoretically, any other number of occupational levels or fields could be adopted, providing that proper definitions can reliably discriminate between any two.

The second step is to construct or select the appropriate items for the new inventory. It is recommended that the selection of these items be made by a panel of three to five experts who are familiar with both the occupational world (fields and levels) and the associations attached to the various wordings.

Each new item should fulfill the following conditions:

1   Have a clear meaning for 'naive' respondents as to content.
2   Be neither too attractive nor too unpleasant in meaning and associations.
3   Be unbiased in gender meaning (unless separate inventories for males and females are to be developed).
4   Adequately represent the occupational clusters and definitions of level and field determined in the first step, and be perceived as such by 'naive' respondents. Items need not necessarily represent the actual labor market and employee distribution (indeed there is little chance that the employment distribution will coincide with the distribution of interests among candidates for the labor market).
5   Be of a constant number to represent each combination of level and field (e.g., three items for each combination of level and field, that is, 3x4x8=96 items). As Roe's (1956) model is to be used as the theoretical basis of the inventory, all four levels and eight fields should be represented in the inventory. However, as participants generally refrain from responding positively to low level items, the level of semi- and unskilled occupations, in all fields, can be left out (reducing the number of items accordingly).

The next step in constructing a new interest inventory is the theoretical examination of the instrument. For this purpose, the chosen items should be presented in random order to a different panel, who will then be asked to classify them into levels and fields. An item should be included in the experimental version of the inventory only if the members of the second panel agree on its classification by both level and field, and this classification is in accord with the intention of the first panel. At this stage some items will undoubtedly have to be rejected and replaced by new items which must again be subjected to a similar test. Since in the course of the empirical examination of the items (see below), even more items may have to be rejected and replaced, it is recommended that the first panel select at least one or two alternative possibilities for each combination of level and field.

Another task for the second panel is to determine the content validity of the group of items for each combination of level and field, i.e., they have to judge the extent to which all the items pertaining to the same cluster represent the population of occupations in that cluster. If the items within a given cluster are too similar, they might not adequately represent the entire population of occupations that belong to that cluster in the occupational world.

To illustrate, using Roe's (1956) classification, the developers of the English version of the Ramak (Meir, Rubin, Temple, and Osipow, 1997) selected Social Worker, Psychologist, and Physical Therapist to represent the professional and managerial level in Service, and Electronics Technician, Automobile Mechanic, and Electrician to represent the semi-professional level of Technology, believing each group to be sufficiently indicative of its category.

The following step is the empirical examination of the items in the inventory. It is recommended that the inventory be administered to a sample of potential counselees with a heterogeneous educational background (providing they can respond to a pencil and paper test) and with assumed different interests. In other words, the respondents should not be culled, for example, from a specific educational program such as engineering students or medical staff.

The instructions should emphasize that what is being measured is the level of interest in each of the items, independent of any potential fulfillment of that interest, and that there is no limit to the number of positive responses. The scale on which respondents indicate their interest can be dichotomous (e.g., Yes and No), or consist of three (e.g., Yes, Doubtful, and No) or more ranks. Following administration, the inventories should be scored according to the scale chosen (e.g., 0 for No and 1 for Yes; or 2, 1, and 0 for Yes, Doubtful, and No, respectively). Each respondent is assigned a score on each cluster of occupations equal to the sum of his or her scores on the items in that particular cluster.

The scores can range from zero (no interest in any of the items in the cluster) to a figure equaling the number of items in the cluster multiplied by the highest score on the scale; the higher the score, the higher the interest level of the respondent in the occupations in a particular cluster. The cluster scores are then summed up horizontally to arrive at level scores, and vertically to produce field scores. The sum of the level scores and field scores must, of course, be the same. This figure indicates the total interest, or general baseline, of the individual respondent towards all items in the inventory.

At this stage, the scores should be subjected to reliability tests: horizontally for each of the level scores and vertically for each of the field scores, using the conservative split-half or Cronbach alpha method. Other reliability tests can be designed to achieve test-retest reliabilities. If more than a single inventory is constructed, the equivalent test reliability should also be measured. It must be emphasized that whatever the measure employed, reliability should be tested separately for each level and each field. The series of reliability measures can be represented in brief by means of their median.

An even more crucial test of the new interest inventory is item analysis. Meir and Gati (1981) suggest six rules for determining the fitness of an item for an interest inventory. These are:

1   the mean score on an item should not be too extreme;
2   the standard deviation of responses on any item should not be too low;
3   all within field (and level) items should correlate positively among themselves;
4   the correlation between each item and its field score should be sufficiently high;
5   the correlation between any item and any other field score should be sufficiently low;
6   there should be a sufficient difference between the correlation of an item with its own field score and its correlation with any other field score.

Naturally, the meaning of 'sufficient' must be determined for the last three requirements. Meir and Gati (1981) suggest that for item (6), for example, the difference between the square of the correlation coefficient of an item with its field and its correlation with any of the other fields should be at least 10 per cent.

To illustrate, an experimental version of the Ramak interest inventory (based on Roe's, 1956, occupational classification) contained 99 items to be marked on a scale of Y ? N (yes, doubtful, no) with scores of 2, 1, and 0, respectively. Each field score was derived from nine items: three for each of the professional-managerial, semi-professional, and skilled workers levels. The responses of a sample of 128 respondents showed that for the item Psychologist (a) the mean score was 1.06, and (b) its standard deviation was .92. In other words, the mean among these respondents was around the '?' response, with a distribution of about 50 per cent responding Y and another 50 per cent responding N. (Statistically the highest possible standard deviation is half the range, a situation that occurs when the sample is divided equally between the two extreme scores.)

The correlation between the score on Psychologist and the field score of Service was .63, while the correlations between Psychologist and the other seven field scores were .23, .13, .49, .41, .11, .22, and .21 with Business, Organization, General-Cultural, Arts and Entertainment, Outdoor, Science, and Technology, respectively. This demonstrates empirically that, at least in this sample, the image of Psychologist is linked much more to Service than to any of the other fields in Roe's (1956) classification of occupations. In contrast, the item Systems Analyst yielded a mean score of .75 with SD = .82, and correlations of .08, .32, .19, 04, .16, .33, .50 and .47 with Business, Organization, General-Cultural, Service, Arts and Entertainment, Outdoor, Science, and Technology, respectively. The small difference between the last two correlations made it impossible to include this item under either Science or Technology, and it therefore had to be dropped from the final version of the inventory.

The next step is to examine the inventory's validity. There are five possible methods for doing so:

1 Correlating it with existing proven inventories. (If any happen to be available, why put so much effort into developing a new one?)
2 Analyzing the structure of the scores to see whether the internal correlations fit the known structure of correlations (e.g., the circular arrangement of fields; the hierarchical order of levels).
3 Determining whether people engaged in a certain field score higher on that than on any of the other fields, and also higher than people engaged in other fields.
4 Examining the concurrent validity, that is whether there is a positive correlation between field scores and well-being measures (e.g., satisfaction, stability, or achievement) or negative correlations between field scores and well-being measures with negative connotations (e.g., burnout, absenteeism).
5 Examining the predictive validity by using the same method as above but with a gap of several years between the measurement of interests and that of the well-being measures. This obviously requires time, resources, facilities, and the wherewithal to overcome the difficulty of locating the respondents after several years.

The steps outlined above are meant to convey the message that the process of designing a good interest inventory should be guided by solid theoretical considerations rather than by a trial-and-error method. Indeed, Osipow (1991) reaches the same conclusion.

It is hoped that this discussion, along with the practical tips offered, will encourage researchers to undertake the daunting, yet feasible, task of interest measurement. Although the investment, in terms of time and effort, may be high, the 'interest' that may accrue from it will be no less considerable.

References

Assouline, M. and Meir, E.I. (1987). 'Meta-Analysis of the Relationship Between Congruence and Well-Being Measures'. *Journal of Vocational Behavior*, 31, pp. 319–32.

Barak, A. and Meir, E.I. (1974). 'The Predictive Validity of a Vocational Inventory 'Ramak': Seven Year Follow-up'. *Journal of Vocational Behavior*, 4, pp. 377–87.

Bouchard, T.J., Jr. (1997). 'Genetic Influences on Mental Abilities, Personality, Vocational Interests and Work Attitudes'. In C.L. Cooper and I.T. Robertson (eds.), *International Review of Industrial and Organizational Psychology*, 12, pp. 373–95.

Crites, J.O. (1997). 'Definition of Interests'. Paper presented at the meeting of The Society for Vocational Psychology, Bethlehem, PA.

Edwards, J.R. (1991). 'Person-Job Fit: A Conceptual Integration, Literature Review, and Methodological Critique'. In C.L. Cooper and I.T. Robertson (eds.), *International Review of Industrial and Organizational Psychology*, 6, pp. 283–357.

Fouad, N.A., Cudeck, R., and Hansen, J.C. (1984). 'Convergent Validity of the Spanish and English Forms of the Strong-Campbell Interest Inventory for Bilingual Hispanic High School Students'. *Journal of Counseling Psychology*, 31, pp. 339–48.

Fouad, N.A. and Dancer, L.S. (1992). 'Cross-Cultural Structure of Interests: Mexico and the United States'. *Journal of Vocational Behavior*, 40, pp. 129–43.

Gati, I. (1991). 'The Structure of Vocational Interests'. *Psychological Bulletin*, 109, pp. 309–24.

Gay, E.G. et al. (1971). 'Manual for the Minnesota Importance Questionnaire'. *Minnesota Studies in Vocational Rehabilitation*, 54.

Hansen, J.C. (1987). 'Cross-Cultural Research on Vocational Interests'. *Measurement and Evaluation in Counseling and Development*, 19, pp. 163–76.

Holland, J.L. (1972). *Professional Manual for the Self-Directed Search*. Palo Alto, CA: Consulting Psychologists Press.

Holland, J.L. (1973). *Making Vocational Choices: A Theory of Careers*. Englewood Cliffs, NJ: Prentice-Hall.

Holland, J.L. (1985). *Making Vocational Choices: A Theory of Vocational Personalities and Work Environments*. Odessa, FL: Psychological Assessment Resources.

Holland, J.L. and Gottfredson, G.D. (1990). *An Annotated Bibliography for Holland's Theory of Vocational Personalities and Work Environments*. Johns Hopkins University.

Holland, J.L. and Gottfredson, G.D. (1992). 'Studies of the Hexagonal Model: An Evaluation (or, The Perils of Stalking the Perfect Hexagon)'. *Journal of Vocational Behavior*, 40, pp. 158–70.

Hunter, J.E. (1986). 'Cognitive Ability, Cognitive Aptitude, Job Knowledge, and Job Performance'. *Journal of Vocational Behavior*, 29, pp. 340–62.

Jensen, A.R. (1986). 'G: Artifact or Reality?' *Journal of Vocational Behavior*, 29, pp. 301–31.

Khan, S.B., Sabir, A.A., Shaukat, N., Hussain, M.A. and Baig, T. (1990). 'A Study of the Validity of Holland's Theory in a Non-Western Culture'. *Journal of Vocational Behavior*, 36, pp. 132–46.

Kuder, F. (1970). 'Some Principles of Interest Measurement'. *Educational and Psychological Measurement*, 30, pp. 205–26.

Kuder, F. (1988). *Kuder and General Interest Survey General Manual*. Chicago: SRA/Pergamon.

Lykken, D.T., Bouchard, T.J., Jr., McGrue, M. and Tellegen, (1993). 'Heritability of Interests: A Twin Study'. *Journal of Applied Psychology*, 78, pp. 649–61.

Meir, E.I. (1968). *Structural Elaboration of Roe's Classification of Occupations*. Jerusalem: Israel Program for Scientific Translations.

Meir, E.I. (1973). 'The Structure of Occupations by Interests: A Smallest Space Analysis'. *Journal of Vocational Behavior*, 3, pp. 21–31.

Meir, E.I. (1975). *Manual for the Ramak and Courses Interest Inventories*. Ramat Aviv: Tel-Aviv University, Department of Psychology.

Meir, E.I. (1989). 'Integrative Elaboration of the Congruence Theory'. *Journal of Vocational Behavior*, 35, pp. 219–30.

Meir, E.I., Bar, R., Lahav, G. and Shalhevet, R. (1975). 'Interest Inventories Based on Roe's Classification Modified for Negative Respondents'. *Journal of Vocational Behavior*, 7, pp. 127–33.

Meir, E.I. and Ben-Yehuda, A. (1976). 'Inventories Based on Roe and Holland Yield Similar Results'. *Journal of Vocational Behavior*, 8, pp. 269–74.

Meir, E.I. and Gati, I. (1981). 'Guidelines for Item Selection in Inventories Yielding Score Profiles'. *Educational and Psychological Measurement*, 41, pp. 1011–16.

Meir, E.I. and Melamed, S. (1986). 'The Accumulation of Person-Environment Congruences and Well-Being'. *Journal of Occupational Behavior*, 7, pp. 315–23.

Meir, E.I., Melamed, S. and Abu-Freha, A. (1990). 'Vocational, Avocational and Skill Utilization Congruences and their Relationship With Well-Being in Two Cultures. *Journal of Vocational Behavior*, 36, pp. 153–65.

Meir, E.I., Melamed, S. and Dinur, C. (1995). 'The Benefits of Congruence'. *The Career Development Quarterly*, 43, pp. 257–66.

Meir, E.I., Rubin, A., Temple, R. and Osipow, S.H. (1997). 'Examination of Interest Inventories Based on Roe's Classification'. *Career Development Quarterly*, 46, pp. 48–61.

Meir, E.I., Sohlberg, S. and Barak, A. (1973). 'A Cross-Cultural Comparison of the Structure of Vocational Interests'. *Journal of Cross-Cultural Psychology*, 4, pp. 501–8.

Meir, E.I. and Stauffer, E. (1980). 'Strukturelle Messung der Berufsinteressen (Structural Measurement of Vocational Interests)'. *Diagnostica*, 26, pp. 85–92.

Meir, E.I. and Tziner, A. (1997). Cross-Cultural Assessment of Interests. Ramat Aviv: Tel-Aviv University, Unpublished manuscript.

Melamed, S., Meir, E.I. and Samson, A. (1995). 'The Benefits of Personality-Leisure Congruence: Evidence and Implications'. *Journal of Leisure Research*, 27, pp. 25–40.

Osipow, S.H. (1991). 'Developing Instruments for Use in Counseling'. *Journal of Counseling and Development*, 70, pp. 322–6.

Peiser, C. and Meir, E.I. (1976). 'A Spanish Version of the Ramak Interest Inventory'. *Interamerican Journal of Psychology*, 10, pp. 9–15.

Peiser, C. and Meir, E.I. (1978). 'Congruency, Consistency and Differentiation of Vocational Interests as Predictors of Vocational Satisfaction and Preference Stability'. *Journal of Vocational Behavior*, 12, pp. 270–78.

Plomin, R., Pedersen, N.L., Lichtenstein, P. and McClearn, G.E. (1994). 'Variability and Stability in Cognitive Abilities are Largely Genetic Later in Life'. *Behavior Genetics*, 24, pp. 207–15.

Roe, A. (1956). *The Psychology of Occupations*. New York: Wiley.

Rounds, J.M. and Tracey, T.J. (1993). Prediger's Dimensional Representation of Holland's RIASEC Circumplex'. *Journal of Applied Psychology*, 78, pp. 875–90.

Rounds, J. and Tracey, T.J. (1996). 'Cross-Cultural Structural Equivalence of RIASEC Models and Measures'. *Journal of Counseling Psychology*, 43, pp. 310–29.

Spokane, A.R. (1985). 'A Review of Research on Person-Environment Congruence in Holland's Theory of Careers'. *Journal of Vocational Behavior*, 26, pp. 306–43.

Strong, K. E (1943). *Vocational Interests of Men and Women*. Stanford: Stanford University Press.

Subich, L.M. (1992). 'Holland's Theory: "Pushing the Envelope"'. *Journal of Vocational Behavior*, 40, pp. 201–6.

Super, E.K. and Crites, J.O. (1962). *Appraising Vocational Fitness*. New York: Harper.

Tracey, T.J. and Rounds, J. (1993). 'Evaluating Holland's and Gati's Vocational Interest Models: A Structural Meta-Analysis'. *Psychological Bulletin*, 113, pp. 229–46.

Tracey, T.J. and Rounds, J. (1994). 'An Examination of the Structure of Roe's Eight Interest Fields'. *Journal of Vocational Behavior*, 44, pp. 279–96.

Tranberg, M., Slane, S. and Ekeberg, S.E. (1993). 'The Relation Between Interest-Congruence and Satisfaction: A Meta-Analysis'. *Journal of Vocational Behavior*, 42, pp. 253–64.

Tziner, A. (1983). 'Correspondence Between Occupational Rewards and Occupational Needs and Work Satisfaction: A Canonical Redundancy Analysis'. *Journal of Occupational Psychology*, 56, pp. 49–56.

Tziner, A. and Meir, E.I. (1997). 'Work Adjustment: Extension of the Theoretical Framework'. In C.L. Cooper and I.T. Robertson (eds), *International Review of Industrial and Organizational Psychology*, 12, pp. 95–114.

Waller, N.G., Lykken, D.T. and Tellegen, A. (1995). 'Occupational Interests, Leisure Time Interests, and Personality: Three Domains or One? Findings from the Minnesota Twin Registry'. In D.L. Lubinski and R.V. Davis (eds.), *Assessing Individual Differences in Human Behavior: New Concepts, Methods and Findings*. Palo Alto, CA: Davies-Black, pp. 233–59.

Walsh, W.B. and Osipow, S.H. (eds) (1986). *Advances in Vocational Psychology*, Hillsdale, NJ: Lawrence Erlbaum.

3 Work Adjustment: Essence and Outcomes

AHARON TZINER AND ELCHANAN MEIR

One of the most well-established areas of research in the work environment involves the individual employee's adjustment to the job and the work context. Indeed, worker adjustment has long been construed as an essential component of effective organizational functioning (Cascio, 1991). In an extensive review of the underlying theoretical framework for the term 'work adjustment', Tziner and Meir (1997) call attention to the basic concept of 'fit'. Often labeled person-environment (P-E) or person-organization (P-O) fit, this concept relates to the interaction between an individual's work-related characteristics and the attributes of the work environment in which he or she functions.

The term 'fit' generally has positive connotations. Thus, a person manifesting fit shows signs of successful adjustment or well-being at work, such as organizational commitment and high performance. In contrast, misfit between an individual's work-related characteristics and the organizational environment may result in any manner of negative attitudes and behaviors, such as dissatisfaction or absenteeism. Numerous examples of such fit-related positive and negative outcomes in the workplace have been demonstrated in recent years (Tziner, 1990; Edwards, 1991; Edwards and van Harrison, 1993; Kristoff, 1996).

Both the Theory of Work Adjustment (Dawis and Lofquist, 1984) and Holland's (1973, 1985) Congruence Theory have served as models to describe the causal relationships between these outcomes and employee characteristics. In the former, fit/misfit is referred to as correspondence/discorrespondence; in the latter, as congruence/lack of congruence (or incongruence). In their review of these theories, Tziner and Meir (1997) outline some of these research findings and add their own amendments in an attempt to synthesize the two parallel approaches. Below is a synopsis of this review, along with a survey of some of the latest research in the field.

The Theory of Work Adjustment – Dawis and Lofquist, 1984

Correspondence and Work Adjustment

The central tenet of the Theory of Work Adjustment is that for a harmonious relationship to exist between the individual and the work environment, that individual must be suited to the environment and the environment must be suited to the individual. This 'correspondence', as Lofquist and Dawis (1969) originally termed the association, is a 'reciprocal and complementary relationship between the individual and his environment' (pp. 4–5). Underlying the theory is the assumption that workers seek to achieve and maintain this mutual correspondence in an ongoing process.

It follows from this theoretical foundation that work adjustment is predicated on two types of correspondence. These have been termed:

Correspondence I: The individual's skills, knowledge, abilities and personality traits must match the requirements of the job, as well as the expectations deriving from the organization's culture and particular structural features (e.g. managerial procedures, communication systems, etc.).

In an interesting recent development, Cable and Judge (1997) found that even interviewers' *perceptions* of the congruence of applicants' values to those of the organization were the best predictors of hiring decisions:

Correspondence II: The job and organizational environment must satisfy the employee's work-related needs.

For instance, work environments that reward individual competitive effort have been found to attract employees with a high need for achievement (Bretz, Ash, and Dreher, 1989; Turban and Keon, 1993). Tziner (1983) also demonstrates that in the case of social workers, the better the correspondence between occupational rewards and individual occupational needs, the greater the degree of employee satisfaction at work (canonical coefficient, $R_c = 0.84$, $P<0.01$).

Dawis and Lofquist postulate that Correspondence I leads to *satisfactoriness*, denoting the degree to which the individual employee actually meets job requirements and organizational expectations. Correspondence II is said to lead to *work satisfaction*, the extent to which workers experience fulfillment of their work-related needs. Both work satisfaction and satisfactoriness are necessary conditions for the development of work adjustment. Operationally, these states can be observed in employees who deliberately opt for a particular job or organization over alternative possibilities, although this choice may not always be directly in their hands.

The notion of correspondence is neatly incorporated into Schneider's (1983, 1987) attraction-selection-attrition (ASA) conceptual scheme, which clearly demonstrates that forces within the organization operate over time to attract, select, and retain those workers who are the most compatible with the organization's characteristics and expectations. Specifically, the ASA scheme posits that persons are attracted to and selected by organizations to the extent that their personal characteristics are suited to the corresponding attributes of the organization, such as culture and climate. That is to say that people tend to select those kinds of organizations and occupations that suit their personalities, interests, and capabilities. Conversely, organizations, for their part, hire those candidates with anticipated fit in outlook and behavior.

It has been noted that in some cases, individuals displaying characteristics unsuited to organizations may still gain entry. However, they exhibit a higher propensity to leave than others (Schaunbroeck et al., 1998). Generally speaking, therefore, the outcome of these mutually attracting elements results in the natural creation of increasingly homogeneous groups of employees with respect to attitudes, work values, and work abilities, since, in the long run, those who do not fit tend to leave. Among senior staff, this homogeneity of 'work personality' has been substantiated in a recent empirical study of the personalities of the managers hired by certain organizations (Schneider, Smith, Taylor, and Fleenor, 1998).

The Role of Personality as a Moderator

Clearly, personality moderates a worker's ability to adjust to the job environment (Correspondence I). Holland (1985), for example, describes the realistic personality, whose personality and functional attributes (interests, skills, abilities, and traits) produce the type of person who attempts to create a congruent environment that allows needs and interests to be satisfied. Friedman and Rosenman (1974) speak of the Type A personality, the highly competitive and aggressive achiever who expresses excessive hostility in response to frustration and authority. Burke and Dezca (1982) posit that such a personality type might best achieve in a loosely structured work environment that would probably be perceived as minimally coercive, restrictive, and frustrating. Moreover, high achievers appear to prefer organizations that reward workers according to accomplishments, rather than seniority (Bretz, Ash, and Dreher, 1989), and that are smaller and perceived as providing more opportunities for personal responsibility, accountability, feedback, and rewards (Turban and Keon, 1993). Turban and Keon also found that, conversely, employees with low self-esteem are more attracted to decentralized structures in which responsibility is more likely to be diffused or shared, and where the participatory nature of the decision-making process tends to offer increased opportunities for recognition and satisfaction.

Personality factors also play an important role in the ongoing process of work adjustment (the P-E fit), which reflects the mutual readjustment of both the employee and employers to changes in the work environment. According to their personality style, individuals may opt to change either their organizational environment (active adjustment) or their reactions to it (reactive adjustment). Whatever the approach adopted, as delineated by Dawis and Lofquist, four distinct responses to an adjustment crisis can be distinguished: (1) the degree of speed in acting/reacting (celerity); (2) the level of activity exhibited while acting/reacting (pace); (3) the typical pattern of pace displayed while acting/reacting (rhythm); and (4) the duration of the action/reaction process (endurance). If an individual's personality style corresponds to the personality profile required for adequate functioning in a particular organizational environment, then attainment of work adjustment becomes probable; otherwise, either the individual or the environment will have to change to avoid strain.

Two additional personality factors may be configured into the individual's response in respect to work adjustment. First, Dawis and Lofquist note that the timing of the readjustment process reflects the employee's degree of 'flexibility', which denotes the amount of discorrespondence with the organizational environment that an individual is able to tolerate before being motivated to do something about it. Second, if readjustment fails, the employee will probably quit the frustrating work environment. The extent to which a person will persist in the attempt to readjust before deciding to leave is termed 'perseverance'.

Tziner and Meir stress the importance of incorporating personality into the correspondence equation. They argue that personality style 'constitutes an essential component of the individual's personality which, along with skills, knowledge and abilities, determines Correspondence I, assuming respective job and organization requirements for these factors are satisfied' (p. 98).

The Role of the Work Environment

In regard to the work environment, Tziner (1987) emphasizes the subjective element of the worker's view of the job context by distinguishing between *preferred* and *perceived* ('actual') organizational climate. Results of a survey conducted on 400 employees from a large industrial company revealed that preferred and perceived achievement climates (both alone and together) made the major contributions to the prediction of the workers' attitudes and behavior at work. The employees' congruency (as operationalized via a self-calculated discrepancy measure) also added a unique value to the relationship.

Two related studies similarly address this notion of subjective perception. The first, by Bretz and Judge (1994), illustrates empirically that individuals to whom the organizational environment appears congruent with their organizational preferences report a higher level of job satisfaction and have longer tenure with their organizations than those experiencing less congruence of this type. Moreover, Bretz and Judge's (1994) data confirm an indirect effect of the P-E fit between organizational preferences and organizational environment on certain indicators of career success, such as salary and job level.

In the second study, Tziner and Falbe (1990) demonstrate that individuals acting in an organizational milieu that they perceive as corresponding to their achievement orientation exhibit higher levels of performance, work satisfaction, and organizational commitment than counterparts who display incongruency. Of particular interest in this study is the distinction made between individuals from two different occupational strata: Group A, whose work was complex and required a high level of skill, and Group B whose work was routine and repetitive. The researchers found a moderate but significant relationship between satisfaction and achievement orientation for both groups, indicating that satisfaction does not weaken the orientation toward achievement. This finding brings into question motivational theories that are assumed to apply to higher-skilled employees rather than the lesser-skilled.

In another investigation of the relevance of sociodemographic variables on workers' perceptions, Tziner and Dolan (1984) conducted a study on 628 randomly selected estate agents in Montreal in which they examined the relationship of level of education and length of real-estate experience with six perceived climate dimensions, and their individual and combined effects on work performance (real-estate earnings and total transactions). Overall, notwithstanding interpretations of causality and specific findings directly related to the real-estate profession, the data indicate the following:

1   Organizational climate is likely to be perceived differently as respondents vary along the two independent variables, and especially with length of real-estate experience.
2   The climate dimension is associated with performance measures directly rather than indirectly through its relationship with performance measures.
3   The variance explained in both of the work performance measures when all six perceived climate dimensions and two sociodemographic variables are entered (added) together is significantly higher than the variance explained by each alone (i.e., when combined, the variables relate to substantially higher levels of work performance than either of the independent variables).
4   The performance criterion used may determine which type of variable – sociodemographic or climate – will play a more substantial role in predicting performance.

Lastly, in an extension of the examination of sociodemographic factors to different international contexts, Falbe, Nobel, and Tziner (1988) caution against the over-generalization of results in studies of performance, especially for findings relating to achievement motivation. In their study, 132 middle managers from the United States were compared with a comparable group of 210 Israeli middle managers on different aspects of achievement motivation and behavior modalities in the workplace (preference for, undertaking of, and satisfaction with certain tasks). The motivational aspects included: uncertainty of outcome, difficult versus easy tasks, taking risks, problem solving, and satisfaction of the need to succeed.

The major differences found between the two groups concerned the dimensions of uncertainty and calculated risk, where inconsistencies were evident in the behavior modalities. While American managers expressed a *preference* for tasks involving uncertainty ($t = 3.26$, $p < .01$) and calculated risk ($t = 3.58$, $p < .001$), Israeli managers were more likely to express *satisfaction* with them ($t = 6.56$, $p < .001$ and $t = 2.54$, $p < .05$, respectively), and reported considerably more *undertaking* of such tasks ($t = 2.80$, $p < .05$ and $t = 2.10$, $p < .05$. for uncertainty and calculated risk, respectively). In short, the two groups of managers varied not only on elements of achievement motivation, but also on behavior modalities. Furthermore, a preference for a particular task was not necessarily accompanied by report of either more satisfaction with, or undertaking of, that task.

Falbe et al. (1988) posit that these differences in achievement motivation might be explained in terms of the values of the sociocultural context in which the managers work and the reward systems of organizations in different cultures. They note, for example, that despite the stereotypical portrait of the American manager as a risk-taker (which may reflect a socially desirable response), the reality is that American organizations discourage risk-taking at the level of middle management by failing to provide rewards for such behavior (Kanter, 1983; Hayes and Wheelwright 1984; Pinchot 1985).

In contrast, previous research indicates that Israelis are caught in the contradiction of wishing to avoid uncertainty (Hofstede, 1980), possibly because of a low threshold for it, and being confronted with a high degree of uncertainty and risk in everyday life (Breznitz, 1983). This contradiction offers a plausible explanation for the fact that managers express a lower preference for, yet a higher undertaking of, risky tasks. Moreover, in the smaller, more homogeneous Israeli society, managers at all levels of organizations are, of necessity, faced with risk and uncertainty. Performing under such conditions may not be preferred, but the ability to do so is valued by society. This kind of social reward may, in itself, be conceived of as a special instance of incentive, in line with other findings that indicate a link between achievement and recognition from the group (Ramirez and Price-Williams, 1976).

A recent empirical study conducted by Christiansen, Villanova, and Mikuky (1997) strongly supports the proposition that compatibility between preferred organizational climate and actual climate affects work attitudes, work satisfaction, and turnover. Moreover, based on a sample of Belgian health care organizations, Vandenberghe (1999) also demonstrates that nursing recruits whose work values profile is closer to that of the employing organizations are more likely to remain in the workplace than those with a less similar profile. This study provides further confirmation of the suggestion that quitting or staying in a job is linked to the person-culture fit, where culture is operationalized in terms of the perception of compatible work values.

Antecedents and Outcomes of Work Adjustment

Tziner and Meir list four antecedents of work adjustment: satisfaction, satisfactoriness (after Dawis and Lofquist, 1984), organizational commitment, and job involvement (after Saks, 1995), along with several common behavioral manifestations of its outcomes, including: lateness, absenteeism, quality and rate of performance (and alterations in them), voluntary turnover (or voluntary tenure), intentional organizational misbehavior, and organizational citizenship behavior. All these are amenable to observation and measurement.

Satisfaction Work satisfaction is generally considered to represent the collection of attitudes held by individuals concerning particular aspects of their work, including working conditions, organizational policy, recognition, supervision, and pay. These attitudes may be more or less favorable, depending on the discrepancy between the individual's work-related needs, desires, and expectations, and what is actually attainable from a specific job in a particular organizational setting. Stated briefly, work satisfaction is a function of the degree of correspondence between a worker's needs and the need-gratifying capacity of the work setting (Betz, 1969; Porter, 1963).

The relationships between work satisfaction, absenteeism, and turnover have been well researched (see: Clegg, 1983; Hanisch and Hulin, 1991; Mitra, Jenkins, and Gupta, 1992; Koslowsly et al., 1997; Sagie and Koslowsky, 1998). Mitra et al. (1992) performed a meta-analysis in which 33 correlations from 17 studies were combined, yielding a corrected mean correlation of 0.33 between absenteeism and turnover. Three additional meta-analyses (Hackett and Guion, 1985; McShane, 1985; Scott and Taylor, 1985) provide reasonable support (estimated correlation coefficient slightly exceeding 0.20) for the work satisfaction-employee absenteeism relationship. Similarly, work satisfaction has also been shown to affect turnover (Lum et al., 1998).

The findings of a negative relationship between work satisfaction and turnover appear to corroborate the connection between the level of work satisfaction and the voluntary decision to stay in an organization, which, according to Dawis and Lofquist, should be mediated by work adjustment. Hom et al. (1992), however, suggest that work maladjustment is a necessary but insufficient mediating factor to account for work dissatisfaction that results in turnover. They concur with Mobley, Horner, and Hollingsworth (1978) that withdrawal cognitions (thoughts of quitting, the intention to leave a job or seek another one) would have to evolve as mediating precursors for turnover to occur.

The wider contextual framework in which these mediating behaviors manifest themselves has been studied by Gerhart (1990), who notes that dissatisfied employees generally try to hold on to their jobs when the job market is tight. Similarly, Hulin (1991) argues that 'dissatisfaction should lead to organizational turnover only if the dissatisfied individual perceives that there are better alternatives available' (p. 446). While these observations do not preempt the possibility of a satisfied worker being tempted by better career prospects elsewhere, in general it can be said that the satisfied tend to stay and the dissatisfied tend to leave (Blau and Boal, 1987).

Organizational commitment   Organizational commitment, a psychological state that characterizes an employee's relationship with the organization, has been found to be an important variable linked to both work satisfaction (Hom, Katerberg, and Hulin, 1979; Cheloha and Farr, 1980) and turnover (Cohen, 1993). Tziner and Meir contend that, based on recent empirical research, it seems appropriate to treat the term 'organizational commitment' as a three-dimensional structure consisting of: (1) affective commitment, (2) continuance commitment, and (3) normative/moral commitment (Allen and Meyer, 1990; Jaros, Jermier, Koehler, and Sincich, 1993; Hackett, Bycio, and Hausdorf, 1994).

Strong affective attachment evolves as the consistency between employees' goals, values, and expectations on the one hand, and their positive experiences in an organization on the other, increases. A state of continuous commitment develops as employees come to realize that they have accumulated investments or benefits that would be lost if they quit. Normative/moral commitment emerges as a result of (1) socialization experiences that emphasize the appropriateness of remaining loyal, and (2) the receipt of benefits that create a subjective need to reciprocate. Empirical research has corroborated the outcomes of these forms of attachment. From a positive perspective, employees with a strong *affective* commitment identify with and voluntarily stay with the organization; those with a strong *continuance* commitment stay on because they need to; and those with a strong *normative/moral* commitment remain because they feel they ought to (Allen and Meyer, 1990).

A number of the negative links between voluntary turnover and both affective and normative/moral commitment have also been documented (Sommers, 1995). Tziner and Meir argue that the accumulated knowledge of the connection between organizational commitment and work satisfaction (Mathieu and Zajac, 1990) indicates that the relationship between work satisfaction and voluntary stay (tenure) with an organization is also partially accounted for by some of these affective components of organizational commitment.

Job involvement   Job involvement is defined as the extent to which the individual identifies psychologically with his or her job (Kanungo, 1979; Blau, 1985). Since it has been causally linked to work satisfaction (Kanungo, 1982), job involvement may also be responsible in part for turnover. This suggestion is borne out by Cotton and Tuttle's (1986) finding that lack of job involvement is thought to partially account for voluntary turnover, though less so than organizational commitment.

In a review of previously published studies, Hackett (1989) uncovered a reasonably substantial correlation between absenteeism and job involvement (r = 0.36), in contrast to a much weaker correlation between absenteeism and organizational commitment (r - 0.12). He concludes that absenteeism is most affected by the intrinsically motivating aspects of the work itself (as reflected by job involvement). Tziner and Meir regard this correlation with caution, however, since Hackett employed an overall measure of organizational commitment, rather than the three independent manifestations of the relationship between absenteeism and job involvement-affective, continuance, and normative/moral-described above.

In bringing together all the available findings associated with three of the antecedents[1] and their outcomes, Tziner and Meir point out that both organizational commitment and job involvement share a natural frame of reference to work satisfaction. Organizational commitment draws on the belief that the organization can aid individuals in meeting some of their existence needs (Alderfer, 1969), while job involvement draws on the belief that the job has the ability to fulfill growth or psychological needs. The existence needs underlie continuance commitment and correspond to the extrinsic aspects of work satisfaction, while the self-actualization needs are gratified by job content, and correspond to the intrinsic aspects of work satisfaction.

The Progressive Model of Withdrawal

These research findings should make it possible to discern a pattern of causal relationships between the various manifestations of withdrawal behaviors in the workplace. Researchers currently stress that negative feelings or aversive attitudes, such as disenchantment or resentment, can be considered a form of psychological withdrawal that precedes any form of behavioral withdrawal (Tziner and Vardi, 1984). Conversely, in terms of the personal motives of the employee, workers' expressions of job dissatisfaction or low level of organizational commitment, such as absenteeism, may be the conscious or unconscious reflections of these 'invisible' feelings (Hanisch and Hulin, 1991). From this perspective, it stands to reason that employees who are highly satisfied with their jobs, or who are strongly committed to the organization, avoid psychological withdrawal in order to maintain continued attachment to work (Blau and Boal, 1987).

Psychological withdrawal appears to signal or predict a large range of objective withdrawal behaviors (Brooke and Price, 1989; Gellatly, 1995). They begin with relatively 'mild' forms, such as withholding efforts at work or 'social loafing' (Rosse, 1988; Kidwell and Bennett, 1993; Birati and Tziner, 1996), whereby employees appear at work but do not carry out their duties to the best of their ability. In other words, they are physically present but may be mentally absent, either totally or partially. Such a state will obviously hamper effective organizational functioning.

The next two phases in the sequence are lateness (including early leaving; Shafritz, 1980) and absenteeism. These behaviors indicate that the employee is retreating from work but still maintains organizational and job-role affiliations. The final stage of this progressive retreat (see Fig. 1) is the most severe withdrawal behavior, voluntary or involuntary turnover, termed full- or job-withdrawal by Hanisch and Hulin (1991).

As is apparent from Figure 3.1, the process is reversible. Individuals may backtrack to earlier phases of retreat from later manifestations of withdrawal; for example, they may resume manifestations of lateness rather than absenteeism. However, psychological withdrawal is likely to appear at each stage. In their investigation of the interrelationship between withdrawal behaviors in the progressive model, Koslowsky et al. (1997) found that late behavior correlates both with affective manifestations of psychological withdrawal (e.g., dissatisfaction, poor commitment, intent to quit) and with withdrawal behaviors (poor performance, absenteeism, and turnover). However, it was found to be more closely associated with adjacent behaviors in the withdrawal path than with more distant variables (e.g., correlation of mean lateness with absence = .40; correlation of mean lateness with later turnover = .07).

Figure 3.1 is useful in that it also presents, in the right-hand box, the impact of the focal employee's withdrawal upon the psychological and behavioral withdrawal of others in the work team or organization. These manifestations, related to work attendance, formal rules, norms, and values, may occur all along the withdrawal path. Simultaneously, the conduct and misconduct of other workers influence the withdrawal behaviors of the focal employee (Sagie and Koslowsky, 1998). The mutual influence between the individual employee and work group peers in the context of group norms in the workplace is a moderating factor increasingly used to explain withdrawal behaviors (Nicholson and Johns, 1985; Haccoun and Jeanrie, 1995; Markham and McKee, 1995). This is certainly an area ripe for further research.

Other models, in addition to progression, can also be used to describe the interrelationships among withdrawal behaviors (Johns, 1997; Koslowsky et al., 1997). For example, the compensatory approach alludes to the negative relationships between the various forms of withdrawal at work (Hill and Trist,

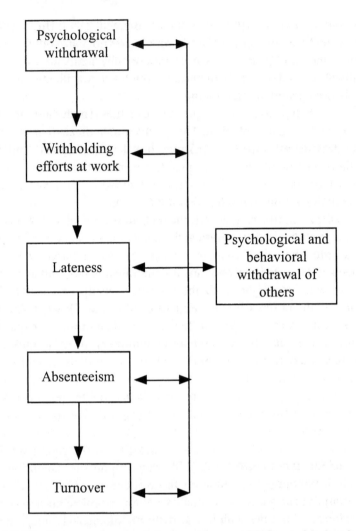

Figure 3.1 The Progressive model of employee withdrawal behavior

1955; Nicholson and Goodge, 1976), claiming that people can make use of different withdrawal behaviors to satisfy the same needs. Thus, some are more likely to come to work late, and others to take more days off. By opting for one form of withdrawal, people tend to avoid other forms. Furthermore, if workers cannot satisfy personal needs by means of partial withdrawal, they may then choose to withdraw fully from the workplace.

In contrast, according to the independence model (March and Simon, 1959; Sheridan, 1992), the different forms of withdrawal are not consistently related to each other. Hence, the adoption of one form does not necessarily indicate an inclination to use or avoid others. The 'spillover' model, on the other hand, assumes a positive relationship between withdrawal behaviors, without specifying any temporal or sequential order (Beehr and Gupta, 1978). Unlike the previous models, this approach implies that an individual is likely to react to certain antecedents (related to personality or situation) with a *set* of withdrawal behaviors rather than a singular response (Blau, 1964; Knatz, Inwald, Brockwell, and Tran, 1992).

The majority of recent empirical findings provide support for the progressive model (Rosse and Miller, 1984; Larson and Fukami, 1985; Rosse, 1988; Mitra et al., 1992), although not exclusively (Johns, 1997). Moreover, Koslowsky et al.'s (1997) meta-analysis demonstrates the dominance of the progression model in the mainstream of research. Accordingly, in line with the progressive approach, we conceive here of the withdrawal phenomenon as a set of correlated and relatively ordered behaviors. Indeed, on the basis of the meta-analytic results, it is even possible to arrive at tentative estimates of the interrelations among the various measures of psychological and behavioral withdrawal.

The Moderating Effects of Workers' Characteristics on Withdrawal Behaviors

In a series of studies on withdrawal behaviors, Tziner and associates investigated the moderating effects of specific qualities that may have a bearing on the generalized results. For instance, Tziner and Vardi (1984) demonstrated that, in a 6-month period, altruistic social workers vented their frustrations at work (as measured by two facets of satisfaction) in directions other than absenteeism (total number of work days vs. total number of absences). In another study, Dolan and Tziner (1988) focused on the impact of previous experience with automation on experienced stress associated with different work aspects among a group of secretaries at a large Canadian university. As expected, those without the appropriate background reported higher levels of experienced stress related to aspects such as task difficulty and interest in the task. Those with experience of automation, however, also displayed high levels of concern regarding proper training and information, presumably since their previous experience of technology had so conditioned them.

These findings clearly indicate that the concept of work satisfaction prescribed by the Theory of Work Adjustment actually represents an entire spectrum of work-related attitudes, including work satisfaction, job involvement, and organizational commitment, that underlie a range of withdrawal behaviors, most notably absenteeism and turnover. As we have noted, work satisfaction is a product of Correspondence II, which reflects the organization's attractiveness for the employee. All of this is summed up succinctly by Tziner and Meir in the following graphic statement:

> *Correspondence II* $\prod$ work satisfaction (and additional work-related attitudes, e.g. job involvement, organizational commitment) $\prod$ work adjustment/maladjustment $\prod$ voluntary tenure with the organization, absenteeism, or voluntary turnover.

Satisfactoriness

It will be recalled that in contrast to Correspondence II, the concept of satisfactoriness concerns the extent to which the organization is satisfied with the performance of the employee, defined as Correspondence I. According to the Theory of Work Adjustment, a high level of satisfactoriness is also conducive to work adjustment, the outcome of which will be voluntary tenure with the organization. Conversely, as demonstrated by Bycio, Hackett, and Alvares (1990), a low level of satisfactoriness engenders work maladjustment and consequent voluntary turnover ($r = -0.31$, $r = -0.26$, in two separate studies) or involuntary turnover ($r = -0.51$, $r = -0.52$, in two separate studies). Moreover, the mean correlation coefficient of $r = 0.25$ found in this study between satisfaction (workers' perception of the job) and satisfactoriness (employer's perception of workers' performance) further sustains the proposed relationship between these two concepts.

There is also support for a strong relationship (mean $r = -0.36$) between performance and organizational commitment (Brett, Cron, and Slocum, 1995), which may be moderated by what Bycio et al. (1990) label the 'extent of economic dependency on work'. According to these researchers, this variable also moderates the performance-work satisfaction relationship. In one particular study, Williams and Livingstone (1994) investigated the degree to which productivity and tenure are related, and note that the more productive a professor, the greater the likelihood that their potential salary would increase by moving on to another university, making them more prone to quit their present job. They also found a propensity of untenured poorly performing professors to leave because of the lack of organizational commitment engendered by the lack of work security.

In general, then, the Theory of Work Adjustment suggests that the probability that individuals will be *forced out* of their work environment is inversely related to satisfactoriness. On the other hand, the probability that individuals will leave their work environment *voluntarily* is inversely related to work satisfaction.

Satisfactoriness may lead to two other possible outcomes, termed organizational intentional misbehavior and organizational citizenship behavior, phenomena that appear to be located at opposite poles of a continuum. Vardi and Wiener (1992) define organizational intentional misbehavior as any deliberate action by members of the organization that defies or violates shared organizational norms, expectations, core societal values, mores, or standards of proper conduct. These organizational misbehaviors typically consist of such elements as sabotage, lying about hours worked, verbal abuse, stealing from co-workers or the company, intentionally working slowly, and wasting resources (Robinson and Bennett, 1995). Such misbehaviors are common when employees exhibit dissatisfaction resulting from a low level or lack of Correspondence I, that is, when they perceive a lack of fulfillment of work-related needs or when their work values clash with those of the organization.

Conversely, organizational citizenship is characterized by unrewarded behaviors essential for organizational effectiveness that go beyond the call of duty or job descriptions (Smith, Organ, and Near, 1983). In line with social exchange theory (Gouldner, 1960; Blau 1964), this exemplary behavior may be seen as an example of the sense of reciprocity felt by a satisfied employee, reflecting the subjective fulfillment of work-related needs (see: Organ, 1988).

The negative effects of work maladjustment on the individual are well documented, and include psychological manifestations (e.g., burnout, depression), psychological disorders (e.g., elevated blood pressure, high level of cholesterol), and behavioral strains (e.g., excessive drinking, smoking). According to the Theory of Work Adjustment, these manifestations are interpreted as the result of Discorrespondence I, the lack of fit between work ability requirements and the employees' actual work-related competence, or of Discorrespondence II, the lack of fit between work-related interests/needs and commensurate organizational/occupational rewards (French and Caplan, 1972; Blau, 1981; Meir and Melamed, 1986; Tziner, 1990; Smith and Tziner, 1998).

For example, Smith and Tziner's (1998) study on nurses in a Canadian hospital examined the moderating effects of affective disposition and social support on the relationship between fit and strains. Person-environment fit was measured in terms of occupational needs and reinforcers, and both positive affectivity (Brief et al., 1988) and negative affectivity (Watson and Clark, 1984) were investigated. Consistent with previous findings, fit was found to be related to work satisfaction and to all but one measure of psychological strain. The study also produced some support for the moderating effects of positive affectivity on work satisfaction and burnout, and scores on both positive and negative affectivity showed significant main effects on strain measures. A model of the process involved in linking strains with the two types of discorrespondence was developed by Tziner and Dawis (1988), with several of its predictions recently corroborated by Sutherland, Fogerty, and Pithers (1995).

Correspondence: Concluding Remarks

In the introduction to their survey, Tziner and Meir graphically portray the classic definition of Correspondence I as follows:

> *Correspondence I*   ∏   satisfactoriness   ∏   work adjustment/ maladjustment ∏ voluntary tenure with the organization or voluntary/ involuntary turnover.

In light of many of the findings described above, however, they argue for a need to amend the overall Theory of Work Adjustment so as to incorporate all the antecedents and outcomes of work adjustment elaborated upon with respect to both types of correspondence. The latest empirical and theoretical observations, as outlined here, reinforce this recommendation. The interrelationships of the components in such an extended theory are depicted in Figure 3.2.

Holland's Congruence Theory (1973, 1985)

Congruence and Well-being

As noted above, Holland (1973, 1985) offers an alternative conceptualization of individual-work environment correspondence whereby people flourish in an environment that fits their type. The fit between personality type and environment type is labeled congruence. In general, congruent person-environment interactions are conducive to positive outcomes in the workplace, as indicated by satisfaction, stability, and achievements; incongruent

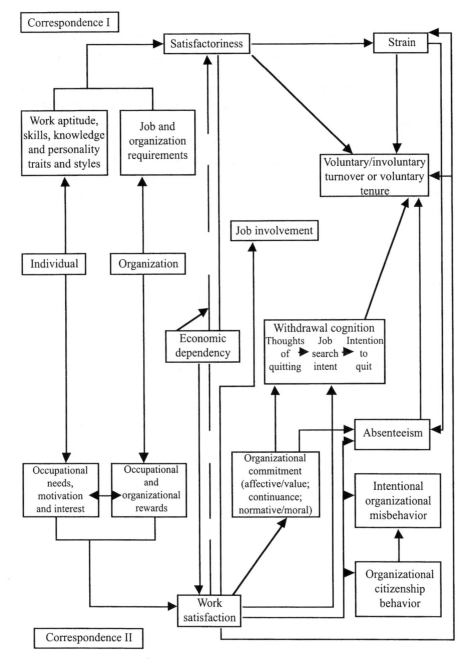

Figure 3.2   The Interrelationships of the extended Theory of Work Adjustment

interactions lead to negative outcomes, such as burnout, absenteeism, and turnover. This concept of congruence has received considerable attention in the study of occupational behavior and attitudes (e.g., Holland, 1973, 1985; Meir, 1989, 1995; Tziner and Falbe, 1990).

Holland conceptualizes the person component of congruence in terms of the individual worker's personality, classified as one of six types: R (Realistic), I (Investigative), A (Artistic), S (Social), E (Enterprising), or C (Conventional). The environment component of congruence is construed in comparable terms, that is, as six environment types labeled in the same way. Thus, as Holland puts it: 'Different types require different environments. For instance, Realistic types flourish in Realistic environments because such an environment provides the opportunities and rewards a Realistic type needs' (p. 5).

Holland's Congruence Theory has gained impressive empirical support (see the reviews by: Spokane, 1985; Edwards, 1991; and the annotated bibliography by Holland and Gottfredson, 1990). In their meta-analysis of 41 different studies, Assouline and Meir (1987) found a total of 77 correlations between congruence and relevant variables, including satisfaction (53 correlations), stability (17 correlations), and achievements (7 correlations). The breakdown of the 53 correlations between congruence and satisfaction yielded a mean correlation of 0.21 (total $N = 9,041$; 95 per cent confidence interval from -.09 to .51). In another meta-analysis, Tranberg, Slane, and Ekeberg (1993) found a mean correlation of .20 between congruence and job satisfaction (20 studies, $N = 8,608$), with a mean correlation of .33 (7 studies, N not reported) for the Social type, and much lower correlations for the other types.

It should be noted that these studies incorporated investigations of both environmental and occupational congruence. Conceptually, however, Tziner and Meir distinguish between the two, defining *environmental congruence* as the fit between personality type and environmental type, and *occupational congruence* as the fit between vocational interests and the requirements of an occupation.

By way of preamble to Tziner and Meir's treatment of this theory, two further remarks are in order. First, in light of the preponderance of studies in the area that employ satisfaction as the indicator of well-being, the interpretations and recommendations suggested by Tziner and Meir focus primarily on this concept. Second, the authors note that it is important that any attempt to discern the qualitative nature of the relationship between work satisfaction and congruence relate to both the variance among established findings on the relationship between these two factors, and the significance of the consistently low correlations found between congruence and either stability or achievements, in contrast to satisfaction (p. 105). The following sections bring the reader up to date with some of the latest theoretical and empirical findings pertaining to this relationship.

Environmental Congruence

Tziner and Meir base their explanation of the relationship between environmental congruence and satisfaction on three primary sources, Holland and Gottfredson (1976), Meir (1989), and Meir and Yaari (1988). The explanation can readily be framed in the language of learning theory: 'An individual receives positive reinforcements from his/her environment for congruent behavior, and negative reinforcements for incongruent behavior. The positive reinforcements give rise to satisfaction and further congruent behavior, as well as the desire to remain in the environment ... Where the environment is important to the individual, such reinforcements cannot be disregarded' (Meir, 1989, pp. 226–7).

An employee's environmental congruence is measured empirically in three steps. First, the personality type of all the people in the environment is established. Second, the environmental type is defined by finding the specific type with the highest frequency. Finally, the individual's type is compared with that of the environmental type. Responses to an adequate inventory derived from Holland's (1973, 1985) Self-Directed Search is usually the preferred tool for determining an individual's personality type. Furthermore, most studies either make do with expert judgments as to the environmental type (as the comparative basis for assigning individual congruence scores), or rely on the measurement of available respondents, since the measurement of all the people in a given environment is often an unwieldy process.

Both measures of types require that the environment be defined as a single entity. Consequently, the 20 correlations between environmental congruence and job satisfaction reported in the meta-analysis by Assouline and Meir (1987) are based on 20 specific environments. Within each of these, the independent variable is the similarity to, or proximity between, each individual's personality type and his or her environmental type, and the dependent variable is job satisfaction.

This meta-analysis found the mean correlation between *environmental congruence* (congruence with the others in one's environment) and satisfaction to be 0.29 (20 correlations, total N = 995, 95 per cent confidence interval between 0.20 and 0.38). It may be recalled that the overall mean correlation between congruence (of both kinds) and satisfaction was found here to be only 0.21. Thus environmental congruence would seem to correlate more with satisfaction than occupational congruence, perhaps because employees can more easily disregard incongruent reinforcements in the workplace (by compensating through avocational activity, for example) than in social environments.

In a recent study, Meir, Tziner, and Glazner (1997) propose that the relatively high variance of the correlation coefficients, even after the breakdown by environmental reference or personality type, could stem from the existence of a moderating variable that is likely to affect the relationship between congruence and behavioral or attitudinal outcomes. Meir, Keinan, and Segal (1986) suggest one such variable when they report a positive correlation of .77 between group importance and the relationship of environmental congruence with job satisfaction (concurrent measurements). In other words, a higher correlation was found for groups whose members attached greater importance to being associated with the group than for those whose members felt this to be of less significance. Consequently, Meir et al. (1986) conclude that if the group is important to its individuals, the reinforcements given by the group members for congruent or incongruent behavior produce a meaningful positive or negative impact, respectively, on the individual member.

In an attempt to ascertain the extent to which this trend is replicated in a different cultural milieu (specifically, the Francophone in Canada), Fournier and Tziner (1995) conducted a similar study in which the measures of environmental congruence, group importance, and job satisfaction were collected at the same time. They found that job satisfaction was insignificantly related to environmental congruence, yet did correlate significantly with group importance. Thus, group importance did not emerge as a moderator, but rather as an additional independent predictor of job satisfaction. In light of this finding, Meir et al's (1997) study chose to focus on the relative role of group importance and environmental congruence as *independent variables* in determining job satisfaction, and on the unique contribution of these two variables to its explained variance.

In addition, in contrast to studies of occupational congruence (often regarded as a predictor of job satisfaction), the same researchers underscore the empirical fact, noted above, that measures of environmental congruence and job satisfaction in previous studies were conducted concurrently. Accordingly, they attribute the inherent long-term instability of the levels of these variables to changes in personnel or in the personality type of other members in the work environment. Meir et al. (1997) therefore departed from the norm by comparing the relationship between environmental congruence and job satisfaction both shortly after the employees joined their chosen occupation *and* following several months of adaptation to the new occupational setting. Remarking on the heuristic and practical implications of such an investigation for personnel hiring and placement, the researchers suggest that (1) both environmental congruence and group importance are positively related to job satisfaction, and (2) the relationships between environmental congruence and group importance to job satisfaction increase with time. As this comprehensive investigation can serve as a useful illustration in terms of methodology, it is described here in some detail.

Participants were 156 individuals almost equally distributed along Holland's (1985) six RIASEC personality types (Realistic, Investigative, Artistic, Social, Enterprising, and Conventional). Four inventories were used: *Holland's (1973) Self-Directed Search (SDS) in its Hebrew version,* which contains 10, 10, and 12 items for the Activities, Competencies, and Occupations sections, respectively, for each of the six RIASEC personality types, with different versions for men and women. The split-half reliability of the Hebrew version of the inventory yielded .88 as the median of the six RIASEC reliability coefficients.

Environmental Type Inventory (ETI), especially devised for the study with the purpose of obtaining the participant's judgment of his or her environment type. A three or four line description of Holland's six personality types was formulated by 10 experts, and participants were asked to mark the type that best described their own environment. In this way deficiencies in both the census and expert methods of determining the environment type were avoided (see: Meir, Tziner, and Glazner, 1997, p.347).

The reliability of participants' judgments was examined by the test-retest method, which found that 133 of the 156 participants (85.2 per cent) assigned the same type to their environment after a lapse of 5 to 7 months. Moreover, when the distance between the participant's first and second judgments along the RIASEC structure was compared (e.g., first time R and second time A represents a gap of 2), the correlation between judgments was .95 (N 156). Although several studies (Camp and Chartrand, 1992; Brown and Gore, 1994) have demonstrated the advantages of congruence measures based on two or even three letters of Holland's RIASEC types, it was feared here that as the participants were unfamiliar with this technique, many would be unable to assign two or three letter codes to their environments with an acceptable degree of accuracy.

Group Importance Inventory (GII; Meir et al., 1986*)*, on which participants respond on 9-point scales to questions such as 'To what extent do you care about how your group members relate to you?' and 'To what extent is it important to you that your group members care about the quality of your family life?' A modified inventory was designed for this study to suit its formulation to those participants for whom an educational rather than work environment was the reference group. The split-half reliability coefficients of this inventory were .85 in the original study by Meir et al. (1986), .81 and .89 in the first and second administrations in the present study, respectively, and .86 in the test-retest comparison (N = 156).

Job Satisfaction Inventory, specifically, the Meir and Yaari (1988) Satisfaction Inventory on which participants respond to 10 nine-rank items regarding their satisfaction with their jobs or studies (e.g., 'To what extent are you satisfied with the challenges you meet in your work/studies?'). The split-half reliability of the inventory in its original form (20 ranks per item) was .92 (Meir and Yaari, 1988), and in this study, .88 and .90 for the employee and student versions, respectively.

Each participant responded to the SDS, the ETI, the GII, and the Job Satisfaction Inventory, and then performed the same procedure about half a year later. Environmental congruence scores were assigned to each participant according to the level of fit between his or her first letter code on the SDS and the type that he or she indicated for the environment. A congruence score of 4 was assigned where both letters matched, 3 if the letters were adjacent in the circular arrangement of RIASEC types, 2 if there was one letter between them, and 1 if two other letters intervened between the participant's first letter code and the environmental type as he or she perceived it. As indicated above, only the first letter of each subject's code was used to describe personality type. In the case of tied scores on the SDS, the median of the respective congruence scores was used.

The correlation between environmental congruence scores in the two administrations was found to be .85 (N = 156), and the reliability of all the measures, as examined either by the split-half method or the test-retest method (gap of 5-7 months), was again about .85. In addition, group importance scores were assigned to each participant according to the sum of his or her scores on the GII (median importance score = 83).

The results of the study revealed that the correlations between environmental congruence and job satisfaction were .215 and .224 for the first and second measurements of congruence, respectively. These coefficients are very close to the .21 and .20 mean correlations between environmental congruence and job satisfaction found in the two meta-analyses by Assouline and Meir (1987) and Tranberg et al. (1993), respectively. Here, however, although environmental congruence was significantly related to job satisfaction ($r = .22$, $p < .05$), it did not account for a unique part of the explained variance.

The study also confirmed the predictive validity of environmental congruence, as it was found that of the participants with low congruence scores (1 and 2), only 64 per cent were available for the second administration of the inventories. In contrast, 93 per cent of the participants with high environmental congruence scores (3 and 4) were still in the same job or educational setting five to seven months later ($X^2 = 8.55$, $p < .01$). This finding is in line with Holland's hypothesis of a positive relationship between environmental congruence and stability.

The intercorrelations found in this study between environmental congruence and group importance were .24 and .37 for measurements 1 and 2, respectively. However, the regression analysis results indicated that the beta associated with environmental congruence was not statistically significant ($\beta = .02$). Group importance, on the other hand, produced an impressively high correlation coefficient in the *second* measurement ($r = .57$, $p < .01$), and strongly and uniquely contributed to explaining the variance of job satisfaction ($\beta = .569$, $p < .01$). Contrary to this second measurement of group importance, both measurements of environmental congruence, as well as the first measurement of group importance, contributed negligibly to predicting job satisfaction. Thus group importance acted as an independent determinant of work satisfaction, and not as a moderator, as had previously been posited by Meir et al. (1986).

Meir et al. (1997) suggest that although environmental congruence appears necessary for the existence of job satisfaction, it is insufficient for its enhancement. Just as individuals first seek to satisfy basic needs before turning to psychological growth needs, in job satisfaction they first attempt to ensure congruence with the work environment and only later become concerned with the social aspects of work, such as those encompassed in group importance. The researchers therefore propose that the impact of group importance on job satisfaction will not be revealed immediately upon an individual's joining an organization, but rather after some adaptation time has elapsed. Thus, environmental congruence apparently accounts for job satisfaction in the short run, whereas group importance comes into play at a later point in time.

Social support would therefore seem to buffer the adverse effects of organizational life (e.g., negative outcomes of stress at work; Koeske and Koeske, 1991). The fact that in this context it has its source in the work group may explain why group importance might be a considerable factor in determining job satisfaction. Placing importance on the work group stems from the perception that it can provide social identity and opportunities for social interaction, as well as help the individual to surmount psychological and functional obstacles encountered in organizational life. Thus, although the contention that fit with the organizational context affects job satisfaction has already gained firm empirical support (Schneider, 1983; 1987), it appears reasonable to assume that the immediate organizational environment, represented by the work group, exerts a stronger impact on job satisfaction than the more remote general organizational environment. This effect is likely to be even stronger when the individual attaches importance to membership in a particular work group. Therefore, when environmental congruence and group importance are allowed to display their effects on job satisfaction concurrently, the effect of the latter will most likely overshadow that of the former. This can probably also account for the unique portion of the explained variance of job satisfaction in Meir et al's study, even though both group importance and environmental congruence revealed statistically significant correlations with job satisfaction. The authors recommend that future studies include several types of congruence (e.g., specialty congruence) with various types of participants and in different work milieus, and that they employ time series designs. This, they claim, would allow for a better examination of the causality of the relationship among the variables in the study. In addition, they recommend exploring the possible effects of environmental congruence and group importance on facets of well-being other than job satisfaction (e.g., performance, achievements, stability, and somatic complaints).

Other future avenues of research include controlling for the possible impact of personality on job satisfaction. Staw and Ross (1985) and Holland and Gottfredson (1990) indicate that some people might be more prone to experiencing job satisfaction than others. Moreover, according to Costa and McCrae (1980), extroverts exhibit a high level of positive affectivity that has been found to affect reported job satisfaction. In other words, positive affectivity results in higher levels of job satisfaction than does negative affectivity, regardless of organizational and occupational contexts. Similarly, Hesketh (1995) found that Enterprising and Social types tend to be more satisfied at work, regardless of their level of congruence. It would therefore seem desirable for the type of personality (e.g., affective disposition) to be explicitly incorporated into future studies of environmental congruence, group importance, and measures of well-being.

Occupational Congruence

It will be recalled that Tziner and Meir define occupational congruence as the fit between vocational interests and occupational requirements. Shartle (1956) makes the following distinctions between three related terms: 'position' is the set of tasks that a single worker has to fulfill in his or her work; 'job' is the set of similar positions in a given organization; and 'occupation' is the group of similar jobs in different organizations. Thus, the number of tasks a worker is expected to fulfill depends on the position. And while the requirements of an occupation obviously vary according to the job, as a rule, the higher the position, the greater the number of tasks to be performed.

Tziner and Meir suggest that an individual's degree of satisfaction in a particular position is reflective of the extent of demands made on his or her time, unique skills, and training. Senior professionals are more likely to be satisfied if the greater proportion of their time and effort is devoted to the substantive content of their profession (on which, among other considerations, their reputation rests), as opposed to, say, the administrative side of their work. Alongside the material benefits and status they offer, jobs defined as 'high-level' also often present workers with the choice of either contending with the position's organizational and decision-making demands or of 'burning out', with all the inevitable negative consequences on satisfaction, stability, and achievement.

Tziner and Meir note that lower-level occupations are characterized not only by simpler tasks, but also by other typical features: training is on-the-job, no higher education is required, the work is monotonous and repetitive, and the status and income of the worker are low. Similarly, unlike senior staff, lower-level workers are usually characterized by limited education and lower abilities, so that promotion opportunities are more restricted. Thus, the abilities and education of lower-level workers are generally congruent with task requirements. As a result, satisfaction may well prevail, requiring fewer incentives to keep such employees in their jobs.

When individual potential exceeds the requirements of the position, or when workers feel under-utilized or under-fulfilled for some other reason, they are unlikely to perceive their jobs as a source of satisfaction, and are more apt to quit. If there are insufficient extrinsic gratifications in the workplace to 'compensate' dissatisfied employees and serve as a justification for staying with the organization, employers may then need to increase external incentives, such as salary, security, and status, in order to retain their workers. Dissatisfied employees may also remain if they lack the self-confidence or the initiative to move on, are afraid of losing real or assumed fringe benefits, perceive a lack of viable alternatives, or are heavily instrumentally committed to their jobs, despite the apparent limitations. However, central to the notion of congruence are the negative outcomes that can be expected in such a situation, such as decreased motivation and performance.

Since moving to the *same* position in another organization offers only a slim chance of additional material benefits, disgruntled employees are only prone to do so if the new job is perceived as more compatible to the their set of task preferences, for example, if less attention needs to be paid to distasteful tasks. A full professor with tenure, for instance, might move to a different university if less emphasis is placed there on teaching undergraduates. From the perspective of Holland's Congruence Theory, we might assume that the former university's board provided insufficient organizational (or environmental) congruence with respect to the teaching of undergraduates.

Meir and Navon's (1992) investigation of the degree of congruence between 'personality type' and 'bank type' in two bank branches provides further illustration of the relationship between satisfaction and congruence. The researchers found that the degree of congruence in the two branches, one defined as Conventional-Social and the other as Conventional-Enterprising, was related both to tellers' satisfaction and to their supervisors' evaluations.

Tziner and Meir argue that the general notion of 'satisfaction' is, in fact, a construct combining various aspects of this psychological state. They posit that within any particular individual, the aspects of satisfaction are positively interrelated; that is, a matrix of all positive correlations among the many aspects of satisfaction can be assumed to exist. According to this line of thinking, an individual's *true* satisfaction score is the personal weighted sum of the various aspects, while the same individual's *empirical* satisfaction score may vary along with the salience of each one. Thus, for example, with respect to the 'salience of satisfaction' associated with the probability of being promoted, it might be suggested that the degree of an employee's (empirical) salience would change with the knowledge that a colleague was about to be promoted.

The more specific term 'occupational (or job) satisfaction' can also be said to incorporate a variety of feelings, from a momentary good feeling to a general state of optimism that such a feeling will persist at work without expectations of future frustrations. Occupational satisfaction is often measured in terms of workers' evaluations of the conditions that might prevail in alternative work settings. For example, employees might be asked to estimate the extent to which their current positions offer the opportunity to exploit their specific skills or task preferences as compared to other places of employment, or the extent to which current good feelings would be felt in a similar occupation in a different organization. Other measures of occupational satisfaction are associated with work conditions, salary, status, work values, and the perception of promotion possibilities.

Satisfaction, whether of a general or specific nature, is a state of mind that varies in response to contextual changes in the workplace, including developments such as changes in job description as a result of technological advances, burnout, and perceived promotion options. Tziner and Meir note that the transient nature of the aspects of satisfaction makes it impossible, when employing correlations, to define a single measure that could predict any specific kind of satisfaction, beyond the stability of satisfaction itself as a measure (notwithstanding the problem of error effect, present in any measuring process).

As we have seen, occupational satisfaction in the workplace depends on the level of fit (congruence) between the tasks employees perform in their positions and their particular skills and preferences. It follows that this level of fit is the plateau for the relation between congruence and satisfaction that, as Tziner and Meir remind us, is 'a limen which cannot be reached (p.108)'. This idea, they note, was behind Spokane's (1985) reference to the '0.30 magic correlational plateau' (p. 335) between congruence and satisfaction. Tziner and Meir offer this observation as a possible explanation for the low values of the mean congruence-satisfaction correlations reported in the meta-analyses by Assouline and Meir (1987) and Tranberg et al. (1993) -r = 0.21 and r = 0.20, respectively.

As noted above, Tziner and Meir also offer a possible explanation for the variance between the results in these studies, suggesting the existence of a moderating variable associated with 'group importance', as indicated by Meir, Keinan, and Segal's (1986) finding of a correlation of 0.77 (rank order) with the correlation between congruence and satisfaction. The moderating effect of group influences on workers' behavior is an area deserving of much further empirical research, the results of which may also help clear up questions regarding the utility of scientific methods for predicting congruence and satisfaction in the workplace.

For some people, it appears, landing a position or choosing an occupation is a matter of chance, the result of a fortuitous encounter or unexpected offer from an employer. For others, however, it involves a careful weighing of plans and options, increasing the probability of congruence between the occupation and the individual's particular skills and preferred activities. That is to say that those making a studied choice can be expected to reach higher mean levels of satisfaction, stability, and achievements in their occupational choice than those who fail to do so or whose choice of job was more random.

In view of the low correlations between congruence and satisfaction, Tziner and Meir raise the question of whether the attempt to achieve a positive relationship between them in the workplace, without professional counseling, is a worthwhile goal. Despite the weakness of this relationship, the authors nevertheless assert that its attainment should be placed high on the agenda of human resource personnel, especially since 'differences in satisfaction may be significant (p.109). They believe this finding is critical, and is borne out by a closer examination of the results of Assouline and Meir's (1987) meta-analysis in which the correlation coefficients were transformed into Binomial Effect Size Display (BESD; Rosenthal, 1990). Employing this technique, Assouline and Meir demonstrated that 'the ratio of satisfied people among those who made congruent occupational choices compared to those whose choices were incongruent was 60.4: 39.6' (p. 343).

Revising the Theoretical Framework

Tziner and Meir (1997) conclude their review of the two theories of work adjustment by juxtaposing them as follows.

According to the **Theory of Work Adjustment**, two kinds of correspondence are conceived as prerequisites for work adjustment:

1 *Correspondence I* Employee abilities, knowledge, skills and personality traits must correspond to work (job and organization) requirements and expectations.
2 *Correspondence II* Employee desires (needs, interests) must correspond to the work (job and organization) gratifications available to fulfill these desires.

According to the **Congruence Theory**, two kinds of congruence are essential preconditions for well-being:

1 *Occupational congruence* There must be correspondence between employee work-related interests and the features of the work available to meet them.
2 *Environmental congruence* There must be correspondence between employee personality and the dominant personality type in the work milieu.

A comparison of the two theories reveals that occupational congruence perfectly matches Correspondence II, particularly if the term occupation is extended to incorporate the organizational milieu in which the work is performed. Environmental congruence, however, accounts only partially for the domain subsumed by Correspondence I, since it is restricted only to personality traits or attributes.

Consequently, Tziner and Meir suggest that Holland's theory be extended to encompass a variety of additional congruencies, for example:

1   between *attitudes, beliefs or values* concerning modes of conduct on the one hand, and *prevailing organizational norms and values* in the relevant organizational milieu on the other;
2   between the *employee's abilities, skills, or knowledge* on the one hand, and *work requirements* on the other.

Following Hesketh's (1995) observation that the Theory of Work Adjustment offers a broader theoretical framework of early career development than Feij et al.'s (1995) model, Tziner and Meir then rationalize that the incorporation of Holland's Congruence Theory into the Theory of Work Adjustment would make it possible to conceptualize and measure more efficiently both individuals' personality traits and the corresponding traits of the organization in the latter theory. They argue that from empirical findings such as those reviewed in this chapter, it is clear that the degree of well-being experienced by an individual in the workplace may be reflected in outcomes beyond work satisfaction, such as absenteeism, physiological strains, voluntary tenure, and organizational citizenship. Thus, the same indicators that describe the construct of well-being at work may also describe the outcomes of work adjustment. In this amended form, Holland's Congruence Theory becomes consistent with, and could in fact be integrated into, the Theory of Work Adjustment.

In light of the more recent findings that reinforce the conclusions reached in Tziner and Meir's review, the modified model clearly appears to lay a coherent conceptual theoretical groundwork for a better understanding of the nature of work adjustment, as well as for devising more efficient means for predicting and fostering this state. The amended Work Adjustment Theory also offers considerable potential for further empirical investigation (especially with respect to the moderating effect of groups), and even for the incorporation of other, non-work related factors, that may impinge on well-being in the workplace, such as what Judge and Waternabe (1993) term 'life satisfaction'.[2]

Notes

1 The fourth antecedent, satisfactoriness, is discussed separately below.
2 This chapter is devoted to the conceptual and theoretical aspects of congruence, and the integration of two dominant theories, the Theory of Work Adjustment and Holland's Congruence Theory. For a discussion of the issues surrounding the operationalizing of congruence and the associated methodological problems, the reader is referred to Edwards (1991) and Hesketh and Gardner (1993). An examination of these papers, along with the current chapter, can afford a comprehensive treatment of both the theoretical and the practical aspects of work adjustment.

References

Aldefer, C.P. (1969). 'A New Theory of Human Needs'. *Organizational Behavior and Human Performance*, 4, pp. 142–75.

Allen, N.J. and Meyer, J.P. (1990). 'The Measurement and Antecedents of Affective Continuance and Normative Commitment to the Organization'. *Journal of Occupational Psychology*, 63, pp. 1–18.

Assouline, M. and Meir, E.I. (1987). 'Meta-Analysis of the Relationship Between Congruence and Well-Being Measures'. *Journal of Vocational Behavior*, 31, pp. 319–32.

Beehr, T.A. and Gupta, N. (1978). 'A Note on the Structure of Employee Withdrawal'. *Organizational Behavior and Human Performance*, 21, pp. 73–9.

Betz, E. (1969). 'Need-Reinforcer Correspondence as a Predictor of Job Satisfaction'. *Personnel and Guidance Journal*, 47, pp. 878–83.

Birati, A. and Tziner, A. (1996). 'Withdrawal Behavior and Withholding Efforts at Work: Assessing the Financial Cost'. *Human Resource Management Review*, 6, pp. 305–14.

Blau, G.J. (1981). 'An Empirical Investigation of Job Stress, Social Support, Service Length, and Job Strain'. *Organizational Behavior and Human Performance*, 27, pp. 279–302.

Blau, G.J. (1985). 'A Multiple Study Investigation of the Dimensionality of Job Involvement'. *Journal of Vocational Behavior*, 27, pp. 19–36.

Blau, G.J. and Boal, K.B. (1987). 'Conceptualizing How Job Involvement and Organizational Commitment Affect Turnover and Absenteeism'. *Academy of Management Review*, 38, pp. 261–71.

Blau, P. (1964). *Exchange and Power in Social Life*. New York: Wiley.

Brett, J.F., Cron, W.L. and Slocum, J.W. (1995). 'Economic Dependency on Work: A Moderator of the Relationship Between Organizational Commitment and Performance'. *Academy of Management Journal*, 38, pp. 261–71.

Bretz, R.D. Jr, Ash, R.A. and Dreher, G.F. (1989). 'Do People Make the Place? An Examination of the Attraction-Selection-Attribution Hypothesis'. *Personnel Psychology*, 42, pp. 561–81.

Bretz, R.D. Jr and Judge, T.A. (1994). 'Person-Organization Fit and the Theory of Work Adjustment: Implications for Satisfaction, Tenure and Career Success'. *Journal of Vocational Behavior*, 44, pp. 32–54.

Breznitz, S. (1983). *Stress in Israel*. New York: Van Nostrand Reinhold.

Brief, A.P., Burke, M.J., George, J.M., Robinson, B.S. and Webster, J. (1988). 'Should Negative Affectivity Remain an Unmeasurable Variable in the Study of Job Stress?' *Journal of Applied Psychology*, 78, pp. 402–12.

Brooke, P.P., Jr. and Price, J.L. (1989) 'The Determinants of Employee Absenteeism: An Empirical Test of a Causal Model'. *Journal of Occupational Psychology*, 62, pp. 1–19.

Brown, S.D. and Gore, P.A., Jr. (1994). 'An Evaluation of Interest Congruence Indices: Distribution Characteristics and Measurement Properties'. *Journal of Vocational Behavior*, 45, pp. 310–27.

Burke, R.J. and Dezca, E. (1982). 'Preferred Organizational Climates of Type A Individuals'. *Journal of Vocational Behavior*, 21, pp. 50–59.

Bycio, P., Hackett, R.D. and Alvares, K.M. (1990). 'Job Performance and Turnover: A Review and Meta-Analysis'. *Applied Psychology: An International Review*, 39, pp. 47–76.

Cable, D.M. and Judge, T.A. (1997). 'Interviewers' Perceptions of Person-Organization Fit and Organizational Selection Decisions'. *Journal of Applied Psychology*, 82, pp. 546–61.

Camp, C.C. and Chartrand, J.M. (1992). 'A Comparison and Evaluation of Interest Congruence Indices'. *Journal of Vocational Behavior*, 41, pp. 162–82.

Cascio, W.F. (1991). *Managing Human Resources: Productivity, Quality of Work Life, Profits*, 3rd edn, New York: McGraw-Hill.

Cheloha, R. and Farr, J. (1980). 'Absenteeism, Job Involvement, and Job Satisfaction in an Organizational Setting'. *Journal of Applied Psychology*, 65, pp. 467–73.

Christiansen, N., Villanova, P. and Mikuky, S. (1997). 'Political Influence Compatibility: Fitting the Person to the Climate'. *Journal of Organizational Behavior*, 18, pp. 709–30.

Clegg, C.W. (1983). 'Psychology of Employee Lateness, Absence, and Turnover: A Methodological Critique and Empirical Study'. *Journal of Applied Psychology*, 68, pp. 88–101.

Cohen, A. (1993). 'Organizational Commitment and Turnover'. *Academy of Management Journal*, 36, pp. 1140–57.

Costa, P.T. Jr and McCrae, R.R. (1980). 'Influence of Extraversion and Neuroticism on Subjective Well-Being: Happy and Unhappy People'. *Journal of Personality and Social Psychology*, 38, pp. 668–78.

Cotton, J.L. and Tuttle, J.M. (1986). 'Employee Turnover: A Meta-Analysis and Review With Implications for Research'. *Academy of Management Review*, 11, pp. 55–70.

Dawis, R.V. and Lofquist, L.H. (1984). *A Psychological Theory of Work Adjustment*. Minneapolis: University of Minnesota Press.

Dolan, S. and Tziner, A. (1988). 'Implementing Computer-Based Automation in the Office: A Study of Experienced Stress'. *Journal of Organizational Behavior*, 9, pp. 183–7.

Edwards, J.R. (1991). 'Person-Job Fit: A Conceptual Integration, Literature Review, and Methodological Critique'. In C.L. Cooper and I.T. Robertson (eds), *International Review of Industrial and Organizational Psychology*, 6. Chichester: Wiley, pp. 283–357.

Edwards, J.R. and Van Harrison, R. (1993). 'Job Demands and Worker Health: Three-Dimensional Reexamination of the Relationship Between Person-Environment Fit and Strain'. *Journal of Applied Psychology*, 78, pp. 628–48.

Falbe, C.M., Nobel Ben-Yoav, O. and Tziner, A. (1988). 'Achievement Motivation of Managers: A New Approach to Assessing Cross-Cultural Differences'. *International Journal of Management*, 5, pp. 304–9.

Feij, J.A., Whitely, W.T., Peiro, J.M. and Taris, T.W. (1995). 'The Development of Career Enhancing Strategies and Content Innovation: A Longitudinal Study of Recruits'. *Journal of Vocational Behavior*, 46, pp. 231–56.

Fournier, S. and Tziner, A. (1995). 'La Congruence Individu-Environement, l'Importance du Groupe de Travail et la Satisfaction au Travail. [Person-Environment Congruence Work Group Importance and Work Satisfaction.] Unpublished Manuscript, University of Montreal.

French, J.R.P., Jr. and Caplan, R.D. (1972). 'Organizational Stress and Individual Strain'. In A.J. Marrow (ed.), *The Failure of Success*. New York: Amacon, pp. 30–66.

Friedman, M. and Rosenman, R.H. (1974). 'Job Stress and Employee Behavior'. *Organizational Behavior and Human Performance*, 23, pp. 372–87.

Gellatly, I.R. (1995). 'Individual and Group Determinants of Employee Absenteeism: Test of a Causal Model'. *Journal of Organizational Behavior*, 16, pp. 469–85.

Gerhart, B. (1990). 'Voluntary Turnover and Alternative Job Opportunities'. *Journal of Applied Psychology*, 75, pp. 467–76.

Gouldner, A.W. (1960). 'The Norm of Reciprocity'. *American Sociological Review*, 25, pp. 165–67.

Haccoun, R.R. and Jeanrie, C. (1995). 'Self Reports of Work Absence as a Function of Personal Attitudes Forward Absence, and Perceptions of the Organization. *Applied Psychology: An International Review*, 44, pp. 155–70.

Hackett, R.D. (1989). 'Work Attitudes and Employee Absenteeism: A Synthesis of the Literature. *Journal of Occupational Psychology*, 62, pp. 235–48.

Hackett, R.D., Bycio, P. and Hausdorf, P.A. (1994). 'Further Assessment of Meyer and Allen's (1991) Three-Component Model of Organizational Commitment'. *Journal of Applied Psychology*, 79, pp. 15–23.

Hackett, R.D. and Guion, R.M. (1985). 'A Reevaluation of the Absenteeism-Job Satisfaction Relationship'. *Organizational Behavior and Human Decision Processes*, 35, pp. 165–7.

Hanisch, K.A. and Hulin, C.L. (1991). 'General Attitudes and Organizational Withdrawal: An Evaluation of a Causal Model'. *Journal of Vocational Behavior*, 39, pp. 110–28.

Hayes, R. and Wheelwright, S. (1984). *Restoring Our Competitive Edge*. New York: Wiley.

Hesketh, B. (1995). 'Personality and Adjustment Styles: A Theory of Work Adjustment Approach to Career Enhancing Strategies'. *Journal of Vocational Behavior*, 46, pp. 274–82.

Hesketh, B. and Gardner, D. (1993). 'Person-Environment Fit Models: A Reconceptualization and Empirical Test'. *Journal of Vocational Behavior*, 35, pp. 315–442.

Hill, J.M. and Trist, E.L. (1955). 'Changes in Accidents and Other Absences with Length of Service: A Further Study of Their Incidence and Relation to Each Other in a Iron and Steel Works'. *Human Relations*, 8, pp. 121–52.

Hofstede, G. (1980). *Culture's Consequences*. Beverly Hills, CA: Sage.

Holland, J.L. (1973). *Making Vocational Choices: A Theory of Careers*. Englewood Cliffs, NJ: Prentice-Hall.

Holland, J.L. (1985). *Making Vocational Choices: A Theory of Vocational Personalities and Work Environment*. Englewood Cliffs, NJ: Prentice-Hall.

Holland, J.L. and Gottfredson, G.D. (1976). 'Using a Typology of Persons and Environment to Explain Careers: Some Extensions and Clarifications'. *The Counseling Psychologist*, 6, pp. 20–29.

Holland, J.L. and Gottfredson, G.D. (1990, August). 'An Annotated Bibliography for Holland's Theory of Vocational Personalities and Work Environments'. Paper presented at the annual meeting of the American Psychological Association. Boston, MA.

Hom, P.W., Caranikas-Walker, F., Prussia, G.E. and Griffith, R.W. (1992). 'A Meta-Analytical Structural Equations Analysis of a Model of Employee Turnover'. *Journal of Applied*

Psychology, 77, pp. 890–909.

Hom, P.W., Katerberg, R. and Hulin, C.R. (1979). 'Comparative Examination of Three Approaches to the Prediction of Turnover'. *Journal of Applied Psychology*, 64, pp. 280–90.

Hulin, C.L. (1991). 'Adaptation, Persistence, and Commitment in Organizations'. In M.D. Dunnette and L.M. Hough (eds), *Handbook of Industrial and Organizational Psychology*, 2. Palo Alto, CA: Consulting Psychologists Press, pp. 445–505.

Jaros, S.J., Jernier, J.M., Koehler, J.W. and Sincich, T. (1993). 'Effects of Continuance, Affective and Moral Commitment on the Withdrawal Process: An Evaluation of Eight Structural Equation Models'. *Academy of Management Journal*, 36, pp. 951–95.

Johns, G. (1997). 'Contemporary Research on Absence from Work: Correlates, Causes and Consequences'. In C.L. Cooper and I.T. Robertson (eds), *International Review of Industrial and Organizational Psychology*, 12, pp. 115–74.

Judge, T.A. and Watanabe, S. (1993). 'Another Look at the Job Satisfaction-Life Satisfaction Relationship'. *Journal of Applied Psychology*, 78, pp. 939–48.

Kanter, R. (1983). *The Change Masters*. New York: Simon and Schuster.

Kanungo, R.N. (1979). 'The Concept of Alienation and Involvement Revisited'. *Psychological Bulletin*, 86, pp. 119–38.

Kanungo, R.N. (1982). *Work Alienation*. New York: Praeger.

Kidwell, R.E. and Bennett, N. (1993). 'Employee Propensity to Withhold Effort: A Conceptual Model to Intersect Three Avenues of Research'. *Academy of Management Review*, 18, pp. 429–56.

Knatz, H.F., Inwald, R.E., Brockwell, A.L. and Gran, L.N. (1992). '/P/ and /MMP/ Predictions of Counterproductive Job Behaviors By Racial Groups'. *Journal of Business and Psychology*, 7, pp. 189–200.

Koeske, G.E. and Koeske, R.D. (1991). 'Underestimation of Social Buffering'. *Journal of Applied Behavioral Science*, 27, pp. 475–89.

Koslowsky, M. (1987). 'Antecedents and Consequences of Turnover: An Integrated Systems Approach'. *Genetic, Social, and General Psychology Monographs*, 113, pp. 271–92.

Koslowsky, M., Sagie, A., Krauz, M. and Dolman, A. (1997). 'Correlates of Employee Lateness: Some Theoretical Considerations'. *Journal of Applied Psychology*, 17, pp. 81–91.

Kristoff, A.L. (1996). 'Person-Organization Fit: An Integrative Review of Its Conceptualizations, Measurement, and Implications'. *Personnel Psychology*, 49, pp. 1–49.

Larson, E.W. and Fukami, C.V. (1985). 'Employee Absenteeism: The Role of Ease of Movement'. *Academy of Management Journal*, 28, pp. 467–71.

Lofquist, L.H. and Dawis, R.V. (1969). *Adjustment to Work*. Minneapolis: University of Minnesota.

Lum, L., Kevin, J., Clark, K., Reid, F. and Sirola, W. (1998). 'Explaining Nursing Turnover Intent: Job Satisfaction, Pay Satisfaction or Organizational Commitment'. *Journal of Organizational Behavior*, 19, pp. 305–20.

March, J.E. and Simon, H.A. (1958). *Organizations*. New York: Wiley.

Markham, S.E. and McKee, G.H. (1995). 'Group Absence Behavior and Standards: A Multi-Level Analysis'. *Academy of Management Journal*, 38, pp. 1174–90.

Mathieu, J.E. and Zajac, D.M. (1990). 'A Review and Meta-Analysis of Antecedents, Correlates and Consequences of Organizational Commitment'. *Psychological Bulletin*, 108, pp. 171–94.

McShane, S.L. (1985). 'Job Satisfaction and Absenteeism: A Meta-Analytic Reexamination'. *Canadian Journal of Administrative Sciences*, 2, pp. 68–77.

Meir, E.I. (1989). 'Integrative Elaboration of the Congruence Theory'. *Journal of Vocational Behavior*, 35, pp. 219–230.

Meir, E.I. (1995). 'Elaboration of the Relation Between Interest Congruence and Satisfaction'. *Journal of Career Assessment*, 3, pp. 341–6.

Meir, E.I., Keinan, G. and Segal, Z. (1986). 'Group Importance as a Mediator Between Personality-Environment Congruence and Satisfaction'. *Journal of Vocational Behavior*, 28, pp. 60–9.

Meir, E.I. and Melamed, S. (1986). 'The Accumulation of Person-Environment Congruences and Well-Being'. *Journal of Occupational Behavior*, 7, pp. 315–23.

Meir, E.I. and Navon, M. (1988). 'A Longitudinal Examination of the Congruence Hypotheses'. *Journal of Vocational Behavior*, 41, pp. 35–47.

Meir, E.I., Tziner, A. and Glazner, Y. (1997). 'Environmental Congruence, Group Importance, and Job Satisfaction'. *Journal of Career Assessment*, 5, pp. 343–53.

Mitra, A., Jenkins, D.G. and Gupta, N. (1992). 'A Meta-Analytic Review of the Relationship Between Absence and Turnover'. *Journal of Applied Psychology*, 77, pp. 879–89.

Mobley, W.H. (1982). *Employee Turnover: Causes, Consequences, and Control*. Menlo Park, CA: Addison-Wesley.

Mobley, W.H., Horner, S.O. and Hollingsworth, A.T. (1978). 'An Evaluation of Precursors of Hospital Employee Turnover'. *Journal of Applied Psychology*, 63, pp. 408–14.

Nicholson, N. and Goodge, P. (1976). 'The Influence of Social, Organizational and Biographical Factors on Female Absence'. *Journal of Management Studies*, 13, pp. 234–54.

Nicholson, N. and Johns, G. (1985). 'The Absence Culture and the Psychological Contract-Who's in Control of Absence?'. *Academy of Management Review*, 10, pp. 397–407.

Organ, D.W. (1988). *Organizational Citizenship Behavior*. Lexington, MA: Lexington.

Pinchot, G. (1985). *Intrapreneuring*. New York: Harper & Row.

Porter, L.W. (1963). 'Job Attitudes in Management: Perceived Importance of Needs as a Function of Job Level.' *Journal of Applied Psychology*, 47, pp. 144–8.

Price, J. and Mueller, G. (1986). *Absenteeism and Turnover of Hospital Employees*. Greenwich, CT: JAI Press.

Ramirez, M. and Price-Williams, D.R. (1976). 'Achievement Motivation in Children of Three Ethnic Groups in the U.S'. *Journal of Cross-Cultural Psychology*, 7, pp. 49–60.

Robinson, S.L. and Bennett, R.J. (1995). 'A Typology of Deviant Workplace Behaviors: A Multidimensional Scaling Study'. *Academy of Management Journal*, 38, pp. 555–572.

Rosenthal, R. (1990). 'How Are We Doing in Soft Psychology?' *American Psychologist*, 45, pp. 775–6.

Rosse, J.G. (1988). 'Relations Among Lateness, Absence, and Turnover: Is There a Progression of Withdrawal?' *Human Relations*, 41, pp. 517–31.

Rosse, J.G. and Miller, H.E. (1984). 'An Adoptive Cycle Interpretation of Absence and Withdrawal'. In P.S. Goodman and R.S. Atkin (eds), *Absenteeism: New Approaches to Understanding Measuring and Managing Employee Absence*. San Francisco: Jossey-Bass, pp. 194–228.

Sagie, A. and Koslowsky, M. (1998). 'Participation and Empowerment in Organizational Settings: Modeling, Effectiveness, and Applications'. Thousand Oaks, CA: Sage.

Saks, M.A. (1995). 'Longitudinal Field Investigation of the Moderating and Mediating Effects of Self-Efficacy on the Relationship Between Training and Newcomer Adjustment'. *Journal of Applied Psychology*, 80, pp. 211–15.

Schaubroeck, J., Ganster, D.C. and Jones, J.R. (1998). 'Organization and Occupation Influences in the Attraction-Selection-Attribution Process'. *Journal of Applied Psychology*, 83, pp. 869–91.

Schneider, B. (1983). 'Interactional Psychology and Organizational Behavior'. In B.M. Staw and L.L. Cummings (eds), *Research in Organizational Behavior*, 5. Greenwich, CT: JAI Press, pp. 1–31.

Schneider, B. (1987). 'The Road to a Radical Approach to Person-Environment Fit'. *Journal of Vocational Behavior*, 31, pp. 353–61.

Schneider, B., Smith, D.B., Taylor, S. and Fleemor, J. (1998). 'Personality and Organizations: A Test of the Homogeneity of Personality Hypothesis'. *Journal of Applied Psychology*, 83, pp. 462–70.

Scott, K.D. and Taylor, G.S. (1985). 'An Examination of Conflicting Findings on the Relationship Between Job Satisfaction and Absenteeism: A Meta-Analysis'. *Academy of Management Journal*, 28, pp. 588–612.

Shafritz, J.M. (1980). *Dictionary of Personnel Management and Labor Relations*. Oak Park, IL: Moore.

Shartle, C.L. (1956). *Occupational Information*. New York: Prentice-Hall.

Sheridan, J.E. (1992). 'Organizational Culture and Employee Retention'. *Academy of Management Journal*, 35, pp. 1036–56.

Smith, C.A., Organ, D.W. and Near, J.P. (1983). 'Organizational Citizenship Behavior: Its Nature and Antecedents'. *Journal of Applied Psychology*, 68, pp. 653–63.

Smith, D. and Tziner, A. (1998). 'Moderating Effects of Affective Disposition and Social Support on the Relationship Between Person-Environment Fit and Strain'. *Psychological Reports*, 82, pp. 963–83.

Sommers, M.J. (1995). 'Organizational Commitment, Turnover and Absenteeism: An Examination of Direct and Indirect Effects'. *Journal of Organizational Behavior*, 16, pp. 49–58.

Spokane, A.R. (1985). 'A Review of Research on Person-Environment Congruence in Holland's Theory of Careers'. *Journal of Vocational Behavior*, 26, pp. 306–43.

Staw, B.M. and Ross, J. (1985). 'Stability in the Midst of Change: A Dispositional Approach to Job Attitudes'. *Journal of Applied Psychology*, 70, pp. 469–80.

Sutherland, L.F., Fogarty, G.J. and Pithers, R.T. (1995). 'Congruence as a Predictor of Occupational Stress'. *Journal of Vocational Behavior*, 46, pp. 292–309.

Tranberg, M., Slane, S. and Ekeberg, S.E. (1993). 'The Relation Between Interest Congruence and Satisfaction: A Meta-Analysis'. *Journal of Vocational Behavior*, 42, pp. 253–64.

Turban, D.B. and Keon, T.L. (1993). 'Organizational Attractiveness: An Interactionist Perspective'. *Journal of Applied Psychology*, 78, pp. 184–93.

Tziner, A. (1983). 'Correspondence Between Occupational Rewards and Occupational Needs and Work Satisfaction: A Canonical Redundancy Analysis'. *Journal of Occupational Psychology*, 56, pp. 49–56.

Tziner, A. (1987). 'Congruency Issue Retested Using Fineman's Achievement Climate'. *Journal of Social Behavior and Personality*, 2, pp. 63–78.

Tziner, A. (1990). *Organizational Staffing and Work Adjustment*. New York: Praeger.

Tziner, A. and Dawis, R. (1988). 'Occupational Stress: A Theoretical Look From the Perspective of Work Adjustment Theory'. *International Journal of Management*, 5, pp. 423–30.

Tziner, A. and Dolan, S. (1984). 'The Relationship of Two Sociodemographic Variables and Several Perceived Climate Dimensions to Performance: An Investigation Among Real-Estate Agents'. *Canadian Journal of Administrative Sciences*, 1, pp. 272–87.

Tziner, A. and Falbe, C.M. (1990). 'Actual and Preferred Climates of Achievement Orientation and Their Relationships to Work Attitudes and Performance in Two Occupational Strata'. *Journal of Organizational Behavior*, 11, pp. 159–67.

Tziner, A. and Meir, E.I. (1997). 'Work Adjustment: Extension of the Theoretical Framework'. In C.L. Cooper and I.T. Robertson (eds), *International Review of Industrial and Organizational Psychology*, 12, pp. 95–114.

Tziner, A. and Vardi, Y. (1984). 'Work Satisfaction and Absenteeism Among Social Workers: The Role of Altruistic Values'. *Work and Occupations*, 11, pp. 461–70.

Vandenberghe, C. (1999). 'Organizational Culture, Person-Culture Fit and Turnover: A Replication in the Health Care Industry'. *Journal of Organizational Behavior*, 20, pp. 175–84.

Vardi, Y. and Wienner, Y. (1992*).* 'Organizational Misbehavior (OMB): A Calculative-Normative Model'. Paper presented at the annual meeting of the Academy of Management, Las Vegas.

Watson, D. and Clark, L.A. (1984). 'Affectivity: The Disposition to Experience Aversive Emotional States'. *Psychological Bulletin*, 16, pp. 465–90.

Williams, C.R. and Livingstone, L.P. (1994). 'Another Look at the Relationship Between Performance and Voluntary Turnover'. *Academy of Management Journal*, 37, pp. 269–98.

4 Perspectives on Groups and Work Teams in the Workplace

AHARON TZINER

Introduction

Research on groups has shifted in recent decades from the investigation of rather small, static entities, to the study of organizational work teams striving to solve problems or complete tasks in rapidly changing real-time situations. The research described below reflects these changes, as well as some of the underlying theoretical concepts and models that assist human resource personnel to understand the influences and processes involved in efficient teamwork. Of greatest importance are the various performance outcomes, which reflect both the characteristics of the groups themselves, and the qualitative nature of the tasks they undertake. These outcomes include not only the degree to which tasks are achieved, but also the level of satisfaction of the team members. Both are consequences that impinge on the productivity and economic viability of the organization.

In the course of this historical review, the reader will notice that the nomenclature regarding groups varies with respect to both the conceptual framework and the classical or contemporary nature of the research. Later studies of organizations tend to adopt a view of the group as an instrumental task-oriented entity created to achieve tasks that promote the organization's interests. As such, the use of terms such as 'team', 'work team', and 'crew members' are more appropriate than 'groups' or 'group members', the concepts classically employed to describe collective entities that are more person-oriented and of a socio-emotional character. Nevertheless, the body of research cited in this chapter has largely subsumed the work team into the generic term 'group'. Thus, the more general usage of the term 'group' will be found here more frequently, even when the thrust of the discussion clearly indicates reference to a set number of employees constituting a work team.

The Group as a Dynamic Entity

The group may be conceptualized as a system, following Katz and Kahn (1966), who suggest that all systems are organized on energetic input/output structures, one of whose functions is the assurance of resources for activation of the system. Their activity is thus cyclical. While the input is generally aimed at making resources available (affording resources) for the operation of intra-system processes that are accompanied by certain products which are 'exported' out of the system, some of the end products are absorbed by the system itself, as components of new input to restore the activation. Consequently, a non-cyclical activity pattern cannot constitute an integral part of a system, since it is essentially based on the idea of cycles and recurrent activation.

Another salient characteristic of systems is engagement in an active, constant, and intense struggle with external environmental forces, incurring a dynamic process of adaptation to an ever-changing environment. The components of the system are required to exert a concerted effort to overcome environmental pressures, sometimes compelling the entire system to redefine its goals. Finally, every system also has a definite boundary that differentiates it from the surrounding environment. Accordingly, all reciprocal processes between the system and its environment are dependent on the degree to which this boundary is penetrable.

A group (of which a work team is an example) can also be treated as a system influenced by external environmental forces. Here we would adopt the core characteristics of the systems theory outlined above, and examine the functional and constitutional changes that a group undergoes over a period of time.

Wolfe (1970) argues that research into groups requires application of the 'structural time' approach, whereby it is necessary to distinguish phases in the creation of 'links'. In his opinion, it must never be assumed that any segment of the network of interpersonal links that develop between individuals in the group framework is likely to remain invariant over a period of time. Even the single link between two individuals, as a constituent of a set, is not invariant over time. Each link, from the moment of its inception, is subject to constant development as a result of the influence of the experiences undergone by the two individuals in the interaction. These experiences are liable to force the individuals to adapt their link to the situation, and may thus again make it necessary to redefine goals.

According to Wolfe, it is possible to distinguish between phases along a continuum of changes, an approach supported by Turner (1966), who claims that events and processes in the group's external environment are likely to leave their mark on the behavior patterns of its constituent individuals. For example, Russo (1967) notes that changes in personal space and group territories are important factors in determining group behavior. In his study, changes in the seating arrangements of the individuals in the research groups led to alterations in communication patterns. Changes in personal space or group territory may be caused by pressures exerted by individuals or groups around the subject group, or by physical changes requiring re-evaluation of spatial range. According to Russo (1967), as well as Mehrabian and Diamond (1971), even apparently irrelevant events may be highly significant, since their influence may be reflected in a continuum of changes in the group (such as modifications of communication patterns or adaptation to situational circumstances). Furthermore, following Dion (1972), the intensity and frequency of intergroup conflicts may also affect group dynamics.

In addition to these external stimuli, the intrinsic nature of group tasks also has implications for group performance (Collins and Guetzkow, 1964; Roby and Lanzetta, 1968). Some tasks constitute obstacles to group achievement because of either inherent attributes or the task environment. Consequently, they induce friction on the socio-emotional interpersonal level of interaction. This emphasis on tasks challenged the classical approach to group performance, where socio-emotional interpersonal relationships were generally regarded as a separate unit, isolated from the influence of events in the task environment.

It appears, then, that alterations in the external situation affect the group since they act as inputs into the group system. Thus, it can be hypothesized that obstacles encountered during task performance, or changes in the nature of the tasks performed by the group, may lead to internal structural changes, even in groups characterized predominantly by socio-emotional interaction. Here these changes would take the form of modifications in the nature of the interpersonal relationships. Furthermore, they might result in the redefinition of goals, because they constitute the code that directs the homeostasis. As a result, both the internal activity patterns and the output of the system will be altered. Given this causal relationship, effective coping with a task requires that the intragroup communication system be appropriate to the nature of the task (Shaw, 1964).

While Homans (1950) stressed the effect of response to activity, interactions, or sentiments in the group structure as determinants of internal group behaviors, the above theoretical contributions and empirical observations, which emphasize external influences on group processes, gave rise to a model that presents the concept of the group as a dynamic entity. As Shaw (1976) puts it: 'Group formation does not stop with the affiliation of members. The group develops over a moderately long period and probably never reaches a completely stable state.' This dynamic model relates to both the structural aspect (interpersonal interaction, communication flow, and leadership patterns) and to the instrumental, task-oriented dimension that turns attention to the goals and the fact that they are constantly modified, frequently in response to new contextual-environment stimuli.

Communication patterns therefore play a part in group effectiveness. Shultz, Ketrow, and Urban (1995), for example, have recently provided evidence that the quality of group decisions may suffer when communication is constrained, thereby leading to inadequate exploration and evaluation of possible courses of action. With respect to the product of these decision-making processes, namely group performance, it appears that centralized communication networks are more effective for simple assignments, while decentralized networks are more effective for complicated tasks (Faucheux and Moscovici, 1960; Shaw, 1964, 1976; Collins, 1970). If we invoke the dynamic model, it would then seem that a change in the nature of both tasks and goals will generally be accompanied by *parallel* changes in interpersonal communication patterns.

It is similarly probable that the kinds of leadership abilities required for effective group action also vary with type of task (Shaw, 1976, p.275), group goals (Stogdill, 1974; Bass, 1990), and members' attributes (e.g., cultural orientations, collectivistic vs. individualistic tendencies: Jung and Avolio, 1999). As indicated, the leader evolves from the group through the pressure exerted on it to tackle certain forces inherent in the external environment. Leaders fulfill a variety of functions, such as serving as the structural crystallizer of the group, the catalyst of intergroup processes that lead to the development of interpersonal links, and the coordinator and mediator of activities. Thus, in a group designed to afford socio-emotional satisfactions and provide its members with a suitable framework for interactive processes, the pattern of leadership is likely to be person-oriented, and essentially different from that which will evolve in an instrumental group committed to the attainment of specific task-oriented goals.

Recently, Jung and Avolio (1999) have demonstrated clear-cut relationships between particular leadership styles (transactional and transformational) and specific types of groups (individualistically-oriented and collectivistically-oriented). Transactional leaders tend to emphasize goal setting, clarification of links between performance and rewards, and provision of constructive feedback to keep group members on target. Transformational leaders incline toward developing personal relationships between themselves and the group members, the relationship being built on mutual trust and personal commitment (rather than on contractual and formal arrangements or guidelines). As for the group styles, individualistically-oriented groups generally consist of members who value individual success, initiative, and personal accomplishment, and who tend to look out for themselves and their own interests. In contrast, collectivistically-oriented groups consist of members who value interpersonal relationships, emphasize in-group solidarity, and attain gratification of achievement needs through the success and accomplishments of the other group members or the group as a whole. According to Jung and Avolio, transactional leadership is particularly effective in managing individualistically-oriented group members, while transformational leadership is better suited to collectivistically-oriented group members.

In a similar vein, Bales (1955) contends that the leadership style suitable for a group characterized by a socio-emotional structure (socio-emotional cohesiveness) is not necessarily suitable for a group requiring organization toward task performance. Stogdill notes that 'person-oriented' leaders tend to see their central function as nurturing a framework that will enhance socio-emotional satisfactions; however, they do not always feel it necessary to contribute to group productivity. On the other hand, 'task-oriented' leaders tend to suppress socio-emotional satisfaction and emphasize the tasks of the group. Indeed, there appears to be little doubt that an interaction between style of leadership (type of leader) and the basic structure of the group (socio-emotional or instrumental) does in fact exist (Katz and Kahn, 1966; Stogdill, 1974; Hare, 1976; Fiedler, 1978).

One way of typifying groups, therefore, relates to the most critical aspect of group functioning, namely, cohesiveness. Using the dynamic model, two different types of cohesiveness can be distinguished: (a) expressive cohesiveness on a socio-emotional basis, whereby affiliation focuses on the central aspiration to derive emotional satisfaction from participation in the group; and (b) instrumental cohesiveness, in which group affiliation is based on task-goal orientation. Tziner (1982) stresses that groups displaying the latter type generally crystallize as a result of mutual dependence, that is, individuals group together for the purpose of attaining goals which *cannot be attained effectively outside of the group context.*

Tziner asserts that each type of cohesiveness can be measured on a continuum, since different levels prevail in different groups. The continuum of instrumental cohesiveness, for example, can be typified at one extreme as a group entity with no formal structure. For a group of individuals described by Mayer (1961) as ego-centered, the only structure is a certain interest, a common orientation that motivates them to cooperate for the attainment of specific goals. The existence of the group is thus dependent on the relevant task orientations, and interactions are limited solely to whatever is necessary to attain the goals. Leadership patterns and communicative structure are similarly determined in accordance with the requirements of the goals. Taken to the extreme, this type of group can be viewed as consisting exclusively of situational characteristics, such as the ideal types of bureaucratic organizations described by the Weberian model. In these organizations, reciprocal relations are entirely formal and alienation is almost absolute. The relationships between individuals are impersonal, conducted on a purely rational and instrumental basis, and are determined solely by the nature of the tasks and goals.

At the other extreme of the continuum is another egocentric network, a collection of individuals who initially group together around an economic, social, or political orientation but, in time and through instrumental interactions, also develop interpersonal lateral relations (Wolfe, 1970). The instrumental orientation, however, remains the dominant basis of the group (see: Terborg et al., 1976). This structure might be exemplified by the Society of Jesus, which maintains minimal connections with the outside world while exhibiting expressive relations among the monks within the order. Nevertheless, the Society of Jesus is involved primarily in instrumental activities: all personal resources and interests are devoted to the attainment of the group goal of missionary work (Coser, 1974, p. 125). This type of group structure is dependent on situational tasks and motives that are frequently altered by the external environment. The dependence, however, is not absolute, as mutual relations are also created beyond those required by the task-goal orientation.

The continuum of expressive (socio-emotional) cohesiveness is similar, or even parallel, to that of instrumental cohesiveness. At one extreme, we find groups characterized by a mixture of expressive and instrumental relations in which the expressive element is dominant. Consider, for example, a group that is organized for the purpose of playing bridge on a fixed day of the week, yet whose members develop close friendly relations in the course of this activity. Eventually, the personal relations become focal, while the bridge game becomes a secondary goal, although the importance of the task in hand is not completely eliminated. At the other extreme of this continuum would be a group such as the Quakers Society of Friends, whose existence is not dependent on time or environment, and whose goals are in no way influenced by the external environment (Vann, 1969).

An underlying assumption of the theoretical dynamic model of group functioning, which serves as our basis for the study of group cohesiveness, is that expressive and instrumental cohesiveness should not be treated in static terms, as the opposite poles of a single continuum. Rather, research should include the entire range of types of groups, which are characterized by *varying levels* of instrumental and expressive components. In dynamic terms, these continua are differential and orthogonal; each reveals unceasing dynamic processes powered by situational changes in the environment or within the system. These processes are followed by changes in the nature and intensity of the basic components of the group structure: interactions between members, communication patterns and channels, leadership structure, and goals. Thus, over time, it can be expected that certain individuals will join a group, while others will leave it; that some kinds of interactive and communicative relations will develop, while others will be discontinued; and that an effective leadership system in one situation will become dysfunctional in other circumstances, so that it will be replaced with a new system with alternative goals.

If we apply this approach to the context of group cohesiveness, we can hypothesize that from a diachronic perspective, changes in group structure will be located two-directionally along the continuum of expressiveness or instrumentalism. Thus, a certain group initially located at one end of the continuum, especially if it is originally constituted to represent one extreme, might gradually change until it is characteristic of the other extreme. Moreover, we could predict transitions between the two continua. For instance, under the influence of situational circumstances, a group of the socio-emotional type may undergo metamorphosis until it is eventually characterized primarily by elements associated with the instrumental type. Similarly, if the socio-emotional links between group members are limited to task-oriented activities, and the values of the individual group members are not opposed to task achievement, then relationships could develop that are primarily instrumental (task-oriented). Conversely, individuals in a group may be brought together on the basis of a common instrumental goal, but if the group is open and the tasks are successfully performed, lateral socio-emotional ties could develop that would endure even in the absence of instrumentally-related goals. These transformations can be identified both by the diachronic features of the verbal and behavioral interactions between the group members, and by related internal and external processes.

Group Cohesiveness

The diachronic nature of cohesiveness serves as the anchor of the dynamic model of group behavior, and also underpins much of the earlier theoretical and empirical studies outlined in this chapter. It will therefore be useful to examine in greater detail some of the thinking behind the development of this concept.

Early interest in cohesiveness concentrated mainly on its sources and its influence on intragroup interactive processes, such as interpersonal communication, group pressure for uniformity, and interpersonal attraction (Festinger et al., 1950, 1952; Schachter et al., 1951; Shaw and Shaw, 1962). However, even the earliest literature in this field reveals considerable debate over the conceptual definition of cohesiveness.

Festinger et al. (1950), for instance, presented a very general and comprehensive approach, viewing cohesiveness as the product of the entirety of forces operating on the individual to remain in the group. The generality of this definition, however, was its weak point, as it made empirical research of the phenomenon very difficult. Thibaut (1950) and Back (1951) defined cohesiveness more operationally as the desire to remain in or belong to the group because of its specific characteristics: belonging, they posited, affords higher status or mediates in the attainment of personal goals.

An examination of these two approaches reveals an essential difference: Thibaut and Back regard cohesiveness as a drive urging the individual to stay in the group (or to join it). Cohesiveness is thus a kind of internal force or set of forces that originate in the characteristics of the group and that operate on the members to do their utmost not to be driven out of it. On the other hand, Festinger et al. see group characteristics as only part of the entirety of forces operating on the individual to stay in the group. In their view, a similarity of attitudes, socio-economic status, values, and personality all contribute to an interpersonal attraction that motivates people to seek a common social framework (Byrne, 1961; Byrne and Nelson, 1965; Byrne and Clore, 1966; Byrne et al., 1969). Accordingly, these factors also constitute forces operating on the individual to remain in the group.

Moreover, the term 'product' (product of total forces), used as the equivalent of cohesiveness, includes other meanings in addition to the forces pressuring one to remain in a group, such as patterns and strengths of interpersonal interaction and group norms of behavior. Thus, group cohesiveness is characterized not only by an individual's act of remaining in the group or striving to belong to it, but also by a more comprehensive range of behavioral patterns than those considered by Thibaut and Back.

Gross and Martin (1952) later claimed that there was no theoretical or empirical justification for treating cohesiveness as a unitary concept. Viewing it as a social phenomenon based on a variety of forces, they gave birth to the distinction between the two types of cohesiveness defined according to the forces operating on the individual to remain in the group. These types match the diachronic nature of group structure discussed above. Gross and Martin offered the following definitions:

1 Cohesiveness on the basis of *interpersonal attraction* between members of the group. Belonging to the group and the desire to do so are based on considering this affiliation as a goal with its own value, independent of the actual activities involved, the prestige or status afforded members of the group, etc. This definition corresponds to expressive (socio-emotional) cohesiveness.
2 Cohesiveness based on the potential of the group to mediate in the *attainment of material personal interests and goals* that cannot be attained in the individualistic framework. This definition corresponds to instrumental cohesiveness.

Gross and Martin's suggestion appears valid if, for example, we imagine a high status group, such as a university senate, which is characterized by high cohesiveness according to Thibaut and Back's definition, but not necessarily by personal attraction between the members. In keeping with Festinger et al., however, a group characterized by a low level of interpersonal attraction can not be considered cohesive. This logical contradiction further illustrates the problem of a unitary view of the concept of cohesiveness.

In their study, Gross and Martin voiced three criticisms of Back's (1951) investigation which have a bearing on this discussion of the unitary nature of cohesiveness:

1 The intercorrelations between the three different indices of cohesiveness presented in Back's study vary from 0.69 to 0.37.
2 Each group was ranked on each of the three indices in terms of level of group cohesiveness. Surprisingly enough, the same group received a different rank on each index.
3 Back emphasized that in 73 per cent of the groups characterized by low cohesiveness, the behavior of the participants was characterized by deliberate restriction of the communication flow (little communication throughout the process of performing tasks), as compared with the same patterns in only about 41 per cent of the groups characterized by high cohesiveness. However, Back completely disregarded the fact that in some 27 per cent of the groups with a low level of cohesiveness, the flow of

communication was not of a deliberately restricted type, and at the high level, such behavior was found in 41 per cent of the groups.

These three criticisms corroborate, albeit only theoretically, the contention that cohesiveness cannot be treated as a unitary concept, but rather that various patterns of cohesiveness must be examined in accordance with the factors on which it is based. Eisman (1959) found support for this assertion in a replication of Gross and Martin's study in which he employed a number of indices of cohesiveness, some based on interpersonal attraction and others on attraction to the goals of the group. The correlations between them, however, did not attain the generally accepted level of significance. The implication of this finding is that different processes of intragroup interaction are found in groups characterized by expressive cohesiveness than in those based on instrumental cohesiveness.

It has been claimed that the earlier paucity of empirical support for a non-unitary approach to cohesiveness was a reflection of a deliberate lack of attention paid in the literature to both the factors that produce different types of cohesiveness and the behavioral implications deriving from them (Hackman, 1976; Evans and Jarvis, 1980). In practice, most of the studies designed to examine the factors involved in the crystallization of cohesiveness and its influence on the behavior of group members were directed at socio-emotional based cohesiveness. Cohesiveness was typically induced from the use of sociometric choice as an indicator of interpersonal attraction. Indeed, there appears to have been a disregard for studies that rebutted the assumptions of previous investigations of socio-emotional cohesiveness, as well as of research into instrumental cohesiveness, which tended to contradict earlier findings.

In order to correct for this tendency, Tziner (1982) offered a review of studies that employed the theoretical framework introduced by Gross and Martin (1952) to examine the influence of cohesiveness on various behaviors of group members. Tziner further investigated the implications for interactive processes that derive from the existence of two types of cohesiveness. This research covered three areas: (1) interpersonal communication, (2) processes of social influence, and (3) performance. In all three areas the effects of high and low functioning were analyzed. As the outcomes of these processes have a direct bearing on the theoretical framework advanced here, we offer a more detailed presentation of the findings of this review, paying particular attention to performance, as it is the most relevant to organizational research in the workplace.

Tziner (1982): Behavior Patterns Compared in Groups Displaying One of Two Types of Cohesiveness

Interpersonal Communication

Tziner reviewed a number of experiments on interpersonal communications conducted on groups varying in degree of cohesiveness. The indices of behavior included group cooperation in creating stories (Back, 1951), patterns of communication (Pepitone and Reichling, 1955), communication flow based on interpersonal attraction (Lott and Lott, 1961), and task activity vs. non-task activity (Shaw and Shaw, 1962). It was found that across these early studies, different patterns of interpersonal communications emerge in groups representing the two types of cohesiveness.

Socio-emotional cohesive groups are characterized by:

1 a high percentage of non-formal communication (where the group is involved in the completion of tasks assigned by external factors);
2 relative equality in the distribution of communicative messages between members of the group (reactive mutuality); messages are not directed at any one dominant figure, nor is there one group member who relays most information;
3 a higher percentage of positive rather than negative socio-emotional communication;
4 a lower threshold of emotional exposure (authenticity).

On the other hand, instrumental cohesive groups are characterized by:

1 a dominant person who holds a central position in the communication network;
2 a relatively small amount of communication in general, since it is perceived as counterproductive for attaining the group goals and a 'waste of time';
3 communication that is not divided equally among the participants (lack of reactive mutuality); a dominant person usually emerges as the center of the exchange of communication;
4 a considerably greater amount of negative socio-emotional communications, especially toward those individuals perceived as not contributing to, or perhaps even reducing, the effectivity of the group (particularly in the case of failure to attain group goals);

5   a formal, very informative type of communication intended to relay information necessary for proper functioning;
6   a high threshold of emotional exposure.

Processes of Social Influence

Tziner also reviewed studies of the processes of social influence, such as the pressure for uniformity and conformity of cognitive and behavioral patterns. These included mutual recognition and attraction (Festinger et al., 1950), conformity (Bovard, 1951; Hackmann, 1976), and status and consensus (Shelley, 1960).

Analysis of the findings of these studies similarly suggests differences between the two types of groups.

In groups characterized by socio-emotional cohesiveness:

1   pressure is exerted on individuals to maintain a uniformity of ideas and attitudes;
2   pressure to conform also applies to perceptual and other cognitive processes;
3   pressure is exerted on members to conform to group norms of behavior.

In contrast, in groups characterized by instrumental cohesiveness:

1   there is pressure for cognitive uniformity of opinions and attitudes, perceived as necessary to assure harmonious personal interaction and effective group performance;
2   there is pressure for conformity of behavior patterns relevant to task-activities, i.e., the group will exert pressure on its members to conform to group norms of behavior only if it is necessary for effective performance.

Performance

Finally, Tziner reviewed early studies on the relationship between cohesiveness and performance, beginning with Schachter et al. (1951), who posited that if one relates to the group product as a function of the group's success in influencing its members, then cohesiveness constitutes a major causal factor of the performance level. Accordingly, if groups that assign a high valence to performance are cohesive, they will exert greater pressure on their members to increase productivity. Similarly, if a cohesive group wishes to reduce productivity, its performance will be of a lower level than that of a group that is not cohesive. Schachter et al. constructed four types of groups, representing the possible permutations of high and low cohesiveness and valence of performance. As in most of the studies reviewed, the cohesiveness manipulated was of the socio-emotional type.

In contrast to the predictions, no connection was found between cohesiveness and high performance. Groups that place high valence on performance do not appear to differ in terms of performance level, even if they do in terms of cohesiveness. However, if the group has a negative orientation toward the performance of formal tasks assigned it by an external force (places negative valence on them), the productivity of its members will be lower if it is cohesive.

In Berkowitz's (1954) replication of this study, groups characterized by a positive orientation toward performance demonstrated a continuous increase in group productivity at both levels of cohesiveness; the higher the cohesiveness, the higher the increase rate. In groups characterized by a negative orientation toward performance, there was a drop in group productivity at both levels of cohesiveness in the first session of the experiment. At a later stage, however, an increase in productivity was found at both levels of cohesiveness, with this trend steeper at the high level than at the low level.

In light of the disparate findings of the two studies, Tziner concludes that no consistent results were produced regarding the relation between cohesiveness and performance. This might be due to the variation in the samples: Schacter's respondents were all female students, while Berkowitz investigated only male students.

Using a different approach, Goodacre (1951) organized army units on the basis of sociometric choices. The effectiveness of these units was then evaluated in the framework of their performance of the tasks assigned to them. Analysis of the association between the levels of unit cohesiveness and the quality of performance revealed correlations varying from 0.62 to 0.78. The researchers therefore concluded that there is a causal connection between cohesiveness and effectiveness of performance, since the high correlations were derived through manipulating the independent variable (cohesiveness). Hemphill and Sachrest (1952) conducted a correlative study of army personnel that was somewhat similar to Goodacre's investigation. Here, the level of cohesiveness of 94 bomber crews was gauged by means of a sociometric index based on interpersonal choice of those pilots the respondents would prefer to have in their crew. Simultaneously, data were collected regarding the precision of the bombings of group targets. The interpersonal attraction among pilots in organic crews relative to that among pilots belonging to different teams (number of intergroup as opposed to intragroup choices) was used as an index for the level of team cohesiveness. This index was found to correlate with the criteria data ($r = 0.36$). While the association is significant, it is not as high as that produced by the previous study, perhaps because other variables were not controlled for.

In a similar vein, Speroff and Kerr (1952) and Van Zelst (1952) organized factory work groups on the basis of sociometric choices. In the course of their work performance, functioning indices were gathered, such as the level of turnover, savings in cost of production, and number of accidents. The findings of these studies validated the assumptions that the more cohesive the work group, the lower the turnover, the greater the savings in cost production, and the fewer the work accidents ($r = 0.54$ between cohesiveness and accidents).

It should be noted that not all of the initial studies examining socio-emotional cohesiveness were successful in identifying significant correlations between cohesiveness and performance effectiveness. Seashore (1954), for example, based his study on organic work groups in an auto assembly plant, and evaluated their performance effectiveness at three-month intervals using the measure of group production. The data did not support the hypothesis that group productivity would increase along with the intensification of interpersonal interaction. In his theoretical discussion, Seashore suggests that it is also necessary to take into account the group's orientation to the performance of formal tasks (assignment of positive or negative value to the attainment of goals set by external factors).

In another study of the relationship between cohesiveness and performance, Cohen et al. (1960) used a laboratory setting, hoping thereby to ensure maximal experimental control. Brainstorming teams formed according to sociometric choices were assigned problem-solving tasks, some of them 'ego-involving' and some 'non-ego-involving'. The researchers hypothesized that as individualism makes working together difficult, the mutual attraction in cohesive groups would lead to less of an inhibition to express individual ideas, thus producing more creativity. However, this hypothesis was not upheld in the experimental test. In contrast to predictions, the cohesive brainstorming teams did not produce a significantly greater number of ideas, nor more original ones, than the non-cohesive groups.

Analysis of the small number of later studies that were designed to ascertain the impact of instrumental cohesiveness on group performance (Ball and Carron, 1976; Bird, 1977) revealed more conclusive findings. In light of all the studies reviewed in this section, Tziner (1982) concludes that:

1 The reason for the inconsistency of the earlier findings may reflect the fact that virtually all of them manipulated only socio-emotional cohesiveness in the attempt to ascertain how it affects the level of group performance (George, 1990; George and Brief, 1992). Moreover, the possibility of a reversed direction of causality, i.e., group performance as a determinant of cohesiveness level (Backeman and Helmreich, 1975), may also contribute to this inconsistency. Tziner thus suggested that an association between cohesiveness and performance does not necessarily exist in a group characterized by socio-emotional cohesiveness, where group motivational orientation (negative or positive valence) toward performance of formal goals (the goal orientation) appears to constitute a mediating factor between cohesiveness and group performance.

2 Much less research has been devoted to the pattern of relationships between the level of cohesiveness and performance indices in groups characterized by instrumental cohesiveness, where group motivational orientation is less significant since, by definition, high cohesiveness indicates a high task orientation of the individuals in the group. Thus factors such as goal path clarity (Anderson, 1975) may contribute significantly to the association between cohesiveness of this type and performance level, as it is reasonable to assume that the more well-defined the routes to the goals, the stronger this association will be. Conversely, if the paths are unclear, the connection can be expected to be weaker.

In summing up the significance of the findings in these three areas of group behavior, Tziner reaffirms that the two distinct types of group cohesiveness serve different functions. Socio-emotional cohesiveness evolves whenever individuals join the group in order to derive emotional satisfactions that can be provided by the very act of participating in the group, such as self-image, recognition, and security. This type of cohesiveness is the product of personal attraction, which, in terms of learning theories, creates a framework of positive reinforcements (rewards). The continued existence of a socio-emotionally cohesive group is thus perceived by its members as a goal and challenge in and of itself, while the activities in which they are involved are of secondary importance; they serve the existential goals of the social framework.

In contrast, instrumental cohesiveness is task-oriented and is the product of the relations of mutual dependency created between various individuals associated for the achievement of common goals that can not be attained effectively outside the group context. The participants therefore emphasize factors that contribute to successful completion of the task, and attribute little importance to interpersonal attraction.

From the review of these early studies, Tziner delineates possible distinct patterns of behavior and interaction that are implied by the two types of cohesiveness. For instance, in a cohesive group of the first type, the relationships are affective, congenial, open, organic, and authentic. In instrumental cohesive groups, where interactions focus mainly on goal attainment, all resources are invested in the creation of optimal conditions for effective performance, including the coordination of individuals' activities, the development of normative patterns of performance-relevant behavior, and the maximal reduction of informal relations that constitute irrelevant investment. Moreover, the later studies reconfirm the significant role of group cohesiveness in task achievement where the group is instrumental in nature. In a more recent series of experiments by Zaccaro and Lowe (1988), Zaccaro and McCoy (1988) and Zaccaro (1991), impressive support was, in fact, found for several of the hypotheses proposed by Tziner regarding differences in group processes and outcomes that result from the two types of cohesiveness.

The Effects of Group Composition on Task Performance

In a more recent development, Tziner (1982) notes that small group research also tends to focus on groups established in order to satisfy members' socio-psychological needs rather than production, despite the practical value of knowing the effects of group composition on group outcomes. As early as 1976, Terborg et al. noted that 'little has changed in this regard over the intervening years' (p. 783). Furthermore, Tziner (1986) points out that the few attempts to assess more outwardly directed performance outcomes have been restricted to groups that are experimentally contrived and assigned simplistic tasks requiring little coordination or communication (e.g., Goldman, 1965; Johnson and Torcivia, 1967). In these studies, group members cooperate by sharing the whole task, in what is termed collaborative tasks. It has been noted, however, that this research literature on small groups is only tangentially related to the dynamics surrounding group outcomes in complex natural settings (Tziner and Eden, 1985).

In complex task structures, successful performance necessitates synchronization of the activities of all group members, each playing a distinctive, separate, and independent role. These activities are subsumed by the larger category of cooperative tasks (coordinated tasks) for which there are specific relationships governing the performance of the subtasks in terms of time or precedence. (This distinction between collaborative and coordinated task structures was first introduced by O'Brien, 1984.)

According to Tziner (1986), whereas the extensive literature on individual efficacy indicates the dominant influence of talent or ability on output (Guion, 1983), the relative dearth of work on group composition leaves basic questions regarding the relevance of the nature of group characteristics to performance unanswered. Tziner argues that while it seems reasonable to expect ability to play an equally central role among the determinants of group efficacy, the multiple requirements of sophisticated group task settings introduce complexities not always apparent in the discussion of individual abilities at the group level. Principal among these is the question of aggregation: In what fashion do individual capacities combine, or aggregate, to determine group efficacy? Do certain skill groupings perform better than others? And if so, why?

Surprisingly enough, the limited empirical evidence of simple task situations (commonly of a collaborative nature) provide equivocal answers to the question of aggregation. Hill (1982), Shaw (1976), and Steiner (1972) conclude that members' task-relevant abilities simply combine in an additive manner. In their view, each member contributes to group production in direct proportion to his or her task-relevant ability, irrespective of other members' task-relevant abilities; the higher a given member's task-relevant ability, the better the group's performance.

Other research indicates that group performance often deviates from this model of simple additivity (Rohrbaugh, 1981), both for better and for worse. On the one hand, there are reports of positive non-additivity, when groups seem to accomplish more than the sum of their parts (Egerbladh, 1976). On the other hand, cases of negative non-additivity have been reported, where efficacy falls below that predicted from individual task relevant skills and talents. (See also the discussion of 'process loss' in Hackman and Morris, 1983.)

These findings have elicited several *ad hoc* theoretical explications. Laughlin and Johnson (1966), for example, link positive non-additivity to the combination of unique resources, each necessary for a separate task facet. Alternatively, Secord and Backman (1974) argue that negative non-additivity, or the inhibition of group production, stems from the feelings of anger evoked by pairing with inferior partners.

Although these speculations highlight interesting dynamics, they fail to elaborate a unified understanding of the phenomenon. At the very least, they do not offer a simultaneous explanation of positive and negative non-additivity. For this purpose, social psychological approaches may be helpful.

Social Psychological Explanations of Non-additivity

That non-additivity often appears in tasks involving coordinated activity suggests that a thorough understanding of the effects of group composition must ultimately address the issue of interpersonal relationships. At least two approaches in social psychology deal with the issue of individual characteristics and their impact on the quality of interpersonal bonds: Similarity Theory and Equity Theory. Their application to the subject of group composition leads to significantly different conclusions regarding the value of heterogeneity and homogeneity among group members.

Similarity Theory

According to the basic tenets of Similarity Theory, homogeneity among group members is desirable because it evokes positive forms of mutual attraction, whereas heterogeneity introduces divisive tensions. Indeed, the research literature on dyads indicates the validity of the commonsense notion that 'likes like likes'. Similarity on a variety of physical and psychological dimensions, including ability, and particularly among people who are instrumentally motivated, has been found to facilitate liking and attraction (Nahemow and Lawton, 1983).

Byrne (1961) and Byrne, Griffitt, Hudgins, and Reeves (1969) claim that individuals sharing common attributes are attracted to one another because they receive reinforcement for traits such as similarity and communality. The experience of realizing that others are similar in personality, outlook, and behavior is reassuring; it is a form of consensual validation. Based on research findings, Earley (1993) notes that individuals sharing similar traits and backgrounds are likely to derive mutual satisfaction from working together. This feeling enhances group cohesiveness which, in turn, impacts positively on team performance.

A parallel body of research indicates that attraction facilitates many desirable interpersonal dynamics, including the evolution of expressive relationships, effective communication and norms of cooperation, and a pleasant interpersonal atmosphere (see: Tziner, 1982). Not surprisingly, these benefits of attraction are identical to those features thought to promote effective team performance on complex tasks requiring high interdependence (Dyer, 1977; Cummings, 1978). The conclusion that homogeneity of skills leads to positive relations and enhanced performance thus seems a straightforward one.

Nevertheless, close examination of the similarity and attraction literature suggests that the influence of homogeneity is somewhat more complex than meets the eye. Secord and Backman (1974) state that 'the attraction between similar persons may rest on the fact that the trait or ability allows them to engage in an activity which is mutually rewarding' (p. 221). Indeed, homogeneity of traits is not a sufficient condition to guarantee the attainment of mutual rewards under any circumstances. For example, when group members are all similarly lacking in the traits necessary for completion of a task into which they have put considerable effort, this negative similarity may prevent mutual reward and even make work a source of mutual friction and irritation (on the assumption that the goal is not achieved). Senn (1971) argues that positive similarity, because it is doubly reinforcing, 'would yield greater liking than negative similarity' (p. 121). His hypothesis of a link between positive similarity and positive non-additivity, however, appears to have overlooked the parallel hypothesis that negative similarity also evokes negative non-additivity.

Furthermore, this discussion of distinct forms of homogeneity does not answer the question of group heterogeneity. As it seems probable that more conflicts will arise between dissimilar than between similar people, one is tempted to accept the simplistic notion that differences breed contempt. Indeed, it has been shown (e.g., Hoffman and Maier, 1961; Szilagyi and Wallace, 1982) that the heterogeneity of individual characteristics frequently creates a breeding ground for interpersonal conflict that is detrimental to performance. These conflicts may interfere with performance because the members' resources (e.g., abilities) available for team coordination are invested in the conflict resolution of interpersonal matters rather than in promoting performance, particularly in the pursuit of smooth and timely synchronization of activities and interactions (Morgan and Lassiter, 1992). As such, heterogeneity, like negative homogeneity, is expected to yield negative non-additivity.

Similarity Theory thus addresses composition effects in terms of their influence on positive attraction and conflictual tension. Positive homogeneity is thought to enhance relationships beneficial to production, whereas negative homogeneity and heterogeneity increase divisive tension and ineffective performance. The assumption that tension is counterproductive, however, is not universally accepted. Equity Theory challenges this proposition, a stance that impacts significantly on the analysis and interpretation of the influence of group composition on performance.

Equity Theory

Equity Theory, as proposed by Adams (1965), deals with tensions arising from unfavorable interpersonal comparison and their motivational impact. Individuals are said to compare themselves with significant others in respect to the ratio or balance of personal inputs to outcomes. The subjective judgment of equality between one's own ratio and that of the significant other produces feelings of equity (Hatfield, 1983), while a perception of unequal ratios induces intense and distressful feelings of under- or over-reward. This tension of inequity then motivates an effort aimed at restoring equity.

By way of illustration, let us consider the implication of this argument in the case of a three-man team engaged in performing a cooperative task that demands synchronization of the activities of its members, who carry out distinct, interdependent roles that are perceived as comparable. Here, each member's two teammates are likely to represent the significant others for comparison. The analysis of input/output ratios can be simplified by assuming that all team members share equally in the rewards. Thus, the equity considerations will focus primarily on the issue of relative effort and contribution to the final product. Feelings of inequity will arise from a perception of disproportionate investment (i.e., task-relevant talents), and are likely to result in uneven performance (Leventhal, 1976).

In reviewing the strategies that individuals employ to restore equity, Steers and Porter (1979) note two important drives at work. In situations in which a team is performing poorly, individuals may change their own level of input effort or may exert pressure on others to augment their efforts. Thus, the under-rewarded can restore equity by reducing their own efforts or by urging others to increase theirs. Alternatively, the over-rewarded can increase their own efforts, or pressure others to cut back on their contribution. As a result, both over-reward and under-reward contain the potential for enhancing or restricting group performance, depending on the specific strategies adopted by the group members. Empirical research has shown that a disparity of reward perceptions does indeed lead to both types of variation in group performance (Mowday, 1979).

The manner in which individuals choose a particular strategy is also of relevance here. One principle would seem to be the frequently reported tendency of groups to bring errant members back into step with the others (Steers and Porter, 1979). According to this approach, groups dominated by individuals who feel under-rewarded will attempt to increase the efforts of lagging members, whereas groups dominated by over-rewarded individuals will seek to restrain overly enthusiastic members in order to assuage their consciences.

In general, Equity Theory can be used to make predictions concerning performance in heterogeneous groups by determining the ratio of members with high task-related attributes (e.g., personality traits, ability, motivation) to those with poor task-related attributes. The case of the three-man team presented above can be used to illustrate the performance predictions produced by applying the theory's principles of additivity. For instance, groups with two high- and one low-ability members will strive to increase the efforts of the low member, thereby leading to a case of positive non-additivity. In contrast, groups with two low- and one high-ability members will attempt to restrict the efforts of the high-ability member, with resulting negative non-additivity. Because inequity is not expected to appear in groups in which all members share equal ability levels, simple additivity should characterize all-high or all-low ability teams.

Applying the Theories

The Similarity and Equity theories offer quite distinct pictures of the effect of group composition on group performance. At the dynamic level, Similarity Theory employs concepts of beneficial attraction and disruptive tension. In contrast, Equity Theory deals solely with tension, but treats it as a motivational force with both positive and negative outcomes.

In both cases, however, the shared thesis is that these interpersonal forces have an impact on the transformation of members' abilities into performance. More specifically, the motivational effects of group composition are seen by both theories as the key reason that group performance frequently falls above or below what is expected from the simple addition of members' abilities.

The differing dynamics of the two social psychological theories generate contrasting predictions as to the ultimate relation between group composition and performance. Table 4.1 presents the relevant theory-based hypotheses regarding the additivity or non-additivity of performance outcomes for three-member groups composed of high- or low-ability individuals. As can be seen, the two theoretical approaches differ in almost every case in respect to the expected outcomes.

It will be recalled that the starting point for this social psychological analysis of group composition and performance was the simple additivity model. Yet both the empirical evidence and the thrust of the arguments do not seem to support this intuitively pleasing model. Indeed, it would appear that

Table 4.1   Performance hypotheses of Similarity and Equity approaches for three-member groups varying in ability composition

PERFORMANCE PREDICTION

Composition	Equity Theory	Similarity Theory
Hi Hi Hi	Additivity	Positive Nonadditivity
Hi Hi Lo	Positive Nonadditivity	Negative Nonadditivity
Hi Lo Lo	Negative Nonadditivity	Negative Nonadditivity
Lo Lo Lo	Additivity	Negative Nonadditivity

non-additivity, or the deviation from group outcomes predicted by the simple sum of group abilities, may be an equally valid perception of extant phenomena. This conclusion does not deny the importance of the additivity model. However, social psychologists commonly promote the notion that in task structural situations, non-additivity should increase in cases of mutual interdependence. This idea is reinforced by task structuralists, who couch it in terms of the 'weak link' model of conjunctive efforts.

From both the Similarity and Equity theories, we can infer that different forces may work against additivity in different collaborative tasks. Similarity would seem to be most important in tasks where members' efforts are easily compared to each other, a case that is obtained when members perform interchangeable functions (e.g., when they are capable of replacing each other). Equity considerations would appear to be more dominant in cases in which each member's contribution is unique but outcomes are shared. Thus, social psychology draws our attention to the potential importance of the relative uniqueness or interchangeability of workers in the cooperative effort as determinants of the driving forces behind non-additivity.

One might ask, of course, at what point social-psychological considerations become particularly salient in task settings. Research by Kerr (1983) indicates the possible influence of one such factor, namely, reward systems. He found that group reward systems lead to a reduction of the 'free rider effect', whereby individuals believe that their contributions to team performance are dispensable or unnecessary, and therefore do not contribute to the collective goal although other members are striving to do so. A similar phenomenon is known as 'social loafing' (Levene, Resnick, and Higgins, 1993). This occurs when some members of a team do not invest all their efforts, or do not give the team the benefit of all their performance potential. These terms must be distinguished from shirking, which is typified as a more individualistic form of withholding effort at work that is related to possible monitoring difficulties or self-interested behavior, rather than to a perception of team parameters (Jones, 1981).

Social loafing and free riding are similar types of dysfunctional behavior that appear under the more general heading of a propensity to withhold effort, PWE (after Kidwell and Bennett, 1993), and which lead to a loss in team performance. Team performance is thus lower than what could be expected based on the individual competence and level of performance of the individual members. It is tempting to argue that group reward systems are just the sort of incentive likely to induce equity, or similarity comparisons, by individual workers interested in increasing personal gain within a group framework. In that case, we would also expect a reduction in social loafing and free riding.

Knoke (1990) offers a comprehensive framework for understanding PWE in the workplace based on an integration of theory and research in various disciplines, including economics, social psychology, and management. He describes several sources of motivation for this negative behavior that emphasize both the formal and informal contextual elements which impinge on an employee's performance at work. Among them are rational choice, normative conformity, and affective bonding. Of particular import is Knoke's observation that before a decision is made to withhold effort, the employee does a rational cost-benefit analysis based on group size, wage premiums, task visibility, and interdependence (p. 450). This suggestion is quite similar to Kerr's (1983) emphasis on reward systems. What is unique here, however, is the reference to the relationship between this kind of calculation and other variables that tap employees' decision-making apparatus, such as personality traits, normative conformity, and affective bonding.

Barry and Stewart (1997) found that social loafing and free riding are less likely to occur in work teams whose members are high on the personality trait of conscientiousness. In addition, Erez and Somech (1996) contend that social loafing is less likely in collectivistic cultures, because individuals in these cultures achieve self-actualization through collective achievements. These researchers also demonstrate empirically that social loafing can be reduced in individualistic cultures if individuals work in teams with others who are familiar to them. In this way, intragroup communication is improved, and incentives for good performance are more apt to be linked to specific performance goals. Since social loafing and free riding are conceptually similar, it is reasonable to assume that the circumstances conducive to diminishing social loafing apply equally to free riding. Thus the same measures undertaken to reduce social loafing can probably be used to reduce free riding.

These studies should alert us to the fine differences between tasks and groups, and to the possibility that subtle fluctuations in team interactions may impact strongly on performance results. What this means is that in order to assess the value of different approaches to group behaviors and team efforts, greater attention must be paid to the empirical assessment of the dynamic interpersonal factors that characterize them. In one striking example, LePine and Van Dyne (1998) found that when employees are *forced* to interact with others in their work groups in order to perform cooperative types of tasks, this interdependence serves as a major source of either low or high satisfaction. It goes without saying that a group member's level of satisfaction is bound to affect the amount of effort he or she is willing to exert in teamwork.

Tziner (1993): The Effects of Interpersonal Communication, Social Influence, and Performance on Group Interactive Processes

In view of the above conclusions, Tziner (1982), Tziner and Vardi (1982), and Tziner and Eden (1985) investigated the influence of various group factors, both internal and external, on group performance. These team studies were conducted in real settings, unlike the artificial settings used in most previous research in the area (cf. Hare, 1976; Rorhbaugh, 1981). All three investigations concerned the actual functioning of tank crews in the Israeli army, on the assumption that their internal relationships and subsequent performance would have a direct bearing on the survival of the group, as well as serious consequences for the organization as a whole (Shaw, 1976; Shirom, 1976). Tank crews were selected because they are small, formal, instrumental groups with a high internal interdependency. Performance depends on the coordinated effort of all crew members, requiring not only task specialization and technical skills, but also team spirit and the continuous and direct involvement of the tank commander (leader) in their activities.

In such teams, the tasks can not be accomplished unless all members make an effective concerted effort (Tziner, 1982). Thus, in this instance, the nature of the relationship between the cohesiveness of a task-oriented group and its performance level is more than just a question of academic concern (cf.: Schriesheim, Mowday, and Stogdill, 1979; Greene and Schriesheim, 1980).

As noted above, while some previous research supported the notion that group performance is positively related to socio-emotional cohesiveness (Landers and Grum, 1971; D'Augelli, 1973; Krichevskii, 1973; Greene and

Schriesheim, 1980; Mullen and Cooper, 1994), possibly because of the strong communication channels that characterize such groups (Hare, 1976; Paulus 1980), other research found negative relationships or no relationships at all (Warwick, 1964; Lott and Lott, 1965; Stogdill, 1972; Tziner and Vardi, 1982). In light of this conflicting evidence, it was suggested that expectations regarding the instrumentality of cohesive groups in attaining organizationally defined goals is largely a function of the social norm prevailing in the group (Anderson, 1975; Hare, 1976; Steers and Porter, 1979). Thus, a cohesive group is likely to be productive if its members identify with the organization; if they do not, such groups can 'use' their cohesiveness to successfully become counter-productive or harmful, or even to sabotage the organization (Berkowitz, 1954; Stogdill, 1972; Tziner, 1982). Tziner and Vardi (1982) contended, however, that while this argument assigns socio-emotional processes a crucial role in determining performance, it tends to ignore the instrumental aspect of the group's performance and the role of the group's ability to carry out the duties expected of it.

In the first study, Tziner and Vardi tested the hypothesis that the ability level of a task-oriented group serves as a moderator between its socio-emotional cohesiveness and its performance effectiveness, proposing that the weak or non-existent relationships between cohesion and outcomes in previous studies resulted from inadequate capability. Drawing on studies that found positive relationships between group ability and performance level (e.g., Laughlin and Branch, 1972; Graham and Dillon, 1974; Egerbladh, 1976; Hoffman, 1979), the researchers argue that even when a group experiences both high levels of socio-emotional attraction and high motivation to perform formal organizational goals, low ability in crucial activities will lead to poor task outcomes (Secord and Backman, 1974; Hackman and Morris, 1975). This poor level of performance may, in turn, affect interpersonal bonds, thereby reducing effectiveness even more (Tziner, 1982). However, if ability is high, poor performance can be more easily handled (and possibly corrected) by a cohesive group than by one which is loosely knit, a proposition supported conceptually by Schultz (1998, p. 300). It was thus expected that in the tank crews, which represent groups with high inter-task dependence, the relationship between group level of performance and the socio-emotional bonds among its members would be affected by the group's ability.

Crews were formed by self-selection following a sociometric procedure using intensity of reciprocity in selection as the measure of cohesiveness. Crew ability level was determined by the average ability of its members. Performance was defined by the team ratings of a superior officer.

The results of this study indicated that, significantly, performance was best explained by crew cohesiveness ($r = 0.30$), although the moderating effect of crew ability level on performance was also strongly substantiated by the high correlation between group cohesiveness and ability ($r = 0.52$). Although Hare's (1976) definition of cohesiveness in socio-emotional terms was followed, Tziner and Vardi claim that it is likely that the soldiers' choice of crewmates also reflects the advantage of working with potentially capable peers. New soldiers, anxious about their future organizational performance as individuals and as crew members, would therefore appear to base their choices on instrumental, as well as emotional considerations (cf.: Borgatta, Couch, and Bales, 1954, Bjerstedt, 1956, Hollander, 1956, Secord and Backman, 1974). The moderating role effects of group ability could be easily clarified if the amount of objective information available to candidates regarding the ability of the others was manipulated prior to a sociometric selection procedure.

The second, quasi-experimental, study (Tziner and Vardi, 1982) examined the question of how leadership style and group cohesiveness interact to affect the performance effectiveness of self-selected crews that carry out clearly defined and interdependent tasks under the supervision of formal leaders, in this case, in the military. An interactive model of these relationships is presented in Figure 4.1.

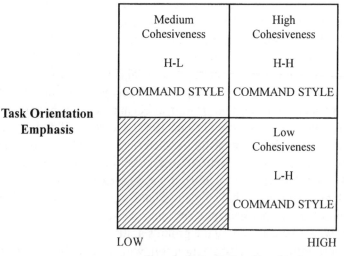

Figure 4.1   Combinations of command style and group cohesiveness expected to yield high performance effectiveness

Relying on the model of group cohesiveness outlined at the beginning of this chapter, the investigation rested on the assumption that leadership style is characterized by two dimensions, emphasis on task performance and emphasis on people orientation (see, for example: Fiedler, 1967; Reddin, 1970; Stogdill, 1974; Luthans, 1979). In general, it is held that when task performance is emphasized, a leader will concentrate on task-relevant aspects of the crew members' activities, on instrumental exchanges of information, and on the need to overcome various obstacles encountered in the course of completing the task (Kerr and Schriesheim, 1974; Katz and Kahn, 1978). When people orientation is emphasized, the leader will be attentive to subordinates' needs as individuals and as a crew, and will be friendly and approachable (Kerr and Schriesheim, 1974; Katz and Kahn, 1978). Furthermore, a leader's behavior can be conceived in terms of a high (H) or low (L) degree on each of the two dimensions, thus resulting in four leadership styles (Katz and Kahn, 1978). Thus, an H-H style is one in which leaders emphasize both a high task and a high people orientation; H-L denotes a task-oriented style; and L-H, a people-oriented leadership style. The fourth style, L-L, is not considered viable for leading groups of the kind that was investigated in this study (e.g., Festinger, Schachter and Back, 1950; Back, 1951; Bennis and Shepard, 1964; Schriesheim, 1980).

As they were investigating a task structure that requires high interdependence (Thompson, 1967), Tziner and Vardi posited that high (superior) performance effectiveness would be found in groups with: (1) high cohesiveness and an H-H leadership style; (2) medium cohesiveness and an H-L leadership style; and (3) low cohesiveness and an L-H style. The first possibility was based on the assumption that in highly cohesive groups, roles are clear, contingencies are spelled out, there is a shared understanding of the use of various resources, and individual differences can be tolerated. Given this type of group task and a positive social attitude, a leader may exercise high involvement both in the process of task accomplishment and in the interpersonal arena. Moreover, under such favorable conditions, both the leader and the group would be ready and able to meet demands for even better performance.

The second possibility was based on the notion that the H-L leadership style (high on task, low on people orientation) was most suited to a medium cohesiveness group, because task-orientation would serve as a common goal encouraging greater cooperation. If tasks are well defined and members are moderately attracted to each other, the leader's emphasis on results will not harm the still weak social foundations, and might even strengthen them. On the other hand, concentrating on socio-emotional activities without pressing for accomplishment (L-H) might jeopardize the moderate level of cohesiveness already established.

Finally, under normal circumstances, if cohesiveness is initially low, the leader will first demonstrate a task orientation by clarifying the task and role structure (Schachter and Back, 1950; Bennis and Shepard, 1964; Festinger and House, 1971; Schriesheim, 1980). However, Tziner and Vardi were investigating instrumental groups in which tasks and individual roles were already well defined. Low cohesiveness in the tank crews was characterized, rather, by a lack of interpersonal attraction, misunderstandings, and mutual misconceptions. In these circumstances, task orientation would be less effective (if not actually detrimental; Blau, 1954; Lott and Lott, 1965) than creating a social context conducive to performance effectiveness.

In this study, 94 crews consisting of three male soldiers who had undergone similar training were formed through a self-selection sociometric procedure; the command style of tank commanders was assessed by means of questionnaires; and crew performance was appraised by unit commanders. The crews were then studied throughout their performance of routine military duties. The results revealed only interaction effects of cohesiveness and command style on performance effectiveness (Table 4.2).

Table 4.2   Two-way analysis of variance of the effects of command style and group cohesiveness on performance effectiveness

Source of variance	*df*	*MS*	*F*
Command style (A)	2	1.743	1.636
Cohesiveness (B)	2	2.130	2.000
A × B	4	6.908	6.487 *
Residual	85	1.065	

* $p < .001$.

The F ratios in Table 4.2 indicate that the interaction between command style and cohesiveness is statistically significant, as anticipated in the research model (see Figure 4.1). In other words, variability in performance effectiveness at the group (crew) level appears to be related to different combinations of leadership style and group cohesiveness. This would mean that under conditions of high crew interdependence (as in tank operation), crew performance effectiveness could be enhanced by matching the command style to the prevailing level of cohesiveness in the group. In more general terms, team performance could be enhanced by matching leadership style to the state of interpersonal relations that characterizes a particular work team.

Figure 4.2 presents the empirical effects on performance of three group situations (levels of cohesiveness) and three styles of command.

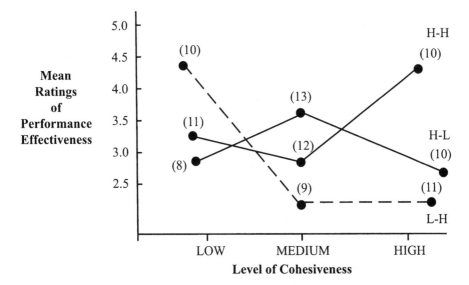

Figure 4.2   Mean ratings of performance effectiveness as related to the combinations of cohesiveness level and command style (Numbers in parentheses represent cell sizes. H-H=high task orientation, high people orientation; H-L=high task orientation, low people orientation; L-H=low task orientation, high people orientation.)

The following patterns emerged from this analysis:

1   Tank crews characterized by high cohesiveness perform best under the direction of an H-H commander (emphasizing both people-orientation and task-accomplishment). Under other cohesiveness conditions, however, this command style is associated with notably lower levels of crew performance effectiveness.

2   Low cohesiveness crews perform most effectively with an L-H commander (low in task emphasis, high in people orientation). This command style is associated with singularly low levels of effectiveness in all other conditions of cohesiveness.
3   Although the relations are not statistically significant, H-L leaders appear to obtain the best performance effectiveness with groups of medium cohesiveness. On the whole, moderate cohesiveness groups did not display high crew performance effectiveness under any of the command styles.

These three trends were highly consistent with the predicted expectations, despite the rigid constraints associated with the design of a study in any natural organizational setting, and particularly in the military. One of these limitations was the need to employ cross-sectional data and a static notion of group cohesiveness, precluding the possibility of extrapolating conclusive evidence as to how, or to what extent, changes in crew cohesiveness across time affected the results. Nevertheless, the authenticity of the procedure, the real-life environment, and the originality of the data provide insights that would be unobtainable in 'neater' environments. The fact that crew cohesiveness served quite effectively as a situational variable lends further support to the situational approach to organizational leadership (e.g., Reddin, 1970; Fiedler, 1971). Tziner and Vardi suggest that in future investigations, in addition to task structure (Fiedler, 1971), task type (Gilmore, Beehr and Richter, 1979), and leader-subordinate relationships (Fiedler, 1971), levels of cohesiveness (including 'rejected' individuals) also be considered as a determinant of group performance effectiveness, in order to extend the generalizability of the results.

The concept of group cohesiveness in self-selected groups focuses attention on interpersonal relationships. In this study, for example, performance effectiveness was not significantly affected by either group cohesiveness or command style taken separately, but only by their interaction. Yet much research has shown that group cohesiveness does not necessarily contribute directly to performance effectiveness (e.g., Schachter, Ellerston, McBride and Gregory, 1951; Berkowitz, 1954; Seashore, 1954). Several moderating effects appear to intervene here, including group norms, task related competence (abilities), and group size.

As already noted, Seashore (1954) and Anderson (1975), for instance, have shown that cohesiveness can lead to productivity when the emerging social norm is identification with the formal goals of the organization. In a more recent study, Mullen and Cooper (1994) found a small but significant positive relationship between cohesiveness and performance, which might have been higher had the researchers distinguished between teams whose norms favored increase of performance and those lacking these norms. However, even when such necessary conditions as goal congruence, cohesiveness, and supportive leadership are fulfilled, level of skill and ability can still make a unique contribution to accomplishment. In Tziner and Vardi's study (1982), there is a certain implication that the initial choice of team members may have as much to do with individuals' perceptions of how well their prospective partners will be able to carry out their tasks (instrumental considerations) as it does with social considerations. Although the effect of group size was not measured in this study since all the tank crew groups were of equal size, it is also well established that group size similarly moderates the way in which other group attributes affect performance (e.g., Laughlin and Branch, 1972; Egerbladh, 1976). These are fruitful areas for future research.

The Assembly Bonus Effect (Michaelsen, Watson and Black, 1989) may shed further light on the possible contributions to group performance of the original make-up of a team and its members' respective skills. This effect can be found when members of a group collectively accomplish a task or successfully obtain a goal that they would have been very unlikely to achieve had each member worked alone (Collins and Guetzkow, 1964). Indeed, when the Assembly Bonus Effect is observed, group performance should exceed the performance of the most capable member, or any additive combination of the individual performances of the members. The group as a whole should reach levels of attainment or yield solutions that none of the individual members would have been capable of realizing independently.

As we have seen, positive group interaction is one of the key factors contributing to successful group performance, as motivation and effort are increased, knowledge is gained, skills are initiated, and task-related individual competencies are channeled and applied to the task (Hackman and Morris, 1983). Interaction, therefore, should contribute to a group performance that is superior to that of individual members, and to the achievement of better, and otherwise unlikely, outcomes.

Nonetheless, a number of empirical studies have shown that groups frequently do not reach the task relevant potential of which they are capable, given the level of talent of the individual members. Tziner (1993) suggests that many of the studies that fail to demonstrate the Assembly Bonus Effect may involve groups characterized by initially poor group composition and process, or 'process loss' (Steiner, 1972). Process loss has been attributed to ineffective task performance strategies, wasteful use of the knowledge and skills of the group members, poor rapport among the individuals in the group (Davis, 1969; Hill, 1982; Hackman and Morris, 1983; Tziner, 1986), and poor group composition that induces negative interpersonal reactions (Tziner and Eden, 1985; Tziner, 1986; Levine and Moreland, 1990).

Tindale and Larson (1992a, 1992b) propose that if an Assembly Bonus Effect does exist, it should manifest itself and be identified primarily at the level of task components, rather than at the completion of the task. By focusing on item-by-item performance, it would be possible to discern how a group can consistently perform no better (and sometimes even worse) than its best member on each component part, and yet still outperform its best member on the overall task (p. 102). This approach assumes that the task in hand can be broken down into its operational components, so that a correct solution or method of handling the sub-task can be described or measured. Thus, group performance would be indicative of whether the group as a whole succeeds at sub-levels or tasks in a way that one individual could not perform alone.

Of course, not all tasks lend themselves to such sub-task dissection, as noted by Michaelsen, Watson, Schwartzkopf and Black (1992), who devised problems for their research that required judgmental solutions rather than 'intellective' tasks. They defined the latter sort as tasks 'involving a definitive objective criterion of success within the definitions, rules, operations and relationships of a particular conceptual system; that is, the answers are relatively straightforward' (p. 107). Similarly, Tziner (1993) argues that complex cooperative task structures (in contrast to collaborative tasks which require little communication or coordination between group members; Johnson and Torcivia, 1967; Goldman, 1971) do not easily lend themselves to a step-by-step analysis either, and are better examined at the overall performance level. As most of the early research into group performance concentrated on collaborative task structures (Johnson and Torcivia, 1967; Goldman, 1971; Hoffman, 1979), this may account for the elusive nature of the Assembly Bonus Effect.

Several more recent studies describe the processes and outcomes of groups performing cooperative type tasks (O'Brien, 1968; Kabanoff and O'Brien 1979; Tziner and Eden, 1985), which usually demand more interdependence among group members than do collaborative tasks (see: Shiflett, 1979). Significantly, these investigations were also conducted in real-life situations, in contrast to the studies of collaborative tasks that were performed by groups in laboratory settings.

In the third experiment, what they call 'a good example of the study of the impact of *a priori* and systematic manipulations of real-life group structures',

Tziner and Eden (1985) investigated how various tank crew compositions affect crew performance. They varied group composition according to the members' level of ability and motivation, since both had been found to be positively, but not clearly, related to group productivity (O'Brien and Owens, 1969; Steers and Porter, 1979; Hill, 1982). As explained above, three-man military tank crews engage in real collaborative tasks that demand a high level of interdependence among the members.

As we have seen, there is evidence that ability composition effects impinge on group performance in either an additive or non-additive fashion, a finding that received support in a recent meta-analysis which revealed a correlation coefficient of $r = 0.33$ between group ability and group performance (Devine, Philips, and Fogel, 1998). The positive correlation, however, appears to be far greater for collaborative tasks than for cooperative tasks (Shaw, 1976; Hill, 1982). From research indicating that each member contributes independently to group production in direct proportion to his or her ability (Johnson and Torcivia, 1967; Bouchard, 1972), one could posit that the higher the levels of ability and motivation of crew members, the better the performance effectiveness of the group. Consequently, if the ability and motivation of each crew member are treated as separate independent variables, the additive effects should be manifested in significant main effects and non-significant interactions.

It will be recalled, however, that group performance on complex tasks has also been found to exceed or lag behind predicted performance expectations based on the ability levels of individual members (Goldman, 1971; Laughlin and Branch, 1972; Egerbladh, 1976; Rohrbaugh, 1981). This is apparently due, respectively, either to the effects of a unique pooling of resources (Steiner, 1972), or to conflict arising from members' frustrations (Secord and Backman, 1974). In both cases, if significant interactions were found between ability and motivation, it would indicate that combinations of ability result in more (or less) productivity than expected, thereby offering evidence of group composition, or non-additive, effects on group performance.

Applying this alternative non-additive conceptual approach, Tziner and Eden (1985) hypothesize that some combinations of ability and/or motivation would yield a crew performance effectiveness that is higher (or lower) than could be anticipated by a simple aggregation of the ability and/or motivation levels of the crew members. Thus, in addition to the significant main effects (i.e., the ability and motivation of each crew member), interactions were also expected to contribute significantly to the variation in crew performance effectiveness.

Given the equivocal nature of the results of previous research, Tziner and Eden therefore attempt to ascertain whether the ability and motivation of crew members combine additively or interactively, or both, to affect group performance. All possible combinations of both ability and motivation levels were deliberately generated (with no other interventions), providing a sound basis for a causal interpretation, in contrast to earlier studies. The investigation focused on 208 crews performing real military tasks that required the synchronization and coordination of all three group members. The effectiveness of their performance was ranked by the unit commanders after two months of military activity.

It was found that both ability and motivation had an additive effect on crew performance, even though each member had a clearly defined and separate role. In addition, two crew composition effects were found for ability, but not for motivation: (1) the performance of uniformly high-ability crews far exceeded the levels expected by the individual members' ability; and (2) the performance of uniformly low ability crews fell considerably below the expected level.

It was also found that replacing one member of a high-ability crew with a low-ability individual diminished crew performance disproportionately. Conversely, replacing one member of a low-level group with a high-ability soldier boosted effectiveness by about the same amount as replacing one low ability member in a crew with a high-low-low composition. In both cases, the increased effectiveness was less than could be gained by turning a high-high-low crew into a group of uniformly high-ability composition. This finding that 'concentrated talent is more effective' in collaborative situations runs counter to the commonsense notion of 'spreading talent around' (Jones, 1974; Nevin et al., 1982).

The fact that composition effects were found for ability and not for motivation reinforces the findings of the effects of ability on group performance (Bouchard, 1972; Tziner and Vardi, 1982). The fact that no composition effects were found for the combination of ability and motivation strengthens the utility group approach to collaborative (cooperative) tasks and calls into question the oft-quoted dictum that 'Performance = Ability X Motivation' (Vroom, 1960). Furthermore, noting the considerable number of 'statistical cards stacked against significant interactions' in their research design, Tziner and Eden (1985) conclude that the two significant interactions found in the study are sufficient evidence that crew members' ability and/or motivation may combine in a non-additive manner with respect to tasks of the type investigated (p. 92).

These deviations from additivity support previous findings and their theoretical underpinnings attributed, among others, to Laughlin and Johnson (1966) and Secord and Backman (1974). Moreover, they add credence to the contention that in task structural situations characterized by mutual interdependence, non-additivity should increase, and that from the social psychological perspective, equity considerations predominate when each member's contribution is unique, but outcomes are shared.

Increasing support is being reported for the hypotheses suggested in the investigations by Tziner and associates (see, for example: Bass, 1985; Yukl and Van Fleet, 1992). Furthermore, a recent study by Barrick, Stewart, Neubert, and Mount (1998) upholds several of Tziner and Eden's (1985) conclusions and casts further light on the relationship of various parameters to group performance. Barrick et al. found that the teams which received higher supervision ratings for team performance were not only those that were higher in general ability, but also those that were higher on personality attributes, such as conscientiousness, agreeableness, extraversion, and emotional stability. In other words, high ability is not sufficient in and of itself to lead to superior team performance; the personality traits of team members also have an impact on performance. From a negative perspective, this means that team members who lack desirable interpersonal attributes may affect the team process in such a way that cohesiveness diminishes, more interpersonal conflict is generated, and less open communication develops among members. As a consequence, less of the work load is shared and, ultimately, team performance suffers.

Despite the relative paucity of research on how the 'personality composition' of work groups affects team performance, some progress has been reported. For example, Barry and Stewart (1997) found a curvilinear relationship between team performance and the proportion of extroverts in teams completing disjunctive problem solving tasks (single-solution cooperative/collaborative type tasks in groups where members are completely interchangeable). A similar trend was found in teams performing conjunctive tasks, characterized by the potentially equal and essential, yet distinct, contribution of each team member.

Additional personality attributes found to link to effective group performance include adjustment, ambition, achievement orientation, and sociability (Dryskell, Hogan and Salas, 1987; Thomas, Moore and Scott, 1996). Researchers have also demonstrated that work team members who are relatively high on achievement motivation show more concern for group success (Zander and Forward, 1968), and that groups composed of members with high achievement motivation scores solve complex problems more efficiently than those with lower scores (Schneider and Delaney, 1972).

Finally, recent research also highlights the team members' subjective perceptions of 'objective' personality attributes, such as level of achievement motivation or the ability to perform successfully. Gibson (1999), for example, demonstrates that perceptions of group members regarding their ability to perform group tasks tend to be related to how much effort the group expends and, ultimately, to the group's overall effectiveness. These perceptions appear to evolve through group processes, such as collaborative interaction aimed at developing a working plan for accomplishing the group's tasks. Interactions of this sort lead to the creation of communication channels for sharing information, resources and assistance, and mechanisms for conferring socially satisfying rewards, such as positive feedback and a warm accepting atmosphere, among other positive intragroup processes. Self-perceptions are more likely to evolve the greater the task complexity (with achievement more dependent on higher levels of group member interdependence), and the higher the degree of uncertainty regarding the means of accomplishing the tasks.

Conclusion

Studies of group composition, such as those described in this chapter, lend credence to the notion that, in addition to motivation and abilities, the personality composition of teams also has an impact on team performance (Neuman and Wright, 1999). The essential point here is that there needs to be a match between team members' task related attributes, including motivational aspects, personality traits, and abilities on the one hand, and the requirements of the group task on the other.

Furthermore, the results of the studies on tank crews have implications far beyond the immediacy of the research findings. They add a critical dimension to the study of small groups in clearly defined cooperative group situations in the real world. The specific findings have significance for a life and death reality, where the wrong combination of team members not only affects productivity, but could have disastrous effects for the group's very survival. The degree to which the experimental conclusions can be generalized to different work settings will have to be determined by further structured research in this field. Ultimately, it is hoped, the synthesis of theoretical models and empirical research will enable human resource personnel to elicit maximum advantage from minimum resources.

Teams today perform an increasing number of organizational tasks in the workplace. It is crucial, therefore, that future research be directed to a more thorough examination of how they operate. Future endeavors, based on classic group research, as described here, should take several directions, each drawing on the others. First, researchers should continue to explore both the team's *internal* composition (as reflected, for example, in size and location, homogeneity, interchangeability of workers, task-related abilities, personality traits that impinge on group functioning, and work motivation), and *external* factors (including nature of task, reward systems, and supportive leadership), and their effects on intragroup processes such as type of cohesiveness, communication networks, goal congruence, and normative behavior. Moreover, there may also be reason to further investigate the effect on team processes of non-task-oriented aspects of personality (designated 'life'), as well as of other relatively uncharted cultural areas of influence, such as individualistic vs. collectivistic group orientation.

In addition, future research should also be directed at pinpointing the degree and quality of influence that various *combinations* of these factors have on team effectiveness, incorporating criteria related to both performance *and* member satisfaction (see also: Banker, Field, Schroeder and Sinha, 1996). Recalling that teams are basically dynamic, changing entities, it is clear that the thrust of future investigations should also be aimed at the effects of internal and external *changes* on the variables. Undoubtedly, the outcome of these avenues of research will provide human resource personnel with additional tools with which to create the most efficient working conditions for different types of tasks and teams. As more and more research comes to incorporate real-life situations, there is no question that the application of the results will increasingly benefit organizations operating in today's highly competitive marketplace.

References

Adams, J.S. (1965). 'Inequity in Social Exchange'. In L. Berkowitz (ed.), *Advances in Experimental Social Psychology*. New York: Academic Press.

Anderson, A.B. (1975). 'Combined Effects of Interpersonal Attraction and Goal-Path Clarity on the Cohesiveness of Task-Oriented Groups'. *Journal of Personality and Social Psychology*, 31, pp. 68–75.

Back, K.W. (1951). 'Influence Through Communication'. *Journal of Abnormal and Social Psychology*, 46, pp. 9–23.

Backeman, R. and Helmreich, R. (1975). 'Cohesiveness and Performance: Covariation and Causality in our Undersea Environment'. *Journal of Experimental and Social Psychology*, 11, pp. 478–89.

Bales, R.F. (1955). 'Adaptive and Integrative Changes as Sources of Strain in Social Systems'. In A.P. Hare, E.F. Borgotta and R.F. Bales (eds), *Small Groups: Studies in Social Interaction*, New York: Knopf, pp. 127–31.

Ball, J.R. and Carron, A.V. (1976). 'The Influence of Team Cohesion and Participation Motivation Upon Performance Success in Intercollegiate Ice Hockey'. *Canadian Journal of Applied Sport Sciences*, 1, pp. 271–5.

Banker, R.D., Field, J.M., Schroeder, R.G and Sinha, K.K. (1996). 'Impact of Work Teams on Manufacturing Performance: A Longitudinal Field Study'. *Academy of Management Journal*, 39, pp. 867–90.

Barrick, M.R., Stewart, G.L., Neubert, M.J. and Mount, M.K. (1998). 'Relating Member Ability and Personality to Work-Team Processes and Team Effectiveness'. *Journal of Applied Psychology*, 83, pp. 377–91.

Barry, B. and Stewart, G.L. (1997). 'Composition, Process, and Performance in Self-Managed Groups: The Role of Personality'. *Journal of Applied Psychology*, 82, pp. 62–78.

Bass, B.M. (1985). *Leadership and Performance Beyond Expectations*. New York: The Free Press.

Bass, B.M. (1990). *Bass and Stogdill Handbook of Leadership: Theory, Research, and Managerial Applications*. New York: Free Press.

Bennis, W.G and Shepard, H.A. (1964). 'A Theory of Group Development'. In C. Shepard (ed.), *Small Groups: Some Sociological Perspectives*. San Francisco: Chandler.

Berkowitz, L. (1954). 'Group Standards, Cohesiveness and Productivity'. *Human Relations*, 7, pp. 509–19.

Bird, A.M. (1977). 'Development of a Model for Predicting Team Performance'. *Research Quarterly*, 48, pp. 24–32.

Bjerstedt, A. (1956). 'The Interpretation of Sociometric Status Scores in the Classroom'. *Acta Psychologica*, 12, pp. 1–14.

Blau, P.M. (1954). 'Cooperation and Competition in a Bureaucracy'. *American Journal of Sociology*, 39, pp. 530–35.

Borgotta, E.F., Couch, A.S. and Bales, R.F. (1954). 'Some Findings Relevant to the Great Man Theory of Leadership'. *American Sociological Review*, 19, pp. 755–9.

Bouchard, T.J. Jr (1972). 'Training, Motivation, and Personality Determinants of the Effectiveness of Brainstorming Groups and Individuals'. *Journal of Applied Psychology*, 56, pp. 418–21.

Bovard, E.W. Jr (1951). 'The Experimental Production of Interpersonal Affect'. *Journal of Abnormal and Social Psychology*, 46, pp. 521–8.

Byrne, D. (1961). 'Interpersonal Attraction as a Function of Affiliation Need and Attitude Similarity'. *Human Relations*, 14, pp. 285–9.

Byrne, D. and Clore, G.L. (1966). 'Effect of Economic Similarity-Dissimilarity on Interpersonal Attraction'. *Journal of Personality and Social Psychology*, 4, pp. 220–24.

Byrne, D., Griffitt, W., Hudging, W. and Reeves, K. (1969). 'Attitude Similarity-Dissimilarity and Attraction: Generality Beyond the College Sophomore'. *Journal of Social Psychology*, 79, pp. 155–61.

Byrne, D. and Nelson, D. (1965). 'The Effect of Topic Importance and Attitude Similarity-Dissimilarity on Attraction in a Multistranger Design'. *Psychonomic Science*, 3, pp. 449–50.

Cohen, D., Whitmyre, J.W. and Funk, W.H. (1960). 'Effect of Group Cohesiveness and Training Upon Creative Thinking'. *Journal of Applied Psychology*, 44, pp. 319–22.

Collins, B.E. (1970). *Social Psychology*, Reading, MA: Addison-Wesley, pp. 180–226; 230–40.

Collins, B.E. and Guetzkow, H. (1964). *A Social Psychology of Group Processes for Decision Making*. New York: Wiley.

Coser, A.L. (1974). *Greedy Institutions*. New York: Free Press, pp. 117–35.

Cummings, T.G. (1978). 'Sociotechnical Experimentation: A Review of Sixteen Studies'. In W.A. Pasmore and J.J. Sherwood (eds). *Sociotechnical Systems: A Sourcebook*. San Diego, CA: University Associates.

D'Augelli, A.R. (1973). 'Group Composition Using Interpersonal Skill: An Analogue Study on the Effects of Members' Interpersonal Skills on Peer Rating and Group Cohesiveness'. *Journal of Counseling Psychology*, 20, pp. 531–4.

Davis, J.H. (1969). *Group Performance*. Reading, MA: Addison-Wesley.

Devine, D.J., Philips, J.L. and Fogel, M.C. (1998). *Cognitive Ability and Team Performance: A Meta-Analysis and Preliminary Model*. Unpublished manuscript, Indiana University.

Dion, K.K. (1972). 'Physical Attractiveness and Evaluations of Children's Transgression'. *Journal of Personality and Social Psychology*, 24, pp. 207–13.

Dryskell, J.E., Hogan, R. and Salas, E. (1987). 'Personality and Group Performance'. In C. Hendrick (ed.). *Group Processes and Intergroup Relations*. Newbury Park, NJ: Sage, pp. 91–112.

Dyer, W.G. (1977). *Teambuilding: Issues and Alternatives*. Reading, MA: Addison-Wesley.

Earley, P.C. (1993). 'East Meets West Meets Mideast: Further Explorations of Collectivistic and Individualistic Work Groups'. *Academy of Management Journal*, 36, pp. 319–48.

Egerbladh, T. (1976). 'The Function of Group Size and Ability Level in Solving a Multidimensional Complementary Task'. *Journal of Personality and Social Psychology*, 34, pp. 805–8.

Eisman, B. (1959). 'Some Operational Measures of Cohesiveness and Their Interrelations'. *Human Relations*, 12, pp. 183–9.

Erez, M. and Somech, A. (1996). 'Is Group Productivity Loss the Rule or the Exception? Effects of Culture and Group-Based Motivation'. *Academy of Management Journal*, 39, pp. 1512–37.

Evans, N.J. and Jarvis, P.A. (1980). 'Group Cohesion: A Review and Reevaluation'. *Small Group Behavior*, 11, pp. 359–70.

Festinger, L., Schachter, S. and Back, K. (1950). *Social Pressures in Informal Groups: A Study of Human Factors in Housing*. New York: Harper & Row.

Fiedler, F.E. (1971). *Leadership*. New York: General Learning Press.

Fiedler, F.E. (1978). 'The Contingency Model and the Dynamics of the Leadership Process'. In L. Berkowitz (ed.). *Advances in Experimental Social Psychology*. New York: Academic Press.

George, J.M. (1990). 'Personality, Affect, and Behavior'. *Journal of Applied Psychology*, 75, pp. 107–16.

George, J.M. and Brief, A.P. (1992). 'Feeling Good-Doing Good: A Conceptual Analysis of the Mood at Work-Organizational Spontaneity Relationship'. *Psychological Bulletin*, 112, pp. 310–29.

Gibson, C. (1999). 'Do They Do What They Believe They Can? Group Efficacy and Group Effectiveness Across Tasks and Cultures'. *Academy of Management Journal*, 42, pp. 138–52.

Gilmore, D.C., Beehr, T.A. and Richter, D.J. (1979). 'Effects of Leader Behavior on Subordinate Performance and Satisfaction: A Laboratory Experiment with Student Employer'. *Journal of Applied Psychology*, 64, pp. 166–72.

Goldman, M. (1965). 'A Comparison of Individual and Group Performance for Varying Combinations of Initial Ability'. *Journal of Personality and Social Psychology*, 1, pp. 210–16.

Goldman, M. (1971). 'Group Performance Related to Size and Initial Ability of Group Members'. *Psychological Reports*, 28, pp. 551–7.

Goodacre, DAM. III (1951). 'The Use of a Sociometric Test as a Predictor of Combat Unit Effectiveness'. *Sociometry*, 14, pp. 148–52.

Graham, W.K. and Dillon, P.C. (1974). 'Creative Supergroups: Group Performance as a Function of Individual Performance in Brainstorming Tasks'. *The Journal of Social Psychology*, 93, pp. 101–5.

Greene, C.N. and Schriesheim, C.A. (1980). 'Leader-Group Interactions: A Longitudinal Field Investigation', *Journal of Applied Psychology*, 65, pp. 50–59.

Gross, N. and Martin, W.T. (1952). 'On Group Cohesiveness'. *American Journal of Sociology*, 57, pp. 546–54.

Guion, R.M. (1983). 'Recruiting, Selection, and Placement'. In M.D. Dunnette (ed.), *Handbook of Industrial and Organizational Psychology*. Chicago: Rand McNally.

Hackman, R.J. (1976). 'Group Influences on Individuals'. In M.D. Dunnette (ed.), *Handbook of Industrial and Organizational Psychology*. Chicago: Rand McNally, pp. 1455–525.

Hackman, R.J. and Morris, C.G. (1975). 'Group Tasks, Group Interaction Process, and Group Performance Effectiveness: A Review and a Proposed Integration'. In L. Berkowitz (ed.), *Advances in Experimental Social Psychology*, Vol. 8. New York: Academic Press.

Hackman, R.J. and Morris, C.G. (1983). 'Group Tasks, Group Interaction Process and Group Performance Effectiveness'. In H.H. Blumberg, A.P. Hare, V. Kent and M.P. Davies (eds), *Small Groups and Social Interaction*. New York: Wiley.

Hare, A.P. (1976). *Handbook of Small Group Research*, 2nd edn. New York: Free Press.

Hatfield, E. (1983). 'Equity Theory and Research: An Overview'. In H.H. Blumberg, A.P. Hare, V. Kent and M.P. Davies (eds), *Small Groups and Social Interaction*. New York: Wiley.

Hemphill, J.K. and Sachrest, L.B. (1952). 'A Comparison of Three Criteria of Air Crew Effectiveness in Combat Over Korea'. *Journal of Applied Psychology*, 36, pp. 323–7.

Hill, M. (1982). 'Group Versus Individual Performance: Are N + 1 Heads Better Than One? *Psychological Bulletin*, 91, pp. 517–39.

Hoffman, L.R. (1979). *The Group Problem Solving Process: Studies of a Valence Model*. New York: Praeger.

Hoffman, L.R. and Maier, R.F. (1961). 'Quality and Acceptance of Problem Solutions by Members of Homogeneous and Heterogeneous Group'. *Journal of Abnormal and Social Psychology*, 62, pp. 401–7.

Hollander, E.P. (1956). 'The Friendship Factor in Peer Nominations'. *Personnel Psychology*, 9, pp. 435–47.

Homans, G.C. (1950). *The Human Groups*. New York: Harcourt, Brace, & World.

House, R.J. (1971). 'A Path-Goal Theory of Leader Effectiveness'. *Administrative Science Quarterly*, 16, pp. 321–38.

Johnson, H.H. and Torcivia, J.M. (1967). 'Group and Individual Performance on a Single Task as a Function of Distribution of Individual Performance'. *Journal of Experimental Social Psychology*, 3, pp. 266–73.

Jung, D.I. and Avolio, B.J. (1990). 'Effects of Leadership Style and Followers' Cultural Orientation on Performance in Group and Individual Task Conditions'. *Academy of Management Journal*, 42, pp. 208–18.

Kabanoff, B. and O'Brien, G.E. (1979). 'Cooperation Task Structure and the Relationship of Leaders and Member Ability to Group Performance'. *Journal of Applied Psychology*, 64, pp. 526–32.

Katz, D. and Kahn, R. (1966). *The Social Psychology of Organizations*. New York: Wiley.

Kerr, N.L. (1983). 'Motivation Losses in Small Groups: A Social Dilemma Analysis'. *Journal of Personality and Social Psychology*, 45, pp. 819–28.

Kerr, N.L. and Schriesheim, C. (1974). 'Consideration, Initiating Structure, and Organizational Criteria – An Update of Korman's 1966 Review'. *Personnel Psychology*, 27, pp. 555–68.

Kidwell, R.E. Jr and Bennett, N. (1993). 'Employee Propensity to Withhold Effort: A Conceptual Model and Three Avenues of Research'. *Academy of Management Review*, 18, pp. 429–56.

Knoke, D. (1990). *Organizing for Collective Action*. Berlin: De Gruyter.

Krichevskii, R.L. (1973). 'The Problem of Cohesiveness in Small Groups in Non-Soviet Social Psychology'. *Psikhologii*, 19, pp. 174–84.

Landers, D.M. and Grum, T.F. (1971). 'The Effects of Team Success and Formal Structure on Interpersonal Relations and Cohesiveness of Baseball Teams'. *International Journal of Sport Psychology*, 2, pp. 88–96.

Laughlin, P.R. and Branch, L.G. (1972). 'Individual Versus Tetradic Performance on a Complementary Task as a Function of Initial Ability Level'. *Organizational Behavior and Human Performance*, 8, pp. 201–16.

LePine, J.A. and VanDyne, L. (1998). 'Predicting Voice Behavior in Work Groups'. *Journal of Applied Psychology*, 83, pp. 853–68.

Leventhal, G.S. (1976). 'The Distribution of Rewards and Resources in Groups and Organizations', In L. Berkovitz and E. Walster (eds), *Advances in Experimental Social Psychology, Vol. 9*. New York: Academic Press, pp. 92–101.

Levine, J.M. and Moreland, R.L. (1990). 'Progress in Small Group Research'. *Annual Review of Psychology*, 41, pp. 585–634.

Levine, J.M., Resnick, L.B. and Higgins, E.T. (1993). 'Social Foundation in Cognition'. In M.R. Rosenzweig and L.W. Porter (eds), *Annual Review of Psychology*, 44, pp. 585–612.

Lott, A.J. and Lott, E.B. (1961). 'Group Cohesiveness Communication Level and Conformity'. *Journal of Abnormal and Social Psychology*, 62, pp. 408–12.

Lott, A.J. and Lott, B.E. (1965). 'Group Cohesiveness as Interpersonal Attraction: A Review of Relationships with Antecedent and Consequent Variables'. *Psychological Bulletin*, 64, pp. 259–309.

Luthans, F. (1979). *Organizational Behavior*, 2ND edn. New York: McGraw-Hill.

Mayer, A.G. (1961). 'The Significance of Quasi-Groups in Study of Complex Societies'. In M. Banton (ed.), *The Social Anthropology of Complex Societies*. New York: Praeger.

Mehrabian, A. and Diamond, S.G. (1971). 'Effects of Furniture Arrangement, Props and Personality on Social Interaction'. *Journal of Personality and Social Psychology*, 20, pp. 18–30.

Michaelsen, L.K., Watson, W.E. and Black, R.H. (1989). 'A Realistic Test of Individual Versus Group Consensus Decision Making'. *Journal of Applied Psychology*, 74, pp. 834–39.

Michaelsen, L.K., Watson, W.E., Schwartskopf, A. and Black, R.H. (1992). 'Group Decision Making: How You Frame the Question Determines What You Find'. *Journal of Applied Psychology*, 77, pp. 106–8.

Morgan, B.B. and Lassiter, D.L. (1992). 'Team Composition and Staffing'. In R.W. Sweezey and E. Salas (eds), *Teams: Their Training and Performance*. Norwood, New York: Ablex.

Mullen, B. and Cooper, C. (1994). 'The Relation Between Group Cohesiveness and Performance: An Integration'. *Psychological Bulletin*, 115, pp. 210–27.

Nahemow, L. and N.P. Lawton (1983). 'Similarity and Propinquity: Making Friends with 'Different' People'. In H.H. Blumberg, A.P. Hare, V. Kent and M.P. Davies (eds), *Small Groups and Social Interaction*. New York: John Wiley.

Neuman, G.A. and Wright, J. (1999). 'Team Effectiveness: Beyond Skills and Cognitive Ability'. *Journal of Applied Psychology*, 84, pp. 376–89.

Nevin, A., Johnson, D.W. and Johnson, R. (1982). 'Effects of Group and Individual Contingencies on Academic Performance and Social Relations of Special Needs Students'. *Journal of Social Psychology*, 116, pp. 41–55.

O'Brien, G.E. (1968). 'The Measurement of Cooperation'. *Organizational Behavior and Human Performance*, 3, pp. 427–39.

O'Brien, G.E. (1984). 'Group Productivity'. In M. Gruenberg and T. Wall (eds), *Social Psychology and Organizational Behavior*. New York: Wiley, pp. 37–70.

O'Brien, G.E. and Owens, A.G. (1969). 'Effects of Organizational Structure on Correlations Between Members' Abilities and Group Productivity'. *Journal of Applied Psychology*, 53, pp. 525–30.

Paulus, P.B. (1980). *Psychology of Group Influence*. NJ: Lawrence Erlbaum Associates.

Pepitone, A. and Reichling, G. (1955). 'Group Cohesiveness and the Expression of Hostility'. *Human Relations*, 8, pp. 327–38.

Reddin, W.J. (1970). *Managerial Effectiveness*. New York: McGraw-Hill.

Roby, T.B. and Lanzetta, J.T. (1958). 'Considerations in the Analysis of Group Tasks'. *Psychological Bulletin*, 55, pp. 88–101.

Rohrbaugh, J. (1981). 'Improving the Quality of Group Judgment: Social Judgment Analysis and the Nominal Group Technique'. *Organizational Behavior and Human Performance*, 28, pp. 272–88.

Russo, N.F. (1967). 'Connotations of Seating Arrangements'. *Cornell Journal of Social Relations*, 2, pp. 37–44.

Schachter, S., Ellerston, N., McBride, D. and Gregory, D. (1951). 'An Experimental Study of Cohesiveness and Productivity'. *Human Relations*, 4, pp. 229–38.

Schneider, F.W. and Delaney, J.G. (1972). 'Effect of Individual Achievement Motivation on Group Problem Solving Efficiency'. *Journal of Social Psychology*, 86, pp. 291–8.

Schriesheim, C.A. (1980). 'The Social Context of Leader-Subordinate Relations: An Investigation of the Effects of Groups Cohesiveness. *Journal of Applied Psychology*, 65, pp. 183–94.

Schriesheim, C.A., Mowday, R.T. and Stogdill, R.M. (1979). 'Crucial Dimensions of Leader-Group Interactions'. In J.C. Hunt and L.L. Larson (eds), *Cross Currents in Leadership*, Carbondale IL: Southern Illinois University Press.

Schultz, D.P. and Schultz, S.E. (1998). *Psychology and Work Today: An Introduction to I/0 Psychology*, 7th edn. Upper Saddle River, NJ: Prentice Hall.

Seashore, S.E. (1954). *Group Cohesiveness in the Industrial Work Groups*. Ann Arbor, MI: Survey Research Center, University of Michigan.

Senn, D.J. (1971). 'Attraction as a Function of Similarity-Dissimilarity in Task Performance'. *Journal of Personality and Social Psychology*, 18, pp. 120–23.

Shaw, M.S. (1964). 'Communication Networks'. In L. Berkowitz (ed.), *Advances in Experimental Social Psychology, Vol. 1*. New York: Academic Press, pp. 11–47.

Shaw, M.S. (1976). *Group Dynamics. The Psychology of Small Groups*. New York: McGraw-Hill, pp. 92–106.

Shaw, M.S. and Shaw, L.M. (1962). 'Some Effects of Sociometric Grouping Upon Learning in a Second Grade Classroom'. *Journal of Social Psychology*, 57, pp. 453–58.

Shelley, M.W. (1960). 'Leadership and Cohesiveness in Small Groups'. *Sociometry*, 23, pp. 209–16.

Shiflett, S. (1979). 'Towards a General Model of Small Group Productivity'. *Psychological Bulletin*, 86, pp. 67–79.

Shirom, A. (1976). 'On Some Correlates of Combat Performance'. *Administrative Science Quarterly*, 21, pp. 419–32.

Shultz, B., Ketrow, S.M. and Urban, D.M. (1995). 'Improving Decision Quality in the Small Group'. *Small Group Research*, 26, pp. 521–41.

Speroff, B. and Kerr, W. (1952). 'Steel Mill 'Hot Strip' Accidents and Interpersonal Desirability Values'. *Journal of Clinical Psychology*, 8, pp. 89–91.

Steers, R.M. and Porter, L.W. (1979). *Motivation and Work Behavior*, 2nd edn. New York: McGraw-Hill.

Steiner, I.D. (1972). *Group Process and Productivity*. New York: Academic Press.

Stogdill, R.M. (1972). 'Group Productivity, Drive, and Cohesiveness'. *Organizational Behavior and Human Performance*, 8, pp. 26–43.

Stogdill, R.M. (1974). *Handbook of Leadership: A Survey of Theory and Research*. New York: Free Press, pp. 327–420.

Szilagyi, A.D. and Wallace, M.Y. (1982). *Organizational Behavior and Performance*. Glenview, IL: Scott Foresman.

Terborg, J.R., Castore, C. and De Ninno, J.A. (1976). 'A Longitudinal Field Investigation of the Impact of Group Composition on Group Performance and Cohesion'. *Journal of Personality and Social Psychology*, 34, pp. 782–90.

Thibaut, J.W. (1950). 'An Experimental Study of the Cohesiveness of Underprivileged Groups'. *Human Relations*, 3, pp. 251–78.

Thomas, P., Moore, K.S. and Scott, K.S. (1996). 'The Relationship Between Self-Efficacy for Participating in Self-Managed Work Groups and the Bif Five Personality Dimensions'. *Journal of Organizational Behavior*, 17, pp. 349–62.

Thompson, J.D. (1967). *Organizations in Action*. New York: McGraw-Hill.

Tindale, R.S. and Larson, J.R. Jr (1992a). 'Assembly Bonus Effect of Typical Group Performance? A Comment on Michaelsen, Watson, and Black (1989)'. *Journal of Applied Psychology*, 77, pp. 102–5.

Tindale, R.S. and Larson, J.R. Jr (1992b). 'It's Not How You Frame the Question, It's How You Interpret the Results'. *Journal of Applied Psychology*, 77, pp. 109–10.

Turner, W.V. (1966). 'Ritual Aspects of Conflict Control in African Micropolitics'. In M. Schwartz, W.V. Turner and A. Tuden (eds), *Political Anthropology*. Chicago: Aldine, pp. 239–47.

Tziner, A. (1982a). 'Differential Effects of Group Cohesiveness Types: A Clarifying Overview'. *Social Behavior and Personality*, 10, pp. 227–39.

Tziner, A. (1982b). 'Group Cohesiveness: A Dynamic Perspective'. *Social Behavior and Personality*, 10, pp. 205–11.

Tziner, A. (1986). 'How Team Composition Affects Task Performance: Some Theoretical Insights'. *Small Group Behavior*, 17, pp. 343–54.

Tziner, A. (1993). 'The Assembly Bonus Effect: A Comment on the Dispute Between Michaelsen, et al. (1989, 1992) and Findale and Larson (1992)'. *International Journal of Selection and Assessment*, 1, pp. 241–3.

Tziner, A. and Eden, D. (1985). 'Effects of Crew Composition on Crew Performance: Does the Whole Equal the Sum of its Parts?'. *Journal of Applied Psychology*, 70, pp. 85–93.

Tziner, A. and Vardi, Y. (1982). 'Effects of Command Style and Group Cohesiveness on the Performance of Self-Selected Tank Crews'. *Journal of Applied Psychology*, 67, pp. 769–75.

Van Zelst, R.H. (1952). 'Validation of a Sociometric Regrouping Procedure'. *Journal of Abnormal and Social Psychology*, 47, pp. 299–301.

Vann, R.T. (1969). *The Social Development of English Quakerism, 1655–1755*. Cambridge, MA: Harvard University Press.

Vroom, V.H. (1960). *Some Personality Determinants of the Effects of Participation*. Englewood Cliffs, NJ: Prentice-Hall.

Warwick, C.E. (1964). 'Relationship of Scholastic Aspiration and Group Cohesiveness on the Academic Achievement of Male Freshmen at Cornell University'. *Human Relations*, 17, pp. 155–68.

Wolfe, A.R. (1970). 'On Structural Comparisons of Networks'. *Canadian Review of Sociology*, 4, pp. 226–44.

Yukl, G. and Van Fleet, D.D. (1992). 'Theory and Research on Leadership in Organizations'. In M.D. Dunnette and L.M. Hough (eds), *Handbook of Industrial and Organizational Psychology, Vol.3.*, Palo Alto, CA: Consulting Psychologists Press, pp. 147–97.

Zaccaro, S.J. (1991). 'Nonequivalent Associations Between Forms of Cohesiveness and Group-Related Outcomes: Evidence for Multidimensionality'. *Journal of Social Psychology*, 131, pp. 387–99.

Zaccaro, S.J. and Lowe, R.H. (1988). 'Cohesiveness and Performance on an Additive Task: Evidence for Multidimensionality'. *Journal of Sport Psychology*, 6, pp. 103–17.

Zaccaro, S.J. and McKoy, M.C. (1988). 'The Effects of Task and Interpersonal Cohesiveness on Performance of a Disjunctive Group Task'. *Journal of Applied Social Psychology*, 18, pp. 837–51.

Zander, A. (1994). *Making Groups Effective*, 2nd edn. San Francisco: Jossey-Bass.

Zander, A. and Forward, J. (1968). 'Position in Groups, Achievement Motivations, and Group Aspirations'. *Journal of Personality and Social Psychology*, 8, pp. 282–8.

5 Organization Staffing Methods and Instruments

AHARON TZINER

Introduction

Over the last few decades, staffing (i.e., employee selection and placement) methods have become increasingly objective and systematized, with a steadily growing array of instruments and methods gradually replacing the somewhat intuitive practices traditionally used by managers for these purposes. Furthermore, following the classic research of Ghiselli (1966) and others, the experience accumulated through the use of valid staffing instruments has enabled researchers to outline in detail the demands imposed on employees by their specific occupations in a variety of job settings. In particular, job analysis outcomes and performance appraisal ratings have been used to portray the characteristics of satisfactorily performing individuals to a desirable degree of accuracy.

Two factors may impact on the quality of an organization's staffing process. The first relates to the suitability of the staffing instruments to the specific organization, and the second to the economic constraints bearing on the choice of instruments. Indeed, the high cost of using a staffing instrument may cause organizations to limit the number of devices employed, resulting in the loss of valuable information on prospective employees. Thus, before choosing the particular instruments to be used, it is wise to pay careful attention to two issues of suitability: (1) how well do the instruments measure the suitability of applicants' functional qualities, such as abilities, skills, knowledge, interests, and personality traits, to the functional demands of the job; and (2) how well do the instruments measure the suitability of the candidates' attributes, in terms of personality and interests, to the culture, climate, and structure of the organization.

Schneider (1987) suggests that individuals are attracted to and selected by organizations to the extent that their personal attributes fit the organization, a notion supported by empirical investigations (Schaubrock, Ganster, and Jones, 1998; Schneider, Smith, Taylor and Fleenor, 1998). Furthermore, on the basis of the Work Adjustment theory (Lofquist and Dawis, 1969), Tziner (1990) contends that if the two types of suitability (functional and personal) do not exist, the worker can be expected to display a strong inclination to leave the organization. Given these facts, the importance of choosing appropriate staffing instruments is beyond doubt. The following analysis is an attempt to assist in this endeavor.

Staffing instruments can be categorized into eight major clusters: (1) biodata; (2) reference checks; (3) interviews; (4) psychological tests; (5) graphological tests; (6) peer evaluation; (7) assessment centers (including situational tests); and (8) integrity tests. Each of these will be considered below.

Moreover, in view of the increasing role played by the assessment center, a clear distinction is made here between the more traditional methods of assessment and the assessment center itself. Finally, in the following review, particular attention is paid, where appropriate, to the research findings of the author and his associates.

Traditional Methods

(1) Biodata

Dailey (1960) defines biodata as a representative body of observations on unplanned events typical of an individual's everyday life. According to a more recent definition, biodata items are those 'that pertain to historical events that may have shaped the person's behavior and identity' (Mael, 1991, p. 763). Broadly speaking, biodata constitute an account of behaviors reflecting past situations to which the individual was exposed and the way he or she coped with them. The use of biodata is predicated on the assumption that relevant past behavior validly predicts future behavior and performance in a specific occupation. As early as 1944, in a review by Guthrie, the author claimed that biographical information emerged as a more reliable predictor than other available factors. More contemporary studies by Eberhardt and Muchinsky (1982) on model vocations, and Neiner and Owens (1985) on post college choice of jobs, appear to confirm that past life-history experiences are related to later employment. A recent meta-analysis also demonstrates the validity of biodata across organizations and various sub-groups (e.g., gender, education), as well as over time (Rothstein, Schmidt, Erwin, Owens, and Sparks, 1990).

Biographical information is generally collected by one of two standard methods the Application Blank or the Biographical Information Blank.

Application Blank, or Weighted Application Blank (WAB)

This method entails weighting the possible responses on each item of information, such as demographic information, number of years of schooling, number of previous jobs, number of months in last job, reason for leaving the last job, and military experience. The weights, which represent the relative predictability of job performance, or any other measure of effectiveness, of the information on the application blank, are typically determined by the use of multiple regression analysis or by a panel of experts.

The form is intended for preliminary screening, as an initial judgment of whether or not a candidate has the minimum requirements to qualify for further steps in the staffing process. The form itself asks mainly for factual data, such as age, gender, education, family status, professional experience, membership in social organizations, and references. This is then scored by weighting the responses and encapsulating them in a total score to be used in the consequent hiring decision process (Gatewood and Field, 1994).

Biographical Information Blank (BIB)

This method employs a more detailed version of the application blank to collect more diversified data on the applicant. It enables the employer or analyst to find out as much as possible about the applicant's past and the influences of various life experiences on professional and economic achievements, opinions, motivations, inclinations, preferences, and interests. All candidates are asked the same questions. The items on the form allow them to describe themselves not only in terms of facts, but also by voicing their opinions on various subjects, such as political, social, and economic issues. The empirical conclusions are then inferred by standardized scores, which are intended to ensure that only those questions that relate to criteria of successful work adjustment are incorporated in the BIB.

For each job, a unique list of biodata considered to be valid predictors must be created. The ample information thus obtained usually enables an optimal understanding of the candidate's character, often beyond a predicted criterion measure. The information derived from the BIB also serves to validate data obtained from other staffing instruments, including data on maturity, social mobility, work values, and so on. Generally speaking, it has been found that the information provided by candidates corresponds with information collected by other means, such as previous employers (see, for example, Cascio, 1976).

Studies by Owens (1976), Owens and Schoenfeldt (1979), and Brush and Owens (1979) have shown that the scores on biodata factors form life history subgroups, each representing a different pattern of life experience. As membership in specific life history subgroups has been found to correlate with success in particular jobs, this information can be used to seek members of the appropriate subgroups to fill vacancies in specific positions.

The literature is full of studies reporting how well BIB predicts job performance (e.g., Ghiselli, 1966; Davis, 1984; Hunter and Hunter, 1984). Cascio (1978) and Reilly and Chao (1982) highlight the versatility of this instrument by demonstrating its validity in a variety of areas of prediction, including wage increment, perseverance in the job, and success in training, for groups of engineers, clerks, managers, salespeople, and military professionals (with predictive ability ranging from 0.32 to 0.46). More recently, in their meta-analysis, Hunter and Hunter (1984) report a predictive validity of about 0.37.

In general, then, the ease of development, low cost, potentially impressive and stable predictive validity, and easily accessible data make WABs and BIBs especially attractive staffing procedures (Mael, Connerly, and Morath, 1996; Wilkinson, 1997).

(2) Reference Checks

One common form of reference check is the letter of recommendation (Kopelman, 1986). This is considered highly important for supplementing the available information on an applicant, particularly with respect to his or her adjustment to the organization and work team, level of motivation, and degree of job involvement. Perhaps the most useful additional information relates to the way the worker's professional career evolved. Letters of recommendation, however, are less informative in regard to potential abilities.

In general, reference checks should be treated with caution, as they mainly elicit information from the past (Dreher and Kendall, 1995), and often in jobs different from the one currently sought. It must be remembered that recommendations rely on a subjective evaluation, which makes them susceptible to bias. In particular, the personality of the referee and his or her relationship with the candidate highly influence the formulation of the reference. Favorable recommendations may be given for diverse, if not irrelevant, reasons, such as the wish to dispose of an employee, the desire to preserve a climate of interpersonal harmony, or the fear of the legal consequences of slander. Thus the bias may well be of a negative nature, indicative of revenge, rivalry, or resentment.

Furthermore, the referee is under no strict obligation to provide valid information, even though this can usually be verified simply by picking up the telephone. Telephone calls have their advantages. First of all, they are cheap and speedy, and they also enable the listener to catch further clues about the candidate from the tone of voice and intonation of the previous employer. It goes without saying, of course, that reference checks acquired close to the time of an employee's leaving an organization are more accurate, especially when the requesting party succinctly indicates the desired parameters.

A more useful type of reference check is a structured recommendation form filled out by the referee. In addition, approaching more than one referee in the organization may also enhance the degree of validity of a recommendation used as a staffing device, along with its unique contribution to the improvement of prediction. By using these more systematic approaches, more comprehensive data is obtained, often accrued from different perceptions of the same individual, and the inherent biases plaguing reference checks are held to a minimum (Dolan and Schuler, 1987).

Studies have revealed that 76 percent of organizations who utilize staffing procedures rely heavily on information obtained from previous employers. Moreover, validity investigations based on ten correlation results (n = 5,389) reveal a mean validity of 0.26 for reference checks in predicting job performance (Hunter and Hunter, 1984). Thus, despite their drawbacks, reference checks are a prevalent source of information and, if used correctly, may constitute a valuable additional predictor.

(3) The Job Interview

For practical and economic purposes, job interviews continue to be one of the most widely used staffing devices (Arvey and Campion, 1982; MacDaniel, Whetzel, Schmidt and Mauser, 1994), and serve as a highly informative tool. Especially under conditions in which the number of applicants is either very low or very high, or when the competition is particularly stiff, interviews reveal personality traits and behaviors that cannot be detected by other instruments.

When an organization has a small number of candidates for a certain job, assessment of the predictive validity of personality tests and cognitive tests may be quite cumbersome, as it must rely on synthetic validity, which is often also costly. Under these circumstances, it is easier and cheaper to conduct employment interviews. Paradoxically, it has also been found that when an organization is inundated with applicants, it is preferable, again for economic reasons, to first interview them in order to screen out those who seemingly have the least chance of adjusting to the organization. Then only the remaining applicants can be processed through the more extensive staffing system.

When competition in the labor market is tough and there is a high demand for manpower, the use of job interviews serves to create an informal vehicle through which to 'introduce' the organization to prospective employees. This interview meeting enables a representative of the organization to listen to the applicants' expectations and needs and to convey messages to them beyond the standard employment procedures. Furthermore, certain specific behaviors and personality can be accessed more easily by the interviewing technique, such as fluency of speech, richness of language, self-confidence, appearance, adjustment to interactive situations, and work motives. In short, the interview is a useful tool for enriching the repertoire of data on the applicant under scrutiny.

However, it must be remembered that an interview is a meeting between two people, and like all interpersonal interactions it is affected by attitudes and stereotypes, needs and vested interests, and by the self-perceptions of both parties that lead them to behave in certain ways. Each participant's behavior impinges on that of his or her counterpart by generating positive or negative responses. Typically, the interviewer integrates data elicited during the interview to formulate a subjective impression and prediction of the candidate's likely adjustment as an employee.

Nevertheless, despite the obvious advantages, there continues to be substantial criticism of the use of personal interviews as a staffing instrument. Mainly due to methodological considerations, the interview, unless it is structured, is considered to be of low reliability and of poor predictive validity (see the reviews by: Mayfield, 1964; Schmitt, 1976; Campion, Palmer and Campion, 1997). The factors held to mar reliability include positive-negative information, contrast effects, interviewer-interviewee similarity, visual cues, interviewer experience, and form of interview.

First, events or attitudes that precede the actual dialogue may shape its outcome. While information on the interviewee's education, professional experience, and psychological test scores, which reach the interviewer from a variety of sources, may be crucial for the interviewing process, it also serves to create a first impression. After this impression is formulated, interviewers often tend to emphasize whatever reinforces it and play down any information that is likely to refute their original evaluation. First impressions, formed by definition at the initial stage of an interview, are of decisive importance, especially since the interviewee also acts upon the interviewer's reactions and displays the kind of behavior supportive of, and reinforcing to, a situation which he or she believes to be beneficial to the outcome.

Secondly, it has also been found that interviewers tend to prefer applicants who resemble them in certain aspects, such as education or membership in the same union or club. These preferences naturally tend to influence the manner in which the interviewer views and assesses the applicant.

In addition, interviewers are often influenced by stereotypes, such as their own perception of what the ideal applicant should look like. They subsequently judge the real applicant against this stereotype, which may be of little or no relevance to work adjustment. Moreover, researchers have also demonstrated the effect whereby previously interviewed applicants strongly influence the judgment of those who follow them. This contrast effect is most evident in the evaluation of mediocre applicants. A mediocre applicant immediately following a brilliant one will almost certainly be evaluated as a failure. However, if the same applicant is fortunate enough to be interviewed directly after a weak candidate, he or she may well be overevaluated.

Other variables likely to generate stereotypical evaluations include gender, age, and race (Dipboye, 1992; Huffcutt and Roth, 1998). Younger applicants are often perceived more favorably than older ones (Arvey, 1979), and generally receive higher evaluations (Haefner, 1977; Avolio, 1982). Similarly, men are often perceived more favorably than women, particularly for jobs that have traditionally been filled by men, and thus they generally receive higher evaluations than female candidates (Dipboye, Fromkin and Wilback, 1975). Interviewers also tend to rate more positively those applicants they consider more intelligent (Keenan, 1977), and physically attractive candidates are more likely to be recommended and hired, regardless of gender (Dipboye et al., 1975).

Roza and Carpenter (1987) advance a model suggesting that demographic variables directly impact on attractiveness ratings, causing a domino affect: Attractiveness ratings, it appears, directly affect likeability ratings. These in turn affect intelligence ratings, which directly influence skill and employability ratings, which directly impinge on the potential to be hired. According to this model, ratings on specific individual characteristics, such as attractiveness, likeability, intelligence, and skills, can be traced back to culturally-bound demographic variables. Thus demographic variables merely help elucidate the process by which the ratings of individual attributes (e.g., intelligence and skills) are formed.

Moreover, the kind of information elicited in the course of the interview, in terms of positive and negative, has also been found to influence decision-making. It has been shown, for instance, that interviewers tend to attach more importance to negative than to positive information, where negative information is data presented by the interviewee that lowers his or her chances of being accepted for the job in the eyes of the interviewer. This phenomenon is explained by Webster (1964) as the tendency to react to the extensive information revealed in the interview by becoming alert to negative or 'knock-out' clues.

Interviewers are also influenced by verbal and nonverbal cues. Hollandsworth et al. (1979) conducted an examination of the significance of these signals and found that information is analyzed according to the following order of importance: content of the spoken words, fluency of speech, body language, eye contact, loudness of speech, and overall appearance. Valenzi and Andrews (1973) also found substantial variety in the use of such signals by the interviewers, leading to differences in candidate evaluations. The use of nonverbal forms of silent consent by the interviewer, for example, created a more relaxed atmosphere and incurred the trust of the interviewee. The result was that the interviewee was more likely to vent opinions and ideas that would not have been divulged in a tense, hostile atmosphere.

In general, the literature in this field suggests that an applicant displaying a high degree of non-verbal communication, such as eye contact, smiling, speech fluency, voice modulation, or nodding, is more likely to be rated as showing more initiative and being more alert, assertive, confident, and responsible (Amalfitano and Kalt, 1977; Young and Beier, 1977; Forbes and Jackson, 1980). Moreover, Gifford, Ng and Wilkinson (1985) show that an applicant's nonverbal cues in the interview are conducive to the formation of a more accurate assessment of his or her social skills. These cues include features such as formality of dress, time spent talking, and rate of gestures.

On a somewhat different level of critique, Schmitt (1976) notes that interview results are characterized by low interrater reliability, and concludes that interviewers must be weighting information differently. Furthermore, Tziner (1990) contends that the weights assigned to the factors incorporated into the synthesis of the interview information are not explicit, and that they may change from time to time, even in the same interview.

These conclusions suggest that differences among interviewers need to be studied in terms of what information they use and how that information is combined and integrated. The research on individual differences and information processing, however, is limited. The few issues that have been studied include the influence of scholastic standing, interests, and business experience on interviewers' ratings of overall suitability (Hakel, Dobmeyer and Dunnette, 1970); the effect of aptitude test results and eight personal history items on ratings of potential job success (Carlson, 1971); the influence of typing skills, shorthand skills, social skills, experience, and education on the evaluation of the potential to be hired (Valenzi and Andrews, 1973); and the effect of an applicant's sex, physical attractiveness, and scholastic standing on ratings of suitability for a managerial position (Dipboye, Fromkin and Wiback, 1975). The results reveal that the amount of accountable variance varies from one per cent for gender in the study by Dipboye et al. (1975), to 47 per cent for scholastic standing in the study by Hakel et al. (1970). These investigations also indicate considerable individual differences, i.e., there was substantial variation in the utilization of information across interviewers in each of the studies.

The problem of individual differences has also been examined by Mayfield, Brown, and Hamstra (1980), who analyzed the standard deviations of interviewer evaluations on 39 items, and found that potential interviewers disagreed in their ratings of candidates on items requiring inferences, as opposed to factual information. The reasons offered for the differences are that either the interviewers could not make inferences, or that they had different frames of reference.

These studies, however, suffer from several limitations. One problem pertains to the nature of the interviewers and the interviewees. Although some investigations employed real interviewers, they were asked to evaluate either a bogus resume (Hakel et al., 1970; Dipboye et al., 1975) or hypothetical applicants (Carlson, 1971; Valenzi and Andrews, 1973). Thus, none of the interviewers had face-to-face contact with 'real' people; in other words, none of the interviewers were interviewed. In other studies, undergraduates role-played the interviewers of hypothetical applicants described in booklet form (Rothstein and Jackson, 1980).

Rothstein and Jackson (1980) chose to conduct their study in an experimental setting because of several problems they noted with regard to field research, namely: (1) interviewers' unfamiliarity with job-related activities; (2) interviewers' use of idiosyncratic judgmental standards; (3) fallible criterion measures; and (4) the undependability of estimates of validity due to frequent failures to obtain criterion data on all applicants. I would argue, however, that these problems probably stem from the design, and not necessarily the setting, of the research. In fact, they may emerge in both field and laboratory settings. In light of Dunnette and Borman's (1979) call for the testing of the 'real world' applicability of experimental results obtained in contrived settings, it might be said that if the interview format, procedure, or data are not useful, then the root of the problem is most likely to be found in the developmental stages of the interview process itself.

Given these considerations, Zedeck, Tziner and Middlestadt (1983) conducted a study of interpersonal differences in the data-processing strategies employed by interviewers. This investigation departed from previous research in three ways. First, the exchange was real, i.e., it took place in an ongoing organization with candidates who were applying for real positions. Thus the interview decisions were made in an actual face-to-face interview situation and were subsequently acted upon.

Secondly, the information assessed was determined to be significant on the basis of analysis of the position involved, and included factors that were not evaluated in the test situation. A systematic job analysis was performed to develop the factors, questions, and scales to be assessed in the interview. The specific procedure was a behaviorally anchored rating format (Maas, 1965) that is consistent with the critical incident methodology used by Latham, Saari, Pursell and Campion (1980). Such a procedure: (1) facilitates the attainment of content validity for the device; (2) is a mechanism by which to devise a relatively more structured interview guide; (3) facilitates the interviewers' understanding of the requirements of the job; and (4) results in a standardized, quantifiable mode for assessment. These objectives overcome the previously cited concerns of Rothstein and Jackson (1980). Moreover, they are consistent with Schmitt's (1976) suggestions for improving the interview.

The third distinctive feature of this study was the use of regression analysis to capture an individual interviewer's strategy or policy for information utilization. This procedure, previously adopted in a variety of settings to study information processing and judgment strategies (Slovic and Lichtenstein, 1971; Zedeck and Kafry, 1977), permitted the assessment of the reliability and validity of specific, individual interviewers.

An interview is indeed a form of test, but this is the extent of the similarity in measurement models. Whereas paper-and-pencil tests can be developed and administered for the purpose of obtaining information in a standardized manner, Zedeck et al. (1983) argue that it may be unreasonable to assume that the interview can be viewed in a similar fashion. While structuring the interview procedure and training interviewers to achieve standardization and commonality may be a personnel goal, it is not realistic to imagine that having different interviewers use the same interview guide in the same situation is comparable to repeated administrations or parallel forms of a test.

Zedeck et al. conceive of the interview as a situation in which interviewers must accommodate and take advantage of the information being conveyed and received. Thus, their study regarded each interviewer as an independent assessment device, rather than analyzing 'the interview', per se, or the results, collapsed across all interviewers. That is to say, in this investigation the interviewer was the test, instead of having all interviewers considered parallel to each other. The researchers argue that if the strategy of an 'effective' (reliable and/or valid) interviewer or group of interviewers can be identified, then that strategy can serve as a model for other, less effective, interviewers.

Accordingly, Zedeck et al. studied interviewer reliability, validity, and strategy for information integration by means of analyses of data both within and across interviewers. The participants consisted of 412 candidates for a military division of a national defense organization who were interviewed by 10 female interviewers and assessed on 9 behaviorally anchored dimensions. Of these, 131 candidates who were subsequently admitted to officers' training school were again evaluated on 19 dimensions and on an overall assessment instrument after six and after twelve weeks.

Interestingly enough, the study reveals that the interviewers tended to formulate their evaluations using only part of the information gathered in the interview. The researchers also noted personal differences among interviewers in their choice of the personal attributes they incorporated into their summary assessments, and in the weights they ascribed to these attributes.

In contrast, the authors demonstrate that although individual interviewers weigh information differently, they do tend to display a high degree of judgmental consistency with respect to dimension rating; overall interview assessment, as measured by the multiple correlation coefficient, yielded coefficients ranging from 0.90 to 0.98. Generally speaking, these findings are supported by Dougherty, Ebert, and Callender (1986).

Nevertheless, analysis across interviewers of the relationship between the interview and six and twelve-week training performance evaluations indicated no predictive validity for the interview decision. Analysis of the individual interview strategies revealed differences between interviewers only at the six-week point.

Zedeck et al. suggest several reasons for the time frame discrepancies, all of which relate to Ghiselli's (1956) notion of criteria dimensionality: criteria are static, dynamic, and individual. While performance at any one time can be evaluated over several separate dimensions, these dimensions may have changed over time. Moreover, the researchers also note that the aggregation of data across interviewers may mask pertinent differences, stating that individual differences between interviewers are 'implicitly recognized and utilized for the purposes of determining who is most effective as an interviewer' (p. 369).

Despite repeated criticism of the technique, the continued popularity of the interview has led to many attempts to improve its reliability and validity (e.g., Orpen, 1976; Wanous, 1980; Schneider, 1987; Maurer, Solamon and Troxtel, 1998). Perhaps the most relevant factor stressed in these studies is the importance of carefully structuring interviews on the basis of a thorough job analysis. It has also been suggested that interview questions probe consistently and systematically into what the applicant has actually done in situations similar to those described in the job analysis. Other recommendations include:

1 the interviewer should attend to all details and nonverbal cues during the entire interview;
2 the questions should be formulated in advance of the interview session and in a manner that will enable full control of both the interviewing process and subject matter;
3 the interviewer should seek applicant information only on those aspects relevant to successful work adjustment, leaving less room for 'disturbing' interviewer-interviewee dynamics;
4 the interviewer should be trained to take detailed notes and to rate each answer of an interviewee or to use multiple scales to rate interviewee reactions and performance (Campion, Palmer and Campion, 1997). Indeed, it has been shown that when note taking is done voluntarily (and not imposed), interviewers who take notes produce ratings that are more valid than those who do not.

Janz (1982) and Orpen (1985) provide two examples of careful preparation. They demonstrate that specifically referring to critical incidents in the applicant's experiences that are predictive of future job behavior leads to an improvement in interview effectiveness. The structured interview, consisting of prearranged and predefined questions, has been shown to enhance the interviewer's judgment of a candidate's suitability for a job (Kaemar and Hochwarter, 1995; Tziner 1990). An example of such a structured interview can be found in Appendix 5.1. Notwithstanding Zedeck, Tziner and Middlestadt's (1983) emphasis of the importance of tapping individual differences among interviewers, the validity and reliability of employment interview outcomes appears to be improving (for a review, see: Arvey and Campion, 1982). Landy and Bates (1973), for example, report the valid outcomes of interviews employed in the selection of police officers from a relatively large sample of 399 applicants, where interviewers shared their findings with others. The improvement in validity is explained by the fact that when interviewers involve others in their deliberations as to how to analyze the information obtained in interviews, they are better able to process out the unwarranted influences that lower the predictive validity and reliability of the interview.

Other means of improving the interview's psychometric qualities include interviewer training (Maurer, Solamon and Troxtel, 1998; Stevens, 1998), and the use of various statistical procedures for integrating the information and components involved in the final stages of decision making in respect to particular candidates. Although it is not yet clear exactly how much these measures improve reliability, their overall contribution has been shown to be appreciable (Campion, Palmer and Campion, 1997). Indeed, using all of these recommended measures for standardization and structuring, Harris (1989) was able to report a predictive validity of about 0.41.

Undoubtedly, most employers consider the interview to be an indispensable component of the staffing process, despite the biases of various sorts to which it is prone. The contribution of the interview is especially significant when it is used to detect behaviors and capacities that cannot be measured by other means, and when high importance is attached to face-to-face interaction with the candidate. Ratings and assessment derived from the interview also play an important role in the validation and cross-validation of predictive data obtained from other sources.

(4) Psychological Tests

Psychological tests are generally used to measure a sample of an individual's specific behavior objectively, thus making it possible to draw inferences about the applicant's characteristics from the test results. Schneider (1976) defines objectivity as the consistent application of *a priori* agreed-upon rules (scoring keys, interpretations, and so forth) to the results of samples of specific behaviors to yield the test scores. The purpose of such a test is to create a procedure for eliciting responses that can be measured in a standardized manner.

Of course, a relationship must be assumed to exist between the tested and actual behavior. In fact, test tasks do not generally measure actual behavior directly; rather, they evoke inferences regarding various aspects of future job performance or organizational behavior. Accordingly, psychological tests do not yield an absolute score. Performance on these tests is typically relative, that is, scores are described and have significance only in terms of some normative reference. For instance, in order to interpret the test scores obtained for an applicant for the position of teller at a bank branch, it would be necessary to compare the candidate's raw score (number of correct answers on the test) with the scores of many other past applicants for the same job. The individuals with whom this applicant is compared thus constitute the normative population, and the scores generated in relation to a normative population are denoted test norms. In practical terms, test norms are derived by transforming the number of correct answers – the raw score – into a relative ranking index in the reference group. The two normative transformations most frequently used are percentiles and standard scores.

A percentile score designates the percent of individuals in the normative population scoring at or below a particular raw score. Standard scores indicate individual performance relative to the mean and standard deviation of the score distribution of the normative population. However, when testing for qualities, a distinction must be made between what a person can do at the present time, and what he or she will be able to do after training. This is usually reflected in the differentiation between scholastic abilities and job-relevant knowledge. Gatewood and Field (1994) distinguish between achievement tests, which measure what a person can do at present as a result of formal learning experience, and aptitude tests, which assess the accumulation of non-formal learning experience.

Psychological tests are usually categorized as personality tests, general mental ability tests (intelligence tests), specific aptitude tests, or occupational interest inventories. (For a detailed discussion of interest inventories, see Chapter 2.) The outcomes obtained are generally grouped as follows:

1 Cognitive ability outcomes, comprising learning ability, problem solving, logical thinking, and spatial abilities, which, according to Guion (1991), are reflective of the 'remembering of ideas or solutions to problems, perceiving, comparing and evaluating stimuli' (p. 341).
2 Motor, sensory and physical ability outcomes, comprising sense-perceptive reactions and psychomotor reactions, such as limb dexterity and reaction speed.
3 Affective attributes outcomes, comprising personality traits, motives, needs, and occupational interests.

Siegel and Lane (1982, p. 165) stipulate five fundamental standards or conditions which must be met for psychological tests to be considered fair:

1 The questions or items should be carefully chosen to constitute a sufficiently large and representative sample of the behavior being analyzed (e.g., knowledge, skills).
2 The conditions of the test administration should be standardized and the test itself be uniform in all respects, in order to permit meaningful and fair comparisons between testees.
3 The test must be reliable.
4 Test norms should be generated to enable conversion of the raw scores into standard scores for interpreting test results. When the test is to be used for selection purposes, the cutoff score (i.e., the passing/failure critical score) must be empirically established.
5 Clear evidence of test validity (both construct and predictive) must be provided.

The Structure of Mental Abilities

The research conducted on the underlying structure of cognitive abilities, as well as on the structure of psychomotoric aptitudes, is a topic of considerable significance for those using psychological tests for staffing purposes, for two primary reasons. First, testers and counselors need to understand clearly what each psychological test examines. This enables them to decide in a systematic and rational manner which tests to include in the staffing process and what kind of new tests need to be developed to measure abilities that are not, or are only partially, measured by existing tests.

Secondly, human resource personnel need to probe the possibility of using a universal test that is applicable to all situations and whose outcomes are indeed relevant to any possible performance criterion, regardless of individual qualities such as age, level of education, gender, or race.

The classic search for such a test was first initiated by the distinguished English psychologist Spearman (1904, 1927), who found by means of factor analysis that when different types of tests were administered to the same group of testees, there was a high correlation between the scores. This led him to postulate the existence of a common factor underlying all the tests. Spearman thus inferred a single common factor shared by all intellectual activities which he called the general or G factor.

Spearman also maintained that some marginal factors are related to specific mental operations, and these he termed S factors. At a later stage, and drawing on accumulated empirical observations, he admitted the existence of an additional intermediate class of factors common to a specific group of activities, factors that are neither sufficiently universal to be included in the G factor nor specific enough to belong to S factors. Designated group factors, they are said to relate to arithmetic, mechanical, and linguistic abilities. The distinction between these group factors and the general or specific factors, however, is not as simple as it may appear. When dealing with a heterogeneous batch of tests, a specific factor may appear under the heading of group factors, yet when the number of tests is small, the very same factor may emerge as a general factor common to all tests, rather than to only some of them.

From Spearman's structure theory, it is clear that cognitive ability tests may be used to measure the general factor as well as group or specific factors. In contrast to Spearman, Thurstone (1938), conceived of intelligence as composed of several basic mental abilities which he defined as follows:

1   verbal comprehension, which is gauged in tests of reading comprehension, verbal analogies, disarrayed sentences, verbal reasoning, and proverb matching. It is most adequately measured by vocabulary tests;
2   word fluency, which is found in tests such as anagrams, rhyming, or naming words in a given category;
3   numerical aptitude, which is the ability to compute simple arithmetic calculations rapidly and accurately;
4   associative memory, which is the ability to recall clusters of items perfectly;
5   general reasoning, which is the ability to infer and apply abstract rules, such as the underlying principles common to groups of stimuli;
6   spatial visualization, which is the ability to visualize and order spatial relations among objects;
7   perceptual speed, which is revealed in the ability of quick and accurate grasping of visual details, similarities, and differences.

Thurstone's multifactor theory was based on factor analysis and weighted differentiations for the various components of intelligence revealed by cognitive tests. He subsequently developed a battery of tests of his own that had the advantage of treating each of the various mental components separately.

After more than two decades of work with factor analysis, Guilford (1967) arrived at yet another comprehensive conceptual model of the structure of the cognitive abilities on which specific aptitude tests are based. He proposed a three-dimensional model in which all intellectual cognitive abilities are classified along three dimensions: operations, contents, and products; that is, a mental operation is carried out on a specific content that leads to a specific product. According to Guilford, these three dimensions represent the structure of the intellect and can be portrayed in a three-dimensional cube within a boxlike model (see: Guilford, 1967, p. 63).

This model combines five categories of mental operations, four content categories, and six product categories to yield 120 possible factors, each described in terms of all three dimensions and each designated a specific ability. However, no suitable tests have yet been designed for a considerable number of these factors. Furthermore, certain factors, such as creativity tests, which generally demonstrate divergent thinking, are examined without any reference whatsoever to others, such as intelligence tests, which tend to gauge convergent abilities.

Guildford also relates to another type of mental ability which he defines as any mental activity performed on behavioral contents. This is similar to what has been termed social intelligence, a notion conceived as early as the 1920s.

Another model for depicting the underlying structures of the different tests is based on the theory of facet analysis, whereby mathematically derived concepts are applied to the study of social and behavioral phenomena. Developed in the mid-1950s, facet analysis provides researchers with the conceptual and quantitative tools necessary to rigorously define whatever subject or 'universe' they are exploring, using definitional systems in the form of a 'mapping sentence'(for a detailed explanation, see: Tziner, 1987).

Using this approach, Schlesinger and Guttman (1969) classified ability tests into two facets: (1) the language of presentation of the test items, which may be verbal, figural, or numerical; and (2) the mental operation required by the test, namely, rule inference or rule application. The researchers then defined a mapping sentence to corroborate the structural configuration based on these facets. The empirical investigation, carried out on high school students, provided firm support for the hypothesized structural configuration: a radex yielded by the radial arrangement of tests according to the language-of-presentation facet, together with a pattern of concentric circles formed by the mental-operation facet.

The resulting model dramatically reduces the number of intellectual abilities from 120 to a mere six. However, Schlesinger and Guttman's model does not take into account an important differentiation in mental operations introduced by Piaget (1956), who postulated that the rule of application operation entails three levels of cognitive complexity, concrete rule application, clerical rule application, and abstract-cognitive rule application, organized hierarchically from the lowest to the highest level.

To correct this omission, Tziner and Rimmer (1984) extended the model to incorporate Piaget's distinction by restructuring the mental operation so that it is composed of four elements, rather than two. Interestingly enough, when the extended mapping sentence was employed, the most appropriate configuration for the structure of ability tests again proved to be a radex.

This conclusion is further supported by the fact that the radex structure did not evolve by chance; rather, the results of the empirical analysis confirmed what had previously been predicted by the mapping sentence. Moreover, the extended model resulting from the extended mapping sentence emerged in two independent replications, conducted in the same study, even though the specific tests administered to the testees differed greatly, as dictated by the objectives of the testing situations (see Figures 5.1 and 5.2).

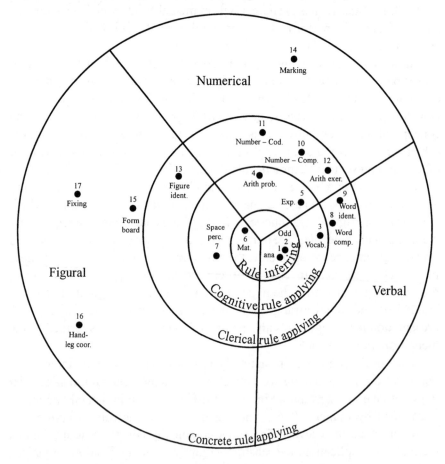

Figure 5.1   SSA map for 17 tests in the first group (vocational guidance)

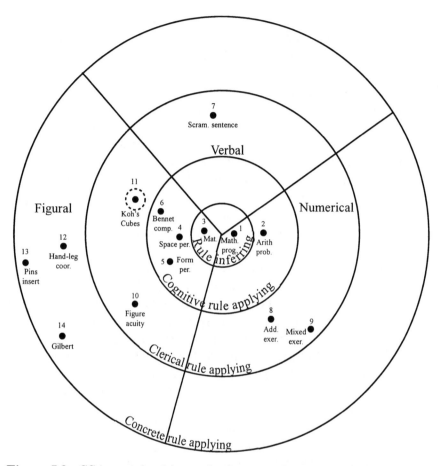

Figure 5.2   SSA map for 14 tests in the second group (selection situation)

In a more recent study, Tziner (1992) examined whether the same underlying structure of ability tests emerges when three different data analysis methods are used. A sample of 335 applicants for vocational guidance were administered a battery of 17 tests, and a matrix of intercorrelations between scores, based on the number of correct answers, was obtained. The matrix was then subjected to factor analysis, Guttman's SSA (smallest space analysis), and tree analysis (for more details of these techniques, see: Tziner, 1992).

The study revealed the structure of ability tests to be markedly dependent upon the method of analysis used; that is, the three methods did not produce a universal structure of abilities. Indeed, on the whole, the three configurations were considerably more dissimilar than similar. The author suggests that this disparity may explain why different theoreticians employing different methods of analysis have found conflicting structures of ability tests (e.g., Spearman, 1927; Vernon, 1965; Schlesinger and Guttman, 1969; Beller and Melamed, 1988; Guttman and Levy, 1992).

In light of these results, Tziner (1992) considered which of these three methods would be most economical in exploring the structure of ability tests. His findings reveal that tree analysis elicited two groupings of abilities, in contrast to six and three for Guttman's SSA and factor analysis, respectively. However, the SSA solution was clearly the most interpretable, revealing a stronger and more coherent logic of inherent structure than the results of tree analysis. Tree analysis also provided the best grouping of ability tests in respect to the percentage of explained variance, as compared to factor analysis, and the goodness-of-fit of the emergent configuration to the initial data matrix, as compared to SSA.

The model that emerged from factor analysis in this study, however, rendered interpretation difficult, as several ability tests loaded high on more than one factor. In general, much fault has been found with factor analysis as a source for the underlying structure of psychological abilities (e.g., Guttman, 1958; Schlesinger and Guttman, 1969; Shye, 1978; Shapira and Zevulun, 1979; Cunningham, 1981; Kelderman et al., 1981; Kim and Mueller, 1981; Tziner, 1987). One criticism of the method is that factor analysis is based on the assumption of linear relationships and the requirement that variables be measured at least at the interval level (Kim and Mueller, 1981), limitations that are not shared by Guttman's SSA (Tziner, 1987). Nevertheless, Tziner (1987) raises the question of the statistical significance of conclusions regarding structures that are obtained by means of Guttman's SSA, noting that 'no statistical tests have yet been devised to compute the probability that a number of different samples of ability tests would exhibit essentially the same structural configuration' (p. 393).

From this discussion it should be clear that measures of general intelligence cannot be accurate for a specific job, insofar as performance in that job may require one or more skills that may not be subsumed in the factors or facets incorporated in the general intelligence measure. Speech fluency, for example, is a skill that would enhance a teacher's performance, but its proficiency could never be scored in a written test of intelligence. Furthermore, since different jobs require different sets of skills, the relationship of general measures of intelligence to future performance must, at best, be considered tenuous.

Over the years, tests have been developed that differentiate between the general and the specific areas of proficiency. Some measure particular abilities, others yield separate scores for the differentiated items, and still others attempt to offer measures of general intelligence. It therefore stands to reason that when choosing an occupational staffing test, we must first determine what data are required. For example, whereas intelligence combined with high on-the-job learning abilities would be tested one way for a potential executive, a completely different set of tests might well be required to test the performance-related intelligence of a heavy-equipment operator.

Ability Measurement Instruments

The major types of cognitive or mental ability tests fall into the following categories:

General intelligence tests For many years, the Stanford-Binet Intelligence Test was the best known and most widely accepted of its kind. Today, additional tests are employed, such as the Wechsler test, the use of which led to the coining of the term intelligence quotient or IQ, which is the ratio between mental age, as determined from a testee's scores, and chronological age. Tests generating this IQ measure gauge an individual's ability for formal learning (largely convergent thinking), and predict his or her future ability to apply in practice the knowledge and specific skills acquired. Most of them measure scholastic potential in the two main cognitive areas of verbal fluency and memory.

An intelligence test widely used in the organizational context is the Wonderlic Personnel Test. This instrument capitalizes on the spiral-omnibus format, whereby the easiest items of each type are presented first, followed by progressively harder items of each type, in an increasingly rising spiral of difficulty (Anastasi, 1988, p. 311). Although the test incorporates items that are used to assess verbal, numerical, and spatial perception capacities, the score is a single overall measure. Empirical data show that the Wonderlic Personnel Test's reliabilities fall in the range of 0.70–0.90, and that its validity excels for clerical jobs.

It must be said, however, that the 'intelligence' tested by intelligence tests encompasses a combination of abilities required to survive and progress in a specific culture. Consequently, these tests obviously vary with cultural milieu and time, a feature that has significant bearing on questions of cultural bias, among other validity related problems.

Specific ability (aptitude) tests These tests are designed to examine the degree of competence likely to be achieved by an individual in performing specific skills following proper training or apprenticeship. Additionally, they separately examine cognitive abilities. The personal scores derived from these aptitude tests are particularly germane when they are used to predict suitability for a particular job.

In the aftermath of the two world wars, the US army invested great efforts in devising such tests, spurred on by the urgency to select and fit millions of people for military jobs. This research formed the foundations on which subsequent testing systems in the US Placement Services were based. The well-known and highly reputed General Aptitude Test Battery (GATB), for example, comprises twelve different tests yielding nine separate and independent factors or abilities: intelligence, verbal fluency, numerical aptitude, spatial aptitude, figural aptitude, clerical skills, motoric coordination, finger dexterity, and manual dexterity.

A comprehensive discussion and samples of specific intelligence and aptitude (ability) tests can be found in Anastasi's (1982) review of the field. There are, however, additional specific abilities not covered in the above list that are measured by some of the following types of tests:

Tests measuring mechanical abilities These tests measure three areas associated with successful performance in jobs involving machines and equipment: the recognition and application of mechanical principles and application, the speed and dexterity of manipulation of physical objects, and the visualization of their relationship in space (Lowenberg and Conrad, 1998, p. 216). The scores on each respective area are collapsed into one summative overall score, using a differential weighting scheme. Two commonly used tests of this sort are the Bennett Mechanical Comprehension Test and the Minnesota Paper Form Board. The reliability of the former is around 0.80, while that of the latter is in the 0.71–0.78 range. Reported validity coefficients for the Bennett Mechanical Comprehension Test vary between 0.30 and 0.60, and for the Minnesota Paper Form Board between 0.30 and 0.34 (Lowenberg and Conrad, 1998).

Tests measuring clerical abilities These tests encompass subtests designated to predict successful performance of office tasks and paperwork. Among other things, the testees are required to concentrate for a long time on small details, to correct typographical errors, to perform routine tasks, and to inspect simple bills.

Tests measuring psychomotoric and psychosensoric abilities In these tests it is important to differentiate between the combination of skill and knowledge, defined as the present level of performance, on the one hand, and ability, defined as the potential or capability for attaining the skill level, on the other. Ability is broken down into eleven elements: (1) control precision, (2) reaction time, (3) speed of arm movement, (4) manual dexterity, (5) finger dexterity, (6) hand/arm steadiness, (7) speed of hand movement, (8) aiming, (9) rate control, (10) multilimb coordination, and (11) response orientation. To the list of psychomotor abilities we might also add fine hand and finger dexterity, such as that involved in marking a map with pins and attaching little flags to the pins (Crawford and Crawford, 1946, 1949), and gross motor coordination as measured by the Stromberg Dexterity Test (1951). Here the testee first has to place circular blocks in holes, then remove and turn them over, and finally replace them in the holes. Reliabilities range between 0.80 and 0.90 (Lowenberg and Conrad, 1998).

Achievement tests These tests attempt to gauge achievement on tasks based on the knowledge of specific items, often acquired in the course of a training or instruction program. Hence, achievement tests measure the effects of standardized or packaged sets of experiences, such as courses in word processing, accounting, or computer programming. Whereas ability tests measure the effect of learning under uncontrolled and unknown conditions, achievement tests seek to measure the cumulative influence of learning in controlled and known conditions.

A second distinction between achievement and ability tests pertains to the purpose for which they are designed: ability tests are employed to predict future work performance, whereas achievement tests are used to ascertain the extent to which individuals have gained knowledge and skills from a defined training or instruction program, and are usually administered in order to identify the most suitable candidates for admission to universities, schools or colleges, government agencies, or public organizations. Other well-known achievement tests examine knowledge levels in a particular profession (engineering, law, accounting, and so on), and are generally administered by employers or trade associations, often to secure benefits for members of these organizations (e.g., tests conducted by the Association of Accountants for the status of certified public accountant).

Personality Tests

Personality tests include a wide variety of instruments designed to diagnose affective aspects of the individual's behavior and character, such as extroversion, introversion, dominance, altruism, sociability, masculinity/ femininity, self-control, anxiety, and emotional stability. In all these tests, assessors seek to probe specific patterns of individual attributes from which a person's most typical and consistent everyday behavior can be predicted. These attributes are measured by three types of inventories: direct self-report personality inventories, indirect self-report personality inventories, and projective tests.

The direct self-report personality inventory This type of instrument, also referred to as a self-presentation questionnaire, requires testees to rate themselves on a personality scale in a straightforward manner, as in the following example: 'Circle the appropriate number 1 2 3 4 5 6 7: "I am usually optimistic"; "I am usually pessimistic".'

The indirect self-report personality inventory A typical inventory of this type contains a large number of statements, and respondents are asked to mark the extent to which they agree with each (i.e., agree, do not agree, undecided). The statements are usually taken from a variety of areas and follow one another without any logical sequence. Indeed, many of them seem to have no psychological implications at all, as in this example: 'Underline the degree to which you agree with each of the following statements: "I prefer summer over winter"; "No one is indispensable".'

These statements are then clustered into factors, and the testee's score is calculated according to a response key as a summative index of responses across statements. The inventories are called 'indirect' because many of the statements do not have any apparent connection to the factor they are meant to measure. Yet each factor has a meaning and significance of its own within the framework of the presumed structure of personality. In fact, the connection between specific statements and a personality factor exists by virtue of empirical research findings, and is not based on the substantive content of the statements. It is therefore assumed that it is hard for candidates to fake their responses, since they can not know what each statement actually measures.

Nevertheless, one cannot overlook the fact that these inventories may have intrinsic methodological flaws. For instance, they may be prone to response sets. These include social desirability on the one hand, which generates the tendencies to conform to what the respondent deems acceptable, to acquiesce, and to respond with either a 'true' or a 'yes' pattern of answers (Couch and Keniston, 1960), and deviation, or the tendency to produce unusual or untypical responses, on the other (Berg, 1967). Over the years, efforts have been made to reduce these response sets by means of psychometric or statistical techniques.

It has, however, also been argued that response sets are themselves indicators of broad and durable personality attributes which are worth measuring in their own right (Anastasi, 1982). For example, the tendency to respond with perceived socially desirable responses might well be linked to a general personality trait of social conformity. Indeed, empirical evidence lends support to the notion of personality differences between individuals who choose to respond with commonly accepted or frequently used responses, and those who produce uncommon responses (Berg, 1967).

The most widely used personality self-inventories, both direct and otherwise, include the MMPI (Minnesota Multiphasic Personality Inventory), the CPI (California Psychological Inventory), the 16 PF (16 Personality Factors), the Personality Research Form (PRF) and the Jackson Personality Inventory (JPI). A meta-analysis recently conducted by Tett, Jackson and Rothstein (1991) reveals reliability coefficients of 0.51 to 0.85 and a mean predictive validity of 0.24 across various self-report personality inventories.

A new personality test, the NEO Five-Factor Inventory, has been playing an increasingly significant role in assessing work-related personality. Its creators, Costa and McCrae (1988), claim that only five major dimensions are necessary to offer an exhaustive description of human personality: neuroticism (emotional stability vs. instability), extraversion (sociable vs. introverted), agreeableness (cooperative vs. competitive), openness to experience (intellectual curiosity vs. preference for routine) and conscientiousness (organized and deliberate vs. unorganized and careless). Costa and McCrae's assumption that each of these five dimensions measures a separate facet of personality is empirically supported by the low correlations found between them. Furthermore, there is growing empirical evidence that these tests indeed predict individuals' work performance reasonably well once they are hired by an organization (Barrick and Mount, 1991; Salgado, 1997; Caldwell and Burger, 1998).

Projective tests Projective tests are the oldest, and probably most controversial, of the instruments used to assess personality. Although there are a number of different projective techniques, they all share two common elements. First, regardless of the measure, individuals are asked to respond to ambiguous stimuli by attempting to give them meaning in an open and unrestricted response format. Secondly, the purpose of the construct being assessed is unknown to the individual being tested. A typical example of the projective technique is the familiar inkblot test, in which subjects are asked to relate to the examiner what they see in an inkblot. The testee may react to the whole blot or to part of it. Each description is scored on the basis of its location in the blot, its response determinant (shape, color, movement, and so on), and the quality of its correspondence with the chosen part of the blot.

The two best-known inkblot tests are the Rorschach and Holzman tests, consisting of 10 and 45 cards, respectively. Critics of projective techniques suggest that the typically standard interpretive procedures associated with these tests inevitably lead to poor reliability, both between scorers and between subsequent retests. Despite the criticism, however, there are those who contend that the evidence actually supports the use of projective assessment devices. Cornelius (1983), for instance, closely examined projective technique studies, including the reviews written by Guion and Gottier (1965) and Kinslinger (1966), and concluded that projective devices perform reasonably effectively in the prediction of performance.

The value of personality testing of some kind in employment is no longer contested, although with respect to the appropriate ways of assessing it, two schools of thought exist. The first, represented by Ones and Viswesvaram (1996), among others, supports the use of broad (as opposed to narrow) measures of personality in personnel selection. The adherents of this approach maintain that since performance in most jobs is complex, only broad and general personality measures can predict it.

In contrast, other scholars hold that each job requires unique personality attributes, so that those needed in one job might not be related to successful performance in another work situation. For instance, the extravert personality may be particularly critical for salespersons, while only marginally, if at all, necessary for successful performance in fashion design. Similarly, conscientiousness may be crucial to a successful quality controller, yet of less importance to a bartender.

Ashton (1988) compared the two approaches and found that broad personality traits are not more valid predictors of performance than narrow measures. However, in respect to mental ability testing (Landy, Shankster and Kohler, 1994), it has been shown clearly that some of the variance in performance can be attributed to broad traits, while the remainder can be explained by specific narrower personality traits. This may turn out to be equally applicable to work personality assessment. It remains for future research in this field to find a well-documented answer to the as yet unresolved question of which of the two approaches is more effective in the context of employment.

Direct Interest Inventories

Another type of psychological test particularly relevant to the world of work is the interest inventory. For a thorough discussion of this instrument, see Chapter 2.

Psychological Testing Procedures

The success of a test lies not only in its heuristic or empirical potential; the way in which it is administered is also very likely to affect the results in a manner which may lead to questions of reliability. Several different techniques are used in an attempt to overcome the problems related to the test situation itself. Each, naturally, has both advantages and disadvantages. Some of the more common procedures are discussed below.

Group and individual tests Group tests were developed during World War I, when it became necessary to test millions of people for military jobs. The technique was later adjusted for civilian use. (Army Alpha and Army Beta are among the best-known group tests from this period.) Group tests are constructed in a way that allows them to be administered simultaneously to several individuals and requires minimal supervisory tasks, such as monitoring time schedules and reading instructions to respondents. They are also characterized by simple answering methods, such as multiple-choice answer sheets.

In individual tests, the instrument is administered to a single testee separately. In addition to relating to the specific outcomes, the test also scrutinizes the entire response process. The procedure is usually applied when such detailed personal attention to the process is crucial, or when the technical testing devices are very complicated or costly. In such individualized tests, positive tester-testee interaction is, of course, vital both to ensure the respondents' test motivation and to enable them to overcome anxiety, and so forth.

Speed and power tests Speed tests restrict the amount of time that testees are allowed to spend on the test items, even if they do not manage to complete them all. The results consequently reflect performance as a function of both accuracy and time; the score equals the number of items answered correctly within the allotted time. In contrast, the power test allows testees ample time to complete the tasks, with accuracy, determination, and other traits more highly weighted than speed. Here the score is calculated simply as the total number of items answered correctly. Normally the items on power tests are of a higher level of difficulty than those on speed tests.

Paper-and-pencil and performance tests In paper-and-pencil tests, the answers are given in writing, while performance tests generally require the manipulation of physical objects.

Supervision and Control of Psychological Testing

Supervision of, and control over, the use of psychological tests are motivated by the need to protect both the testee and the organization or company administering the tests. This is a complex and weighty issue that involves numerous ethical problems and regulations. For example, the sale and distribution of tests is limited and controlled to prevent the public from acquiring knowledge of their contents and scoring methods. The testers themselves must also be highly skilled in the correct, objective, and standard use of the testing material in order to eliminate the possibility of external factors contaminating outcomes. Since confidentiality of scores must be insured, they may be released only to qualified professionals with a full understanding of their theoretical and structural meaning. The professionals are then also responsible for conveying the results and feedback to the testees.

Test Validation

The use of psychological tests for employee selection and placement is both traditional and widespread, with such instruments serving as essential components of most every staffing program. In order to make efficient use of their outcomes, however, several procedures need to be complied with. These include employing several tests or staffing tools, choosing the suitable instruments for clearly defined occupational criteria within the specific organization, and using varied, independent, sources of information in order to cross-validate the data obtained. It must be remembered that test results are measures of a static test situation, whereas the ultimate aim of the process is to predict future performance under predominantly dynamic conditions. The question of validity is thus a key issue that must accompany every staffing program.

Petterson and Tziner (1995) recently attempted to assess the stability of the predictive ability of job performance over time of two specific intelligence tests, OTIS (measuring general intelligence) and BETA (gauging non-verbal intelligence). Specifically, they were testing the notion of a 'dynamic criterion', a concept first advanced by Ghiselli (1956). Ghiselli contended that the predictive validities of measures used in the staffing process, such as cognitive ability test scores, diminish over time, and that the greater the lapse of time between the administration of the staffing instruments and the collection of criteria measures, the less valid they become. He based this assumption on the fact that market needs change, so that the abilities that were critical for successful performance at the assessment point would become less relevant as time progresses.

Petterson and Tziner suggested, however, that predictive ability might vary as a function of practice, and that while specific skills might be temporally bound, they might still influence successful performance both close to assessment, and at a remote time. Thus in their investigation of the validity of the cognitive tests, they also explored the moderating effects of job tenure and job complexity.

Two measures of job performance that tapped cognitive aspects of competence were used as criteria for 255 production employees of a paper manufacturing plant, producing a one-to-one correspondence between predictors and criteria. Hierarchical moderated regressions were generated in order to ascertain the extent to which the validity of the two intelligence tests changed as a function of tenure and of job complexity. The results upheld the predictive validity of the two tests. Tenure was found to affect the predictive validities only as job complexity increased, but not where this moderator remained stable over time. Thus, this study did not support Ghiselli's proposition, while the cognitive tests were shown to be useful predictors, especially with respect to performance in complex jobs.

(5) Graphological Tests

Practitioners of graphology, the science of handwriting analysis, seek to understand the characteristics of an individual's personality by analyzing the peculiarities of handwritten text. If we define handwriting as the impressions left after the act of writing, then the writing sample can be seen as the final product of a specific behavior, and is generally assumed to be the result of expressive hand movements that in some way reflect aspects of the writer's personality. The underlying rationale is thus not dissimilar to that on which the entire system of projective techniques (such as the inkblot test) is founded. In fact, it has been suggested that handwriting is an expression of the brain's 'language', in which personality attributes and thought are logically and comprehensively reflected, and through which motoric and projective expression are unified (Frederick, 1965).

Two approaches to handwriting analysis prevail in the literature of graphology. The holistic (or gestalt) approach favors a global, overall impression of the handwriting, without delineating its specific features. The holistic school conceives of a person as a whole, dynamic entity, so that the individual features that go to make up that person do not collectively reflect his or her true character. For this reason, general handwriting patterns and single signs or features of the script are disregarded. Some graphologists adhering to this school analyze the hand movements and devices employed by the writer, whereas others emphasize the symbolic aspects. All of them, however, interpret the organization of the spatial field covered by the writing, the direction of the hand movements, and the depth and pressure revealed in the script, in an attempt to uncover the writer's unconscious motives, drives, and inclinations.

The analytic (or atomistic) approach emphasizes the 'objective' measurements of writing characteristics, correlating the size, shape, and degree of slant of the letters to the writer's personality attributes. This approach thus presumes a positive relation between various features of letters and specific personality traits.

In evaluating the validity of graphology assessment, four parameters are employed:

1 The consistency of handwriting over time. Do changes in handwriting characteristics reflect changes in personality, or do they reflect inconsistency and a lack of stability resulting from random error?
2 The degree of agreement among graphologists regarding the interpretation of a specific sample of handwriting or specific features of the same script.
3 The degree to which the content of what is written affects the outcomes and conclusions of the analysis.
4 The accuracy of prediction for varied purposes, such as staffing.

Although these issues have been the subject of numerous studies, no indisputable conclusions have yet been reached. What follows is a review of selected findings gleaned from investigations into the reliability and validity of graphological ratings.

Reliability of Graphological Assessment

As we have seen, for graphologists, handwriting represents a form of behavior. Consequently, one crucial question regarding this field concerns the extent to which handwriting remains stable over time. If its features reflect the natural instability of the personality, then any attempt to use graphological assessment for the purposes of staffing will be worthless. This problematic question has been studied by a number of researchers, whose early studies reported a high consistency in handwriting features, with correlations ranging from 0.78 to 0.88 (e.g., Crider, 1941). Similar outcomes have also been obtained by more recent studies – coefficients between r = 0.70 and r = 0.93 (e.g., Currer-Brigs, 1971; Nevo, 1986) – which tend to confirm the notion that the characteristics of handwriting remain relatively stable over time.

Needless to say, if graphologists can not agree on the information to be identified by handwriting analysis and on the interpretation of this information, then both the reliability and the validity of their ratings remains in doubt. Nonetheless, various investigations have attempted to determine reliability, including the three representative studies discussed below.

In the first study by Galbraith and Wilson (1964), 100 students were asked to copy a short paragraph, and these handwriting samples were then rated by three graphologists for five personality attributes: attention to detail, perseverance, self-consciousness, tenacity, and dominance. Inter-graphologist correlations ranged from 0.61 (tenacity) to 0.87 (dominance), with an average correlation of 0.78, indicating a high level of inter-graphologist reliability. This study, however, suffers from the fact that the samples subjected to graphological assessment were copied passages, and that the testees used different types of paper and pens. In other words, there was neither standardization nor spontaneity in the writing conditions, both generally considered by graphologists themselves to be crucial prerequisites for reliable and valid evaluation.

In another study, Hofsommer, Holdsworth, and Seifert (1965) asked three graphologists to rate each of 322 foremen on a seven-point leadership scale, and found an inter-graphologist reliability of 0.74, a result similar to that of the previous investigation. However, although the number of testees was larger and the script samples were not copied passages, here too there were methodological flaws. The researchers used letters of application as the material for their graphological assessment, which again created a lack of standardization. It may also be assumed that the handwriting samples were somewhat artificial, since people would wish to display their best handwriting when applying for a job. Moreover, letters of application refer to life events that may impact on the ratings, thus making the content an additional uncontrolled variable. Finally, again there was a lack of standardization in respect to the type of paper and writing tools, which may well have affected the writing styles as well.

The third study by Rafaeli and Klimoski (1983) corrected for several of these methodological failings. Here use was made of two types of content, one considered neutral and the other non-neutral (CVs), and of identical writing utensils and types of paper, so that the variables of content and writing conditions were fully controlled. This investigation found inter-graphologist reliability coefficients ranging between 0.23 and 0.59, with a median of 0.45. However, it too was by no means methodologically flawless.

Validity of Graphological Assessment

The literature of graphological assessment validation is dominated by three major research techniques: the sorting, matching, and ranking methods.

The sorting method   This technique concentrates on only one personality variable (such as extrovert-introvert). Two groups of subjects known to differ with respect to that trait are chosen, and the graphologist is asked to sort their handwriting samples into the two appropriate groups. If the results are distinctly superior to random classification, the graphological judgment is considered valid (see: Frederick, 1965). The advantage of this method lies in its ease of handling, since it involves only a single dimension on which a judgment must be made (presence vs. absence of a specific trait). However, it has been harshly contested by graphologists, who argue that evaluation of the total personality yields much better validity coefficients.

The matching method   In this technique graphologists are either presented with written personality descriptions of the testees which they must then match with their handwriting samples (Jansen, 1973), or the graphologists compose their own assessments on the basis of samples, and these are then matched to the testees by people who know them well. Although the method has the advantage of employing graphological assessment of the whole personality, it is quite cumbersome. Moreover, it is subject to interdependency between the matchings, so that one incorrect matching increases the probability of other incorrect results. The smaller the number of comparisons, the more likely it is that this deviation will occur. On the other hand, if the number of comparisons is large, the more difficult it becomes to remember the many personality descriptions for matching purposes.

The ranking or rating method The ranking method requires graphologists to rate, on numerical scales, the extent to which a personality attribute deduced from handwriting characterizes an individual. In a subsequent phase, these ratings are validated against the testees' scores on other forms of assessment. Personality test scores or personality descriptions formulated by psychologists and psychiatrists have become accepted in the literature as criteria with which to correlate graphological ratings. In terms of the goal of validation, this method has proved to be a source of great disappointment.

For example, in Kimmel and Wertheimer's (1966) comparison of a graphologist's ratings on five personality traits (based on 22 handwriting samples) with the ratings of two psychologists derived from personality tests, the intercorrelations between the scores of the two psychologists fluctuated between 0.21 and 0.74, while the intercorrelations between the ratings of the graphologist and each psychologist were even lower. The authors conclude that their study does not lend credence to the validity of graphological ratings. It is possible, of course, that the findings stemmed from the low reliability of the criterion measure, or that the fact that only one graphologist and a small number of writing samples were involved in the research affected the reliability of the results.

Further studies have investigated the validity coefficients of graphological assessment against two criteria: the scores of individuals on the Edwards Personality Inventory (EPI), and the extent to which testees agreed that the graphologists' ratings properly portrayed their personality. In this case the validity coefficients of the two criteria were not significant, and it was concluded that it is not advisable to use self-evaluation as a validity criterion on its own, but only in conjunction with other criterion measures (Tziner, Jeanrie, and Cusson, 1993).

In recent years, increasing use has been made of supervisor appraisals as a measure of performance in the occupational system, since supervisors are so readily available in the workplace, and their appraisals would indeed appear to be an obvious criterion for the validation of graphological assessment for staffing purposes. However, numerous studies have shown supervisor assessments to be poorly predicted by graphological ratings. For example, a comprehensive study by Jansen (1973) reports the results of four experiments of this type conducted over the course of ten years. Only in the third experiment, was graphological assessment found to be valid in respect to supervisor appraisal and to significantly correlate ($r = 0.23$) with immediate supervisor ratings. In another study by Flug (1981), a similarly positive but low correlation coefficient was found between graphological assessment and the criterion measure of supervisor appraisal.

Again it is difficult to determine whether the relatively low predictions produced by these studies indicate that the graphological forecast is a poor or invalid tool, or whether supervisor appraisal as a criterion measure is itself hard to predict because of its inherent deficiencies. It could be argued, for instance, that the supervisor's rating might be contaminated by a host of irrelevant factors including:

1 a personal liking for the employee;
2 the 'halo effect': the tendency to evaluate the employee across rating domains in accordance with an overall impression of favorability or unfavorability;
3 first impression and primary errors: a tendency on the part of an examiner to exaggerate certain aspects of behavior or performance exhibited in the early phases of acquaintance with the ratee;
4 the recency effect: the fact that the impression of an employee's recent behavior or performance may override previously formulated evaluations;
5 the proximity error: the effects of previous appraisal outcomes on subsequent ratings;
6 similarity and contrast errors: Similarity refers to raters' tendency to evaluate more positively those testees they perceive to bear a resemblance to themselves. Contrast is conceived as either a tendency to judge others in a manner opposite to the way in which raters perceive themselves (Plum and Naylor, 1968), or to judge employees relative to previously assessed ratees (Landy and Trumbo, 1981). A more in-depth treatment of these cognitive errors can be found in Bernardin and Beatty (1984) and Murphy and Cleveland (1995).

Several investigations have been conducted in Israel that attempt to validate graphological assessments against a wider array of criteria. These include, among others, studies by Flug (1981), Ramati (1981), Bar-Hillel and Ben-Shakhar (1985), Bar-Hillel and Flug (1986), Ben-Shakhar et al. (1986).

In one typical study, both the reliability and validity of graphological assessment in personnel selection were investigated (Flug, 1981). The research sample contained 80 sets of handwriting (CV's), and the evaluators were three graphologists, one clinical psychologist, and the chief psychologist of the

Institute of Applied Psychology in Tel-Aviv. The criterion measure with which their evaluations were correlated were the assessments of the testees' immediate supervisors. The results revealed a positive but low predictive validity for each of the types of evaluators, with the average validity value in the range of $r = 0.2$ to $r = 0.3$. Reliability between the three graphologists was also positive but low. The predictive validity of the assessment attributed to the institute's chief psychologist was found to be only slightly higher than that of the clinical psychologists or of the average rating of the three graphologists.

One interesting result arising from this particular research was that the unique contribution of the clinical psychologist to the prediction of the criterion measure, beyond the percentage of variance explained by the institute psychologist, was very low. However, the clinical psychologist's predictive validity was higher than that attained by the graphologists. According to Flug, these findings demonstrate that although the ratings of the institute psychologist explain only a small part of the variance, and those of the clinical psychologist an additional proportion, these 'contributions' are not redundant.

Flug's study is by no means definitive, however, since of the 80 individuals who were tested, statistical analyses were conducted on only 20 to 58, probably an insufficient sample to warrant generalization of the findings. Furthermore, the lack of information on the quality of the criterion leads Flug herself to question its reliability and validity.

Research has yet to be conducted to ascertain the extent to which graphological and clinical-psychological assessments complement each other by adding uniquely meaningful portions of explained criterion variance. An appropriate research design for this purpose might have both clinical psychologists and graphologists examine the same subjects and rate them on a set of the same behavioral items, gauging various aspects of a work adjustment criterion or other criterion measures.

Flug (1981) thus found no significant variance between the groups of judges. Interestingly enough, a study by Ben-Shakhar, Bar-Hillel, and Flug (1986) produced identical results: the predictions of the graphologists and psychologists were similar, with the psychologists' prediction being only slightly higher than that of the graphologists.

A final endeavor worthy of note in respect to the validity of graphological assessment is the meta-analysis conducted in Israel by Nevo (1986). Combining 14 studies on a total of 9,321 testees, Nevo found an average validity coefficient of $r = 0.15$ between graphological evaluation and job performance criteria.

The Use of Graphological Tests

Despite the severe reservations voiced about their levels of reliability and validity as a staffing tool, graphological tests are widely used in industrial organizations in France, Germany, Holland, and Israel. In a critical review, Nevo (1986) attempts to explain why this is so. He argues that graphologists furnish descriptions containing generalizations that fit most people and would sound reasonable and apt even if they were not based on handwriting samples, a phenomenon known as the Barnum Effect. Another of his contentions refers to the base rate of graphological assessments, as illustrated by the personal attribute of 'honesty'. Nevo claims that if only a very low number of applicants is considered 'absolutely honest', then any case of embezzlement validates the graphological prediction. A third argument is based on the psychological proposition dubbed the 'visibility of success'. People tend to forget, or prefer to ignore, negative evidence, while the dramatically accurate predictions of graphologists are vividly remembered.

Notwithstanding these criticisms, a solution might well be found by combining graphological tests with other staffing measures, a step that might lead to a significant improvement in the level of prediction. This possibility obviously requires thorough empirical scrutiny. For the meanwhile, however, empirical evidence of the reliability and predictive validity of graphological evaluation does not appear to be very promising (see: Rafaeli and Klimoski, 1983).

(6) Peer Evaluation (Sociometric Tests)

In this method, people on the same hierarchical or occupational level in the organization evaluate each other on a set of behavioral dimensions that are observable at work. Each individual evaluates the performance of all the others, but not of him- or herself. Sociometric tests have been found highly efficient, especially for appraising employee promotability (Amir, Kovarsky, and Sharon, 1970; Downey, Medland and Yates, 1976; Love, 1981).

The acquisition of peer assessments requires that proper opportunities exist for peers to observe each other's performance or behavior at work for a period of at least three weeks. Peer evaluations are obtained at a given point in time that ensures that the data are always up-to-date. They may also be collected over a period of several years and at different points in time, thus providing a more dynamic image of the ratee.

Three common methods are in use for obtaining peer evaluations:

1 *Peer nomination*. Each rater chooses those co-workers (e.g., two or three) who in his or her opinion are best suited for a particular position, or who rank highest on a list of pre-specified performance behaviors (or dimensions).

2 *Ranking*. Each rater ranks the others according to their specific performance/behavior abilities, in descending order from the best (highest) to the worst.

3 *Peer rating*. Each group member is rated on a behavior-anchored scale on a series of dimensions related to that member's behavior and performance in the organization.

Studies have shown that friendship considerations do not significantly bias ratings in any of these three methods (Love, 1981). There are, however, contaminating factors that may affect the ratings for better or worse, especially when workers need to maintain good relations or, conversely, in situations where they are competing for the same job.

In general, peer ratings are considered the most reliable and valid predictors of a candidate's future success in a job. In a series of studies conducted by Hollander (1954, 1965), for example, validity coefficients between 0.3 and 0.7 were found for peer evaluation of general performance potential on various performance criteria. Similarly, Lewin and Zwany (1976) found a validity coefficient of approximately 0.4 in 15 studies of peer evaluation effectiveness.

More recently, Tziner (1984) has provided impressive evidence of the ability of assessment center-based peer rating to predict performance in officer training ($r=0.51$; $p=<.001$), although the same predictor failed to account for on-the-job performance. To explain these findings, the author suggests that the assessment center (see below) might better imitate the training course than it does the job. It is interesting to note, however, that the assessment center-based peer rating made no unique contribution to explained variance in performance in training; the information it provided added little to the information already available to assessors.

Tziner proposes three possible explanations for the fact that peer rating was found to have no validity in predicting officer performance:

1 the restriction of the range of the performance criterion to the upper end of the scale, as those in officer positions are, by definition, relatively high performers;

2 the alleged dynamic nature of the criterion (Ghiselli and Haire, 1960);

3 the fact that superior ratings are generally deficient performance measures.

With respect to the first supposition, the author notes that correcting for the range restriction statistically increases the validity coefficient (from .05 to .12), although it still remains non-significant. In order to test the second explanation, Tziner suggests taking criterion measures at several points in time over a longer period, and calculating validities against performance at each point in time. The results should then be inspected to detect whether the measures decrease as more time elapses after the conclusion of the assessment, as might be expected from Ghiselli and Haire (1960).

As for the third explanation, Tziner argues that there may be good reason to suspect the presence of criteria contamination and criteria deficiency in this particular study, since female officers were assessed by men, who may have displayed undue bias. The author suggests that this problem could be overcome by employing objective, rather than subjective, measures of performance, such as how many of the objectives assigned to the officers were accomplished and with what degree of success.

In contrast, Tziner and Dolan (1985) report evidence in support of the predictive validity of peer evaluation, finding a coefficient of 0.43 (p<0.05) against a criterion of officers' training performance. In this study, the criterion was defined in terms of the final grade obtained by the candidate on completion of training. The grade represented a weighted composite of the soldier's scores on objective examinations (indicative of the relative importance of grades to success) and instructors' ratings of performance in field command exercises. The instructors were themselves experienced and successful commanders.

The sociometric score (peer nominations) emerged here as a more valid single predictor than any of the others with which it was compared. Moreover, the peer nominations were relatively superior in terms of their unique contribution to explaining variance in successful performance throughout training, although they still proved limited in terms of their effectiveness for predicting on-the-job efficiency. Three possible explanations were suggested for the impressive predictive validity of peer evaluations in training: (1) peer evaluation consists of an overall assessment that integrates information on behavior over time and across situations; (2) it is based on convergent opinions, which increases its reliability; and (3) it is less contaminated by social and cultural biases than any other predictors yielded by paper-and-pencil instruments.

This staffing measure has its limitations, however, especially in a business or industrial context (Lewin and Zwany, 1976), where objections have been voiced to the use of peer evaluation. People in such organizations have expressed the fear that the data inherent in sociometry might lead to the deterioration of work-team cohesiveness, and consequently affect performance and the organization as a whole (Cederblom and Loundsbury, 1980).

The results of these studies clearly indicate the value of peer assessment. However, they also suggest that it is probably best employed together with other predictor measurements and with the consent of the individuals involved.

Contemporary Methods

(7) Assessment Centers

Assessment centers have greatly increased in popularity in the last two decades, mainly due to their ability to handle a large and varied number of staffing tests, including situational exercises and simulations (such as 'in-basket' and leaderless group discussion), aptitude, intelligence, and personality tests, peer evaluations, and background interviews. Generally speaking, the fact that it makes use of a greater variety of staffing devices gives the assessment center an advantage over traditional methods in that it yields a more accurate and richer description of the applicants' qualities. Not only does it examine their skills and aptitudes, but it also simulates their ability to adjust to a number of situations likely to be encountered in the organization.

Situational Tests

A situational test elicits performance on a sample of job-relevant tasks, thus enabling direct inspection of an applicant's performance and behaviors in a situation closely simulating actual work conditions. The situational tests typically used by assessment centers seek mainly to detect three clusters of job-related behavior: (1) decision making and work supervision; (2) leadership, planning, organization, and initiative; and (3) independence and decisiveness. The tests thus allow for expression of the individual's job-relevant repertoire of knowledge, abilities, and motivation, as well as predicting the probability of adjustment to the particular work environment.

Tziner (1984) notes that, in comparison to a number of different measures used to predict successful officer performance in the military, including consensus ratings on various dimensions and overall assessment, the situational exercise score displayed the highest validity in terms of the predictability of performance in training ($r = .76$ vs. $r = .58$ and $r = .60$, respectively). This score also made a remarkable and unique contribution to explained variance

(35 per cent). In fact, Tziner reports that after its entrance into the hierarchical regression analysis, the other assessment center measures had very little to contribute to the prediction of performance in training. However, with respect to the criteria of officer field performance in the same study, the situational exercise score was neither a valid predictor nor a significant contributor to prediction when entered into the regression analysis after peer rating. The author suggests that the superior result for the training criterion may reflect the fact that the situational exercise score was derived from a statistical combination of assessment data and consensus rating, rather than from a clinical combination of those data (see below).

As a rule, the selection of situational activities is meant to include more of those repertoires that are crucial for success on the job than it does 'routine' behaviors. The difficulties of constructing and standardizing situational tests are therefore legion, as this endeavor must start with the derivation of the job requirements and the behavior dimensions to be observed. Subsequently, sample tasks must be chosen that will not only simulate these requirements and job activities, but will also validly elicit behaviors related to successful work adjustment.

The assessment process clearly demands skillful observations, recording, and analysis of task performance tests. It therefore requires the right choice of competent assessors who are well acquainted with the different aspects of the job for which the applicants are to be tested. Typically, the assessors are managers at two or three organizational levels above the candidates being assessed, and are specially trained for this task. Clinical psychologists may also be included on the assessment team, primarily because they are trained to recognize behaviors which may not be obvious to the untrained eye.

Advantages of Assessment Centers

Notwithstanding the importance of situational exercises, they constitute only one of the components of the assessment center. Indeed, the attractiveness of this method of selection stems from the fact that it offers a wide variety of staffing instruments. Furthermore, it is rooted in sound psychometric principles. Using multiple assessment techniques (static, as well as dynamic instruments such as situational tests), standardizing the procedures for drawing inferences from such techniques, and pooling the judgments of several assessors in rating each candidate's behavior, considerably enhances the likelihood of predicting future performance successfully (Finkle, 1976; Cascio and Silbey, 1979; Sackett and Hakel, 1979; Sackett, 1982).

In general, the psychometric efficiency of the assessment center has been demonstrated empirically by evaluative research, with many studies showing it to be a reliable predictor of professional performance and career advancement (see below). The extent of the assessment center's success, however, depends to a large degree on the specific effectiveness of each of its components, including the situational exercises, the assessors, the accuracy of judgment, the formulation of the evaluations, and so on.

The Process of Assessment

In the course of the assessment, applicants are teamed up into groups of ten to twelve individuals who remain together throughout the stages of the observation. At each stage, the individual applicant's performance is observed by several assessors to ensure independent observation and judgment. Only at the end of the process is an attempt made to formulate a single, overall assessment rating on each scale of observed behavior.

Because of the high cost of this process, assessment centers are operated mainly for the purpose of selecting candidates for managerial positions or highly critical functions in the organization. Since there are generally relatively few applicants for this sort of job, assessment centers are sometimes set up to serve an aggregate of several organizations, a convenient and feasible arrangement, as managerial requirements are similar in most organizations. As a rule, they demand strong leadership, organizational skills, and the ability to function under stress, among other qualities.

The History of Assessment Centers

Assessment center techniques were first employed by the military in the two world wars. It is believed that German psychologists used assessment center procedures in World War I to select officers (Thornton and Byham, 1982), while a well-documented example from World War II is the Office of Strategic Services (OSS), a center set up to screen and evaluate intelligence agents (MacKinnon, 1977). The OSS served as the first prototype for the industrial application of assessment centers, as illustrated by the research-oriented Management Progress Study conducted by American Telephone and Telegraph in 1956 (Cohen, Moses and Byham, 1974). Following Michigan Bell's pioneering experiments in 1958, the industrial use of assessment centers for staff selection mushroomed. The early sixties saw the adoption of this method by such major firms as Standard Oil, IBM, General Electric, Sears, Wickes and J. C. Penney (MacKinnon, 1977). The individual state governments then followed suit, with the result that these centers are now in use throughout the United States (e.g., Byham and Wettengel, 1974). Thornton and Byham (1982) offer an authoritative recounting of the rapid spread of assessment center programs around the world, and the Canadians Slivinski and Ethier (1973) and Slivinski et al. (1977), for example, relate interesting examples of center applications and research within the governmental framework. These international works represent an intriguing extension of the field.

The phenomenal growth and deployment of assessment centers has generated considerable research and debate regarding the manner of their implementation and the nature of their contribution to selection. The sections below highlight selected facets of this compendium of knowledge, with particular attention to such topical areas as assessment process outcomes, the predictive validity of ratings, and the comparison with traditional selection methods.

Assessment Process Outcomes

The assessment process yields a variety of outcomes that differ in number, breadth, and scope. They include individual ratings for each dimension observed in various exercises, overall performance evaluations for each situational exercise, and final consensus ratings made after assessors have discussed candidate performance among themselves. The results of these assessments are used both to make selection and promotion decisions, usually on the basis of an overall assessment rating, and for management development purposes, an application that is becoming increasingly common (Hollenbeck, 1990).

In selection and promotion programs, attribute ratings are derived for the main purpose of ensuring that assessors focus on the appropriate aspects of the managerial performance domain. However, the individual ratings, per se, are not that important. They do take on more significance when assessment centers are used for management development purposes, where an accurate diagnosis of the individual's profile of developmental needs is required. The individual test results then become the basis for developmental planning and the subsequent training and development exercises required for successful assessees.

Not surprisingly, this panoply of outcome measures has raised a number of questions regarding the reliability and construct validity of final attribute ratings, which represent both individual judgments on specific exercises and aggregations of judgments across multiple assessors and multiple exercises.

Moreover, doubts have been voiced concerning the possibility of replicating the results. In addition, the research reveals an ongoing debate over the relative virtues of assessments based on individual exercise ratings, final overall assessment ratings, and final attribute ratings. These concerns, in turn, have raised more fundamental issues regarding the judgmental process itself.

Construct Validity

Individual dimension ratings The assessment center method and its emphasis on behavior sampling ultimately rests on the hypothesis that people exhibit consistent patterns of behavior across situations. However, a disquieting finding relating to convergent validity calls into question basic assumptions which are the very essence of the assessment center approach to individual dimension ratings.

Dreher and Sackett (1983) examined the dimension ratings in each exercise in three assessment centers, hypothesizing that if assessment centers were measuring stable personal characteristics, such as judgment and analytical skills, then the ratings of a particular dimension across exercises should be more highly related to one another than the ratings of different dimensions in the same exercise. Contrary to their hypothesis, however, the ratings of different dimensions in the same exercise were found to be highly correlated, whereas the ratings of a given dimension in different exercises yielded lower inter-correlations. In fact, some of these intercorrelations were so low that they actually called into question the meaningfulness of the assessment dimensions. For example, if a candidate's oral communication skill rating in a group setting produces a low to nonexistent relationship with his/her oral communication skill rating in a one-to-one setting, then assigning a single overall rating of oral communication skill would seem to be highly questionable.

These and similar findings indicate moderate levels of convergent validity, that is, moderate correlations of the same attribute as evaluated in more than one exercise (Archambeau, 1979; Sackett and Dreher, 1982; Turnage and Muchinsky, 1984). Studies report low consistency within dimensions across exercises, and high consistency across dimensions within exercises. High correlations among the ratings of several attributes observed in the same exercise is also indicative of high levels of method variance (Sackett and Dreher, 1982; Russell, 1987). Moreover, researchers who have conducted factor analyses of within-exercise attribute ratings note that they tend to yield exercise factors rather than attribute factors (Bycio, Alvarez and Hahn, 1987; Robertson, Gratton and Sharpley, 1987).

On the basis of their research findings, Dreher and Sackett (1983) conclude that effective performance is situational. They argue that anyone responsible for developing assessment centers, as well as anyone intending to make use of them, should consider changing their focus from the rating of effectiveness on global dimensions to the rating of effectiveness on specific exercises. Moreover, Sackett and Wilson (1982) recommend that if performance varies across situations, then it is also crucial to sample all the important situations or work roles that effectively constitute the job.

In contrast, Bycio, Alvarez and Hahn (1987) pursued a totally different avenue in attempting to explain the low correlation of dimension ratings across exercises relative to those within exercises. They demonstrate that the various procedures used to evaluate the candidates account for the observable differences in both the convergent and discriminant validities, as well as in the dimensionality of the assessment center ratings. In their view, differing types of evaluation methods may force raters to process and organize assessment center data in ways that reflect the methodological process. For example, if a within-exercise method of evaluation is used, it might force the assessor to organize assessment information by exercise. Alternatively, use of the within-dimension method would impose the requirement of organizing observations in terms of dimensions.

Results of this kind have led some people to conclude that assessment centers in their present form indeed lack construct validity, and should thus be set up in a different manner. Tziner (1990), for example, recommends that they be designed so as to better assess the contingency of leadership and managerial performance. Certain critics have even suggested abandoning human attributes as the organizing concepts for the design and implementation of assessment centers (Sackett and Dreher, 1982; Russell, 1987).

Thornton, Tziner, Dahan, Clevenger and Meir (1997), however, argue that such drastic measures are premature for several reasons. First, while some studies of within-exercise attribute ratings reveal questionable psychometric properties, others have revealed quite acceptable levels of reliability (Borman, 1982; Kehoe, Weinberg and Lawrence, 1985; Konz, 1988) and convergent validity (Hinrichs and Haanpera, 1976).

Secondly, there are indications that the psychometric properties of attribute ratings are determined to some extent by the method of observation and integration (Silverman, Dalessio, Woods and Johnson, 1986). In the studies cited above, for instance, the system of observation was the 'within-exercise attribute rating method', whereby assessors give within-exercise attribute ratings after observing one candidate in one exercise. The unit of analysis in these construct validity studies is therefore the rating by one assessor of one attribute after viewing one exercise. However, there is another procedure known, as the 'behavior reporting method' (used in the original American Telephone and Telegraph studies; Bray and Grant, 1966), which does not call for within-exercise attribute ratings, and thus may enable assessors to focus on specific behaviors and avoid evaluations at the exercise level. Using this technique, in the integration discussion assessors report only behaviors relevant to each attribute, but not ratings. They then compare behaviors relevant to each attribute across exercises, giving attribute ratings only after behaviors have been reported across all exercises.

Because the within-exercise rating method requires assessors to make attribute ratings after each exercise, it may encourage them to think in terms of overall exercise performance. As a result, it may cause observers to generalize from some overall impression of doing well (or poorly) on situational-related characteristics in a given exercise to the evaluation of all attributes. Like Thornton (1992), we might surmise that behavioral reports generate a different process of human judgment that may improve the discriminability of final attribute ratings. Of course, if within-exercise attribute ratings are not made, researchers cannot study construct validity in the form of convergent and discriminant validity for this unit of analysis.

Final attribute ratings In contrast to within-exercise attribute ratings and final overall assessment ratings (see below), many assessment center organizations today place the emphasis on final attribute ratings, which are derived from the combined judgment of multiple assessors integrating behavioral observations across multiple exercises. Thus, the relevant issue here is the quality of the final attribute ratings after all assessors have integrated information from all exercises. There are indications that the use of final attribute ratings along with the behavioral reporting method may produce more reliable and differentiated assessments than the other techniques described thus far.

First, there is considerable evidence of a high level of interrater agreement on final attribute ratings (McConnell and Parker, 1972; Schmitt, 1977; Neidig and Martin, 1979; Sackett and Hakel, 1979; Kehoe et al., 1985). Second, studies show that final attribute ratings correlate substantially with numerous measures of job performance (Bray and Campbell, 1968; Tziner, Ronen, and Hacohen, 1993), progress in management (Bray and Grant, 1966), promotion potential (Tziner et al., 1993), and ratings of performance on comparable dimensions of subsequent on-the-job performance in managerial positions (Mitchel, 1975). Finally, numerous factor analyses have revealed that assessors' judgments are permeated by meaningful and interpretable factors, ranging in number from two (Sackett and Hakel, 1979; Shore, Thornton and Shore, 1990), to three or four (Russell, 1987), to as many as eleven (Bray and Grant, 1966; Thomson, 1970).

Final attribute ratings also afford the opportunity to determine construct validity by investigating their relationships to alternative measures of comparable constructs, in addition to analyzing the internal structure of assessment center ratings. Studies that have adopted this approach also provide considerable support for the construct validity of assessors' judgments of managerial attributes. Results indicate that assessors' judgments on final attribute ratings are correlated with managerial judgments of similar performance constructs on the job (Mitchel, 1975), with self-ratings (Russell, 1987; Shore, Shore, and Thornton, 1992), with test scores on cognitive ability and personality tests measuring comparable attributes (Shore et al., 1990), and with peer ratings (Shore et al., 1992).

A recent managerial assessment center study conducted by Thornton et al. (1997) in a large organization in Israel throws additional light on the issue of the construct validity of final attribute ratings, particularly in respect to results derived from the behavioral reporting method. Assessors' ratings of 382 middle-level managers being considered for promotion were correlated with cognitive tests and psychologists' evaluations measuring comparable constructs, and the factorial structure of the final attribute ratings was also examined. The following hypotheses were posited:

H1: Final attribute ratings in an assessment center using the behavior reporting method will correlate higher with (a) tests measuring comparable attributes than they will with tests measuring noncomparable attributes (convergent vs. discriminant validity), and (b) psychologists' assessments of comparable attributes than they will with psychologists' assessments of non-comparable attributes.

H2: Factor analyses of final attribute ratings in an assessment center using the behavior reporting method will yield four meaningful factors that are similar to four *a priori* categories of attributes.

Care was taken in this study to avoid contamination by maintaining discretion and independence between the sources of information obtained for the assessees. The results were analyzed in depth to determine construct validity as well as clusters. Because of the important insights revealed by the study, along with its conscientious design, it is described here in detail.

Psychologists who were not members of the assessor teams that observed the situational exercises conducted a background interview and examined the personality test results. They then formed evaluations of eight personality characteristics: maturity and emotional stability; independence; energy level; initiative and willingness to take on challenges; perseverance and dedication; creativity; career ambitions; and assertiveness. The assessors were not made aware of the psychologists' evaluations before they formulated their own ratings.

Well-trained assessors then evaluated sixteen attributes organized into four *a priori* categories:

1 *Managerial Skills*: planning and organizing; routine problem solving; complex problem solving; activating others; decision making; meeting and discussion facilitation.
2 *Communication*: written communication; oral communication.
3 *Work Values*: standards for high performance; reliability; following instructions; organizational identification.
4 *Interpersonal Skills*: interpersonal relations; openness and tolerance to others; teamwork; behavioral flexibility.

One other attribute, general intelligence level, was evaluated but not included in the study because the rating was derived directly from the cognitive test scores.

In the next step, the assessors used the behavioral reporting method to observe, record, and integrate their observations after all the exercises had been completed. Drawing on their notes, each psychologist or manager assessor independently rated each of the assessees on 16 of the 25 attributes. Other psychologists who had not observed the situational exercises evaluated the assessees on the remaining nine attributes based on the results of the general intelligence and personality tests. On the day following the exercises, the assessors met to discuss their ratings and behavioral observations. After considering any discrepancies in the ratings given to each assessee, including behaviors relevant to each dimension, they arrived by consensus at a single rating on each of the 16 attributes for each of the candidates.

The researchers conducted several analyses to determine the construct validity of these final attribute ratings. They first correlated the ratings of the assessors with the cognitive test scores and the psychologists' evaluations of personality characteristics. Each of these three sources of information, it will be remembered, was independent of the others. Although the cognitive tests had been administered before the candidates were referred to the assessment center, the results were not available to the psychologists, who formulated their evaluations of personality characteristics on the basis of the background interviews and personality tests. Similarly, the program administrators withheld the cognitive test results and the psychologists' evaluations from the assessors until after the integration of the behavioral observations.

The authors next obtained ratings of the comparability of assessment attributes and cognitive test scores, and the comparability of assessment attributes and characteristics, from four faculty members and 13 advanced graduate students in the Industrial/Organizational Psychology program at Colorado State University. The judges, all trained and experienced in psychometric principles and test validation, were asked to indicate if each assessment attribute and each test (or personality characteristic) clearly measured comparable constructs. An assessment attribute was considered to measure a construct comparable to that measured by a test (or personality characteristic) if at least two-thirds of the judges (i.e., 12 out of 17) indicated similarity. If five or fewer judges indicated similarity, the test (or personality characteristic) was considered to be noncomparable. Nine of the 16 assessment attributes were judged to have at least one comparable and one noncomparable test measure, and six to have at least one comparable and one noncomparable personality characteristic as evaluated by psychologists.

Factor analyses were then conducted in order to elicit the underlying structure of assessors' judgments regarding the 16 final attribute ratings based on behavioral observations. Confirmatory and traditional factor analyses were performed to test the appropriateness of the *a priori* four-factor model of assessor ratings corresponding to the categories of attributes defined by the organization.

The results of these various analyses were as follows:

Levels of internal consistency Table 5.1 presents the means, standard deviations, and correlations among the assessment center attributes. Alpha coefficients of the subsets of attributes in each of the four *a priori* categories reveal consistently high levels of internal consistency: .87 for Managerial Skills, .74 for Communication, .76 for Work Values, and .79 for Interpersonal Skills.

Correlations of ratings with tests and with psychologists' evaluations Table 5.2 displays the correlations of assessors' ratings with comparable and noncomparable tests, and Table 5.3 the correlations of assessors' ratings with comparable and noncomparable evaluations by psychologists. Average correlations were computed after making the r to Z transformation; the statistical significance of the difference of the averages with t tests was then determined.

The results provide considerable support for construct validity. Table 5.2 shows that for six of the nine comparisons with tests, the correlations of assessors' ratings with comparable sets of test measures were higher (p<.05) than the correlations with noncomparable sets. For example, assessors' ratings of routine problem solving correlated at an average .28 with tests of general intelligence, creativity, and mechanical ability, but only .00 with tests of spatial perception, accuracy of perception, writing ability, oral ability, and graphical ability.

In more general terms, the findings reveal the assessors' judgments about most attributes to be logically related to cognitive test performance. For example, assessments of routine and complex problem solving are related to test measures of logic, creativity, and mechanical ability. The latter test is particularly relevant in the field of manufacturing, where this study was conducted. Similarly, the researchers found assessment of writing, oral, and interpersonal communication skills to be related to test measures of language mastery, oral ability, and logic.

From Table 5.3, it can be seen that for five of the seven comparisons with psychologists' evaluations, assessors' ratings correlated higher with comparable sets of measures (p<.05) than with noncomparable sets. For example, assessors' ratings of standards for high performance show a correlation of .42 with psychologists' evaluations of perseverance and dedication, but only .06 with psychologists' evaluations of creativity, maturity and stability, independence, and energy level. Again, the assessments of most attributes were found to be related to relevant psychological evaluations based on the background interview and personality test scores. For instance, the raters' assessments of standards for high performance and organizational identification are related to perseverance and dedication, and their assessments of reliability and openness are related to evaluations of maturity and emotional stability.

These results suggest that the assessors' judgments about performance on management attributes were based on separate and relevant constructs as measured by independent assessment techniques. Both tests and psychologists' evaluations provide confirmation of these judgments.

Notwithstanding these impressive findings, the ratings on several assessment center attributes fail to demonstrate the predominant pattern of convergent and discriminant validity with tests or psychologists' evaluations.

Table 5.1   Means, standard deviations, and correlations of assessment center dimensions

	Mean	SD	1	2	3	4	5	6	7	8	9	10	11	12	13	14	15	16
1 Planning and organizing	3.29	.96	—															
2 Routine problem solving	3.17	.91	.53	—														
3 Complex problem solving	2.66	.95	.69	.62	—													
4 Activating others	3.04	.99	.35	.68	.47	—												
5 Decision making	3.10	.91	.53	.57	.57	.59	—											
6 Meeting facilitation	2.58	.94	.43	.51	.43	.58	.55	—										
7 Written communication	3.59	1.07	.64	.46	.63	.30	.45	.48	—									
8 Oral communication	4.01	1.00	.43	.39	.54	.49	.43	.51	.60	—								
9 Standards for high performance	3.73	1.05	.25	.32	.19	.45	.31	.19	.17	.17	—							
10 Reliability	3.69	.94	.30	.29	.32	.20	.22	.12	.21	.15	.47	—						
11 Following instructions	3.99	1.00	.09	.02	.00	.01	-.04	-.19	-.01	-.04	.39	.40	—					
12 Organizational identification	3.73	.95	.01	.03	-.04	.04	-.09	-.03	-.08	-.10	.37	.28	.48	—				
13 Interpersonal relations	3.48	.96	.12	.30	.25	.39	.16	.38	.14	.24	.05	.20	.02	.25	—			
14 Openness and tolerance	3.28	1.06	.08	.23	.21	.23	.04	.22	.06	.13	.03	.29	.13	.25	.65	—		
15 Teamwork	3.47	1.00	.21	.43	.21	.61	.31	.34	.18	.24	.58	.33	.13	.29	.46	.46	—	
16 Behavioral flexibility	2.90	1.00	.35	.48	.46	.51	.37	.43	.31	.39	.16	.15	-.11	.07	.45	.44	.48	—

Note: N from 298 to 382; at p < .05, critical value = .10.

Table 5.2 **Correlations of assessors' ratings with comparable and noncomparable tests (N = 49)**

Assessors' Ratings	Comparable Test[a]	r	Noncomparable Test[b]	r
Planning and organizing	Logic	-.04	Spatial perception	-.18
			Accuracy of perception	-.18
			Ability to work fast	-.14
			Numerical ability	.04
			Language mastery	-.03
			Writing ability	-.12
			Oral ability	-.17
			General knowledge	.22
			Creativity	.05
			Basic math functions	.07
			Graphical ability	-.02
			Mechanical ability	.02
			M =	**-.04**
Routine problem solving	General intelligence	.11	Spatial perception	.06
	Creativity	.30*	Accuracy of perception	.02
	Logic	.34		
	Mechanical ability	.36*	Writing ability	-.03
	M =	.28[c]	Oral ability	-.03
			Graphical ability	.02
			M =	**.00**
Complex problem solving	General intelligence	.13	Spatial perception	-.03
	Creativity	.24	Accuracy of perception	.04
	Logic	.51*	Ability to work fast	-.05
	Mechanical ability	.33*	Language mastery	.13
	M =	.30[c]	Writing ability	.15
			Oral ability	.04
			Basic math functions	.28*
			Graphical ability	.03
			M =	**.07**
Activating others	Oral ability	.05	General intelligence	-.12
			Spatial perception	-.14
			Accuracy of perception	-.04
			Ability to work fast	-.07
			Numerical ability	-.16
			Writing ability	-.12
			General knowledge	.09
			Logic	.08
			Basic math functions	.19
			Graphical ability	-.07

Table 5.2 cont'd

Assessors' Ratings	Comparable Test[a]	r	Noncomparable Test[b]	r
			Mechanical ability	.01
			M =	-.03
Decision making	General intelligence	.26	Spatial perception	-.26
	Logic	.22	Ability to work fast	-.14
		M = .24[c]	Numerical ability	-.18
			Language mastery	.02
			Writing ability	-.13
			Oral ability	-.31*
			Creativity	.09
			Basic math functions	.19
			Graphical ability	-.09
			Mechanical ability	-.07
			M =	-.09
Meeting facilitation	Oral ability	.08	Spatial perception	-.05
	Language mastery	.28*	Accuracy of perception	.15
		M = .18	Ability to work fast	.15
			Numerical ability	-.11
			Writing ability	.11
			General knowledge	.09
			Creativity	-.27*
			Logic	.31*
			Basic math functions	.22
			Graphical ability	.16
			Mechanical ability	.07
			M =	-.06
Written communication	Language mastery	.53*	Spatial perception	.19
	Writing ability	.48*	Accuracy of perception	.14
	Oral ability	.40*	Ability to work fast	.13
	Logic	.51*	Numerical ability	.12
		M = . 48[c]	Creativity	.27*
			Basic math	.29*
			Graphical ability	.17
			Mechanical ability	.34*
			M =	.21
Oral communication	Language mastery	.61*	Spatial perception	.06
	Oral ability	.10	Accuracy of perception	.22
	Logic	.48*	Ability to work fast	-.03
		M = .40c	Numerical ability	.15
			Creativity	.24

Table 5.2 cont'd

Assessors' Ratings	Comparable Test[a]	r	Noncomparable Test[b]	r
			Basic math	.18
			Graphical ability	.32*
			Mechanical ability	.16
			M =	.21
Interpersonal relations	Language mastery	.13	Spatial perception	-.01
	Oral ability	.10	Accuracy of perception	.02
	Logic	.43*	Ability to work fast	.02
	M = .22[c]		Numerical ability	-.09
			General knowledge	-.11
			Creativity	.25
			Basic math	.11
			Graphical ability	.18
			Mechanical ability	-.07
			M =	-.01

[a] Correspondence of constructs measured by assessors and test.
[b] Lack of correspondence of constructs measured by assessors and test.
[c] Correlation is higher ($p < .01$) than average correlation for noncomparable tests.
* $p < .05$.s

Table 5.3 Correlations of assessors' ratings with comparable and noncomparable assessments by psychologists (N = 382)

Assessors Ratings	Comparable Evaluation by Psychologists[a]	r	Noncomparable Evaluation by Psychologists[b]	r
Activating others	Initiative and willingness to take on challenges	.44*	Independence	.43*
			Career ambitions	.27*
	Energy level	.38*	M =	.35
	M =	.41		
Meeting facilitation	Assertiveness	.37*[c]	Energy level	.32*
			Perseverance & dedication	.00
			Creativity	.17*
			M =	.16
Standards for high performance	Perseverance and dedication	.42*[c]	Creativity	-.11*
			Maturity and stability	.17*
			Independence	.20
			Energy level	-.00
			M =	.16

Table 5.3 cont'd

Assessors Ratings	Comparable Evaluation by Psychologists[a]	r	Noncomparable Evaluation by Psychologists[b]	r
Reliability	Maturity and stability	.32*	Independence	.11*
	Perseverance and dedication	.35*	Energy level	.02
	M =	.33[c]	Creativity	.21*
			Career ambitions	.12*
			Assertiveness	.09
			Initiative and willingness to take on challenges	.03
			M =	**.10**
Organizational identification	Perseverance and dedication	.49*[c]	Assertiveness	-.23*
			Creativity	-.16*
			Energy level	-.06
			Independence	-.26*
			Maturity and stability	-.24*
			Initiative	-.10*
			M =	**-.09**
Openness and tolerance of others	Maturity and stability	.41*[c]	Independence	.13*
			Energy level	.05
			Creativity	.25*
			Career ambitions	-.01
			Assertiveness	.06
			Initiative	-.04
			Perseverance and dedication	.38*
			M =	**.06**
Behavioral flexibility	Creativity	.18*	Energy level	.21*
			Assertiveness	.18*
			Perseverance	.12*
			Initiative	.23*
			M =	**.19**

[a]   Correspondence of constructs measured by assessors and psychologists.
[b]   Lack of correspondence of constructs measured by assessors and psychologists.
[c]   Correlation is higher ($p < .01$) than average correlation for noncomparable evaluations.
* $p < .05$.s

Thornton et al. suggest that such failures are due primarily to the lack of correlation between a given test or evaluation and the supposedly comparable attribute, which may stem from the inadequacy of the tests to tap such attributes as planning and organizing, the ability to activate people, and behavioral flexibility.

The final step in the investigation was to perform both confirmatory and traditional factor analyses (McArdle, 1996) on the correlation matrix of the 16 attributes rated by the assessors (Table 5.1). For the confirmatory factor analysis (CFA), a model with four uncorrelated factors corresponding to the four categories of attributes listed above was used, with each attribute loaded on one, and only one, factor. The Goodness of Fit Index (.71) was found to be smaller than the conventional standard, and the Root Mean Square Residual (.16) larger than the conventional standard for Goodness of Fit, indicating that this particular categorization scheme does not provide a good fit with the data. Thus the CFA suggests that the assessors were imposing a somewhat different structure on their ratings than the one proposed by the *a priori* categories.

Traditional factor analysis using a principal axis extraction with varimax rotation was employed to examine three-, four-, and five factor solutions in an attempt to determine the structure present in the assessors' judgments. An eigenvalue greater than one was used as the criterion for retaining factors. The residual correlation matrix indicated that the four-factor solution reproduced the original data most accurately: only 15 per cent of the residuals are greater than 0.05, and the solution accounts for 60 per cent of the variability in the data. Moreover, the squared multiple correlations for the factors (ranging from .83 to .88) reveal that they are internally consistent and well-represented by the variables. The four-factor solution also defines the variables reasonably well, as evidenced by the commonalities (ranging from 0.35 for organizational identity to 0.86 for performance standards).

Although the researchers also examined the results of an oblique rotation, the factor matrix from the orthogonal rotation was deemed to provide a better simple structure and greater ease of interpretation of the factors. Table 5.4 displays the four factors, the loadings and commonality of each variable, and the percentage of variance accounted for by each factor. Variables are grouped and ordered by the magnitude of their loading (from high to low, down to .45) on each factor.

The four factors correspond with the *a priori* categories in some ways but not in others. The factor loadings do produce evidence to support the presence of a managerial skills cluster. As predicted, this factor consists of planning and organizing, routine problem solving, complex problem solving, decision making, and meeting facilitation. However, activating others does not load as highly as anticipated. On the other hand, although written communication and oral communication were expected to load on a distinct factor, both attributes emerged as components of the managerial skills factor.

Table 5.4   Factor loading: Commonalities (h^2) and percentage of variance for principal axis factors extraction and varimax rotation for 16 dimensions rated by assessors in an Israeli assessment center (N = 382)

| | *Factors* | | | | |
	Managerial dimension	Leader-ship skills	Inter-personal skills	Work values	H^2
Complex problem solving	**.83**	.09	.16	.07	.73
Planning and organizing	**.79**	.07	.01	.17	.66
Written communication	**.79**	.03	.02	.03	.62
Decision making	**.63**	.42	.00	- .03	.57
Routine problem solving	**.60**	.43	.20	.07	.59
Oral communication	**.62**	.21	.14	-.07	.45
Meeting facilitation	**.54**	.30	.26	-.17	.53
Activating others	.42	**.74**	.24	-.01	.78
Teamwork	.13	**.65**	.39	.21	.65
Standards for high performance	.13	**.64**	-.15	.04	.86
Openness and tolerance	.05	.04	**.85**	.21	.76
Interpersonal relations	.13	.19	**.76**	.07	.63
Behavioral flexibility	.38	-.33	**.48**	-.05	.50
Following instructions	.03	.13	-.03	**.72**	.52
Reliability	.25	.25	.14	**.58**	.44
Organizational identification	.10	.00	.19	**.55**	.35
Percentage of variance	39.10	11.90	8.70	5.40	

Note: Loadings of .45 or larger are printed in boldface to facilitate interpretation.

In addition, the dimensions activating others, teamwork, and standards for high performance loaded on a factor that appears to represent leadership skills. Finally, the two remaining hypothesized factors are also supported by the factor analysis, with openness and tolerance, interpersonal relations, and behavioral flexibility loading on a factor representing interpersonal skills, and following instructions, reliability, and organizational identification loading on a work values factor.

The analyses of the final attribute ratings in this assessment center program thus produced considerable evidence of construct validity. First, the ratings on the 16 attributes correlated with independent measures of comparable constructs measured both by ability tests, and by psychologists' assessments that were based on interviews and personality test scores. Secondly, although confirmatory factor analysis indicated that the structure of assessors' final attribute ratings did not fit the *a priori* categories, traditional factor analysis yielded meaningful groupings that largely conformed to most of these categories. The factors of managerial skills, interpersonal skills, and work values emerged and contained nearly all of the predicted attributes. A fourth factor, not suggested by the original categories, related to leadership attributes. Although this configuration does not match the hypothesized factors precisely, the results reflect much more than a single general halo, and clearly reveal meaningful groups of attributes.

This study may have produced positive results by virtue, at least in part, of the behavioral reporting method, in which the assessors observe behaviors in exercises and share these observations with each other, but do not rate individual attributes after each separate exercise. Thornton et al. (1997) suggest that the combination of managers and psychologists working together as assessors (see below) may also have provided unique perspectives on the assessees' performance.

The evidence of the construct validity of the overall attribute ratings thus argues for the use of the behavioral reporting method. The results obtained here, in conjunction with evidence from other assessment center studies employing the same reporting method (Bray and Grant, 1966; Shore et al., 1990), stand in sharp contrast to the findings that emerge from studies of assessment centers conducted by means of the within-exercise technique. The latter have generally failed to establish the discriminant validity of within-exercise attribute ratings by single assessors after observation of single exercises.

The conclusions to be drawn from this and supporting research, however, are not entirely clear-cut. Dugan (1988) found that even well-trained assessors may not use many dimensions in arriving at final overall assessment ratings, and that factor structures may not conform to *a priori* clusters. There is also some indication in the literature of changes in inter-judge reliability before and after case discussions between assessors. Before discussion, median inter-judge reliability across dimensions falls below satisfactory levels, with specific figures ranging from 0.50 (Tziner and Dolan, 1982) to 0.67 (Schmitt, 1977) and 0.76 (Borman, 1982). However, reliability appears to improve remarkably after assessors have discussed individual candidates' performances, with coefficients of 0.80 or higher recurring consistently (Sackett and Dreher, 1982; Thornton and Byham, 1982; Tziner and Dolan, 1982; Tziner, 1984).

The changes in reliability reported in these studies may, of course, reflect simple artifactual effects of conformity and group pressure. However, we should not overlook the possibility that the differences may also reflect some of the more basic judgmental biases that assessors exhibit. For example, each assessor may collect different kinds of information for given subjects, or evaluate them differently as a result of *a priori* disparities in interpreting a dimension. Alternatively, differential placement, cue perception, or allocation of attention, may all lead to discrepancies in the observations collected. The higher reliabilities obtained after discussion may therefore simply reflect the fact that only by combining data and perceptions can the assessing team arrive at a comprehensive collective image.

Another negative trend affecting reliability is the moderate level of intercorrelations found among the ratings of the various exercises performed by the same candidates. Turnage and Muchinsky (1984) found an average correlation of 0.91 between dimension ratings and the overall assessment rating. This may point to an underlying, common structural component, somewhat similar to Spearman's G. On the other hand, the result may be evidence of undesirable appraisal biases, such as the halo effect or the carryover of judgments, which may cause uncorrelated factors to appear related. Although the former possibility might be considered a theoretical issue deserving of greater attention, the latter artifact can be seen as a methodological problem that must be redressed.

Overall Assessment Ratings (OAR)

The evaluation process in assessment centers usually ends with an overall assessment rating (OAR), best described as the consensus reached by a group of assessors that represents the likelihood of a candidate performing successfully in a position for which he or she has been tested. This overall rating has generally been shown to exhibit a reasonably high criterion-related validity and higher correlations with organizational success criteria than those obtained from ratings on specific dimensions (see below). Direct contamination of this assessment can be avoided if those senior personnel responsible for the ultimate decisions regarding employee advancement, or those to whom the candidates will be responsible, are kept completely ignorant of all of the assessment information gathered.

An example of the utility of the OAR is provided by Tziner's (1984) study of 102 female soldiers accepted for officer training, after first having been evaluated in an assessment center. Several predictor scores were examined, including peer-rating, a composite score of situational exercise ratings, assessor consensus ratings, and intelligence scores. These were validated against performance in training. Sixty-seven of those who successfully completed the course were appraised one year later. The validity coefficients clearly revealed that of all the predictors, OAR alone significantly predicted performance as officers.

Despite its usefulness, the process of summing up individual assessment dimensions to produce overall assessment ratings is called into question by an empirical finding reported by Sackett and Hakel (1979). In their study, the regression of OAR on dimension ratings for a given assessor and for assessor teams revealed that a small subset of dimensions was sufficient to explain the vast majority of variances (namely: leadership, organizing and planning, and decision making). The remaining dimensions added only minutely to the prediction of OAR. Tziner (1984) reports findings of a similar nature. These results cast doubt on the manner in which assessors draw all dimensions into their summative considerations, as well as suggesting that it might be possible to drop some dimensions from the analysis.

In contrast, Thornton and Byham (1982) argue against dropping dimensions on a number of counts. First, at the statistical level they note that regression analyses are based on linear relationships. However, they propose that if the dimensions have a curvilinear association with OAR, their importance may well be underestimated. Secondly, even if the dimensions contribute little to the prediction of OAR, they may still be important factors contributing to the predictive validity of these scores. Finally, they contend that while laggard dimensions may be of little significance to prediction per se, they may have important diagnostic value and may allow for accurate and useful feedback to the assessees once observations have been concluded.

When viewed as a whole, the differing empirical results suggest that the questions of the reliability of process outcomes and the way in which varying outcomes should be taken into consideration, are still far from resolved. In many cases, inconsistencies appear to be linked to deeper issues related to our limited understanding of the judgmental processes at work in the assessment situation. Among the many avenues of future research, therefore, it might be wise to direct particular attention to what could be labeled the dynamics of impression formation.

Predictive Validity

For many, the central issue of assessment centers is their predictive validity. Do assessment center methods, based on behavioral sampling, really predict a person's later performance on the job? Since the answer to this question is so crucial, it is no wonder that a substantial number of reviews appear in the literature (i.e., Cohen, Moses, and Borman, 1974; Sackett and Dreher, 1982; Thornton and Borman, 1982; Tziner and Dolan, 1982; Konz, 1988; Outcalt, 1988). Huck (1977) reviewed almost fifty studies, while in the same year, Klimoski and Strickland (1977) were still able to relate to additional investigations of this critical issue. The latter review revealed a median 0.40 correlation coefficient between overall assessment ratings and such criteria as career progress, salary advance, supervisor ratings, and evaluations of potential progress. Thornton and Byham (1982), and Gaugler et al. (1987) arrived at equally positive estimations of predictive validity based on the latest findings available to them.

Positive results notwithstanding, questions still remain regarding the evaluation of predictive validity itself. The difficulties relate primarily to issues such as the appropriateness of the performance criteria employed, the possible contamination of assessment and performance, and the time lapse between assessment and job performance. Tziner (1994), for example, notes that most of the existing research has employed either contaminated criteria, such as career progress (Moses and Boehm, 1975) or salary progress (Bray and Grant, 1966; Mitchel, 1975), or subjective criteria, such as supervisor ratings (Tziner, 1984; Outcalt, 1988). As McEvoy and Beatty (1989) remark, the contamination results from the fact that assessment center evaluations are often employed to determine promotion and other administrative decisions. Similarly, Thornton and Byham (1982) maintain that supervisor ratings manifest considerable limitations, among them leniency, halo effects, and range restriction errors. Criticisms have also been leveled at the procedure of using overall assessment ratings and their summation by mechanical/statistical means, in contrast to clinical-judgmental methods.

Performance criteria and subjectivity As noted above, research findings indicate that overall assessment ratings predict some criteria better than other assessment techniques. In particular, they appear to predict promotion more efficiently than do actual performance ratings (Sackett and Dreher, 1982; Thornton and Byham, 1982; Tziner, 1990). In other words, assessors at the center may be judging promotability, rather than competence or efficacy. This means that they do not identify the candidates with the highest real potential so much as those individuals that the organizational decision-makers are more likely to promote.

Early prediction of organizational success is not necessarily a negative phenomenon; indeed, there may be great value in the early identification of candidates with high promotional potential. Nevertheless, many organizations turn to assessment centers precisely because they are dissatisfied with internal promoting procedures and wish to employ more objective evaluations of competence.

Moreover, the awkward potential dependence between OAR scoring and promotion might engender a situation in which favorable evaluations cause supervisors to perceive the candidates receiving them more positively, subsequently influencing their recommendations for promotion. This might be seen as a type of self-fulfilling prophecy which, in common with other contamination patterns, tends to lead to artifactual overestimation of predictive success. Support for the existence of a process of this sort, referred to as 'direct criteria contamination' (Klimoski and Brickner, 1987), was found by Turnage and Muchinsky (1984), who demonstrated that OAR scores were more likely than rating of on-the-job performance to predict promotion to the position of foreman. In fact, as McEvoy and Beatty (1989) also note, most assessment center research has been conducted on operational centers 'deliberately designed to aid in determining promotions or arriving at other administrative decisions' (Tziner, Ronen, and Hacohen, 1993, p. 226).

Klimoski and Strickland (1977) identify a parallel form of assessor contamination, 'indirect (subtle) criterion contamination', which they maintain has led to exaggerated claims of the validity of assessment center procedures. The researchers contend that assessment center staff draw on their knowledge of 'what it takes to get ahead' in the organizations whose candidates they observe, thus leading to the 'perpetuation of the inbreeding process ... instead of injecting new blood into the organization' (Tziner, Ronen, and Hacohen, 1993, p. 227). This type of contamination thus derives from the fact that job performance ratings (or job promoting decisions) are the very same criterion measures as used in the validation of assessment centers.

Dunnette and Borman (1979) and Turnage and Muchinsky (1984) independently point to evidence of the inflating effects of subtle criterion contamination on prediction. The former observe that overall assessment rating in assessment centers correlates more highly with organizational success criteria than do ratings on specific dimensions, while the latter report lower average validity coefficients for dimension ratings than for overall ratings. Their finding that OARs predict measures of organizational success better than do ratings of specific assessment dimensions indicates that the overall assessment ratings are probably affected by factors linked to measures of organizational success (i.e., indirect criterion contamination), which are not reflected in the specific dimension ratings.

An additional source of 'contamination' may relate to the type of assessor responsible for the observation and assessment of candidates. Gaugler et al.'s (1987) meta-analysis found evidence that assessment centers employing psychologists as assessors provide significantly more valid outcomes than those employing managers in this capacity. They also demonstrate that the combination of managers and psychologists working together as assessors produces overall assessment ratings with greater predictive validity than is the case when managers alone serve as assessors. These findings run counter to the entrenched view that managers are better equipped to interpret the meaning of behaviors exhibited by assessees because of their more intimate knowledge of the requirements of managerial success. Results of this sort may have led Tziner, Ronen, and Hacohen (1993) to conclude that 'studies of assessment centers should be designed in such a way that each team of assessors consists of outside psychologists together with managers from the organization'. Moreover, they contend that 'use should also be made of criterion measures less susceptible to the policy-capturing phenomenon' (p. 236).

In their seminal investigation, Tziner et al. (1993) add to the understanding of these issues and clearly illustrate the interplay of the various factors operating in the assessment process. One of the research objectives in their study was the examination of the predictive validity of assessment outcomes, utilizing two uncontaminated criterion measures and comparing overall assessment ratings with dimension ratings. In addition, the research design included a long-term test of validity which, besides being of intrinsic interest, also provided a further tool by which light could be shed on the meaning of the results.

In this study of 329 assessees in a large business corporation, psychologists and high-level managers independently formulated 18 assessment ratings, consensus ratings on the same dimensions, and overall assessment ratings. The superiors of the 240 assessees who were eventually promoted then appraised their performance on two uncontaminated criterion measures over a period of four years.

For both psychologists and high-level managers, multiple regression analysis demonstrated a long-term (but somewhat declining) validity for the assessment center. However, no consistent pattern of significant differences was discerned between the predictive validities of the two groups as assessors. Tziner et al. suggest that the choice between psychologist or manager depends on both the criterion measure by which the assessment center is to be validated, and the degree to which either of these categories is more likely to tap the underlying essence of the criterion measure (because of the types of behavioral cues, incidents, and qualities to which they need to attend). In a certain way, this proposition resembles Sackett, Zedeck, and Fogli's (1988) statement with respect to measures of typical and maximum job performance, namely, that each criterion proves to be better forecasted by predictions of a different kind.

Following Klimoski and Brickner (1987), the results also demonstrate a possible effect of indirect (subtle) contamination that may have affected validities even at the dimensional level. Rather than conducting the assessment along all dimensions and following the weighting scheme created at the center, the assessors may have acted in a policy-capturing capacity when according more primacy and attention to those dimensions perceived as strongly determining either performance or potential ratings on the job. This possibility is further substantiated by the fact that only 50 per cent of the OAR variance could be accounted for by the consensus ratings on the dimensions ($R = 0.71$).

An alternative interpretation is also possible if the modest stability indicated by the moderate test-retest reliabilities of both criterion measures over time are considered. This would be to attribute the trend of decrease in validity over time to the dynamic nature of the criteria (Ghiselli and Haire, 1960). Ghiselli and Haire posit that as we move farther away from the assessment process, the criteria for successful performance change as a result of factors such as shifts in customer demands, the need to contend with new competitors, and/or alterations in government regulations that affect the feasibility of financial transactions. Accordingly, the policy captured by assessors at the assessment time (what has been referred to as indirect contamination and may arguably have guided their evaluation process) becomes less and less valid as we distance ourselves from that event. This could thus lead to the lowering over time of the predictive validities of the predictions and assessments derived in the assessment center. It is also plausible that the shifting relations among dimension ratings and criteria over time might be ascribed to the relatively low reliability estimates for dimension ratings (median = 0.57).

Regardless of the extent to which it may have affected individual assessment dimension ratings, subtle criterion contamination can undoubtedly be detected in the overall assessment rating when it is correlated with the rating of potential for upper levels of management. While the predictive validity of OAR for the performance criterion remained quite stable over time, a striking descending trend was observed in relation to the criterion measure of potential for upper management level, which dropped from r = 0.56 (p<0.01) to 0.36 (p<0.01).

This result is in line with the findings of Dunnette and Borman (1979) and Turnage and Muchinsky (1984) reported above, which indicate the superiority of overall assessment ratings over specific dimension ratings in assessment centers, possibly because the overall ratings are more likely to be influenced by factors linked to success in the company, yet not reflected in the individual assessment dimensions. Tziner et al.'s (1993) results, though consistent with this contention, lend only partial support to it, as this effect was not replicated in relation to the second criterion measure, 'overall performance effectiveness rating'. It is possible, however, that the above reasoning applies predominantly to generic criteria, such as the rating of promotion potential, and may be less likely to apply to the more concrete appraisal of criteria directly related to job performance, such as overall performance rating. Furthermore, on statistical grounds, we cannot exclude the possibility that the much higher mean and smaller standard deviation of the overall performance criterion (as compared with the potential criterion) may have restrained the magnitude of the predictive coefficients of the former.

The subjective nature of supervisor ratings is also well-documented (Thornton and Byham, 1982). The issues here, including leniency, halo effects, and range bias restriction, may similarly induce errors in testing the validity of the assessment. These errors are further exacerbated by the tendency of researchers to average supervisor ratings, although these individuals may hold widely divergent views of success. The error and vagary introduced by this averaging is highlighted by Schmidt et al. (1984), who report low correlations between different supervisors assessing the same worker (0.20 to 0.40).

From this discussion, we might conclude that subjective job performance rating is simply a poorer methodological index of job effectiveness than objective data relating to promotion, such as transfers and discharges. Sackett (1982) even argues that, as a rule, advancement measures such as position level achieved or wage change should be used as validation criteria instead of measures of actual performance. Indeed, the majority of assessment center validation studies have in fact employed 'objective' criteria, such as advancement or salary growth. In a long-term study of the predictability of managerial success, for example, Tziner et al. (1994) utilized the 'hard data' criterion of monetary bonuses as one of the criteria against which the predictors were assessed (albeit without success, since not one of the predicting measures was significantly valid for this criterion). Such criteria, however, may well be construed as violating the true notion of behavioral consistency underlying the use of assessment centers as a staffing method. Wernimont and Campbell (1968), for instance, maintain categorically that 'for the consistency notion to be consistent, the measures to be predicted must also be measures of behavior. For example, it would be something less than consistent to use a behavior sample to predict such criteria as salary progression, organizational level achieved, or sub-unit production' (p. 373).

This kind of inconsistency naturally creates theoretical problems in respect to our understanding of how assessment centers work, so that research seeking to demonstrate a point-by-point correspondence between behaviors during and after selection would be highly desirable. Significant correlations of this nature would not only lend increased credibility to the theoretical underpinnings of assessment centers, but would also help to alleviate concerns over criterion contamination, a problem continually overshadowing the interpretation of predictive success.

Timing

Contamination also ties in with another difficulty, that of timing. Over what time period are predictions to be made? If criteria are collected shortly after assessment, candidates may not have had sufficient chance to display their potential. Yet if too much time has elapsed, many extraneous factors will have begun to affect their performances. This issue of optimal timing between the assessment and prediction of collected criteria warrants additional research attention.

As we have seen, studies such as that conducted by Tziner, Ronen, and Hacohen (1993) on promoted candidates in a large business corporation have shown a decrease in validity over time, which has been attributed to the dynamic nature of the criteria (Ghiselli and Haire, 1960). This naturally results in a concomitant lowering over time of the predictive validities of the predictions and assessments derived in the assessment center. Nevertheless, Tziner et al. (1993) conclude that, on the whole, their study demonstrates the long-term validity of assessment center predictions when two uncontaminated criterion measures are used in an organizational setting. In fact, the OAR validity coefficients obtained, despite not being corrected for range restriction and criterion unreliability, closely resembled the figures commonly reported for North American or British assessment centers (e.g., Anstey, 1977; Gaugler et al., 1987; Feltham, 1988), although the study was conducted elsewhere.

Another four-year follow-up study of high level managers in an Israeli corporation (Tziner et al., 1994) found a fluctuation in the magnitude of predictive validity over time for all the predictors employed in the analysis. Although the researchers suspect that it was due to sampling errors, they do not dismiss the possibility that the assessees themselves might also have changed over time, resulting in a concomitant change in the validity of the predicting measures. Indeed, one of the interesting results that had previously emerged from Tziner's (1984) study of female officers during and after training was that, after an interval of one year, only by combining prediction scores statistically and by assigning weights in the regression equation, was it possible to obtain a significant prediction of officer field performance ($R = .34$, $p<.01$).

Finally, the study of the predictive validity over time of two intelligence tests conducted by Petterson and Tziner (1995) in a Canadian manufacturing enterprise found that the predictive ability of the tests was not time-based. However, when job complexity was considered, the validity increased in relation to the complexity of the job.

These studies indicate that while there is some evidence for the long-term validity of both individual predictors and aggregates thereof, the results are clearly not overwhelming. More research is definitely called for, especially in respect to the choice of criterion measures and their careful matching with the predicting measures, as well as to the likely impact of the degree of job complexity and level of management.

Mechanical-statistical vs. clinical-judgmental combination Research findings not only throw light on longitudinal predictions and the problematic issues surrounding predictive criteria, but also on additional difficulties related to the method for combining scores into a predictive index. This question has given rise to a long-standing debate, particularly in regard to the formulation of OAR scores.

There are two opposing schools of thought here, one favoring mechanical-statistical compilation (e.g., Sackett and Hakel, 1979), and the other advocating clinical-judgmental processes (e.g., Thornton and Byham, 1982). Arguments for mechanically derived overall assessment ratings are founded on the premise that the human assessor is a poor integrator of information (e.g., Kaplan and Schwartz, 1975), and therefore a mechanical/standardized process should be used to generate an overall rating which combines the dimensional assessment data both exhaustively and accurately.

Proponents of the judgmental/clinical combination, on the other hand, argue that it is difficult to generate empirically the appropriate cross-validated weights for a mechanical combination, and that the subtleties of managerial performance require attention to complex behavioral nuances that are more amenable to the human integrator than to rote formulae (see Adams and Thornton, 1990). The fact that the literature points consistently to the fact that OARs that are 'clinically' formulated have high predictive validity (Tziner and Dolan, 1982; Borman et al., 1983; Ritchie and Moses, 1983) has often been taken to mean that the clinical-judgmental approach should be preferred. Indeed, Thornton and Borman (1982) take just such a stand.

However, additional research that compares these two data combination techniques has again produced equivocal results. Borman et al. (1983) and Ritchie and Moses (1983), for example, found that clinically formulated OARs have high predictive validity, while Moses (1973) and Huck (1977) found equal predictive validities for the clinical and the mechanical combinations of assessment information, and Mitchel (1975) found virtually no difference.

A number of researchers (Borman, 1982; Sackett and Wilson, 1982; Tziner and Dolan, 1982) have shown that mechanical-statistical procedures can also lead to a successful integration of data, frequently predicting more accurately than clinically-based formulations. We have already seen how the use of regression analysis weights in a study of female officer potential (Tziner, 1984) assisted in the creation of a multiple regression coefficient that provided the only significant predictor, unlike any of the four individual predictor scores. These statistically or 'mechanically' generated validity coefficients are generally higher than the validities of each of the individual ratings and, in particular, higher than comparative procedures of the clinical type, such as consensus ratings.

Nonetheless, Tziner (1984) notes that in this particular study, there was reason to expect a statistical composite score to be more valid, since it combined sources of information that were independent of each other (intelligence scores, peer-rating measures, and assessors' evaluations). Thus, fallacies such as intelligence scores influencing assessors' consensus judgments, which are inherent in the clinical process of combination (Dolan and Roy, 1982) were avoided to some extent. Another contributing factor to the 'success' of the prediction in this study was the well-designed nature of the assessment center, with the situational exercises purpose-made to measure the dimensions required for the role of female officer. The author also suggests that the value of the multiple regression coefficient, $R=.34$ ($p<.01$), might have been even higher had it been corrected for restriction in range. As such, it is argued that the finding also lends support to the conclusion that multi-predictor systems are superior to single predictor schemes (Tziner and Dolan, 1982; Tziner and Dolan, 1985).

In another study, Tziner and Dolan (1982) combined the assessment data, individual exercise ratings, and intelligence scores of potential female military officers using regression analysis weights, resulting in a multiple correlation of .47 (p<.01). This validity coefficient was higher than the validities of each of the overall consensus ratings, which represent clinical combinations of assessment data (r=.47 vs. r=.36 and r=.38, respectively). Similarly, Tziner, Meir, Dahan, and Birati (1994) note in their longitudinal study of candidates for high-level management positions that 'to analyze the utility of the assessment center, we used the predictive validity of the mechanically derived score, as it consistently revealed the highest validity over the four years of study' (p. 239).

Murphy and Davidshofer (1991) contend that the debate has been settled in favor of statistical/mechanical combinations, but, along with Adams and Thornton (1990), they admit there are still grounds to believe in the value of further research comparing the two methods. For this reason, Tziner et al.'s (1994) longitudinal study of candidates for high-level management positions not only compared the predictive abilities of paper-and-pencil tests, assessors' evaluations (on 25 dimensions), and OAR scores, but also specifically compared the validity of two clinically-derived overall assessment scores to that of a mechanically-generated overall score.

The overall assessment ratings consisted of:

OAR-1: a global summary consensus rating agreed on by the assessors for each of the assessees and meant to reflect the overall likelihood of success in high-level management positions in general for 283 assessees (generated on a 2-point Likert scale with 2 denoting suitable and 1 denoting not suitable).

OAR-2: suitability for specific positions of high-level management for 99 of the assessees (formulated on a 5-point Likert scale with 1 denoting very low likelihood of success and 5 very high likelihood of success).

These two overall assessment ratings were considered 'clinical composites'. In addition, an overall 'mechanical composite' was calculated as an equal weights index of the consensus ratings on the twenty-five dimensions. The twenty-five assessment dimensions were clustered into six measures (composites): general intelligence; personality (e.g., emotional stability, stamina, coping with stress, energy level); work values; communication skills; interpersonal interaction abilities; and managerial performance abilities (e.g., problem solving, decision making). (The intercorrelations between the six components [factors] ranged between 0.12 and 0.65.) These factors were scored on a scale from 1 (poor) to 6 (outstanding).

Two criterion measures were used to validate the predicting data: (1) a summary score of performance ratings provided by the immediate supervisor; and (2) the total amount of the yearly bonus allocated to each candidate for his assessed contribution to increased productivity.

Tziner et al. (1994) found that of the three overall scores, only the one derived in a mechanical/statistical fashion displayed superiority in terms of predictive validity over the six measures yielded by the assessment process. While the overall assessment rating of general suitability (OAR-1) proved valid across all four years, it displayed consistently lower validity than the mechanically derived overall assessment score. The latter emerged as the best combination of the assessment data, conforming to results of previous studies and providing further support for the mechanical/statistical method of combining assessment data into an overall assessment score.

As noted, mechanical/statistical derivation helps to overcome inherent deficiencies in human processes of data integration, such as the inability to consider a large number of assessment dimensions simultaneously and integrate them accurately and exhaustively (e.g., Sackett and Hakel, 1979). Tziner et al. (1994) contend that this advantage probably holds true to an even greater extent in the case of the assessment of candidates for intricate positions, such as high-level management.

Despite these findings in favor of the mechanical-statistical compilation of overall scores, the debate surrounding this issue continues to rage. Advocates of the mechanical-statistical technique are often willing to admit that the clinical method may have potential advantages in certain limited instances. The subtleties of performance in higher occupational echelons, for example, may require attention to complex behavioral nuances that are more amenable to clinical insights than to mathematical formulae. Nonetheless, however, doubts are still expressed as a result of the well-known shortcomings of judgmental processes (see: Dolan and Roy, 1982), which would tend to be mitigated by the use of mechanical methods.

In the absence of unequivocal evidence, it seems reasonable to suggest that the best approach would be a combination of the two techniques. Judgmental procedures would seem best suited to the formulation of cross-situational dimensional ratings, as this requires the comparison and contrast of cues over a variety of settings. Statistical-mechanical methods, on the other hand, would appear most suitable for the combination of the resultant dimensional scores into an overall predictive index. Surprisingly enough, this possibility of combining the techniques has not yet been the focus of research, and it remains an option for further study.

In summary, there appears to be support for the predictive validity of assessment center results. This being said, however, a close reading of the literature points to important areas for future development, both empirical and theoretical. Despite the vast literature in the field, there is a strong possibility that renewed attention to the issues of the criteria for success, the criteria for prediction, and the predictive methods themselves would further enhance the efficacy of the assessment center approach.

Traditional Selection Methods Versus Assessment Centers

In order to judge the success of assessment centers, we must take into consideration the efficacy of traditional selection methods. Do some traditional tests predict success better than others? Do some contribute better to overall assessment scores in assessment centers than others? In general, how well do assessment centers compete, for example, with personality inventories, ability tests, internal staff assessments, and the like? In view of the tight economic milieu in which most large companies operate, another question must surely be that of economic payoff: Do the results of center assessments outweigh the costs of operating a battery of expensive tests?

Conventional wisdom suggests that assessment centers compare very favorably indeed with traditional methods. Initial support for this supposition was originally found in Byham's (1977) review of 22 studies, which demonstrated the preferential predictive strength of the assessment center approach. In fact, McNutt (1979) asserts that the most impressive feature of assessment centers is that their predictive validity actually exceeds that of more traditional methods. In contrast, however, Klimoski and Strickland (1981), for example, found that pre-assessment potential ratings were more correlated with later performance ratings than were assessment center scores. In a similar vein, Hinrichs (1969; 1978) found that managerial predictions of future potential based on personal file reviews did a better job of predicting performance one to eight years later than did assessment center methods. Lastly, Gaugler et al. (1987) reported significant yet modest coefficients of validity (around .33) in their meta-analysis of assessment center validity research, a figure 'that falls well within the range of validities found for traditional methods' (Tziner et al., 1994, p. 230). These results clearly challenge the monolithic view of the benefits of the assessment center approach.

As for individual predictors, we have already noted that they fare less well, overall, than multiple predicting measures, and that they are not necessarily consistent in terms of predictive validity across studies. The studies of female officer training by Tziner (1984), Tziner and Dolan (1982), and Tziner and Dolan (1985) attempted to determine which of various predictors significantly predicted success and which most accounted for variance in final aggregate scores. Differentiation was made between success in training and success on-the-job, in this case, performance in the field. Following are some of their more salient results.

Tziner and Dolan (1982): A high multiple correlation (r=.50, p=<.01) was found between assessment center predicting measures and final scores in officer training. This validity was substantially higher than that attained in relation to the same subjects using traditional predictors (e.g. selection interviews). Specifically, paper-and-pencil tests alone yielded a validity coefficient of .40 (accounting for 16 per cent of the variance in performance in officer training), while the inclusion of elements unique to the assessment center procedure (i.e., assessment ratings) increased the multiple correlation to .50, with a squared multiple correlation of .25. Thus a significant increment of a 9 per cent improvement in prediction was gained. Nevertheless, the authors note that from the point of view of utility, this gain is not necessarily sufficient to justify the economic cost of introducing these unique assessment center elements.

Tziner (1984): The situational score and OAR scores, independently, were found to be the most valid predictors in this study of performance in training, while only the OAR scores predicted performance. This investigation also produced impressive evidence of the potential of center-based peer ratings to predict performance in officer training (r=.51; p<.001), although these ratings failed to predict on-the-job performance. The same predictor, however, made no unique contribution to explained variance in performance in training, even though it might be assumed that peers are more likely to be privy to information on aspects of personality and behavior that is not available to assessors.

In contrast, the same study revealed that although none of the intelligence measures as a single predictor related significantly to either of the performance criteria, as a whole they did contribute a unique portion to the explained variance. As the author notes, this occurred only after other components of the assessment center were entered into the regression analysis, indicating the probability that a suppressant effect had to be removed before the contribution of intelligence could emerge. When the contributions of intelligence and consensus measures were compared, however, nearly a measure for measure equivalence was found, leading Tziner to conclude that the center might consider eliminating one of these measures in order to cut costs.

Tziner and Dolan (1985): This study used two samples of female cadets in training in order to allow for cross-validation. Several measures were employed to assess their potential success: a general intelligence score (GIS), a peer nomination score (PNS), a general assessment score of personality fitness to command positions (GASPF), and a predictive-clinical composite score (PCCS) which, by means of clinical judgment, integrated the three previous measures into a single score (with highly satisfactory interjudge reliabilities ranging from .73 to .84).

The first major finding of this study was that the statistical-linear combination of the three predictors (PCCS) yielded a valid and more solid predictive measure of officer success in training than did the clinically obtained GASPF (r=.45 and r=.50 versus r=.28 and r=.26 for samples A and B respectively, both corrected for range restriction). In fact, the multi-predictor selection approach achieved a much higher validity than any of the other alternative selection systems based on only one of the traditional selectors. The peer (sociometric) score emerged as the most valid single predictor (r=.43 for both samples) and, unlike in the previous studies, the intelligence score (GIS) accounted for much of the variance, although it only marginally served as a valid predictor. It is particularly interesting to note that the psychologists' evaluation of personal fitness failed to serve as a serious predictor.

If we move away from the military arena, we may recall Tziner et al.'s (1994) comprehensive longitudinal study in an Israeli corporation, in which final ratings on 25 assessment dimensions were obtained for 382 candidates for high-level management positions. The dimensions were determined by an assessment center process, two overall clinically derived assessment scores, and an overall mechanically derived assessment score. For 49 of the assessees, scores were also available on a battery of paper-and-pencil cognitive tests administered at the pre-employment stage. For all candidates, data were obtained over a period of four years on two criterion measures: standardized supervisor ratings (formulated by supervisors with no knowledge whatsoever of their subordinate's performance in the assessment center); and monetary bonuses. The standardization of the supervisor ratings was employed in order to minimize the biases which commonly affect these evaluations, thus resulting in a measure which could be expected to be of technical superiority to the supervisor ratings ordinarily used in assessment center validation studies.

In this study, too, the intelligence rating formulated in the assessment center and the scores on the cognitive tests were found to be invalid, failing to reach a significant level of prediction over time. The researchers suggest, however, that this finding may reflect either homogeneity among the assessees, or, following Thornton and Byham (1982), the relative lack of importance that general intelligence plays in high-level management situations, in contradistinction to specific communication skills (see: Bass, 1990). In contrast, the personality measure proved valid, a finding not commonly reported in such studies (Tziner and Dolan, 1982; Gaugler et al., 1987; Tziner, 1990), and may also have been related to the demands of high-level management positions. Only modest coefficients of predictive ability were found for the other assessment center predictors (0.20–0.25). However, an economic utility analysis (see Chapter 6) demonstrated a considerable cost-effectiveness for the assessment center program, revealing a saving of over $300,000 in three years.

The advantages of the assessment center approach notwithstanding, the results of all this research can not be ignored. From the earlier studies, Tziner (1990) concludes that carefully designed traditional selection systems may be the preferable solution, especially when a multi-predictor selection approach is used. This view is supported by a meta-analysis based on studies of different samples, in which Hunter and Hunter (1984) found traditional methods (e.g., ability tests) to be no less valid than assessment center ratings. This raises the possibility that a well-designed system of ability tests, biographical data, structured interview evaluations, supervisor ratings, and similar traditional tools may offer an economically satisfactory substitute for the assessment center approach.

In regard to financial outcomes, the gains of assessment centers may also be less significant than was first thought by their proponents. Tziner and Dolan (1982), for example, found that while assessment center ratings were indeed substantially more valid than interview ratings, potential promotion ratings, or even paper-and-pencil ability tests administered by the centers themselves, the statistical difference did not necessarily translate itself into an economically significant return on the greater investment entailed in assessment center techniques.

On the other hand, Tziner et al. (1994) conclude that 'despite the fact that assessment centers are expensive to operate and sometimes they exhibit only a modest predictive validity, they may outperform traditional methods (e.g., cognitive ability tests) in detecting high-level management'. They add, however, that this blanket conclusion should be restricted to candidates for high-level management positions and to supervisor ratings as the criterion measure of successful performance. The first caveat takes on special significance when we recall the possible positive moderating effect of job complexity on the predictive abilities of intelligence tests (Petterson and Tziner, 1995).

Tziner (1990) argues that the specific answer to the question of what kind of measuring systems to use is ultimately dependent on the task at hand. In certain job classifications, the cost of selection error may far outweigh the additional outlay, and rates of prediction error have indeed been shown to be more stable in assessment center tools than in traditional methods (e.g., Thornton and Byham, 1982; Dreher and Sackett, 1983). It could also be argued that the difference in certainty might itself carry a premium far beyond the monetary cost of the specific selection process, although the benefit of the psychological value of greater predictive certainty is not always clear.

In addition, the assessment center situational exercises appear to exhibit more culture fairness than traditional predictors, such as psychometric tests. Goldstein et al. (1998), for example, found that when the cognitive ability test score was statistically removed from the situational exercise scores, none of the evaluation scores exhibited statistically significant differences between Black and White assessees.

Finally, it should be noted that comparisons between methods frequently overlook the possibility that the differing techniques are by no means incompatible, and that two may be better than one. A Canadian study by Slivinski et al. (1979), for instance, demonstrated that the combination of assessment center and traditional methods provided a notable improvement over the predictive success of either method alone. They conclude that financial considerations notwithstanding, both methods should be viewed as complementary parts of a total evaluation package.

In conclusion, it is clear that the comparison of assessment centers and traditional means is far from straightforward. While the conventional wisdom that assessment centers are more valid may be true, the economic benefits are not necessarily viable. In this light, the possibility of integrating assessment content into various types of hybrids continues to remain an avenue for future exploration and analysis.

Postscript

Frequent mention has been made of the large amount of empirical data available on the assessment center approach to job assessment. This section has therefore related to the three major issues of reliability, predictive validity, and comparisons with traditional methods, and as such it is reflective and representative of the major foci of the extensive body of literature. To students of assessment centers, the very number of studies is not surprising. From the start, assessment centers have reflected an empirical and practical attempt to improve the fit between people and their occupations through more efficient methods of selection. This endeavor has been fueled by the debate over the concerns arising from the evaluation of traditional staffing methods.

There have been times, however, when the sheer number of empirical studies has tended to overshadow the central theoretical issues of critical relevance for the improvement of assessment center techniques. Throughout this section, therefore, repeated reference has been made to the basic problems and lacunae in our understanding of theoretical issues, such as the nature of the assessment-making process, the combination of multiple information sources, and the consistency of behavior across settings. The resolution of the empirical problems in this field must surely progress hand in hand with the clarification of these theoretical issues.

One example of the interplay between theory and practice that could be developed relates to the assessments of managerial candidates, most of which have been based mainly on performance dimensions obtained by practically derived job analysis methods. Yet although it is commonly believed that leadership forms a central facet of management success, few attempts have sought to exploit the current knowledge of theories of leadership (e.g., transformational and transactional theories: Bass, 1990) in order to devise more appropriate assessment center devices. The dialectic between empirical and theoretical advances is a recurring theme in all branches of scientific endeavor. Thus, the call to integrate the two approaches represents the recognition that empirical work in the field has advanced far enough to turn assessment from an art into a science. The practical success of assessment centers can only benefit from further developments of this kind.

(8) Integrity and Honesty Tests

Recent years have seen an increase in the use of integrity and honesty tests for personnel selection, a trend attributed to a substantial rise in disruptive employee behaviors at work, including theft, sabotage, malingering, and the sale of professional secrets. It is estimated that these negative behaviors cost employers in the United States an annual average of 70 billion dollars. Consequently, employers are continually seeking methods and instruments with which to assess new employees or veteran workers designated for promotion to positions where counterproductive behaviors may inflict severe and damaging losses. Integrity and honesty tests, which are designed to evaluate predispositions to inappropriate activities in the workplace through a paper-and-pencil device, have therefore gained in popularity (Camara and Scneider, 1994; Sackett and Harris, 1994).

Sackett, Buris, and Callaghan (1989) classify these tests into two broad categories: overt integrity tests and personality-based integrity tests. Overt integrity and honesty tests are designed to directly assess beliefs and attitudes regarding dishonest behavior. Some ask specifically about illegal or dishonest activities, employing questions such as 'Have you ever stolen from your present employer?' The measure derived from this kind of test draws on the assumption that a person with a past history of counterproductive activities is likely to be prone to recidivism.

Personality-based measures aim to predict a broad range of counterproductive behaviors indirectly, by gauging personality traits such as reliability, adjustment, and sociability. Rather than being asked to directly admit past offenses, the testee is instructed to respond to statements such as: 'I feel it is justifiable for an underpaid employee to take home work equipment or materials for personal use.' The assumption here is that a person holding positive attitudes toward deviant behaviors at work will be more susceptible to this kind of behavior than individuals with a lesser inclination of this sort.

A large-scale meta-analysis by Ones (1993) revealed that the true score correlation between various overt tests was 0.45, between personality-based integrity tests 0.70, and between overt and personality-based tests 0.39. The linear composite scores of overt and personality-based tests correlated 0.64, thus lending credence to the assertion that an integrity/honesty construct actually exists.

Accordingly, an integrity composite was calculated and was found to correlate with the Big Five personality dimensions (see above): 0.87 with conscientiousness, 0.78 with agreeableness, and 0.59 with emotional stability. These results further support the construct validity of the integrity measure, a conclusion that has also been documented by Murphy (1993).

Finally, Ones (1993) also found evidence of the predictive validity of the integrity/honesty measure, noting specifically a correlation of 0.41 between job performance and the integrity composite measure. This outcome is reinforced by Ones, Viswesvaran, and Schmidt's (1993) analysis, which demonstrated that integrity tests are predictive of supervisors' overall performance ratings of counterproductive behaviors across situations, jobs, and organizations. These researchers even judge the predictive validity of integrity/honesty tests in relation to the criterion of overall job performance to be higher than that of any organization staffing instrument other than ability tests, situational tests, and job knowledge tests.

No discussion of integrity and honesty testing can ignore the device of lie-detection (the polygraph). This technique is based on the proposition that an individual's attempts to deceive or lie are accompanied by a change in physiological activity. Considerable empirical research has cast serious doubt on the veracity of this assumption. Ney (1988), for example, maintains that an individual may be able to control his or her physiological reactions (such as respiration rate, blood pressure, and skin galvanic reaction) and thereby affect the results of the process of polygraph measurement. These measures have also proved to be unreliable indicators across time and situations, as well as to vary across similar situations for the same individual.

Moreover, Hampson (1988) notes that the basic assumption underlying the use of the polygraph is that 'if a person is dishonest in the test [then] he/she will behave undesirably in life situations. It is assumed that truthfulness and honesty are inherent qualities of behavior. However, half a century's research into behavioral consistency has shown that it is not possible to make highly accurate predictions. The polygraph may or not be a lie-detector, but it could never be a personality detector' (p. 64). No wonder, then, that this unequivocal conclusion has recently found strong support in Iocono and Lykken's (1997) investigation, which once again demonstrates the untenability of the claims for the predictive validity of the polygraph.

References

Adams, S.R. and Thornton, G.C. III (1990). 'The Assessor Judgment Process: A review of Reliability and Validity of Assessment Ratings'. Paper presented at the National Assessment Conference, Minneapolis, Minnesota.

Amalfitano, J.G. and Kalt, N.C. (1977). 'Effect of Eye Contact on the Evaluation of Job Applicants'. *Journal of Employment Counseling*, 14, pp. 46–8.

Amir, Y., Kovarsky, Y. and Sharon, S. (1970). 'Peer Nomination as a Predictor of Multistage Promotions in a Ramified Organization'. *Journal of Applied Psychology*, 54, pp. 462–9.

Anastasi, A. (1982). *Psychological Testing*, 5th edn, New York: Macmillan.

Anastasi, A. (1988). *Psychological Testing*, 6th edn, New York: Macmillan.

Anstey, A. (1977). 'A 30-Year Follow-up of the CSSB Procedure with Lessons for the Future'. *Journal of Occupational Psychology*, 50, pp. 149–59.

Archambeau, D.J. (1979). 'Relationships Among Skill Ratings Assigned in an Assessment Center'. *Journal of Assessment Center Technology*, 2, pp. 7–20.

Arvey, R.D. (1979). 'Unfair Discrimination in the Employment Interview: Legal and Psychological Aspects'. *Psychological Bulletin*, 86, pp. 227–240.

Arvey, R.D. and Campion, J.E. (1982). 'The Employment Interview: A Summary and Review of Recent Research'. Personnel Psychology, 35, pp. 281–322.

Ashton, M. C. (1998). 'Personality and Job Performance: The Importance of Narrow Traits'. *Journal of Organizational Behavior*, 19, pp. 289–303.

Avolio, B.J. (1982). 'Age Stereotypes in Interview Evaluation Contexts'. *Dissertation Abstracts International*, 42, p. 3020B (University Microfilms, nos. 81–29, 504).

Bar-Hillel, M. and Ben-Shakhar, G. (1985). 'The *a priori* Case against Graphology: Methodological and Conceptual Issues'. Unpublished manuscript, Hebrew University.

Barrick, M.R. and Mount, M.K. (1991). 'The Big Five Personality Dimensions and Job Performance'. *Personnel Psychology*, pp. 44, 1–26.

Bass, B.M. (1990). *Bass & Stogdill's Handbook of Leadership: Theory, Research and Managerial Applications*, 3rd edn, New York: Free Press.

Beller, M. and Melamed, E. (1988). 'A Tree Analysis Representation of Psychometric Tests Used for Selection of University Applicants'. In B. Nevo and Y. Cohen (eds), *Selected Topics in Evaluation and Measurement*. Jerusalem: National Institute for Testing and Evaluation, pp. 361–82.

Ben-Shakhar, G., Bar-Hillel, M. and Flug, A. (1986). 'A Validation Study of Graphological Evaluations in Personnel Selection'. In B. Nevo (ed.), *Handbook of Scientific Aspects of Graphology*. Springfield: Charles Thomas.

Berg, I. (1967). *Response Set in Personality Assessment*. Chicago: Aldine.

Bernardin, H.J. and Beatty, R.W. (1984*). Performance Appraisal: Assessing Human Behavior at Work*. Boston: Kent.

Blum, M.L. and Naylor, J.C. (1968). *Industrial Psychology: Its Theoretical and Social Foundations*. New York: Harper.

Borman, W.C. (1982). 'Validity of Behavioral Assessment for Predicting Military Recruiter Performance'. *Journal of Applied Psychology*, 67, pp. 3–9.

Borman, W.C., Eaton, N.K., Bryan, D. and Ross, R.L. (1983). 'Validity of Army Recruiter Behavioral Assessment: Does the Assessor Make a Difference?'. *Journal of Applied Psychology*, 68, pp. 415–419.

Bray, D.W. and Campbell, J.R. (1968). 'Selection of Salesmen by Means of an Assessment Center'. *Journal of Applied Psychology*, 52, pp. 36–41.

Bray, D.W. and Grant, D.L. (1966). 'The Assessment Center in the Measurement of Potential for Business Management'. *Psychological Monographs*, 80, pp. 1–27.

Brush, D.H. and Owens, W.A. (1979). 'Implementation and Evaluation for an Assessment Classification Model for Manpower Utilization'. *Personnel Psychology*, 32, pp. 369–83.

Bycio, P., Alvarez, K.M. and Hahn, J. (1987). 'Situational Specificity in Assessment Center Rating: A Confirmatory Factor Analysis'. *Journal of Applied Psychology*, 72, pp. 463–74.

Byham, W.C. (1977). 'Application of the Assessment Center Method'. In J.L. Moses and W.C. Byham (eds), *Applying the Assessment Center Method*. New York: Pergamon.

Byham, W.C. and Wettengel, C. (1974). 'Assessment Center for Identifying and Developing Management Potential in Government Operations'. *Public Personnel Management*, 3, pp. 352–562.

Caldwell, D.F. and Burger, J.M. (1998). 'Personality Characteristics of Job Applicants and Success in Screening Interviews'. *Personnel Psychology*, 51, pp. 119–36.

Camara, W.J. and Schneider, D.L. (1994). 'Integrity Tests: Facts and Unresolved Issues'. *American Psychologists*, 49, pp. 112–19.

Campion, M., Palmer, D. and Campion, J. (1997). 'A Review of Structure in the Selection Interview'. *Personnel Psychology*, 50, pp. 699–702.

Carlson, R.E. (1971). 'Effect of Interview Information in Altering Valid Impression'. *Journal of Applied Psychology*, 55, pp. 66–72.

Cascio, W.F. (1976). 'Turnover, Bibliographical Data and Fair Employment Practice'. *Journal of Applied Psychology*, 61, pp. 576–80.

Cascio, W.F. and Silbey, V. (1979). 'Utility of Assessment Center as a Selection Device'. *Journal of Applied Psychology*, 64, pp. 107–18.

Cederblom, D. and Loundsbury, J.W. (1980). 'An Investigation of User Acceptance of Peer Evaluation'. *Personnel Psychology*, 33, pp. 567–79.

Cohen, B.M., Moses, J.L. and Byham, W.C. (1974). *The Validity of the Assessment Center: A Literature Review*. Monograph 2. Pittsburg: Development Dimension Press.

Cornelius, E.T., III (1983). 'The Use of Projective Techniques in Personnel Selection'. In K.M. Rowland and G.R. Ferris (eds), *Research in Personnel and Human Resources Management*. Greenwich, CT: JAI Press.

Costa, P.T. Jr and McCrae, R.R. (1988). 'Personality in Adulthood: A Six-Year Longitudinal Study of Self-Reports and Spouse Ratings on the NEO Personality Inventory'. *Journal of Personality and Social Psychology*, 54, pp. 853–63.

Couch, A. and Keniston, K. (1960). 'Yeasayers and Naysayers: Agreeing Response Set as a Personality Variable'. *Journal of Abnormal and Social Psychology*, 60, pp. 151–74.

Crawford, J.E. and Crawford, D.M. (1946). *Small Parts Dexterity*. New York: Psychological Corporation.

Crider, B. (1941). 'The Reliability of Two Graphologists,' *Journal of Applied Psychology*, 25, pp. 323–5.

Cunningham, W.R. (1981). 'Ability Factor Structure Differences in Adulthood and Old Age'. *Multi-variate Behavioral Research*, 16, pp. 3–22.

Currer-Brigs, N. (1971). *Handwriting Analysis in Business: The Use of Graphology in Personnel Selection*. New York: Wiley.

Daily, C.A. (1960). 'The Life History as a Criterion of Assessment'. *Journal of Counseling Psychology*, 7, pp. 20–23.

Davis, K.R. Jr (1984). 'A Longitudinal Analysis of Biographical Subgroups Using Owens Developmental-Integrative Index'. *Personnel Psychology*, 37, pp. 1–14.

Dipboye, R.L. (1992). *Selection Interviews: Process Perspectives*. Cincinnati, OH: South-Western Publishing.

Dipboye, R.L., Fromkin, H.L. and Wilback, K. (1975). 'Relative Importance of Applicant Sex, Attractiveness, and Scholastic Standing in Evaluation of Job Applicant Resumes'. *Journal of Applied Psychology*, 60, pp. 39–43.

Dolan, S. and Roy, D. (1982). *Managerial Selection*. Montreal: University of Montreal.

Dolan, S. and Schuler, R. (1987). *Personnel and Human Resource Management in Canada*. St. Paul, MN: West.

Dougherty, T.W., Ebert, R.J. and Callender, J.C. (1986). 'Policy Capturing in the Employment Interview'. *Journal of Applied Psychology*, 71, pp. 9–15.

Downey, R.G., Medland, F.F. and Yates, L.G. (1976). 'Evaluation of Peer Rating System for Predicting Subsegment Promotion of Senior Military Officers'. *Journal of Applied Psychology*, 61, pp. 206–9.

Dreher, G.F. and Kendall, D.W. (1995). 'Organization Staffing'. In G.R. Ferris, S.D. Rosen and D.T. Barmen (eds), *Handbook of Human Resource Management*. Cambridge, MA: Blackwell.

Dreher, G.F. and Sackett, P.R. (1983). *Perspectives on Employee Staffing and Selection*. Homewood, IL: Irwin.

Dugan, B. (1988). 'Effects of Assessor Training on Information Use'. *Journal of Applied Psychology*, 73, pp. 743–8.

Dunnette, M.D. and Borman, W.C. (1979). 'Personnel Selection and Clarification Systems'. *Annual Review of Psychology*, 30, pp. 477–525.

Eberhardt, B. and Muchinsky, P.M. (1982). 'Biodata Determinants of Vocational Typology: An Integration of Two Paradigms'. *Journal of Applied Psychology*, 67, pp. 714–27.

Feltham, R. (1988). 'Validity of a Police Assessment Center: A 1-19 Year Follow-up'. *Journal of Occupational Psychology*, 61, pp. 129–44.

Finkle, R.D. (1976). 'Managerial Assessment Center'. In M.D. Dunnette (ed.), *Handbook of Industrial and Organizational Psychology*. Chicago: Rand McNally.

Flug, A. (1981). *Reliability and Validity of Graphological Assessment in Personnel Selection*. Unpublished master's thesis, Hebrew University (Hebrew).

Forbes, R.J. and Jackson, P.R. (1980). 'Nonverbal Behavior and the Outcome of Selection Interview'. *Journal of Applied Psychology*, 53, pp. 65–72.

Frederick, C.J. (1965). 'Some Phenomena Affecting Handwriting Analysis'. *Perceptual and Motor Skills*, 20, pp. 211–18.

Galbraith, D. and Wilson, D. (1964). 'Reliability of the Graphoanalytic Approach to Handwriting Analysis'. *Perceptual and Motor Skills*, 19, pp. 615–18.

Gatewood, R.D. and Field, H.S. (1994). *Human Resources Selection*. Fort Worth, TX: Harcourt Brace.

Gaugler, B.B., Rosenthal, D.B., Thornton, G.C. III and Bentson, C. (1987). 'Meta-analysis of Assessment Center Validity'. *Journal of Applied Psychology*, 72, pp. 493–511.

Ghiselli, E.E. (1956). 'Dimensional Problems of Criteria'. *Journal of Applied Psychology*, 40, pp. 1–4.

Ghiselli, E.E. (1966). *The Validity of Occupational Aptitude Tests*. New York: Wiley.

Ghiselli, E.E. and Haire, N. (1960). 'The Validity of Selection Tests in the Light of the Dynamic Character of Criteria'. *Personnel Psychology*, 13, pp. 225–31.

Gifford, R., Ng, C.F. and Wilkinson, M. (1985). 'Nonverbal Cues in the Employment Interview Links between Applicant Quality and Interviewer Judgments'. *Journal of Applied Psychology*, 70, pp. 729–36.

Goldstein, H., Yusko, K.P., Braverman, E.P., Smith, B.D. and Chung, B. (1998). 'The Role of Cognitive Ability in the Subgroup Difference and Incremental Validity of Assessment Center Exercises'. *Personnel Psychology*, 51, pp. 357–74.

Guilford, J.P. (1967). *The Nature of Human Intelligence*. New York: McGraw-Hill.

Guion, R.M. (1991). 'Personnel Assessment, Selection and Placement'. In M.D. Dunnette and L.M. Hough (eds), *Handbook of Industrial and Organizational Psychology*, 2nd edn, Vol. 2. Palo Alto, CA: Consulting Psychologists Press.

Guion, R.M. and Gottier, R.F. (1965). 'Validity of Personality Measures in Personnel Selection'. *Personnel Psychology*, 18, pp. 49–65.

Guthrie, E.R. (1944). 'Personality in Terms of Associative Learning'. In J. McHunt (ed.), *Personality and Behavior Disorders, Vol. 1.* New York: Ronald.

Guttman, L. (1958). 'What Lies Ahead for Factor Analysis?' *Multivariate Behavioral Research*, 16, pp. 411–35.

Guttman, L. and Levy, L. (1991). 'Two Structural Laws for Intelligence'. *Intelligence*, 15, pp. 79–103.

Haefner, J.E. (1977). 'Race, Age, Sex, and Competence as Factors in Employer Selection for the Disadvantaged'. *Journal of Applied Psychology*, 62, pp. 199–202.

Hakel, M.D., Dobmeyer, T.W. and Dunnette, M.D. (1970). 'Relative Importance of Three Content Dimensions in Overall Suitability Ratings of Job Applicants' Resumes'. *Journal of Applied Psychology*, 54, p. 65–71.

Hampson, S.E. (1988). 'What are Truthfulness and Honesty?' In A. Gale (ed.), *The Polygraph Test: Lies, Truth and Science*. London: Sage, pp. 53–64.

Harris, M.M. (1989). 'Reconsidering the Employment Interview: A Review of Recent Literature and Suggestions for Future Research'. *Personnel Psychology*, 42, pp. 691–726.

Hinrichs, J.R. (1969). 'Comparison of "Real Life" Assessments of Managerial Potential with Situational Exercises, Paper-and-Pencil Tests and Personality Inventories'. *Journal of Applied Psychology*, 53, pp. 425–32.

Hinrichs, J.R. (1978). 'An Eight-year Follow-up of a Management Assessment Center'. *Journal of Applied Psychology*, 63, pp. 596–601.

Hinrichs, J.R. and Haanpera, S. (1976). 'Reliability of Measurement in Situational Exercises: An Assessment of the Assessment Center Method'. *Personnel Psychology*, 29, pp. 31–40.

Hofsommer, W., Holdsworth, R. and Seifert, T. (1965). 'Problems of Reliability in Graphology'. *Psychology and Praxis*, 9, pp. 14–24.

Hollander, E.P. (1954). 'Military Research and Industrial Applications'. *Personnel Psychology*, 7, pp. 385–95.

Hollander, E.P. (1965). 'Validity of Peer Nominations in Predicting a Distant Performance Criteria'. *Journal of Applied Psychology*, 49, pp. 434–8.

Hollandsworth, J.G., Kazerlkis, R., Stevens, J. and Dressel, M.E. (1979). 'Relative Contributions of Verbal, Articulative and Nonverbal Communication to Employment Decisions in the Job Interview Setting'. *Personnel Psychology*, 32, pp. 359–67.

Hollenbeck, G.P. (1990). 'The Past, Present and Future of Assessment Centers'. *Industrial and Organizational Psychologist*, 28, pp. 13–17.

Huck, J.R. (1977). 'The Research Base'. In J.L. Moses and W.C. Byham (eds), *Applying the Assessment Center Method*. New York: Pergamon.

Huffcutt, A.I. and Roth, P.L. (1998). 'Racial Group Differences in Employment Interview Evaluations'. *Journal of Applied Psychology*, 83, pp. 179–86.

Huffcutt, A.I. and Woehr, D.J. (1999). 'Further Analysis of Employment Interview Validity: A Quantitative Evaluation of Interviewer-Related Structuring Method'. *Journal of Organizational Behavior*, 20, pp. 549–60.

Hunter, J.E. and Hunter R.F. (1984). 'Validity and Utility of Alternative Predictors of Job Performance'. *Psychological Bulletin*, 96, pp. 72–98.

Iacono, W.G. and Lykken, D.T. (1997). 'The Validity of the Lie Detector: Two Surveys of Scientific Opinion'. *Journal of Applied Psychology*, 82, pp. 426–33.

Jansen, A. (1973). *Validation of Graphological Judgments*. Paris: Mouton.

Janz, T. (1982). 'Preliminary Comparison of Direct versus Behavioral Estimates of the Standard Deviation of Performance in Dollars'. Paper presented at the Annual Meeting of the Academy of Management, New York.

Kaemar, K.M. and Hochwarter, W.A. (1995). 'The Interview as a Communication Event: A Field Examination of Demographic Effects on Interview Outcomes'. *The Journal of Business Communication*, 32, pp. 207–32.

Kaplan, M.F. and Schwartz, S. (eds) (1975). *Human Judgment and Decision Processes*. New York: Academic Press.

Keenan, A. (1977). 'Some Relationships between Interviewers' Personal Feeling about Candidates and their General Evaluation of Them'. *Journal of Occupational Psychology*, 50, pp. 275–83.

Kehoe, J.F., Weinberg, K. and Lawrence, I.M. (1985, August). 'Dimension and Exercise Effects on Work Simulation Ratings'. Paper presented at the meeting of the American Psychological Association, Los Angeles.

Kelderman, H., Mellenbergh, G.J. and Elshout, J.J. (1981). 'Guilford's Facet Theory of Intelligence: An Empirical Comparison of Models'. *Multivariate Behavioral Research*, 16, pp. 37–61.

Kim, J.D. and Mueller, C.W. (1981). *Factor Analysis: Statistical Method and Practical Issues*, 7th edn, Beverly Hills, CA: Sage.

Kimmel, D. and Wertheimer, M. (1966). 'Personality Rating Based on Handwriting Analysis and Clinical Judgment: A Correlation'. *Journal of Projective Techniques*, 30, pp. 177–8.

Kinslinger, H.J. (1966). 'Application of Projective Techniques in Personnel Psychology Since 1940'. *Psychological Bulletin*, 66, pp. 134–49.

Klimoski, R.J. and Brickner, M. (1987). 'Why do Assessment Centers Work? The Puzzle of Assessment Center Validity'. *Personnel Psychology*, 40, pp. 243–56.

Klimoski, R.J. and Strickland, W.J. (1977). 'Assessment Centers: Valid or Merely Prescient?' *Personnel Psychology*, 30, pp. 353–61.

Klimoski, R.J. and Strickland, W.J. (1981). 'A Comparative View of Assessment Centers'. Unpublished manuscript, Ohio State University.

Konz, A.M. (1988). *A Comparison of Dimension Ratings and Exercise Ratings in Assessment Centers*. Unpublished doctoral dissertation, University of Maryland.

Kopelman, R.E. (1986). *Managing Productivity in Organizations: A Practical, People-Oriented Perspective*. New York, McGraw-Hill.

Landy, F.J. and Bates, F. (1973). 'Another Look at Contrast Effects in the Employment Interview'. *Journal of Applied Psychology*, 58, pp. 141–4.

Landy, F.J., Shankster, L.J. and Kohler, S.S. (1994). 'Personnel Selection and Placement,' *Annual Review of Psychology*, 45, pp. 261–96.

Landy, F.J. and Trumbo, D. (1981). *The Psychology of Work Behavior*. New York: Dorsey.

Latham, G.P., Saari, L.M., Pursell, E.D. and Campion, M.A. (1980). 'The Situational Interview'. *Journal of Applied Psychology*, 65, pp. 422–7.

Lewin, A.Y. and Zwany, A. (1976). 'Peer Nominations: A Model, Literature Critique and a Paradigm for Research'. *Personnel Psychology*, 29, pp. 423–47.

Lofquist, L.H. and Dawis, R.V. (1969). *Adjustment to Work*. Minneapolis: University of Minnesota.

Love, K.G. (1981). 'Comparison of Peer Assessment Methods: Reliability, Validity, Friendship Bias, and User Reaction'. *Journal of Applied Psychology*, 66, pp. 451–7.

Lowenberg, G. and Conrad, K.A. (1998). *Current Perspectives in Industrial and Organizational Psychology*. Needham Heights, MA: Allyn & Bacon.

Maas, J.B. (1965). 'Patterned Scaled Expectation Interview: Reliability Studies on a New Technique'. *Journal of Applied Psychology*, 49, pp. 431–3.

MacDaniel, M., Whetzel, D., Schmidt, F. and Maurer, S. (1994). 'The Validity of the Employment Interviews: A Comprehensive Review and Meta-Analysis'. *Journal of Applied Psychology*, 79, pp. 599–616.

MacKinnon, D.W. (1977). 'From Selecting Spies to Selecting Managers'. In J.L. Moses and W.C. Byham (eds), *Applying the Assessment Center Method*. New York: Pergamon.

Mael, F.A. (1991). 'A Conceptual Rationale for the Domain and Attributes of Biodata Items'. *Personnel Psychology*, 44, pp. 763–92.

Mael, F.A., Connerley, M. and Morath, R.A. (1996). 'None of Your Business: Parameters of Biodata Invasiveness'. *Personnel Psychology*, 49, pp. 613–50.

Maurer, T., Solamon, J. and Troxtel, D. (1998). 'Relationship of Coaching with Performance in Situational Employment Interviews'. *Journal of Applied Psychology*, 83, pp. 128–36.

Mayfield, E.C. (1964). 'The Selection Interview: A Re-evaluation of Published Research'. *Personnel Psychology*, 17, pp. 239–60.

Mayfield, E.C., Brown, S.H. and Hamstra, B.W. (1980). 'Selection Interviewing in the Life Insurance Industry: An Update of Research and Practice'. *Personnel Psychology*, 33, pp. 725–39.

McArdle, J.J. (1996). 'Current Directions in Structural Analysis'. *Current Directions in Psychological Sciences*, 5, pp. 11–18.

McConnell, J.J. and Parker, T. (1972). 'An Assessment Centers Program for Multiorganizational Use'. *Training and Development Journal*, 26, pp. 6–14.

McEvoy, M.G. and Beatty, R.W. (1989). 'Assessment Center and Subordinate Appraisals of Managers: A Seven-Year Examination of Predictive Validity'. *Personnel Psychology*, 37, pp. 45–52.

McNutt, K. (1979). 'Behavioral Consistency and Assessment Centers: A Reconciliation of the Literature'. *Journal of Assessment Methods in Psychology*, 2, pp. 1–8.

Mitchel, J.O. (1975). 'Assessment Center Validity: A Longitudinal Study'. *Journal of Applied Psychology*, 60, pp. 573–9.

Moses, J.L. (1973). 'The Development of an Assessment Center for Early Identification of Supervisory Potential'. *Personnel Psychology*, 26, pp. 569–80.

Moses, J.L. and Byham, W.C. (eds) (1977). *Applying the Assessment Center Method*. Elmsford, NY: Pergamon.

Murphy, K.R. (1993). *Honesty in the Workplace*. Pacific Grove CA: Brooks/Cole.

Murphy, K.R. and Cleveland, J.N. (1995). *Understanding Performance Appraisal: Social, Organizational and Goal-Based Perspectives*. Thousand Oaks, CA: Sage.

Murphy, K.R. and Davidshofer, C.O. (1991). *Psychological Testing: Principles and Applications*, 2nd edn, Englewood Cliffs, NJ: Prentice Hall.

Neidig, R.D. and Martin, J.C. (1979). *The FBI's Management Aptitude Program Assessment Center (Report #21): An Analysis of Assessor's Ratings. (TM 79–2)*. Washington, DC: Personnel Research and Development Center, U.S. Civil Service Commission.

Neiner, A.G. and Owens, W.A. (1985). 'Using Biodata to Predict Job Choice among College Graduates'. *Journal of Applied Psychology*, 70, pp. 127–36.

Nevo, B., Ed. (1986). *Handbook of Scientific Aspects of Graphology*. IL: Charles Thomas.

Ney, T. (1988). 'Expressing Your Emotions and Controlling Feelings'. In A. Gale (ed.), *The Polygraph Test: Lies, Truth and Science*. London: Sage, pp. 65–72.

Ones, D.S. (1993). *The Construct Validity of Integrity Tests*. Unpublished doctoral dissertation, University of Iowa, Iowa City.

Ones, D.S. and Viswesvaram, C. (1996). 'Brandwith Fidelity Dilemma in Personality Measurement for Personnel Selection'. *Journal of Organizational Behavior*, 17, pp. 609–26.

Ones, D.S., Viswesvaram, C. and Schmidt, F.L. (1993). 'Comprehensive Meta-Analysis of Integrity Test Validities: Findings and Implications for Personnel Selection and Theories of Job Performance'. *Journal of Applied Psychology*, 78, pp. 679–703.

Orpen, C. (1985). 'Patterned Behavior Description Interviews versus Unstructured Interviews: A Comparative Study'. *Journal of Applied Psychology*, 70, pp. 774–6.

Outcalt, D. (1988). 'A Research Program on General Motors Foreman Selection Assessment Center: Assessor/Assessee Characteristics and Moderator Analysis'. Paper presented at the 16th International Congress on the Assessment Center Method, Tampa, FL.

Owens, W.A (1976). 'Background Data'. In M.D. Dunnette (ed.), *Handbook of Industrial and Organizational Psychology*. Chicago: Rand McNally.

Owens, W.A. and Schoenfeldt, L.F. (1979). 'Toward a Classification of Persons'. *Journal of Applied Psychology*, 65, pp. 569–607.

Petterson, N. and Tziner, A. (1995). 'The Cognitive Ability Test as a Predictor of Job Performance: Is its Validity Affected by Job Complexity and Tenure Within the Organization?' *International Journal of Selection and Assessment*, 3, pp. 227–36.

Piaget, L.W. (1956). *The Child's Conception of Space*. London: Routledge & Kegan Paul.

Rafaeli, A. and Klimoski, R.J. (1983). 'Predicting Sales Success Through Handwriting Analysis: An Evaluation of the Effect of Training and Handwriting Sample Content'. *Journal of Applied Psychology*, 68, pp. 212–17.

Ramati, Z. (1981). *Reliability and Validity of Graphological Assessment in Selection of Officer Candidate*. Unpublished master's thesis, Tel-Aviv University (Hebrew).

Reilly, R.R. and Chao, G.T. (1982). 'Validity and Fairness of Some Alternative Employee Selection Procedures'. *Personnel Psychology*, 35, pp. 1–62.

Ritchie, R.J. and Moses, J.L. (1983). 'Assessment Center Correlates of Women's Advancement into Middle Management: A 7-Year Longitudinal Analysis'. *Journal of Applied Psychology*, 68, pp. 227–31.

Robertson, I.T., Gratton, L. and Sharpley, D. (1987). 'The Psychometric Properties and Design of Managerial Assessment Centers: Dimensions into Exercises Won't Go'. *Journal of Occupational Psychology*, 60, pp. 187–95.

Rothstein, H.R., Schmidt, F.L., Erwin, F.W., Owens, W.A. and Sparks, C.P. (1990). 'Biographical Data in Employment Selection: Can Validities be Made Generalizable?' *Journal of Applied Psychology*, 75, pp. 175–84.

Rothstein, M. and Jackson, D.N. (1980). 'Decision Making in the Employment Interview: An Experimental Approach'. *Journal of Applied Psychology*, 65, pp. 271–83.

Roza, S.M. and Carpenter, B.N. (1987). 'A Model of Hiring Decisions in Real Employment Interviews'. *Journal of Applied Psychology*, 72, pp. 596–603.

Russell, C.J. (1987). 'Individual Decision Processes in an Assessment Center'. *Journal of Applied Psychology*, 70, pp. 737–46.

Sackett, P.R. (1982). 'The Interviewer as Hypothesis Tester: The Effects of Impressions of an Applicant in Interview Questioning Strategy'. *Personnel Psychology*, 35, pp. 789–803.

Sackett, P.R., Buris, L.R. and Callahan, C. (1989). 'Integrity Testing for Personnel Selection: A Review and Critique'. *Personnel Psychology*, 42, pp. 491–529.

Sackett, P.R. and Dreher, G.F. (1982). 'Constructs and Assessment Center Dimensions: Some Troubling Empirical Findings'. *Journal of Applied Psychology*, 64, pp. 401–10.

Sackett, P.R. and Hakel, M.D. (1979). 'Temporal Stability and Individual Differences in Using Assessment Information to Form Overall Ratings'. *Organizational Behavior and Human Performance*, 23, pp. 120–37.

Sackett, P.R. and Harris, M.M. (1994). 'Honesty Testing for Personnel Selection: A Review and Critique'. *Personnel Psychology*, 37, pp. 221–45.

Sackett, P.R. and Wilson, M.A. (1982). 'Factors Affecting the Consensus Judgment Process in Managerial Assessment Centers'. *Journal of Applied Psychology*, 67, pp. 10–17.

Sackett, P.R., Zedeck, S. and Fogli, L. (1988). 'Relations Between Measures of Typical and Maximum Job Performance'. *Journal of Applied Psychology*, 73, pp. 482–6.

Salgado, J.F. (1997). 'The Five Factor Model of Personality and Job Performance in the European Community'. *Journal of Applied Psychology*, 82, pp. 30–43.

Schaubrock, J., Ganster, D.C. and Jones, J.R. (1998). 'Organization and Occupation Influences in the Attraction-Selection-Attribution Process'. *Journal of Applied Psychology*, 83, pp. 869–91.

Schlesinger, M.I. and Guttman, L. (1969). 'Smallest Space Analysis of Intelligence and Achievement Tests'. *Psychological Bulletin*, 71, pp. 95–100.

Schmitt, N. (1976). 'Social and Situational Determinants of Interview Decisions: Implications for the Employment Interview'. *Personnel Psychology*, 29, pp. 79–101.

Schmitt, N. (1977). 'Interrrater Agreement and Dimensionality and Combination of Assessment Center Judgments'. *Journal of Applied Psychology*, 62, pp. 171–6.

Schmitt, N., Noe, R.A., Meritt, R. and Fitzgerald, M.P. (1984). 'Validity of Assessment Center Ratings for Prediction of Performance Ratings and School Climate of School Administrators'. *Journal of Applied Psychology*, 69, pp. 207–213.

Schneider, B. (1976). *Staffing Organizations.* Pacific Palisades, CA: Goodyear.

Schneider, B. (1987). 'The People Make the Place'. *Personnel Psychology*, 40, pp. 437–54.

Schneider, B. and Schmitt, N. (1986). *Staffing Organizations.* Glenview Scott: Foresman.

Schneider, B., Smith, D.B., Taylor, S. and Fleenor, J. (1998). 'Personality and Organizations: A Test of the Homogeneity of Personality Hypothesis'. *Journal of Applied Psychology*, 83, pp. 462–70.

Shapira, Z. and Zevulun, E. (1979). 'On the Use of Facet Analysis in Organizational Behavior Research: Some Conceptual Considerations and an Example'. *Organizational Behavior and Human Performance*, 23, pp. 411–28.

Shore, T.H., Shore, L.M. and Thornton, G.C. III (1992). 'Construct Validity of Self-and Peer Evaluations of Performance Dimensions in an Assessment Center'. *Journal of Applied Psychology*, 77, pp. 42–54.

Shore, T.H., Thornton, G.C. III and Shore, L.M. (1990). 'Construct Validity of Two Categories of Assessment Center Dimension Ratings'. *Personnel Psychology*, 43, pp. 101–16.

Shye, S. (ed.) (1978). *Theory Construction and Data Analysis in Behavioral Sciences.* San Francisco: Jossey-Bass.

Siegel, L. and Lane, I. (1982). *Personnel and Organizational Psychology.* Homewood: Irwin.

Silverman, W.H., Dalessio, A., Woods, S.B. and Johnson, R.L. Jr (1986). 'Influence of Assessment Center Methods on Assessors' Ratings'. *Personnel Psychology*, 39, pp. 565–78.

Slivinski, L.W. and Ethier, L. (1973*). Development of the Assessment Center for the Career Assignment Program: Descriptive Summary of the Senior Executive Population.* Ottawa: Public Services Commission of Canada, Managerial Assessment and Research Division.

Slivinski, L.W., Grant, K.W., Bourgeois, R.P. and Pederson, L.D. (1977). *Development and Application of a First Level Management Assessment Center.* Ottawa, Canada: Managerial

Assessment and Research Division of the Personnel Psychology Center.

Slovic, P. and Lichtenstein, S. (1973). 'Comparison of Bayesian and Regression Approaches to the Study of Information Processing in Judgment'. In L. Rappaport and D.A. Summers (eds), *Human Judgment and Social Interaction*. New York: Holt, Rinehart and Winston, pp. 16–108.

Spearman, C. (1904). '"General Intelligence" Objectively Determined and Measured'. *American Journal of Psychology*, 15, pp. 201–93.

Spearman, C. (1927). *The Abilities of Man*. New York: Macmillan.

Stevens, C.K. (1998). 'Antecedents of Interview Interactions, Interviewers' Ratings, and Applicants' Reactions'. *Personnel Psychology*, 51, pp. 55–86.

Tett, R.P., Jackson, D.M. and Rothstein, M. (1991). 'Personality Measures as Predictors of Job Performance: A Meta-Analytic Review'. *Personnel Psychology*, 44, pp. 703–42.

Thomson, H.A. (1970). 'Comparison of Predictor and Criterion Judgments of Managerial Performance Using the Multitrait-Multimethod Approach'. *Journal of Applied Psychology*, 54, pp. 496–502.

Thornton, G.C. III (1992). *Assessment Centers in Human Resource Management*. Reading MA: Addison-Wesley.

Thornton, G.C. III and Byham, W.C. (1982). *Assessment Centers and Managerial Performance*. New York: Academic Press.

Thornton, G.C. III, Tziner, A., Dahan, M., Clevenger, J.P. and Meir, E. (1997). 'Construct Validity of Assessment Center Judgments: Analyses of the Behavioral Reporting Method'. *Journal of Social Behavior and Personality*, 12, pp. 109–28.

Thurstone, L.L. (1938). 'Primary Mental Abilities'. *Psychometric Monographs*, 1.

Turnage, J.J. and Muchinsky, P.M. (1984). 'A Comparison of the Predictive Validity of Assessment Evaluations versus Traditional Measures in Forecasting Supervisory Job Performance: Interpretive Implications Criterion Distortion for the Assessment Paradigm'. *Journal of Applied Psychology*, 69, pp. 595–602.

Tziner, A. (1984). 'Prediction of Peer Rating in a Military Assessment Center: A Longitudinal Follow-up'. *Canadian Journal of Administrative Science*, 1, pp. 146–60.

Tziner, A. (1987). *The Facet Analytic Approach to Research Design and Data Processing*. New York: Peter Lang.

Tziner, A. (1990). *Organization Staffing and Work Adjustment*. New York: Praeger.

Tziner, A. (1992). 'A Comparative Examination of Structural Models of Ability Tests'. *Quality & Quantity*, 26, pp. 383–94.

Tziner, A. and Dolan, S. (1982). 'Validity of an Assessment Center for Identifying Future Female Officers in the Military'. *Journal of Applied Psychology*, 67, pp. 728–36.

Tziner, A., Jeanrie, C. and Cusson, S. (1993). *La Selection du Personnel: Concepts et Applications*. Montreal: Editions Agence D'Arc.

Tziner, A., Meir, E.I., Dahan, M. and Birati, A. (1994). 'An Investigation of the Predictive Validity and Economic Utility of the Assessment Center for the High-Management Level'. *Canadian Journal of Behavioural Sciences*, 26, pp. 228–45.

Tziner, A. and Rimmer, A. (1984). 'Examination of an Extension of Guttman's Model of Ability Tests'. *Applied Psychological Measurement*, 8, pp. 59–69.

Tziner, A., Ronen, S. and Hacohen, D. (1993). 'A Four-Year Validation Study of an Assessment Center in a Financial Corporation'. *Journal of Occupational Behavior*, 14, pp. 225–37.

Valenzi, E. and Andrews, I.R. (1973). 'Individual Employment Differences in the Decision Process of Interviewers'. *Journal of Applied Psychology*, 57, pp. 233–36.

Vernon, P.E. (1965). *The Measurement of Abilities*, 5th edn, London: University of London Press.

Wanous, J.P. (1980). *Organizational Entry*. Reading, MA: Addision-Wesley.

Webster, E.D. (ed.) (1964). *Decision Making in the Employment Interview*. Montreal, Canada: Eagle.

Wernimont P.F. and Campbell, J.P. (1968). 'Signs, Samples and Criteria'. *Journal of Applied Psychology*, 52, pp. 372–6.

Wilkinson, L.J. (1997). 'Generalizable Biodata? An Application to the Vocational Interests of Managers'. *Journal of Occupational and Organizational Psychology*, 70, pp. 49–60.

Young, D.M. and Beier, E.G. (1977). 'The Role of Applicant Nonverbal Communication on the Employment Interview'. *Journal of Employment Counseling*, 14, pp. 154–65.

Zedeck, S.A. and Kafry, D. (1977). 'Capturing Rater Policies for Processing Evaluation Data'. *Organizational Behavior and Human Performance*, 18, pp. 269–94.

Zedeck, S.A., Tziner, A. and Middlestadt, S. (1983). 'Interview Validity and Reliability: An Individual Analysis Approach'. *Personnel Psychology*, 67, pp. 752–8.

APPENDIX 5.1

GUIDELINES FOR STRUCTURED INTERVIEWS

INTERVIEW FORMAT

Part I
A. <u>Candidate identification details</u>

_____   _____   _____
           Surname   First name   ID No.

B. <u>Desired position</u>   _____

C. _____   _____
     Name of interviewer   Signature

Note to the Interviewer: Below is a list of suggested information to be gathered or confirmed about the candidate. Additional data may also be requested where appropriate.

1. <u>Service in the army</u>

    (a) <u>Objective information</u>: unit of armed forces in which candidate served, rank achieved by end of duty, specializations, duties, duration of service, etc.

    (b) <u>Events during service (regular or reserve) indicative of adjustment to authority</u>: time spent in units, reasons for transfers, relations with peers and superiors, etc.

2. <u>Professional experience</u>

    (a) <u>Objective information about previous places of employment</u>: description of work done by candidate, type of position held, achieved organizational level, wage brackets, dates of employment (for detecting gaps in continuity of employment).

    (b) <u>Reasons for quitting previous places of employment or positions</u>:

(c) <u>Social adjustment to work</u>: Describe your relations with colleagues and superiors at previous workplaces.

(d) <u>Examination of perceived professional adjustment</u>

    (i) How did past superiors evaluate your performance and on what evidence was this based?

    (ii) Describe jobs performed, issues you dealt with that earned you credits from your superiors.

    (iii) Describe job, issues, or situations that earned you disapproval from your superiors.

(e) <u>Examination of levels of complexity in previous jobs</u>

Describe a typical working day in previous jobs; including skills demanded, kinds of problems encountered and how you coped with them.

(f) <u>Examination of decision-making skills at work</u>

    (i) Describe a number of projects or subjects you were involved in during the last year. What decisions were you required to make?

    (ii) Describe issues in the last year about which you had to make decisions. Describe the possible consequences of wrong decisions.

(g) <u>Examination of motives and attitudes toward work</u>

    (i) What gave you satisfaction in the positions you filled and what disturbed you?

    (ii) What were the most prominent achievements and failures in your previous job?

(h) <u>Examination of initiative demonstrated at work</u>

Which changes and/or innovations did you initiate in your previous job?

3. <u>General state of health</u>

   (a) Describe your current state of health and history of illnesses.

   (b) How would you describe your current state of health?

4	3	2	1
excellent	good	fair	not well

4. <u>General social adjustment</u>
Have you ever been involved in any felonies or been convicted by a court, in the past or present?

Date _____ Signature of interviewer _____

Part II

5. <u>Understanding of requirements of desired position</u>

   (a) Describe what is demanded of you in the job that you are considering.

   (b) How were the duties in this job presented to you?

6. <u>Aspects of performance</u>

   (a) <u>Professional preferences</u>

      (i)   How would you tailor the job to correspond to your needs if you could?

      (ii) Which of your abilities and skills will contribute to your success in the offered position? Which will be counterproductive?

      (iii) Assuming that you obtain the job you apply for, how and in which areas can you make significant contributions immediate, and in which matters would you need additional training?

(b) <u>Plans for the future</u>

   (i)   Given a free choice, how would you plan your career, based on your past experience?

   (ii) Tell us about your plans for the future (scholastic, professional, family-related, personal, etc.) and upon what they are contingent?

(c) <u>Social preferences</u>

   (i)   Describe your capacity for adjusting to new social situations. In what kind of situations do you have difficulty in adjusting to people who are unlike those you are used to?

   (ii) In whose company do you feel most comfortable? Least comfortable?

   (ii) Describe your friends and your relationships with them.

(d) <u>Hobbies and recreation</u>

   (i)   How do you spend your leisure time?

   (ii) Describe in detail activities that you like best and interest you most.

   (iii) Do you have any second profession or hobby that could serve as an alternative occupation?

   (iv) Of what social, professional or sports associations are you a member?

(e) <u>Decision-making ability</u>
   What were the most significant decisions you made in the last five years, and by what means did you reach them?

(f) <u>Ability to manage people</u>
   Suppose that you were commissioned with an urgent assignment for which you would need to draw on the cooperation of other employees, how would you go about it?

(g) <u>Motives and expectations</u>

    (i)   What influences played a part in your decision to apply to us for work? (newspapers, friends, advertisements, etc.)?

    (ii) What motivated you to join our organization?

7. <u>Self-assessment</u>

(a) What makes you think you will adjust to work in our organization?

(b) What are your expectations with respect to wages and benefits?

8. <u>Personal characteristics and life events</u>

(a) One of the earmarks of an adult is that he knows himself and can distinguish between his capacities and limitations. Describe your own positive and negative traits.

(b) Describe those life events that you value as the most outstanding achievements or failures.

(c) Describe life events you conceive as peaks, lows, or turning points in your life.

9. <u>Aspects of health</u>

(a) Describe prolonged or serious sicknesses you had as an adult or as a child.

(b) Describe complications following diseases, operations, accidents, etc.

(c) Describe operations and prolonged hospitalizations, for <u>any</u> health reasons, in the last five years.

(d) Did you or do you suffer from any of the following illnesses: diseases of the nervous system, mental diseases, migraines, insomnia, asthma, other?

REMARK:
If the interviewee points to a specific disease, his present state of health should
be assessed, as well as possible impacts on his performance in the future. The
applicant should be requested to provide medical documents attesting to his
present state of health.

10. Summary of interview

> I have concluded all I intend to ask. If we have omitted any items that you
> still would like to have discussed, you can discuss them now.

Form of the evaluation of an applicant at the end of the interview

Item 1: Evaluation of relevant work-related dimensions
Choose for each dimension, the behavioral anchor that seems to you most
descriptive of the candidate. Mark X in the square opposite the most suitable
behavior.

1. Ability to cope with stress
   The capability to maintain effective performance under pressure, by
   overcoming situational obstacles.

[ ] (a) Even with a regular schedule, will sometimes have difficulty in coping
        with workload. This will affect performance detrimentally.
[ ] (b) Will be able to perform well under a regular workload. However, when
        presented with additional load, performance will be seriously impaired.
[ ] (c) When presented with duties exceeding the daily load, will proceed to
        perform well, but will deal only with part of the load (and not necessarily
        with the right priorities).
[ ] (d) Even in unexpected situations, will be able to proceed with work. Will
        perform effectively and rationally, and set the right priorities.

2. Planning ability
   The ability to establish courses of action for accomplishing work goals,
   and appropriately allocate the time, efforts, and resources involved.

[ ] (a) Will only occasionally plan courses of action such as planning of efforts,
        resources allocation.

[ ] (b) Usually knows goals and how to achieve them. Will use certain planning methods for the allocation of time and resources available.

[ ] (c) Planning will be evident in many of the candidate's projected activities. Will meticulously plan allocations of time and resource involved.

[ ] (d) Planning will be highly evident in all projected activities. Will meticulously plan allocation of time and resources in all activities.

3. Comprehension
   The ability to grasp and understand new issues.

[ ] (a) Has difficulty in grasping and understanding new issues even after extensive explanation and demonstrations.

[ ] (b) Will grasp and understand new issues only after extensive explanation and demonstration.

[ ] (c) Has no difficulty in grasping and understanding new and often complicated issues.

[ ] (d) Has an excellent and quick grasp and understanding of new and complicated issues.

4. Ability for oral communication
   The ability to communicate ideas in a lucid and comprehensible way.

[ ] (a) Will usually be unable to articulate lucidly or communicate well with people

[ ] (b) Will not always convey message in a clear and comprehensible way and will, most of the time, be unconvincing.

[ ] (c) Will be able to convey message in a comprehensible but not fluent manner, and will thus not always be convincing.

[ ] (d) Will be able to convey message in a lucid and convincing manner and communicate fluently with his audience. Will have views accepted, even if opposed to majority views.

5. Initiative
   The ability to come up with new ideas to improve work and performance processes without being requested to do so, or being pressured into applying them.

[ ] (a) Will only occasionally come up with new ideas for the improvement of work and performance processes without being requested to do so.

[ ] (b) Will suggest new ideas for the improvement of work and performance processes without being requested to do so.

[ ] (c) Will suggest new ideas for the improvement of work and performance processes, but will have difficulty in putting them into practice.

[ ] (d) Will often suggest new ideas for the improvement of work and performance processes even when not requested to do so.

6. Ability to make decisions
   The ability to make reasoned and practical decisions, as required by
   . circumstances.

[ ] (a) Will not be eager to decide for fear of erring. Will not take responsibility for decisions.

[ ] (b) Will shirk making unreasoned, hasty or unconsidered decisions. However, tends to be inconsistent in decisions and is liable to revoke them under pressure.

[ ] (c) Will be unflinching in decisions, will stand by them, and believe in them, but will not reconsider them when circumstances so require.

[ ] (d) Will wholeheartedly make reasoned decisions while being willing to reconsider them when needed.

7. Supervisory ability
   The capacity to direct the work of others and to organize and integrate their activities so that the goal of the work group can be attained.

[ ] (a) Will be unable and/or unwilling to direct and organize others to carry out duties assigned to them.

[ ] (b) Will have great difficulty in directing and organizing others to carry out duties assigned to them.

[ ] (c) Will manage to direct and organize others to carry out assigned duties, but the overall performance will often be imperfect and ineffective because will not have assigned the duties in the right way.

[ ] (d) Will always succeed to direct and organize others to carry out duties. The overall performance will be perfect and effective because will have taken care to assign duties in the right way.

8. Ability to perform repetitious jobs
   The degree of perseverance in repetitious jobs while maintaining a high standard of work.

[ ] (a) Will have difficulty in persevering and maintaining a high standard of repetitious work, over a prolonged period of time.

[ ] (b) Will try to persevere, but will succeed only partially to maintain high quality of work over a prolonged period of time.

[ ] (c) Will succeed considerably in persevering and maintaining a high quality of work over a prolonged period of time.

[ ] (d) Will completely succeed in persevering and maintaining a high standard of work in repetitious jobs over a prolonged period of time.

9. Ability for teamwork
   The ability to maintain good working relations with both superiors and colleagues.

[ ] (a) Will not succeed in maintaining good working relations with superiors or colleagues, and will have difficulty in cooperating in team situations.

[ ] (b) Will be able to perform in a team, but with friction and with strained interpersonal relations.

[ ] (c) Will, as a rule, succeed to integrate into teamwork and will relate well to others, but not in every workteam and not with all the employees.

[ ] (d) Will fully integrate into a workteam within a reasonable period. Will relate well to superiors and/or colleagues and will fully cooperate with others in performing duties.

Item 2: General Assessment

Finally, how would you generally evaluated:
A. the candidate's predicted level of performance,
B. the candidate's predicted ability to adjust to work

A. Level of Performance

excellent	extremely good	very good	good	fairly good	fair	fairly low	inadequate
%	%	%	%	%	%	%	%

B. <u>Ability to Adjust to Work</u>

excellent	extremely good	very good	good	fairly good	fair	fairly low	inadequate
%	%	%	%	%	%	%	%

C. If the decision to hire the candidate depended entirely on your recommendation, what would it be?

    4 – I highly recommend hiring the candidate
    3 – I recommend hiring the candidate
    2 – I recommend hiring the candidate, but with some reservations
    1 – I recommend rejecting the candidate

REMARKS:

_____
_____
_____
_____

Date _____ Signature _____
Position in Organization _____

6 Performance Appraisal

AHARON TZINER

Introduction

Once an organization has selected its employees, defined their jobs and positions, trained the work teams, and set them to work, what still needs to be done? Clearly, the next stage is an evaluation of the quality of the employees' performance. In other words, the organization needs to examine to what extent satisfactoriness has been achieved (Dawis and Lofquist, 1984). This is not an unusual step. The fact is that organizations are continually appraising their workers' contribution to the organization, both formally and informally, for the purposes of hiring, firing, and promotion.

Satisfactoriness is commonly determined through a process known as performance appraisal (PA). The aim of performance appraisal is to assist the organization in actualizing its inherent performance potential by facilitating enhancement of employees' motivation and work-related skills. PA also serves to hone the decision-making processes involved in improving the performance of workers in current positions, or assignment to new positions. However, for a PA system to function successfully, it must be based on two fundamental behavioral principles. The first is that increased productivity depends on the existence of a direct link between workers' levels of achievement and the incentives offered to them (such as remuneration, bonuses/stock options, and promotion). The second is that feedback, i.e., knowledge of the results of the performance appraisal, assists in the process of changing behavior and increasing motivation.

This link in the human resources management chain represents more than a transient evaluation of a subordinate's performance on the job, or another step in the estimation of the cost-effectiveness of the production line. On the contrary, the degree to which the appraisal process is 'successful' has significant long-term consequences for an organization. Yet several factors mitigate against such success, and they may include any one or combination of the following scenarios: (1) ratees' negative views of the appraisal system and its outcomes have long-term deleterious effects on their job satisfaction, organizational commitment, and future performance; (2) the immediate results of the PA are dubious because of the questionable reliability and validity of the appraisal tools employed; (3) the raters themselves lack the appropriate tools with which to appraise their subordinates efficiently, and thus are unable to overcome the subjective biases and negative assessment styles that reflect certain beliefs they hold about fellow workers; (4) the appraisal format appears to skirt specific job functions, resulting in frustrations and problems with the feedback process that cause friction between supervisors and subordinates.

In practice, the evaluation of workers' performance within an organization can be considered the product of three basic systems (reflected in the problems cited above) which influence its construction, utilization, and consolidation. These are the appraisal formats, the encounter between the rater and the ratee, and the organizational system. Moreover, the specific processes that occur within each of these systems also contribute intrinsically to the ultimate quality and empirical value of the appraisal process.

This chapter therefore reviews in some detail the processes involved in the construction and operation of a PA system and what it actually measures. The review includes such issues as adjusting the appraisal system to specific applications, and supervisors' abilities to draw appropriate conclusions from the PA process. Various problems encountered in the process of appraisal are also described, as are some suggested solutions. Additionally, we shall explore types of scales, formats, and systems of performance appraisal, with specific reference to approaches in formulating the criteria for performance appraisal.

A major section of this chapter is devoted to an in-depth exploration of two aspects of the PA process that have come under increasing scrutiny in recent years.

The first involves a critical comparison, based on a series of investigations, of two of the most commonly used systems of performance appraisal (behavior-based rating formats and graphic rating scales). Particular reference is made to their influence on a variety of outcomes that have significance for future employee performance on the job. These include rater/ratee attitudes to PA, rater/ratee relationships, feedback and goal setting, and consequent motivation, goal acceptance and job performance. The second issue relates primarily to raters' political considerations in the workplace which, among other considerations, have increasingly been observed to affect the efficiency of performance appraisal. Some recently developed tools designed to measure these attitudes successfully are also described below.

Construction and Operation of a Performance Appraisal System

The following discussion of appraisal systems is based on Tziner's (1990, pp. 107–42) review, in which he defines performance appraisal as a pre-planned formal process designed to acquire as reliable and accurate information about workers' performance as possible. In Tziner's estimation, assessment of satisfactoriness should focus on measuring: (1) the extent to which employees meet task requirements; and (2) the degree to which employees conform to the organization's demands regarding the norms of behavior and rules of conduct that emanate from the organization's value system and organizational structure.

An appraisal system must be based on a representative sampling of characteristics, modes of conduct, or types of output associated with a particular job. By way of introduction, therefore, Tziner notes the importance of distinguishing between job evaluation and performance appraisal. Although performance appraisal would appear to be conceptually similar to job evaluation, the two terms are, in fact, radically different. Job evaluation relates to the *job* from the point of view of the requirements of the organization. Its function is to set the relative value of a job or position in the organization in order to establish remuneration scales (see Chapter 1). The subject of performance appraisal, however, is the *individual worker*. The function here is to measure the employee's performance in the job, distinguishing between successful, average, and poor workers on the basis of parameters that are considered vital for determining satisfaction with their performance.

The PA process should thus both identify and measure the extent to which employee work-related behaviors meet performance standards. Consequently, the appraisal process usually includes: (1) identification of the relevant activities of the worker; (2) identification of the various dimensions and components required for successful performance in the specific job or position being analyzed; and (3) their measurement in a manner that is as objective as possible. The measures should reflect workers' behavior and contribute to determination of the degree of efficacy of the specific behaviors in question. Knowledge of the level of performance also enables feedback to be given to workers with a view to their changing job behavior so as to suit the expectations of the organization.

Construction of an Appraisal System

The appraisal system must be reliable, which means that different analysts or appraisal systems will arrive at the same conclusions about a given worker, despite the constant distracters that influence judgment. The system should also be flexible, in the sense that it is capable of assimilating possible changes in technology or in the structure of the position. Finally, it is important that the appraisal system be lucid enough to be understood by the various employees of the organization, who must be able to trust the process and feel that it is valuable to them in a variety of ways. It is desirable, therefore, that a performance appraisal system be constructed in an atmosphere of cooperation and mutual trust between all levels of the organization.

Constructing and operating a system of performance appraisal is a daunting prospect, and there are several hurdles to overcome in the process. These include: (1) adapting the appraisal system to specific organizational uses; (2) training and guiding the 'appraiser'; (3) assessing the appraiser's ability to analyze information and communicate results to the subjects of the appraisal; and (4) ensuring management's ability to apply the conclusions drawn from the accumulated performance appraisal information to the practical level of decision-making in personnel management.

Constructing Criteria for Performance Appraisal

The first step in the construction is to generate performance appraisal criteria. Here the important job components identified in the course of the analysis must be turned into appropriate measures for the description of the relevant behaviors and outcomes associated with a given job or position.

A PA system must be constructed in accordance with pre-established objectives which will determine its character, criteria, and application. Thus, for example, the measures of the criterion in an appraisal system designed for the purpose of fixing wage scales should reflect the current total effect or contribution of a worker in a particular position in the organization. On the other hand, a PA system designed for the purpose of selecting personnel suitable for advancement to administrative positions would be used to detect and evaluate potential on the basis of achievements. Accordingly, the measures of the criterion would probably relate to those aspects in the performance of the job that reflect the worker's ability to meet challenges in the prospective position.

In all situations, however, appraisal should incorporate two distinct types of performance measures, namely: (1) measures of task performance; and (2) measures of contextual performance. Task performance relates to the proficiency with which individuals perform the specific activities (tasks, duties) that comprise their work roles and jobs. Contextual performance refers to the effectiveness of behaviors that contribute to the accomplishment of broader organizational goals. These might include such behaviors as volunteering to undertake duties not incorporated in the employee's formal job description, facilitating interpersonal communications and the reduction of disruptive emotional responses, and promoting teamwork.

An appraisal system therefore produces ratings that reflect the achievements of each ratee on different performance criteria. These ratings may take one of two possible forms, a composite overall criterion or a multiple criterion.

Composite overall criterion   The composite overall criterion is a single index or global measure of success that reflects the overall contribution of the worker to the organization. The workers are characterized and differentiated by the same global score, which reflects their superiors' ratings on various aspects of performance as combined into one general index. The proponents of this approach attach less value to specific behaviors in evaluating the overall worth of an individual's contribution to the organization. It is thus inconsequential that workers differ from one another along different dimensions of the criterion, since the specific components of the appraisal are assumed to be unimportant. Indeed, a low rating in one dimension of the criterion may be compensated for by a high rating in another. For example, a given supervisor may lack financial finesse, yet have an impressive ability to create a strong cooperative team atmosphere in his group.

Multiple criterion   In contrast, the multiple criterion consists of a series of dimensions characteristic of the criterion being used to describe performance. Each dimension is distinguished from the others, even though there may be a connection or overlap between them. Proponents of this approach maintain that the various aspects of performance are unrelated; therefore, their combination into one index of performance level is untenable. Since the criterion itself is essentially multidimensional, the construction of a single index to combine measures that are not compatible, for the sake of obtaining a single, quantitative grade or score, is not seen to serve any useful purpose (Ghiselli, 1956; Guion, 1961; Dunnette, 1963; Wallace, 1965). For example, detractors of global criteria would take issue with the value of combining a score of attendance with an indicant of performance, or of combining bank tellers' skills in keeping track of transactions with a score that reflects the quality of their conduct with clients.

Formulating Criteria for Performance Appraisal

There are two basic approaches to the formulation of criteria for performance appraisal. The first is the outcome, or performance, oriented approach, which evaluates the final results of performance (over units of time), and the second is the input approach, which measures behavior on the job, including character traits, specific abilities and skills, and degree of effort.

Outcome (performance) oriented approach The advantage of the outcome-oriented approach is its emphasis on results, since the essence of the organization is to attain objectives. This approach is supposed to prevent the paradoxical situation in which workers with low productivity are given good performance appraisals simply because they are socially accepted. However, as Tziner (1990) notes, the drawback of the outcome-oriented approach is linked to the notion of goal achievement itself, as it tends to play down the means taken to achieve the goal, as well as the degree of desirability of these means to the organization. To illustrate, Tziner offers the scenario of very industrious shop floor workers who ignore the dangers of the hazardous machinery they operate, thereby creating a situation that is both illegal and undesirable from the organization's perspective.

According to Tziner, it is relatively easy to formulate criteria in terms of productivity for simple routine jobs. Examples might include the volume and quality of a typist's work, the quantity and quality of the products of a welder on a production line, or the number of trees cut down by a lumberjack in a workday. In complex businesses, however, the formulation of criteria in terms of productivity is difficult and complicated. For example, when considering the evaluation of a department manager's productivity, we would have to ask what work this manager actually does. Similarly, the performance appraisal of one of the skilled workers in a team would inevitably raise the question of the specific contribution of each member to the overall achievements of the team. One interesting method of arriving at a reasonable solution has been to measure performance in terms of negative indicators, such as tardiness, absenteeism, accidents on the job, number of errors, and depreciation of products.

Input approach The input approach, a widely accepted and implemented alternative, formulates an evaluation criterion in subjective judgmental terms. It may take the form of an evaluation of the way specific aspects of the job are undertaken, or an assessment of the quality of general performance. It may also include an appraisal of certain abilities and talents, or even of the potential of the worker being evaluated. Two types of scales are commonly used for this sort of evaluation, trait-based and behavior-based.

Trait-based scales are designed to evaluate personal qualities, professional experience, and education, the assumption being that a connection exists between these qualities and performance. However, there is no operational definition of precisely what a worker must do in order to succeed. Moreover, as Tziner (1990) notes, a variety of factors can alter the relationship between a particular trait (such as initiative) and its effect on performance. For instance, how do superiors who have rated workers as having average initiative understand this rating? What were their expectations of the workers and how do they like to see initiative applied? On the other hand, do the workers understand the requirement to take initiative and its practical implications in the same way as the supervisors? Thus, as a result of differences of perception and expectations, a context may be created in which the evaluators and those being evaluated may give different interpretations of the link between the input variables (such as the traits of the worker) and their outcomes, namely, the level of performance.

Nevertheless, Tziner points out that the trait approach is compatible with the way in which people tend to perceive, judge, and categorize others in terms of qualities such as ambition, friendliness, self-discipline, and so on. It is also relatively easy for assessors to convey their impressions when they are required to make evaluations based on workers' traits. As a rule, however, evaluations based on qualities are more useful for predicting success in a job position than for giving detailed feedback on workers' past performance.

Behavior-based formats, on the other hand, focus on the behaviors essential for successful performance, rather than on personal qualities. They thus facilitate analysis of work-related activities into specific aspects of behavior, and the evaluation of worker performance on each of those aspects. Performance analysis using this type of format is a detailed process that involves determining the different dimensions for performance evaluation, and judgment, and selecting those dimensions that are important for the specific purpose for which the system is constructed. Behavior-based performance formats are especially suited for giving detailed feedback to workers about their performance, and for mapping their future training needs and objectives.

In contrast to the trait approach, this type of appraisal is based on an analysis of behavior and achievement (i.e., how each characteristic of the worker is expressed in actual behavior and how each incident of behavior leads to a certain level of achievement). A specific example of how different aspects can impact on behavior might relate to two qualifications required by engineers, professional knowledge and judgment, the combination of which may enable them to carry out several kinds of operations, including the ability to distinguish between the essential and the inconsequential, to critically examine professional literature in the field, and to know when to compromise or be rigid in applying engineering laws. All these are specific activities that need to be appraised. A recent study suggests that this kind of approach is superior to the trait method, at least with respect to reducing the bias in supervisor ratings.

Systems of Performance Appraisal

When summarizing and processing data obtained from different appraisal systems, the employee population in an organization can be divided into categories according to either their performance potential (behavior, traits, skills, and so on – the input approach) or their level of actual performance (the outcome approach). In a superficial grading, one might obtain two general categories, such as 'workers whose performance is poor' and 'workers whose performance is good'. A more sophisticated classification might differentiate clusters along, for example, eight levels of performance, such as: outstanding, excellent, very good, good, average, fair, poor, and very poor.

In the earlier stages of recording the personal evaluations of each worker, two systems of appraisal may be used, the *absolute* system and the *relative* system. In the absolute system, raters relate directly to the individuals whose performance is being evaluated, disregarding their acquaintance with any other individuals who are also to be evaluated. At every point in the measurement scale, appraisers need to ask whether a specific listed trait or behavioral incident fits the qualities or behaviors exhibited at work by the ratee, and what grade along a numerical continuum best describes it. In this case, judgment is formulated by absolute criteria.

Examples of the absolute system of appraisal include graphic scales, behavioral scales, and weighted checklists. As this method supplies a great deal of information about the worker, it is particularly convenient for examining, evaluating, and providing feedback on the quality of a worker's performance, and for standardizing performance appraisals. The goal of standardization is, of course, to eliminate differences between evaluations that stem from differences in the raters, whether external or internal, and thus to facilitate comparisons between them at the organizational level.

A *relative* system of appraisal, on the other hand, is based on a comparison between different workers belonging to the same work team or hierarchical level or occupying the same position in the organization in order to rank them from the best to the worst performer. Relative evaluation is conducted in one of three ways: rank ordering, forced distribution, or paired comparisons.

Rank ordering This method sorts out the better workers from the less successful ones.

Forced distribution Here the appraiser is required to distribute the ratees among categories that represent different levels of performance in accordance with a predetermined quota. Usually, five levels are normally distributed, as in the following example:

1	2	3	4	5
best		average		poorest
10%	20%	40%	20%	10%

This system is useful when three conditions obtain: (1) the number of workers evaluated by one rater is large (more than 20); (2) only a rough differentiation between the groups is required; and (3) it can be assumed that the performance levels in a group are normally distributed.

Below is an example of the forced distribution system:

Level of performance	Percent of total	Names of workers in each category
Excellent	5	—
Above average	15	—
Average	60	—
Below average	15	—
Poor	5	—

Paired comparisons This process involves the evaluation of a worker's performance relative to every other member of the work team. For each pair of workers, the appraiser has to decide whose performance is better. Thus, in order to compare all the workers, the evaluator must perform $n(n-1)/2$ comparisons (where n=number of workers). For example, if a set of evaluated workers is composed of Dan, Jack, John, Laurie, and Fran, the comparison is performed for $5(4)/2=10$ pairs, as follows:

Dan	——	Jack		Jack	——	Laurie
Dan	——	John		Jack	——	Fran
Dan	——	Laurie		John	——	Laurie
Dan	——	Fran		John	——	Fran
Jack	——	John		Laurie	——	Fran

The results might look something like this:

Number of times each ratee's performance was rated
higher than that of the others

Dan   – 4
Jack   – 2
John   – 1
Laurie   – 0
Fran   – 3

The relative system is easy to apply when the number of rated workers per cluster is very small, or when the categories of performance according to which the workers are classified are clearly defined. It is simply not viable if the performance of a large number of workers is to be rated, as the difference between workers ranked 2.5 and 2.6, for example, can hardly be considered significant. What is more, if 40 workers are to be evaluated, the appraiser would have to make 40(40-1)/2, or 780, comparisons. Furthermore, this system does not illuminate either the real differences between workers or the relative distances between them. For instance, how can we be sure that the gap between the workers ranked first and second is the same as the distance between those ranked tenth and eleventh on the same list? Finally, the relative ranking obtained for one set of workers cannot be compared with that of another set of workers, since the standards and norms of performance, or indeed the human potentials, may be different in the two groups. Tziner (1990) concludes that the relative system is probably best suited to a situation in which a choice has to be made from among the members of a small work team for purposes of promotion, rotation, special assignments, etc.

Sources of Performance Appraisal

Employee appraisal is often associated with the evaluation of workers' performance specifically by their superiors. However, attempts have been made to enrich the evaluation by providing a broader base of information culled from different sources within the organization that can be expected to represent a variety of perspectives and opinions relating to the workers being assessed (Borman, 1974). By using more than one source of appraisal, a number of factors accounting for ratees' behavior in relevant performance areas can be discerned, and may, in turn, contribute to the validation of the entire process. Naturally, for this approach to succeed, goals and principles must be clarified, necessary skills must be taught, and the participants in the system must be well prepared.

Six possible sources of appraisal have been identified: (1) evaluation by superiors; (2) evaluation by peers; (3) evaluation by subordinates; (4) self-evaluation; (5) external evaluation (outlined in Tziner, 1990); and (6) 360-degree performance evaluation.

(1) Evaluation by superiors This is the most popular and accepted form of evaluation. Indeed, the role of evaluator follows from the very definition of the position of superior. They are also the ones responsible for the training and development of their workers, and the ones who have control over a significant part of the job rewards.

Evaluations that are provided by superiors are generally a main source of information for decision-making related to staffing and the distribution of assignments. In view of their status, influence on the system, and work experience, superiors are thus considered legitimate raters. However, as we shall see below, superiors (and especially direct supervisors) are prone to distorting 'objective' data because of overly high expectations or subjective perceptions about their subordinates or about the PA system itself.

(2) Evaluation by peers Workers on the same level of the organizational hierarchy can also evaluate one another. In fact, studies have shown this to be a very accurate form of evaluation, since colleagues are in intimate contact and can follow each other's daily behavior – for better or worse (Tziner, 1984). Furthermore, evaluation by peers can be obtained from several individuals, thereby allowing for a more accurate rating that is relatively free of prejudice and is not based on a single non-routine impression.

Peer evaluation is especially important in technical jobs, where successful appraisal requires the assessor to be familiar with a body of professional knowledge. In the army, for example, this procedure has been practiced for many years in various contexts and for the achievement of a range of objectives. Perhaps one of the most popular implementations has been the use of peer appraisal as a decision-making tool for promotion purposes. Because of the reliability of the method and its high rate of success as a predictor of future success, peer evaluation is also widespread in civilian frameworks, especially among those responsible for choosing administrative personnel (P.C. Smith, 1976; Love, 1981).

Nevertheless, it should be noted that peer evaluation might have detrimental effects on the interpersonal climate because of its tendency to create suspicion and friction, particularly if the ratings are used for competitive reward purposes. In such circumstances, it might also be prejudicial in nature. Another drawback of peer evaluation is that in formulating their ratings, peers and supervisors rely on different sources of information.

(3) Subordinate evaluation This approach has been dubbed 'inverted evaluation', since, unlike conventional evaluation, it has no relation to supervisors or supervision. The very nature of the system raises questions of principle; is it possible, for example, for workers on one level to be allowed to have influence or control over the actions and advancement of workers on a higher level? To what extent do workers on a lower level understand the demands made on those who are above them? Are their evaluations valid and reliable? Nonetheless, it may be very useful for a superior to be made aware of and acknowledge the evaluations and attitudes of subordinates, whether or not the organization attaches much importance to them in respect to the organizational future of that supervisor. Indeed, in Japan, inverted evaluation is common practice, and the results are routinely used for promotion purposes.

Where there is a task-oriented relationship between two hierarchical levels, inverted evaluation naturally takes on different proportions. For example, in institutions of higher education it is common for students to rate their professors. Although these evaluations are not the only factors in determining the status of faculty members, universities are nevertheless interested in receiving information on specific areas of behavior relating to their overall teaching performance.

(4) Self-evaluation No other system can be compared with self-evaluation in terms of the plethora of observations that can be drawn on and the intimate familiarity with the complexities of the job and performance to be evaluated. Nonetheless, in most cases, self-evaluation is not accurate, as people have a tendency to be lenient with themselves and to attribute problems to external factors or to other people (Landy and Farr, 1980; Thornton, 1980).

Most human resource personnel would agree that it is unreasonable to expect workers to rate their own performances negatively, even when this is deserved. However, as noted above, all raters tend to be particularly lenient when appraisals are used for administrative decisions, so that employees are actually likely to inflate their self-ratings in order to attain extrinsic rewards. Yu and Murphy (1993) demonstrate leniency effects in self-ratings even across samples in China, and in so doing contradict previous investigations of Chinese raters which indicated that self-ratings were either only moderately biased or were lower than those generated by peers or supervisors.

Another factor that may bear on leniency is the extent to which ratees believe that self-reported information may be verified against other performance measures (Farr and Werbel, 1986). Self-ratings have, however, been found to be less fraught with the halo error, indicating that individuals do have the ability to differentiate between various aspects of performance (Campbell and Lee, 1988).

(5) External evaluation   External evaluations, given by the clients of an organization or by those who come into considerable contact with the day-to-day workings of a company, are usually partial and based on a very specific point of view. Therein lies both their strength and weakness: while outsiders' evaluations often emphasize aspects that are invisible to workers and supervisors, these factors are not necessarily the main issues mitigating against efficient performance.

(6) 360-degree evaluation   A method of performance appraisal that has been growing in popularity is the 360-degree evaluation, whereby ratings are obtained from all the individuals involved in work relations with the ratee (e.g., supervisors, customers, sales contacts, and project members). It has been shown that when properly designed, the 360-degree evaluation can result in substantially improved performance.

Performance Appraisal Formats (Performance Rating Scales)

Different kinds of performance appraisal systems have been developed with a view to assisting the rater in the task of judging. As noted above, for each assessee, a rater's judgments are meant to distinguish both between different performers and between the different dimensions required for the successful performance of the job. Accordingly, a variety of rating scales have been developed to determine: (1) to what extent ratees meet the requirements of the job; (2) the way in which they perform their assigned tasks; and (3) the measure of their success in doing so. With the help of these scales, the rater is able to base his or her judgments on the broadest possible array of relevant information.

Rating scales (or performance appraisal formats) differ from one another in the type of assistance they provide to the appraiser. The first distinction lies in the goals for which they are constructed, such as the evaluation of candidates for advancement, the provision of feedback, or the preparation of a survey for instructional purposes. The second difference relates more to the extent to which the scales are exploited for the purpose of training and development. This may include adjustment of the scale to a specific organization or job, or it may relate to the extent to which members of the organization or other professionals participate in its construction. Thirdly, the scales often differ with respect to the form and sequence of ratings. The last major distinction concerns the balancing of the ratings and the effectiveness of the scale in terms of its potential for minimizing errors in evaluation. All these issues have played an important role in the attempts to construct new ranking scales. Tziner (1990) breaks down the various scales or formats into eight main categories: (1) trait-graphic scales (GRS); (2) weighted checklist scales; (3) forced choice scales (FCS); (4) mixed standard scales (MSS); (5) behaviorally anchored rating scales (BARS); (6) behavioral expectation scales (BES); (7) behavioral observation scales (BOS); and (8) behavioral description scales (BDS). Below is a description of each of these appraisal formats, followed by a detailed comparison of the three major types: trait-graphic scales (GRS), behaviorally anchored rating scales (BARS), and behavioral observation scales (BOS).

(1) Trait-Graphic Scales

Carroll and Schneier (1982) note that this kind of format, which rates worker output, is one of the oldest and most widely used by organizations for appraising employee performance. The appraisal includes items such as: level or quality of performance; traits of the worker in areas of ability; personal qualities; skills, such as level of precision; attitudes toward work; initiative; and dedication. For each dimension of the appraisal, whether it measures the quantity or the quality of performance, there is a descriptive continuum of ratings in terms that range from 'excellent' to 'poor'. For example:

Trait	Rating				
Independence	1 *very independent*	2	3 *average independence*	4	5 *very dependent*
Precision at work	1 *very precise*	2	3 *average precision*	4	5 *very imprecise*

Level of performance

1 2 3 4 5 6 7 8 9 10 11 12 13 14 15 16 17 18 19 20 21 22 23 24 25
  Poor   *below*   . *average*   *above*   *excellent*
                      average   *average*

   The advantage of the trait-graphic format lies in the basic simplicity both of the construction of the scale and its application. The scale can easily be constructed by a personnel department in cooperation with raters and ratees based on only a very general familiarity with the job under review. No special instruction in the use of the system is needed, the evaluation form is easy to understand, and little time is required to rank the list of outputs or qualities.

   However, the format also has its disadvantages. One is that the levels in the scale are often not defined precisely, so that there is a certain degree of subjectivity, and even obscurity, with respect to the meaning of each level. The meaning and significance of the levels thus usually vary across appraisers, making it very difficult to distinguish precisely between the different levels of the evaluated characteristic *per se,* or to tease out different raters' conceptions of the 'distances' between them.

   Another intrinsic difficulty is that the definition of the term 'evaluation' is not always sufficiently clear to appraisers, since it is often formulated abstractly, without reference to empirically measurable criteria. Consequently, if an appraisal format of the trait-graphic scales type is to be used, it is advisable to define these elusive factors of performance as clearly as possible according to their conceptual and practical concomitants in order to standardize them for different raters. Consider, for instance, the term 'initiative'; it might be more clearly defined as 'devising new ideas for improving work processes without being required to do so'.

   In addition, there are limitations in the trait-graphic format concerning the degree of control the rater has in determining the grade on the scales. Furthermore, it suffers from the inherent difficulty of controlling errors, including the central tendency, that is, the tendency to cluster marks around the middle of the scale, or negative or positive leniency.

(2) Weighted Checklists

This type of form employs a weighted checklist consisting of a list of statements, adjectives, or individual job-related qualities previously scaled for effectiveness. Raters are asked to choose the statements, which, in their opinion, are the most descriptive of each ratee. This form of evaluation, first suggested by Knauft (1948), is intended to increase the objectivity of the assessment procedure and limit the tendency of assessors to over or under evaluate assessees when continuums are used.

The success of appraisal formats of this type is conditional on the degree of correlation between the formulation of the statements, adjectives, and individual qualities described in the checklist and those criteria actually employed by members of the organization to describe effective work or the qualities of workers. Naturally, these criteria must be sufficient to distinguish between different levels, so that ideally, each item should be weighted in accordance with its relative importance to performance. The final ratings are calculated on the basis of the number of items attributed to each of the worker.

Three stages are involved in the production of a weighted checklist. First, a detailed list of effective and ineffective behaviors in the performance of the job must be compiled. Next, a number of raters who are very familiar with the job review each description, determine whether it portrays a desirable or an undesirable behavior, and rank it on a nine-point scale on which '1' stands for 'very undesirable behavior' and '9' for 'very desirable behavior'. Descriptions judged similarly by the different raters can be included in the checklist. For example, a statement ranked 4,4,5,5, and 4 would be chosen, while one receiving inconsistent grades, such as 9,5,4,6, and 5, would be disqualified. Finally, the weight of the statement is determined as an average of the judges' rankings.

Below is an example of a weighted checklist based on a form used to assess the manager of a manufacturing department:

The following list is intended to facilitate the evaluation of the human relations abilities of an employee. The list provides different examples of possible behavior. You are to choose only those statements that describe behaviors you have actually seen displayed by the ratee. (Place an X beside the appropriate statements.)

1   When s/he makes assignments, s/he discusses them at length with his/her subordinates.
2   S/he is not capable of resolving disagreements among his/her subordinates.
3   S/he encourages the ideas of his/her subordinates, and tries to apply them if possible.
4   S/he delegates responsibility for performing an important duty, but refuses to allow the subordinate to perform it without his/her intervention.
5   S/he makes an effort to praise work well done.
6   S/he does not keep the promises s/he makes to his/her subordinates.
7   S/he displays tact and patience when listening to his/her subordinates' complaints.
8   S/he does not apologize to subordinates when s/he has made a mistake.

(3) Forced Choice Scales

Forced choice scales, based on a list of behavioral statements that are usually presented in clusters of three or four each, was introduced by Wherry (1959) as a means of reducing error and increasing the validity of assessment procedures. The collection of statements in each cluster is arranged so that each proposition is weighted equally in terms of its influence on the quality of performance, or so that raters will not prefer any one statement over another when choosing items for the appraisal of workers' performance. However, the items do differ in their potential to enable distinctions to be drawn between levels of performance. In any given cluster, there are usually only one or two statements that clearly distinguish between better and poorer workers.

Accordingly, raters are asked to choose the two statements in each cluster which they believe best describe the ratee's performance. This choice then determines the result of the appraisal within the cluster. It is represented as the sum of the numerical values which designate the ability of the statement to distinguish between high-level and low-level performers, a property labeled 'discriminability'. For example, the following statements might represent a cluster in a scale for evaluating the teaching quality of a university professor:

1   aptient with slow students;
2   lectures fluently and with confidence;
3   holds the students' attention and interest;
4   sets clear goals for each lesson at the beginning of the course.

Now assume that it has been determined that statements 1 and 3 represent the qualities of the best teachers. If the raters choose these two statements to describe a given ratee, he or she scores 2 points. If they choose only one of the statements, say 1 and 2 or 2 and 3, the ratee scores 1 point. If they choose neither 1 nor 3, the ratee receives zero points.

Empirical evidence indicates that the use of forced choice scales for appraisal reduces tendencies both toward the extremes and toward the center. Furthermore, impressive gains in the degree of reliability and validity of performance appraisals have been reported for these scales (Landy and Farr, 1980).

Nevertheless, this appraisal format suffers from serious disadvantages. The first is the enormous amount of effort that has to be invested in order to develop and construct appropriate clusters. In addition, not only is the use of the format extremely complex and time-consuming for raters, but it also implies a lack of trust in their ability to formulate valid appraisals. Insofar as the final numerical values defining the level of performance are determined by means of routine calculations, it essentially turns raters into mere tools for obtaining raw data They do not know how the clusters were formed, nor are they made aware of the weight of each statement in the various clusters. As efficient evaluation requires the initial consent and combined effort of all parties concerned, the raters' awareness that they have no control over the final scores accorded to the ratees must surely reduce the overall effectiveness of this appraisal process. This phenomenon alone might explain the lack of popularity of, and paucity of research on, this format (Zavala, 1965; Bernardin and Carlyle, 1979). Moreover, while forced choice scales are helpful in determining the extent to which someone is suited for a particular position, they are less useful for purposes of development and instruction, as they do not provide a comprehensive picture of the various factors involved in ratees' performance.

(4) Mixed Standard Scales

First introduced by Blanz (1965), mixed standard scales were designed to reduce errors in rating, and particularly the tendency toward leniency, an effect that was indeed substantiated by Blanz and Ghiselli (1972). In this format, each dimension of performance is described by three different propositions which are randomly distributed throughout the appraisal form, so that raters cannot readily perceive that they are being asked to evaluate the same dimension three separate times. Since it is also difficult to discern what level of performance each statement reflects, each proposition is judged on its own merit. Raters are asked to compare the ratee's performance with the description in the statement and score it on a three-point scale: better, as good as, worse.

Mixed standard scales make it a simple matter to check the internal consistency both of the appraiser and of the results for each ratee. For example, if a rater stipulates that a worker performs worse than a statement describing ineffective performance, and better than another statement describing effective performance, it is clear that the appraisal is inconsistent.

(5) Behaviorally Anchored Rating Scales (BARS)

Since its development, the behaviorally anchored rating scales (BARS) format, designed to create standardization both in the observation of the performance of the worker being evaluated and in the interpretation of the information gathered, has received a great deal of attention (e.g., Bernardin and Smith, 1981; Fay and Latham, 1982). The idea here is to employ scales with 'behavioral anchors', that is, propositions that describe specifically, and in the professional language of the evaluators, the activities and behavior entailed in the work of the ratees. The assumption is that with behavioral anchors defined in the rater's own terminology, the alleged lack of ambiguity in the scales will be reduced, and the achievement of relatively error-free performance evaluation ratings will be enhanced.

The construction of the anchors for the purpose of rating performance demands prolonged and complicated efforts, with professionals working together with the department supervisors who will be carrying out the performance appraisal in order to formulate them. Indeed, it is not uncommon for professional evaluators to involve representatives of the ratees themselves in this process of construction.

The guiding principle of the rating scale is to obtain the maximum possible number of specifications of a wide spectrum of dimensions of performance, and then translate each dimension into behavioral terms. Once this goal is achieved, it is then possible to base appraisals on specific, relevant descriptions.

In contrast to trait-graphic scales (from which BARS was derived), the numerical values, or ratings, along the scale are clearly and unequivocally defined with the help of these behavioral anchors, with each anchor exemplifying a distinct level of performance. BARS thus represents an attempt to surmount the basic drawback of trait-graphic scales, whereby raters interpret the statements on the scale as they see fit. (A more detailed description of the stages in the process of developing the BARS type of evaluation can be found in Bernardin and Beatty, 1984.)

Naturally, the joint effort of researcher, raters, and ratees (where relevant) in the process of constructing BARS evaluation forms impacts on the assessors' level of commitment to the process and their motivation to employ the format. It also contributes to the gradual creation of a broad-based frame of reference that clearly defines criteria of effective performance which are acceptable to both raters and ratees. Consequently, the scale helps to generate change in the relationship of the individuals on both sides of the assessment situation, who learn to base their mutual interaction on concrete events, as well as on the analysis of jobs and styles of behavior. This type of interaction stands in sharp contrast to the formation of general impressions through random association.

Furthermore, since it is based on real events at work, BARS positively affects standardization in the processes of observation and scale construction. It also contributes significantly to the readiness with which workers accept criticism. As the scales identify real, specific, and objective behaviors, the feedback process makes it easier for ratees to discern the roots of their performance problems or to discover the keys to improved skill and success. Moreover, the feedback provides workers with details concerning various aspects of their performance. Similarly, the scales specify incidents of behavior and performance at different levels of quality, thus enabling assessors to distinguish between efficient skilled activities and inefficient behavior. The extensive detail in each anchor thus facilitates the feedback process of explaining to specific workers exactly how and why they were graded.

The major advantage of BARS, therefore, lies in the way the scale is constructed and its subsequent use to the organization (Bernardin and Smith, 1981). Surprisingly, however, the many studies that have attempted to determine whether this format is, in fact, significantly better than others in reducing appraisal errors have not yet produced unequivocal findings (see: Borman, 1979; Kingstrom and Bass, 1981; Latham and Wexley, 1981; Tziner, 1984a).

Criticism of the format includes the high cost of its development and the large amount of time required to fill out the questionnaire. Other problems concern the possibility of detecting individual behaviors in each ratee and the degree of accuracy with which the anchors reflect a particular behavior. Oddly enough, BARS can create a paradoxical situation in which behavior represented by anchors such as 'effective' (denoting a high level of performance) or 'ineffective' (a low level of performance) is applicable to the same worker! It is also possible that a ratee who displays behavior represented by the anchor 'excellence' may fail in the job.

(6) Behavioral Expectations Scales (BES)

Another version of BARS is the behavioral expectation scale based on the 'critical incident' technique, which involves selecting those behaviors that are considered critical for success in the job. On the basis of observation of ratees for a period of from six months to a year, raters are asked to indicate what type of behavior they predict from each worker. This prediction does not have to reflect the modes of behavior described in the anchors of the scale; on the contrary, the evaluator is told to make inferences about the future based specifically on observed behavior.

Appraisal formats of this type obviously leave considerable room for perceptual distortions that can bias the appraisals. In the absence of anchors of behavior for all levels of the scales, or in the absence of complete correspondence between the behavioral anchor and what is actually demonstrated, the rater can only make an approximate appraisal based on inference. Another drawback relates to the raters' prior knowledge of the anchors used to represent efficient or low-level behavior, since the statements are arranged in descending order. This allows them to adjust a particular ratee's appraisals on each dimension of performance so as to fit their general impressions. Nevertheless, Ivancevich (1980) reports that a BES-based performance appraisal significantly improved attitudes (such as increasing perceived equity of ratings and reducing job-related tension) in a group of engineers.

(7) Behavioral Observation Scales (BOS)

BOS scales, developed by Latham and Wexley (1981), have a format similar to that of BARS, but with a number of significant differences. Here the evaluator is asked to indicate the frequency with which certain behaviors appear in the course of a ratee's evaluation (from 'very frequently' to 'very infrequently' or from 'always' to 'never'), or the degree of typicality of the ratee's performance (from 'very typical' to 'very atypical'). The scale also directs observation to the quality of the performance.

The BOS format does not actually require appraisers to know the ratee's job well. They can relate to behavioral details without any direct assessment of good or bad performance, but simply rate the frequency with which they observe a particular behavior description or characterization. In essence, however, the process is based on the assumption that 'good' behavior *per se* does not necessarily occur with the highest frequency.

The major advantage of this format lies in the fact that both the observation and the consequent evaluation refer to behaviors that are actually displayed in performance of the ratee's job, without the need for inference or prediction. Furthermore, the appraisal information is totally comprehensive, since specific references to and evaluation of each separate incidence of behavior are required. In this way it is likely that assessors will avoid the type of paradox mentioned earlier, namely, that patently inconsistent behaviors on the same scale would fit a single assessee.

However, the BOS evaluation format has two striking drawbacks. First, for the purposes of standardizing the ratings that distinguish between excellent and poor performance, a sample of several hundred workers is required. The development process is thus very costly. Secondly, the different ranks associated with each behavior are defined in general terms or not at all (as in the trait-graphic scales). This lack of specificity amounts to abandonment of one of the basic advantages of behavioral scales, the designation of evaluations in measurable behavioral terms.

A well-known example of the BOS is the Minnesota Satisfactoriness Scale (MSS), designed by Dawis and Lofquist (1984). The MSS was developed following a search of the literature aimed at identifying the kinds of information that might be indicative of satisfactoriness. Positive indicators include quantity and quality of work, job suitability, promotability, and degree of merit for a pay raise, while negative indices include frequency of absences, lateness, accidents, and disciplinary actions. Experimental rating forms were constructed in order to formulate the items that would sample these indicators. Supervisor ratings were then obtained for almost 1,000 employees in skilled, nonskilled, blue-collar, and white-collar occupations. Preliminary analyses of these data indicated that two factors accounted for the common variance in most employee groups. The first was identified as a performance factor, with loadings on items such as quality of work, promotability, and meriting a pay raise. The second was a conformance factor, with loadings on items like frequency of absences, lateness, and accidents.

Consequent revisions of the experimental scales resulted in the construction of the MSS as a 28-item questionnaire designed to assess the satisfactoriness of an employee. The items are presented in question form, and for most of them, the rater is asked to compare the employee with other members of the work group and to indicate his or her standing on a three-point scale, such as 'not as good, about the same, better', or 'less, about the same, more'. Other items ask the rater to make a decision on such matters as awarding the employee a pay raise or promoting him or her to a position of greater responsibility. The final item asks for an overall rating of the employee's satisfactoriness framed by indicating in which quarter of the distribution of people doing the same work the employee would fall.

The MSS is scored on five scales: general satisfactoriness, performance, conformance, dependability, and personal adjustment. Internal consistency reliabilities for these scales, obtained for several different worker groups, range from 0.69 to 0.95, with a median of 0.87. The validity of the MSS has been demonstrated against a criterion of job tenure in a study of over 1,500 workers (Lofquist and Dawis, 1969). Discriminant validity, indicated by analysis of correlations between the MSS and the Minnesota Satisfaction Questionnaire, have shown that the variance shared by the two instruments ranges from only 2 to 10 per cent for different occupational groups.

(8) Behavioral Description Scales (BDS)

Like the BOS, this format, designed by Kane and Lawler (1979), is meant to eliminate the shortcomings of BARS. In its initial development phase, the BDS normally requires that a large list of behavioral statements describing various levels of performance be generated. Similar items are then combined into 'generic behaviors' in order to reduce the length of the list. For each statement, judges are asked to respond to three questions:

1   During a six-month period, how many times would a ratee have the opportunity to exhibit the behavior described by the statement?
2   On how many of these occasions would it be moderately satisfactory to exhibit this behavior?
3   What level of performance on, say, a seven-point scale from unacceptable to excellent, is described by the behavioral item?

Another group of judges receives the same list of items with the same basic questions. In the second set of questions, however, the term 'satisfactory' is replaced by 'unsatisfactory'. Following this procedure, standard deviations for the occurrence rates of each level of performance are computed for each generic behavioral item in order to obtain a frequency distribution set.

In the form used by the raters, the behavioral statements are randomly distributed. In a blank space next to each statement, the rater is asked to indicate the number of times the ratee exhibits a particular behavior. A ratee's frequency scores are then compared with the opportunity afforded to manifest that behavior, and the frequency for each performance level is computed by means of the derivation process (as described above).

As yet, not much is known about how well BDS fares with respect to its psychometric properties, nor how well it accomplishes the various performance appraisal objectives.

Which Rating Format is Best?

Initial examination of the psychometric properties of behavior-based scales versus graphic rating scales appeared to demonstrate the advantages of the former, although these were less than anticipated (Landy and Farr, 1980). While these early investigations tended to demonstrate the superior reliability (Latham and Wexley, 1981) and validity (Latham, Fay, and Saari, 1979) of BOS, a comparative review of the rating formats along qualitative and quantitative criteria (Bernardin and Beatty, 1984) failed to find a single rating format superior to all others in all respects, despite its emphasis on the comparison between behavior-based and graphic scales (Feldman, 1981; Fay and Latham, 1982). Indeed, thirty years of research into the psychometric properties of the various appraisal methods has not demonstrated conclusively which format is the most appropriate or efficient (see: Landy and Farr, 1980; Latham and Wexley, 1981; Tziner, 1990; Steiner, Rain and Smalley, 1993; Gosselin, Werner and Halle, 1994).

In point of fact, however, an accurate comparison of scale formats was not possible in many studies because of differences both in scale dimension content and anchors and in the number of scale points (see: Borman, 1974). The inconsistency of the findings might also be explained in part by the fact that only few of these studies subjected both forms of scales to the same methodological scrutiny.

Tziner's (1990) review, however, allows a more discerning, albeit tentative, distinction to be drawn between the various formats. Forced choice scales would seem to be better able to inhibit deliberate rating inflation, making them more suitable for administrative purposes, such as promotion, merit pay, and employment termination. Behavior-based formats, on the other hand, would appear to be superior to others in fostering performance improvement, since, by providing data for feedback, they tend to facilitate clarification of work roles, thereby reducing role ambiguity and conflict. Finally, with respect to psychometric characteristics, personnel comparison methods (such as paired comparisons and rank ordering) seem to be less susceptible to intentional leniency, the central tendency, and range restriction biases.

The Effects of Performance Appraisal Formats on Raters, Ratees and Job Performance

Although it is difficult to recommend one appraisal format over another, we have seen that behavior-based scales appear to offer advantages with respect to fostering performance improvement and worker development. In a recent attempt to investigate this relationship further, Tziner and a number of colleagues conducted a series of six studies that compared and contrasted methods and formats of performance appraisal on a variety of rater and ratee outcomes, testing them immediately after the evaluation process took place (Tziner, 1984a; Tziner et al., 1988; 1989; 1993; 1997; 2000). The goal of these studies was not only to throw light on the effectiveness and utility of the specific measuring tools, but also to assist human resource personnel to take advantage of the potential of PA to contribute to the overall work environment and productivity of the employees in their organizations.

This objective was adopted in light of the scant research on the usefulness of PA methods for developmental purposes, and the fact that they are seldom used to assist both supervisors and subordinates to improve their productivity. On the whole, it was hoped that the studies would help to reinforce the contention that, when administered properly, PA serves more than administrative functions in areas such as remuneration or assignment decisions.

Earlier studies had demonstrated that when performance feedback is precise and timely, it may result in behavior change, even though job behaviors are generally difficult to modify (Steers, 1975; Campbell and Pritchard, 1976; Schneier, Shaw and Beatty, 1991). The extant research also indicated that performance appraisal contributes both to employee development (McGregor, 1957) and to the improvement of future job performance (Bernardin and Beatty, 1984; Murphy and Cleveland, 1991). According to Dorfman, Stephan, and Loveland (1986), performance appraisal makes short-term behavior change possible specifically through the following mechanisms: raters' identification of employee strengths and weaknesses; the provision of performance feedback; and the facilitation of exchanges with supervisors. In acknowledging previous research in this field, Tziner et al. (1997) note, however, that evidence regarding the long-term (future) influences of performance appraisal on employee attitudes and performance has yet to be established clearly (Nathan, Morhrman and Milliman, 1991).

Murphy and Cleveland (1995) also point to the relative dearth of investigations on subordinates' reactions to appraisal systems, as compared to the abundance of studies on their psychometric properties and accuracy.

Moreover, Bernadin and Beatty (1984) maintain that ratees' reactions to appraisal systems are more likely than their psychometric qualities to make a significant contribution to sustaining the viability of the appraisal system. Whatever the accuracy of the ratings and their freedom from errors, an appraisal system will be rendered useless, and probably sink into decay, if it does not elicit positive reactions from both raters and ratees (see: Hedge and Borman, 1995). Recently, a large meta-analytic study by Cawley, Keeping, and Levy (1998) has provided further strong support for this contention.

Of the eight types of PA rating tools outlined above, the two currently in greatest use in the field are: (1) behavior-based rating formats, which define job performance in terms of specific, 'pinpointed', observable actions (e.g., 'ratee completes all sections of a crime report'); and (2) trait-graphic rating scales (GRS), which typically identify relatively broad and vague dimensions of performance in specific areas (e.g., 'ratee pays increased attention to details'). In contrast to GRS, which depend on the subjective (and biased) judgments of appraisers, behavior-based appraisal defines job performance in relatively objective, quantitative terms. The two most popular behavior-based formats are: (1) Behavioral Observation Scales (BOS), which ask raters to report the frequency of specific job-related behaviors; and (2) Behavioral Anchored Rating Scales (BARS), which use behavioral statements to illustrate rating levels. BOS, in particular, clarifies for both the appraiser and the worker precisely what activities should (or should not) be performed on the job, in what manner, and how the outcomes link to performance ratings (Latham and Wexley, 1981).

Throughout the series of studies conducted by Tziner and his colleagues, the researchers maintain that these three rating scale formats (GRS, BOS, and BARS) might prove useful in helping raters and ratees to develop rating performance feedback and to fashion their plans and goals for acting on that feedback. The specific characteristics of the three scales and the results of studies of their use provide evidence in support of this position. Thus, particular attention is given in the following account to the specific post-PA outcomes that served as dependent variables in Tziner et al.'s series of investigations.

The suppositions made by the researchers were as follows:

1 *Communications* BOS appears more likely to minimize barriers to communications between superiors and subordinates because it specifically defines the requisite organizational expectations and performance requirements. Consequently, role ambiguity and role conflicts should be reduced and positive employee attitudes toward their work should be enhanced. Moreover, Wiersma and Latham's (1986) finding that managers

and employees prefer BOS (and GRS) to behaviorally anchored rating scales may be indicative.

2   *Performance goals*   Because they differ in the extent to which they focus on specific behaviors and the amount of information they can provide about actual behaviors, different rating scale formats are likely to affect the sorts of performance goals set by both raters and ratees. Although the GRS format is widely used by organizations for performance review purposes (Carroll and Schneier, 1982), such appraisals tend to be generic. Thus, the consequent course of action deriving from the definition of the goals to be accomplished (as reflected in goal clarity) is likely to be fuzzy. On the other hand, it is reasonable to posit that rating scales which focus on specific behaviors (e.g., BOS) should lead to goals that are clearer, more directly observable, and better accepted by ratees than scales that provide less behavioral information. This enhanced clarity should in turn increase commitment to the goals (Carroll and Schneier, 1982; Huber, 1985; Dolan and Schuler, 1987). Indeed, clarity, acceptance, and commitment are all recognized determinants of the success of performance appraisal and feedback (Latham and Wexley, 1981), and consequently, they were also employed as criteria in Tziner et al.'s series of studies.

3   *Feedback*   A behavioral observation scale (BOS) performance appraisal and review process should lead to higher levels of performance and satisfaction with the feedback process than a graphic rating scale approach, for three reasons. First, as noted repeatedly, the BOS-based process conveys more precisely what an individual should do. Rather than enjoining someone to 'improve your sense of responsibility' or 'sharpen your leadership skills', behavior-based feedback identifies the specific desirable or undesirable actions to be taken or avoided (Latham and Wexley, 1981). Secondly, BOS-based feedback is more likely to be accepted because it is seen as more factual, objective, and unbiased (Kopelman, 1986). And thirdly, BOS-based feedback would be more conducive to setting performance goals that are specific and job-related, rather than vague and unrelated (e.g., minimization of the raters' subjectivity; see: Petit and Haines, 1994). These goal properties (specificity and relevance) are likely to further affect the extent to which the appraisee perceives the goals as clear, acceptable, and worthy of commitment (Carroll and Schneier, 1982; Huber, 1985; Dolan and Schuler, 1987).

4   *User satisfaction with the appraisal method*   User satisfaction does not relate only to feedback or goal setting; it concerns the entire appraisal process. The quality of this attitudinal concomitant is critical, since if either the PA

administrators or ratees are dissatisfied with the system, the effectiveness of both the appraisal and the feedback is diminished (Wiersma and Latham, 1986; Gosselin and Murphy, 1994; Petit and Haines, 1994). As behavior-based appraisal defines job performance in relatively objective, quantitative terms, it should be seen by ratees as more accurate and fair, i.e., less prone to problems of rater bias, errors, or inexperience (Tharenou, 1995).

5   *Rater satisfaction* Rater dissatisfaction may emerge, among other things, from anxiety related to a lack of desire or ability to rate one's colleagues. Preliminary evidence indicates that BOS helps decrease evaluators' fear of possible confrontations with their subordinates (Latham, Fay, and Saari, 1979). This suggestion is supported by the observation that raters who are generally uncomfortable carrying out appraisal and delivering appropriate feedback (Napier and Latham, 1986; Arpin, 1994) may find that the use of BOS scales reduces this discomfort, since it directs discussion to the frequency of specific behaviors, rather than to the rater's evaluations of those behaviors. Moreover, the fact that workers might be expected to view behavior-based rating as relatively more factual and incontrovertible than GRS-based appraisals should also facilitate the review process from the perspective of the rater (Wiersma, Van Den Berg, and Latham, 1995). Indeed, to the extent that the performance review discussion is based on relatively objective and quantitative information, rather than ambiguous criteria and subjectively interpreted levels of performance, the feedback should be less acrimonious and more satisfying for both sides.

Tziner, Joanis, and Murphy (2000) note that raters are also likely to be more satisfied with BOS than with BARS because of the relatively objective appearance of the BOS format, which involves recording behavior frequencies that require no extrapolation on the part of the rater (Latham and Wexley, 1981; Petit and Haines, 1994). Moreover, BOS seems easier both to understand and to implement in adequately (Borman, 1986). In addition, in respect to the choice between BARS and BOS, we have already noted Tziner's (1990) comments about raters' difficulties regarding which anchors in the BARS actually reflect the ratee's performance, and the fact that diametrically opposed statements can describe the same worker's behavior. In such cases, the rater may select an intermediate score as most representative, and consequently formulate a goal that is not appropriate. These drawbacks indicate that of the two behavior-based appraisal methods, the BOS format should result in more positive rater satisfaction reactions and higher ratee performance appraisal reviews (e.g., ratee satisfaction, clarification of path to goal).

In their investigations, Tziner and his colleagues tested most of these suppositions empirically, some for the first time, while seeking at the same time to overcome several of the drawbacks inherent in previous studies. The following review highlights a number of the major findings and their implications, especially where they further elucidate theoretical conceptions or indicate avenues for future research. By and large, Tziner et al. compared the three PA formats in real organizational settings, using samples of supervisors (managers) trained to conduct performance rating and their subordinates. With the exception of the first investigation, which still stressed psychometric properties, the studies recorded the post-appraisal responses, reactions, and ratings of assessees (and in some cases of raters as well), in accordance with the particular dependent variables being examined. An overview of the studies can be found in Table 6.1.

The pertinent results and conclusions drawn by the researchers in each of these studies are summarized below. The 'comments' represent the main ideas presented in the discussion of the individual papers.

Tziner (1984)– Psychometric Properties of Rating Scales in a Real Organizational Setting

Description

Fifty-seven managers in an aircraft plant appraised their subordinates using BARS and a graphic scale.

Results

In overall terms, the BARS method appeared less susceptible than the GRS to both halo and leniency effects, and also yielded marginally higher interrater agreement.

Comments

The results stem from the elimination of certain methodological deficiencies apparent in earlier comparative studies (e.g., an equal number of scale points was ensured), a conclusion based on Bernardin and Smith's (1981) suggestion that results not supporting the psychometric superiority of BARS may be accounted for by methodological flaws.

Table 6.1   Independent and dependent variables in a series of studies by Tziner et al. on the effects of rating appraisal formats on work outcomes

Authors	Year	GRS	BARS	BOS	Other independent variables	Hypotheses regarding	dependent variables (outcomes):
Tziner	1984	✓	✓			Leniency, halo effect (Interrater R)	
Tziner and Kopelman	1988	✓		✓	Performance feedback	Goal clarity, acceptance and commitment	
Tziner and Latham	1989	✓		✓	Performance feedback, goal setting		Work satisfaction, org. commitment
Tziner, Kopelman and Livneh	1993	✓		✓		Goal clarity, acceptance and commitment	Ratee appraisal-satisfaction, method performance
Tziner, Kopelman and Joanis	1997	✓	✓	✓		Goal acceptance, path to goal, foal commitment, specificity and observability	Ratee appraisal-satisfaction, rater appraisal-satisfaction
Tziner, Joanis and Murphy	2000	✓	✓	✓		Perception of goals, goal specificity and observability	Ratee appraisal-satisfaction

This evidence does not, however, prove that BARS is unequivocally superior to the GRS format in respect to psychometric properties, since the study found only marginal or non-significant leniency effect (e.g., initiative) differences between the two methods on several performance dimensions. This may be due to the insufficient training of raters. As rating errors are well-ingrained habits, only prolonged and extensive rater training might eliminate them. A comprehensive workshop for rater training may be needed to provide trainees with adequate opportunities to practice the acquired skills, receive feedback on their appraisal performance, and thus ensure a comprehensive acquaintance with the appropriate behaviors to be observed (see: Latham et al., 1975). This issue is addressed at the end of this chapter.

The results may also reflect the reality of the organizational setting in which the study was conducted. Ratees' assumptions that the appraisals were to be used for administrative purposes might have caused an unwillingness to subject themselves to union pressures. That is to say, contextual factors of this kind may have biased the ratings on the BARS, although they are generally regarded as more easily tenable, another indication that real world research, in contrast to laboratory studies (e.g., Fay and Latham, 1982), is critical for valid exploration of the results of training and/or type of rating scale effects on rating errors.

According to Feldman (1981), rating errors will probably creep into overall (global) evaluations of any type, independent of the rating method. Nevertheless, the global performance evaluation, made after the ratings on performance dimensions had been completed, was less contaminated by leniency effects when using BARS than when using the graphic rating scale format. Tziner notes here, however, that since BARS provides a standardized frame of reference for observing, recording, and interpreting behavioral incidents (Bernardin and Smith, 1981), a feature shared by other behavioral approaches (e.g., BOS; Latham and Wexley, 1977; 1981), the ratings on performance dimensions based on these 'incidents' reflect an objective reality (i.e., actual performance and behavior) more efficiently than do GRS. Consequently, they are presumably less contaminated by prevalent rating errors, as described by Feldman (1981).

It appears, therefore, that the BARS method, as one of the broad category of behavioral approaches, better prepares raters to summarize cognitively and abstract adequately from all partial ratings made on dimensions, thus enabling them to incorporate these scores into a 'well-designed' overall (global) evaluation. This quality should express itself in the lower susceptibility of this evaluation to appraisal biases, a proposition that Tziner notes has yet to be submitted to either theoretical elaboration or empirical examination. Moreover, future research might incorporate a measure of 'correct' performance, or a differential accuracy measure in order to examine the replicability of other results revealed by this study.

Tziner and Kopelman (1988) – Effect of Rating Formats on Goal-setting Dimensions

Description

Ten managers and their 62 subordinates participated in a field experiment that examined the effects of PA feedback deriving from BOS and GRS on three goal-setting dimensions: goal clarity, goal acceptance, and goal commitment.

Results

The BOS format yielded significantly higher levels of goal clarity, goal acceptance, and goal commitment.

Comments

In a preliminary analysis of the data, an average intercorrelation of .60 was found among the three perceptual goal-setting dimensions. In light of the high interrelatedness among the dependent variables, the three measures were analyzed together using a multivariate analysis of variance (MANOVA). The results indicated significant differences in perceptions of the set goals across two experimental groups, $F(1,60)=51.14$, $p<.001$, Wilks' lamda=.27.

The results of *a priori* t tests (Wildt and Ahtola, 1978, p. 30), performed separately for the three goal-setting dimensions, indicated that ratees who received performance feedback using a BOS format reported significantly higher levels of goal clarity, goal acceptance, and goal commitment. This supports the notion that the behavior specificity of BOS enables the formulation of more focused goals, a situation that should, in turn, facilitate the improvement of ratees' work behavior and work performance. In contrast, goal setting derived from the generic (and often vague) performance dimensions of GRS-based performance feedback requires supervisors to perform an unpleasant duty, which may therefore often be avoided, postponed, or handled hurriedly (see: Kopelman, 1986).

Tziner and Latham (1989) – Effects of Appraisal Instrument, Feedback and Goal-setting on Worker Satisfaction (with the PA) and Commitment

Description

In light of studies indicating that in the absence of trained appraisers it makes no difference which PA format is used (Fay and Latham, 1982), 20 managers received intensive training in appraising objectively, giving performance feedback, and setting specific goals when conducting PA with 125 subordinates. Following training, they were randomly assigned to one of four conditions: (1) feedback and goal-setting using BOS-based appraisals; (2) feedback using BOS-based appraisals with no goal-setting; (3) feedback and goal-setting using GRS-based appraisals; and (4) feedback using GRS-based appraisals with no goal-setting. Work satisfaction and organizational commitment were measured before and after the performance appraisals were conducted.

Results

Analysis revealed that: (1) BOS-based appraisal increased work satisfaction significantly more than GRS appraisal; (2) feedback followed by goal-setting resulted in significantly higher worker satisfaction and organizational commitment than feedback alone, regardless of the appraisal scale that was used; and (3) the combination of BOS-based appraisal, feedback, and goal setting led to significantly higher work satisfaction than any other experimental condition.

Comments

The results of this field experiment reveal that performance feedback alone generates improvements in ratee organizational commitment and, particularly, in work satisfaction, in keeping with previous findings (Kim and Schuler, 1979). However, performance feedback followed by goal-setting produced even more positive ratee outcomes than feedback alone, perhaps 'because people are basically feedback seekers' (Ashford, 1986). Positive feedback provides information about how well appraisees meet organizational expectations and work requirements, and as the individuals realize that their superiors recognize their accomplishments, a number of attitudinal changes may occur. The results of the appraisals on work satisfaction confirm that these attitudes include such work-related perceptions as ambiguity concerning advancement, work relations with supervisors, the ability to accept criticism, and so on, which serve as motivating factors for self-correction.

Unlike work satisfaction, organizational commitment was only slightly affected by performance feedback alone, although it too was measured on aspects of superior-subordinate relationships. Improper conceptualization and/ or operationalization of organizational commitment do not therefore appear to account for the weaker effects. Organizational commitment has been defined as the extent to which an employee identifies with, and is involved in, his or her work unit and the organization as a whole (Curry, Wakefield, Price and Mueller, 1986). Perhaps, then, feedback alone does not have much of an impact on some of the issues of organizational commitment that were tapped in this research, such as pride in belonging to the work unit or willingness to assume any job so as to stay with the unit. Moreover, it is clear that organizational commitment is a matter of more than just receiving performance feedback.

The process of goal setting seems to give the ratee a broader picture of the work unit and the organization's objectives, and how the set goals contribute to that unit and to the organization's goals. Consequently, we might expect the emergence of the sort of organizational commitment measures that were examined in this study, such as: 'I am proud to tell others that I am part of this work unit', or 'I would accept almost any job in order to stay with this work unit.'

Performance feedback combined with goal-setting contributed most strongly to ratees' measures of work satisfaction. This may derive from the fact that goal-setting fosters feelings of participation in work-related issues (Schneider, 1981; Miller and Monge, 1986) and meaningfulness at work, both of which were components of the study's satisfaction measure.

In respect to the appraisal formats, the BOS-based evaluation proved more beneficial in every instance, and was the only format to produce a significant effect in regard to work satisfaction. The authors again cite the inherent specificity of BOS, which may be expected to affect work satisfaction positively by strengthening ratees' feelings of control at work, dissipating ambiguity about expectations and requirements, and so on.

In passing, Tziner and Latham also note the contribution this study makes by extending the research of behavioral observation scales to the Israeli organizational setting, which differs considerably from its North American counterpart in terms of work value structure (Falbe, Nobel-Ben Yoav and Tziner, 1986). The positive reactions to BOS, as compared to alternative instruments such as GRS, found in both laboratory and field settings in the

US (Bernardin and Beatty, 1984; Wiersma and Latham, 1986), have now been replicated in Israel.

The authors suggest further development and testing of a variety of appraisal instruments that are relevant and free of contamination in a number of different organizations and jobs. This empirical process could provide raters who are unwilling to risk antagonizing their subordinates by negative feedback (Latham, 1986; Napier and Latham, 1986; Wiersma and Latham, 1986) with reliable instruments, as well as furthering the corroboration, clarification, and extension of the underlying conceptual frameworks and mechanisms of the PA process. Moreover, they recommend that the study be extended beyond the effects of appraisal format and performance review on work-related attitudes, to the impact of these variables on employee behavior, such as absenteeism, turnover, and job performance.

Tziner, Kopelman, and Livneh (1993) – Effects of Performance Appraisal Format on Received Goal Characteristics, Appraisal Process Satisfaction, and Changes in Rated Job Performance

Description

As a natural extension of the previous studies, here 16 managers were instructed to use BOS and GRS formats for a PA and review process. The researchers then compared the results of the two types of scales in terms of level of goal clarity, acceptance, and commitment, as well as appraisal process satisfaction and improvement in job performance.

Results

For all three variables it was hypothesized that the BOS-based performance appraisal and review process would yield higher levels of positive outcomes. These predictions were confirmed.

Comments

Again BOS consistently produced higher levels of goal clarity, acceptance, and commitment, and higher levels of satisfaction with the appraisal process than GRS. The authors note add that the results regarding satisfaction are compatible with Mount's (1983) observation that employee appraisal satisfaction is related to a general satisfaction factor, which includes affect toward the appraisal system, the quality of performance feedback, and the extent to which the appraisal form aids discussion of the formulation, performance, and facilitation of personal development plans.

In order to examine the effect of the appraisal formats on performance, the employees were rated at the time of the appraisal (Time 1) and again at a later date (Time 2). Mean performance scores were essentially the same in both the GRS and BOS groups at Time 1 (5.11 and 5.10, respectively). Although no significant subsequent changes in mean rated performance were recorded for the GRS group at Time 2 (5.13, r(106)=.71), the mean performance of those appraised using BOS improved modestly to 5.22, $t(104)=1.12, p=.13$. Analysis of *individual* performance, however, indicated a significant improvement for BOS, to $t(52)=2.77; p<.01$, and only an insignificant improvement for GRS condition, r(53)=.71.

Tziner et al. note that given the widespread use of GRS-based performance appraisals (Teel, 1980), their results give credence to Nathan et al'.s (1991) claim that the typical PA review may not alter performance. On the other hand, the study found that the BOS-based approach did lead to significant (albeit modest) improved job performance (on a within-person basis).

The authors suggest that future research should be based on data amenable to confirmatory factor analysis, and that objective data on goal properties, such as specificity, and job-relatedness should be obtained using reliable external assessment of goal statements. Such information, they argue, would facilitate the process of confirming the overall causal model of linkages between goal properties, perceived goal characteristics, process satisfaction, and improved job performance. In their view, these advances would go a long way to clarifying the processes triggered by BOS and GRS (Murphy and Cleveland, 1991), an issue that has been sadly neglected. Notwithstanding decades of research on the psychometric properties of these (and other) rating formats, the real payoff may be their impact on on-the-job work behavior and job performance.

Tziner, Kopelman and Joanis (1997) – Investigation of Raters' and Ratees' Reactions to Three Methods of PA

Description

In a further extension of the previous studies, attention was given to all three appraisal methods and to raters, as well as ratees. It was hypothesized that, compared to a GRS-based process, BARS and BOS-based performance appraisals and reviews would generate: (1) superior performance goals (in terms of observability and specificity); (2) superior ratee perceptions of set goals (clearer clarification of path to goal, more acceptable, more amenable to commitment/achievement); and (3) more favorable user reactions (ratee and rater satisfaction with the PA review). In addition, given the limitations inherent in BARS, it was posited that both rater and ratee satisfaction would be higher for BOS than for BARS. In this study, as in the previous field investigations, raters were trained intensively in all aspects of the PA and feedback processes prior their administration of the forms.

Specificity of goals was assessed in terms of the extent to which precise courses of action were spelled out (explicit/concrete and desirable/ undesirable behaviors/objectives were defined), and observability in terms of the extent to which the goal described a behavior or action that could readily be discerned. These goal properties were judged independently of raters and ratees. Using the Kappa coefficient, agreement among three judges was found to be $K=.67$ for specificity and $K=.72$ for observability. The ratings of the judges were then averaged to calculate separate scores for the specificity and observability of each of the goals.

Results

1 *Goal specificity* BOS-based reviews yielded significantly higher goal specificity than either GRS or BARS.
2 *Goal observability* None of the three review formats demonstrated an advantage with respect to goal observability, perhaps because the observability of a goal largely reflects the nature of the work situation itself, which is not affected by the appraisal format.
3 *Path to goal* BARS did not yield higher clarification of path to goal than GRS, although the difference was in the predicted direction and approached statistical significance $(p=.063)$. However, the BOS-based review did yield higher clarification of path to goal than GRS.
4 *Goal acceptance and goal commitment* BOS produced higher levels of goal acceptance and goal commitment than either the GRS or the BARS method.
5 *Ratee satisfaction* BOS yielded higher ratee satisfaction than GRS and BARS.
6 *Rater satisfaction* There was no support for the proposition that behavior-

based reviews would produce higher rater satisfaction than GRS, possibly because this variable is so reflective of the overall rating context. Moreover, the fact that the ratings were explicitly conducted solely for developmental purposes and clearly had no administrative implications might have obviated the tensions that often accompany a GRS-based review.

Comments

These findings clearly reinforce previous indication of the superiority of a BOS-based performance appraisal review over one that is either GRS- or BARS-based with respect to user reactions. Tziner et al. recommend the continued collection of data from various sources (in contrast to this study where goal properties were assessed by independent judges, performance review satisfaction data were provided by the raters, and goal characteristics and attitudinal data were supplied by the ratees). Furthermore, they suggest that future research should extend this line of inquiry to include additional cultural settings beyond Canada (this study), Israel (Tziner and Kopelman, 1988), and the Netherlands (Wiersma et al., 1995). Data from all sources could then be matched, thus enabling causal modeling of the entire nomological system.

Tziner, Joannis and Murphy (2000) – A Comparison of Three Methods of Performance Appraisal with Regard to Goal Properties, Goal Perception, and Ratee Satisfaction

Description

A similar comparison of simple graphic scales with either BOS or BARS rating formats was conducted for a sample of police officers. Again the formats were evaluated in terms of goal properties, the ratees' goal perception, and ratee satisfaction with the appraisal process.

Results

Performance improvement goals using BOS were judged by experts to be the most observable and specific. In addition, when BOS was used, the ratees' satisfaction with performance appraisal was highest, and their perceptions of performance goals most favorable. The overall results therefore suggest that behaviorally-oriented rating formats can enhance the developmental applications of performance appraisal. With respect to specific outcomes, the results were as follows:

1 *Specificity* As stated above, and in line with the predictions, the goals set with BOS were more specific than those established by means of either BARS or GRS. Since the BOS format asks the rater to record the frequency with which specific critical behaviors occur, there is indeed a greater likelihood that goals will also be framed in terms of specific, observable behaviors. In contrast, both BARS and GRS ask raters to provide general evaluations (in BARS behavioral statements are used merely to illustrate the meaning of scales and scale levels), making it likely that ratee goals will be tailored toward affecting raters' evaluations, rather than toward displaying the specific behaviors listed on the BOS.

2 *Observability* In terms of goal observability, no reliable difference was found between BOS and GRS, although both of these methods proved superior to BARS.

3 *Ratee perceptions* Ratee perceptions of goals were more favorable with BOS and GRS than with BARS, with no significant differences found between the first two methods. Nevertheless, it could be argued that the increased clarity of goals obtained with BOS may be a sufficiently important reason in and of itself to prefer it over GRS.

4 *Ratee satisfaction* The level of ratee satisfaction with the appraisal system was also higher for BOS and GRS than for BARS. Again, no significant differences were discovered between GRS and BOS on this variable. Wiersma and Latham (1986) also found these two methods to be equally good by virtue of their similar ease of use. In addition, they showed that individuals were most satisfied with BOS because of their ability to minimize personality disputes, assist in the explanation of weak assessments, make feedback easier, and render appraisal sessions more comprehensible.

Comments

In this study, Tziner et al. employed a measure of ratee perception of goals which called for a simple aggregation of the disparate dimensions of goal clarity, goal acceptance, and goal commitment. However, the literature indicates certain ambiguities and contradictions in the definition of these three terms, with some authors asserting that acceptance and commitment are interchangeable concepts (e.g., Huber, 1985), while others argue that they have different meanings (Locke, 1968).

Locke defines acceptance as a state of mind whereby individuals agree to attain the goals set for them, and commitment as the degree of resolve to reach these goals. Although there is no reference here to the person setting the goals, the *a priori* acceptance of them by the ratee is implied. In a later development, Locke, Shaw, Saari and Latham (1981) define commitment more broadly, applying it to any type of goal, independent of its source, whether set by the individuals themselves, their superiors, or in collaboration with others. Acceptance is subsumed under commitment, and is seen as referring specifically to the degree of commitment to assigned goals. Thus commitment here implies goal acceptance (Locke, Latham, and Erez, 1988). This description of the conceptual relationship is borne out by Early and Kanfer (1985). All in all, then, there still remain persistent ambiguities in the definitions of the variables labeled acceptance, commitment, and clarity, and it would therefore be beneficial to undertake a more extensive study to determine whether they are all part of the same concept, or whether it is indeed possible to differentiate between them.

Another acknowledged limitation of goal-setting stems from the accent on individual results, a practice that often engenders a mentality of 'every man for himself', with an adverse effect on cooperation to attain collective goals. Teamwork, which is important in so many settings (such as the police; Kane and Freeman, 1987), thus becomes problematic, as borne out by Petit and Haines (1994), who note the difficulty of applying goal-setting procedures to several categories of personnel.

Finally, Tziner et al. suggest that it would be interesting to employ a cost-benefit analysis approach to the examination of these methods. In effect, we are obliged to ask how BOS can be recommended when GRS is not only easier to use and less costly to develop, but also seems to generate similar results. The authors conclude with a key question for human resource personnel: Are the satisfaction of the ratees and their reactions to the goals set for them enough to justify the time, energy, and effort required for the implementation of BOS?

Conclusions

From the findings of the individual studies in this series of investigations, several generalized conclusions may be drawn regarding the effects of the different rating scales on ratee/rater response to the process of the appraisal:

1 Although on the whole, behavioral rating methods appear to have the advantage over graphic scales, largely due to their precise nature, the specific drawbacks of BARS indicate that it is the least preferable of the three formats studied. This contention is borne out by the fact that in all the studies in which BARS were included, they were always held in the lowest favor and produced the least impressive contributions to the improvement of work habits in the workplace.

2 BOS seem to have the psychometric advantages over GRS of superior reliability and validity. Moreover, because of their specificity (and clearer format), BOS also appear to minimize communication barriers and role ambiguities, and to lead to clearer and more observable goals and consequent ratee commitment to carry them out. What is more, the feedback process with BOS is generally more focused, factual, objective, and unbiased, and thus more likely to garner specific job-related goals that positively influence the appraisees' attitudes to the overall PA process and their resulting work satisfaction. Of particular importance is the finding that goal-setting adds incrementally to feedback, especially with the use of BOS, although the advantage of BOS over GRS was not substantiated in terms of organizational commitment. Raters are also more likely to feel comfortable with BOS because they direct attention to the frequency, rather than the quality, of specific and incontrovertible behaviors, in contrast to the ambiguous and relatively subjective criteria of GRS formats.

3 Tziner et al. argue for clearer definitions and objectification of goal properties, maintaining that objective data on features such as specificity and job-relatedness should be obtained using reliable external assessment of goal statements. Furthermore, in light of the conceptual confusion over the definitions of ratee perception of goals (i.e., acceptance and commitment), the researchers recommend undertaking further research to determine whether these variables are part of the same concept, or whether it is possible to differentiate between them.

4 Tziner et al. note the limitations of stressing individual PA results in respect to goal-setting, the implication being that supervisors need to attend to the individual aspects of commitment and performance, but not at the expense of group concomitants of effective job performance.

5 Despite the overall impression of the superiority of BOS over GRS, several of these investigations found little difference between these two formats on particular dependent variables, including: effect on overall rated performance (Tziner, Kopelman and Livneh, 1993); goal observability (Tziner, Kopelman and Joanis, 1997; Tziner, Joannis and Murphy, 2000);

path to goal (Tziner, Kopelman and Joanis, 1997); rater satisfaction (Tziner, Kopelman and Joanis, 1997; Tziner, Joannis and Murphy, 2000); and ratee perception of goals (Tziner, Joannis and Murphy, 2000). In view of these findings, along with the relative ease and lower cost of producing GRS formats, it might be argued that before the outcomes are examined and one appraisal method or another is opted for, it would be wise to adopt a cost-benefit analysis approach. As stated above, ratee satisfaction may not be sufficient justification for the time, energy, and effort required to implement a BOS-based appraisal.

6　The inferences made about raters being unprepared to administer PA because of the potential negative consequences to themselves highlight the underlying operational aspect of this research. Independent of the academic discussion of the superiority of rating formats, there is the very real consideration of the need to develop reliable and valid appraisal instruments in a number of organizational and cultural settings, the use of which might actually make or break an organization. The matching of data from a variety of sources would contribute significantly to the causal modeling of the entire nomological system.

7　One of the interesting issues to emerge from these studies concerns the relationship between the various outcomes, that is, the overall causal model of linkages between goal properties, perceived goal characteristics, process satisfaction, and improved job performance. Tziner et al. repeatedly suggest that future research should be based on data amenable to confirmatory factor analysis (LISREL), which would go a long way toward clarifying 'the long ignored processes' triggered by the two rating formats, BOS and GRS (Murphy and Cleveland, 1991).

8　Finally, notwithstanding the decades of research on the psychometric properties of rating formats, the real payoff of this avenue of study may well lie in changes in on-the-job work behavior and job performance. Moreover, it may be of considerable value to expand the research into other areas of behavior, such as absenteeism and turnover.

The Appraisal Interview

In the last crucial phase of performance appraisal, supervisors and ratees review together the quality of the employee's performance. The workers are now confronted with the data about their behavior and achievements during a given time period, with their accomplishments judged on the basis of absolute criteria, the existing standards of the organization, or the relative achievements of their peers. The intention of the appraisal interview is to facilitate the pointing of employees' efforts and abilities in directions both desirable to the organization and compatible with their own career aspirations. In many workplaces, this phase is not sufficiently implemented, perhaps because of the lack of awareness of the importance of feedback or because of the unwillingness of supervisors to convey negative information of a personal nature to their workers.

Changes in the behavior of the ratee are likely to occur when a number of conditions obtain. The feedback provided must be based on events and behaviors that are clearly defined and detailed, and operational goals must be prioritized and set for both short- and long-term attainment. Properly conducted, the interview can improve the performance level of workers by as much as 30 per cent (see: Latham and Yukl, 1975; Erez, 1977; Locke et al., 1981). The appraisal meeting may also represent a powerful and uncompromising revelation of the quality of the relationship that has formed between a superior and a subordinate over time. It goes without saying that different kinds of effects will be achieved from an interview based on mutual trust, honesty, and respect, than from one in which suspicion and possibly animosity prevail.

Objectives of the Performance Appraisal Interview

The performance appraisal interview enables feedback to be offered to the workers on a variety of routine activities and behaviors that are not usually considered in the course of daily work. Whereas on a daily basis attention is paid to critical events and unusual assignments, the majority of tasks do not fall into this category. Superiors also make use of the appraisal interview to explain their views on various issues and to invite workers to share their thoughts regarding possible changes in patterns of work and behavior. It should be noted that on this occasion the superior is not only permitted to criticize defective performance, but is obligated to do so for the good of the worker and the organization. However, although a superior may decree the need for change in an interview, it is only with the workers' cooperation that a high degree of commitment and responsibility on the part of all concerned can be achieved. The interview thus has the potential to reinforce organizational discipline.

Insofar as the performance appraisal interview provides a channel of open communication in which the worker, as well as the superior, can discuss their positive feelings and air complaints, the dialogue can enhance motivation by encouraging cooperation, responsibility, and mutual understanding. Ilgen, Fisher, and Taylor (1979) demonstrate that the more supervisors are perceived by ratees as having particular positive qualities, the greater the respect they will earn and the stronger their influence on the ratees. These qualities include professional status, skill in judging job behavior, good intentions, offering criticism constructively, and having a positive influence on the allocation of resources.

To ensure that the goals of the interview are, in fact, achieved, it is desirable for all the parties concerned to prepare themselves for it appropriately. These preparations may be of a general nature, such as improving skills in interpersonal communications and counseling, or of a more specific nature, such as studying relevant data, setting the criteria for the success of a particular assignment, and planning possible options for further progress.

Methods and Principles in Conducting Interviews for Periodic
Performance Evaluation

Following Maier (1976), Tziner (1990) notes the use of three accepted techniques for conducting a performance interview. These are generally labeled 'tell and sell', 'tell and listen', and 'problem solving'. The differences among the techniques are expressed in the extent to which it is possible for a worker to display initiative during the course of the interview.

The 'tell and sell' method gives the superior a significant and dominant role; there is virtually no invitation extended to workers to discuss the findings or what is inferred from them. In this authoritative situation, the superior formulates and communicates the strategy for improvement of the worker's performance, and attempts to convince him or her of its value.

The 'tell and listen' technique emphasizes mutual responsibility and cooperation between raters and ratees. Superiors present describes their evaluations to the ratees, while allowing considerable room for the workers to respond. The discussion incorporates the expression of attitudes and feelings, but does not emphasize the definition of future goals. Although this method generally enhances the satisfaction of workers with respect to their personal connections with the evaluators, it does not necessarily contribute to the improvement of their performance.

In contrast, throughout interviews employing the 'problem solving' technique, workers and superiors are equally active. The interview begins with the shaping of the appraisal process itself; workers are given the opportunity to evaluate themselves on each dimension of their performance. The discussion then concentrates most specifically on those areas where the evaluations of the ratee and the superior differ, and generally conclude with the designation of specific goals for the next performance interval.

Burke, Weitzel, and Weir (1978) highlight several principles that can lead to positive results from the performance appraisal interview:

1 high levels of ratee participation in the process lead to greater ratee satisfaction with the appraisal process and with the rater;
2 ratees are more satisfied with the performance appraisal interview when the rater is respectful, exhibits a friendly, helpful, constructive attitude, and acknowledges good performance (in essence, the rater preserves the worker's self-esteem);
3 little or no performance improvement can be expected in areas that are heavily criticized;
4 mutual setting of specific goals leads to a considerable degree of performance improvement.

Kopelman (1986) and others further recommend:

1 maintaining a reasonable balance between praise and criticism;
2 explaining motives and decisions in a logical and objective way;
3 expressing willingness to assist the workers in any area related to their work;
4 listening with an open mind, thus facilitating the worker's cooperation during the interview;
5 formulating solutions for current problems;
6 setting specific goals for improvement of future job performance and removing job related obstacles;
7 allowing a reasonable time to elapse between one interview and the next (usually half a year);
8 preserving continuity by following up the materialization of agreed conclusions and decisions during the interval between interviews.

Despite agreement on the positive virtues of these techniques, Bernardin and Buckley (1981) and Kopelman (1986) note that managers are still very reluctant to conduct PA interviews. Strangely enough considering their position, the cause might be traced back to a lack of rigorous interviewing skills. This lack may also explain why it is reported that, in practice, performance appraisal interviews often fail to produce the expected positive improvements in subordinate behaviors. As noted above, merely presenting supervisors with the bare essentials and basic principles for conducting an effective interview is unlikely to create a substantial and durable change in their behavior. Furthermore, it has been found that raters in general are very reluctant to provide negative feedback even when they do conduct the interview.

Tziner (1990) suggests several steps toward rectifying the present situation: (1) Training should be aimed at increasing skills and acquiring techniques so that the less competent raters gain confidence in their ability to handle difficult feedback situations successfully; (2) intensive and extensive practice of skills should be given the highest priority; and (3) after completion of a training program, raters should repeatedly be given refresher courses; otherwise, as has been reported, the effects achieved during the initial training will begin to dissipate after six to twelve months.

Organizational Factors Affecting the Appraisal Process

In his review, Tziner (1990) lists a number of organizational factors that tend to influence the appraisal process. These include the climate in the organization, the extent of commitment of both evaluators and assessees to the process (especially the extent of support the supervisors receive from senior administrative officials), the quality of informal communications in the organization, the nature of daily communications and feedback between superiors and subordinates, and the quality of instruction given to superiors. All these factors, and more, determine the extent to which staff are motivated, the evaluation assignment is understood, and the appraisal is conducted in a manner that is both professional and efficient.

By way of introduction to this issue, Tziner makes specific note of the effect of the social climate of an organization on the effectiveness of an appraisal system (Kane and Lawler, 1979). Organizational climates characterized by low levels of trust, either between raters or across organizational levels, can seriously reduce the system's likelihood of being either useful or valid. In the context of the appraisal process, trust has been defined as the degree to which raters believe that fair and accurate evaluations will be, or have been, made in their organization (Bernardin and Beatty, 1984). It has even been suggested that in a low-trust climate, unless objective performance data are available, performance appraisals should not be used for important personnel decisions. Tziner (1990) adds that this suggestion is particularly alarming, given the number of organizations that could be characterized as both having low levels of trust and lacking objective performance data.

As noted above, the purposes of the performance appraisal affect the cues that are looked for in the course of the process. However, when appraisals serve important administrative functions, raters' beliefs about how they are conducted by other raters may influence the way in which they themselves evaluate their own subordinates. For instance, if ratings are to be used for merit pay decisions, the relative comparisons of ratings may become an important concern for each rater. An assessor who believes that other raters are purposely inflating their subordinates' evaluations may therefore be inclined to do so as well. This kind of belief is also a reflection of the degree of the rater's trust in the appraisal process, which, as we have indicated, may be an important predictor of distorted ratings, particularly when used as a basis for personnel decisions (Murphy and Cleveland, 1995).

In contrast, as Tziner points out, when appraisals are used for feedback purposes alone, trust in the appraisal process may be a less significant predictor of rating distortion, since raters may not feel compelled to compare their distributions with those of other raters. Thus, the purposes of appraisal not only affect questions of leniency (see above), but may also serve to moderate the relationship between trust in the appraisal process and rating behavior. The issues of social climate and political beliefs in an organization, and their effects on perceptions of the appraisal process and on its outcomes are discussed at greater length below.

The Influence of the Rater on the Appraisal Process

The process of performance appraisal is clearly a complex one which involves collecting a large amount of diverse information and then integrating and evaluating it. To be valuable, an evaluation must be the combined product of the professional skill and judgment of the assessor, effective measuring instruments, and a well-conceptualized appraisal process. Yet even when each of these elements harmoniously contributes to the overall efficiency of the process, there are no guarantees that it will be accurate. The raters probably play the greatest role in this respect, and their influence should not be underestimated. Not only do they have a decisive effect on the quality of the evaluation produced, but the results of their appraisals often have consequences of far greater significance than the particular job performances being assessed (see: DeNisi, Cafferty and Meglino, 1984).

Rater Qualities

Experience and skill in evaluation   Tziner (1990) reminds us of the predictable finding that raters who are trained and have received feedback about their evaluations, both from ratees and superiors, improve their rating skills as they become more experienced (e.g., Latham, Wexley and Pursell, 1975; Borman, 1979; Ivancevich, 1979; Bernadin and Pence, 1980; Fay and Latham, 1982). Nevertheless, other important qualities of raters that impinge on the effectiveness of observation and appraisal skills, and that operate independently of experience and training, also need to be considered.

Personal variables   In general, it can be said that when raters perceive ratees as different from themselves with respect to certain traits, they tend to assess them as less competent. Landy and Farr (1980), for example, found that appraisers tend to give better ratings to people of their own race, and a meta-analysis found that white raters gave higher evaluations to white ratees than to black, and that black ratees gave higher evaluations to black ratees than to white. However, this finding has also been challenged by studies that have found no favoritism on the part of raters towards ratees of their own race.

The gender of the rater may also be assumed to color his or her expectations of members of the opposite sex, especially when they are performing tasks that have traditionally been considered feminine or masculine. However, the results of a meta-analysis concerning the relationship of gender to performance were mixed, and it has been demonstrated that the gender of raters and ratees explains only a marginal amount of performance rating variance. On the other hand, it has also been observed that women ratees tended to receive lower ratings than men if their appraisals are conducted after a poor performer (male or female). Needless to say, these variables may operate in the opposite direction as well: workers' perceptions of their assessors with respect to age, sex, education, and so forth, may also affect performance levels.

Research into the influence of personal factors on evaluation processes, and closely related topics such as decision making and risk-taking, throw light on these mutual effects. For instance, it has been reported that superior appraisers tend to have 'balanced' personalities and to exhibit high self-confidence, minimal anxiety, and social grace. Poorer appraisers, on the other hand, tend to be characterized by less adaptive and balanced personalities and to react according to their internal needs rather than to the more objective external reality. It has even been claimed that it is this unique encounter between rater and ratee that largely determines the extent to which the ratee's behavior is ultimately perceived as adaptive and appropriate or deviant and ill-suited (Carroll and Schneier, 1982).

This 'rater-ratee acquaintance effect', as it is termed, changes as the rater and ratee become better acquainted, so that some degree of positive or negative attitude toward the ratee is gradually formed. A positive attitude can increase rating accuracy by eliciting a more open response on the part of the worker, which consequently provides the assessor with more information for the formulation of the evaluation. Nevertheless, there is also good reason to assume that a rater's favorable impression of a ratee may result in intentional or unwitting inflation of ratings as a result of the consequent biasing errors (Tsvi and Barry, 1986).

Another aspect of the rater-ratee interaction pertains to the ongoing relationship between them. For example, Fisher (1979) notes that, paradoxically, the evaluations of poor performances are generally more lenient when the rater anticipates having to provide feedback directly to the ratee. He postulates that raters who are anxious about the possible repercussions of a negative rating might shield themselves from unpleasant reactions by deliberately being lenient. The extent to which raters are uncomfortable giving their subordinates justifiable criticism has been conceived as reflective of their self-efficacy as raters (Abbott and Bernardin, 1983).

Cognitive Obstacles in the Appraisal Process

Not surprisingly, in recent decades a number of studies have been devoted to an examination of the various cognitive processes that impact on the accuracy of performance ratings. Without a doubt, the process of observation and appraisal contains many opportunities for distortion. To begin with, human judgment is influenced by the cognitive style of the appraiser. This style relates to the mental acts of perception and observation, aggregation and storage, short- and long-term memory, and the incorporation of these elements into an overall appraisal. When observers focus attention on one person, they perceive only part of the existing stimuli, such as facial expression, posture, dress, and the force and meanings of words. Following is a brief review of both classic and contemporary studies of some of the cognitive variables that have particular bearing on performance appraisal.

As we have seen, evaluation involves a number of stages. Feldman (1981) describes four stages of performance appraisal – attention, categorization, recall, and information integration – which are carried out by means of either an automatic or a controlled process. In the automatic process, the rater notes and categorizes the employee's personality traits and behavior unconsciously, whereas the controlled process is performed consciously.

Feldman goes on to note several sources and forms of rater distortions that affect subsequent recall of the employee. One of these relates to the process used to organize perceptions. The author contends that raters use cognitive categories, prototypes, and schemata that affect the perception and organization (storage and recall) of performance information. A category is a set of familiar, similar objects (i.e., a set of objects organized according to the principle of 'family resemblance'). A prototype constitutes an illustration of a category; it is an abstract image combining the typical features of a category. For example, the category of 'fine whiskies' might be represented by the prototype 'Glenfiddich'. The term schemata refers to the high-level memory structures that incorporate verbal or propositional information (Murphy and Cleveland, 1995).

The process of perceiving and cognitively organizing information (stimuli) relevant to performance behavior is further influenced by the tendency to 'reconcile opposites', which manifests itself by ignoring or adding features in the encoding and 'storage in memory' stages. Another phenomenon is known as the 'assimilation effect', which refers to the adjustment of new facts and data to conform to some preexisting schemata. The assimilation effect thus reinforces first impressions, making them overvalued and dominant during the observation period. Observers tend to strengthen these first impressions throughout the observation process by attending preferentially to information that confirms them, while tending to suppress or ignore perceptions that do not.

A related source of cognitive error has commonly been labeled the 'halo error', and refers to the fact that an assessor's impression of certain dimensions may influence his or her evaluation of others. However, in a review of the definitions of this effect, Murphy et al. (1993) maintain that the major conceptions about the construct are either wrong or problematic, and that the halo error is not pervasive, that inflated correlations among rating dimensions are not the norm, and that contextual factors tend to influence the emergence of this effect. An empirical test of this contention, concluded that the halo effect is best considered a unitary phenomenon and should be defined as the influence of a rater's general impression on ratings of specific ratee qualities.

Taking a different approach, Kane (1994) developed a model of the determinants of rater error, hypothesizing that such error may have conscious antecedents, that is, raters may deliberately decide to introduce distortions into ratings. Drawing on subjective expected utility concepts, his model suggests that raters may evaluate the relative utility of accurate and inaccurate assessment, along with the probability of being caught out for giving inaccurate ratings. This possibility is discussed further below.

Not surprisingly, moreover, it has been demonstrated that the accuracy of dimensional ratings, unlike overall holistic ratings, is a function of the accuracy of memory. Several studies have investigated the effects of memory aids of one sort or another. For example, a field study of the impact of cognitive processes on performance evaluations showed that structured diary-keeping and recall methods helped raters to recall information, differentiate among ratees, and generate more positive reactions to the appraisal process. The study, however, did not measure the cognitive processes directly.

Another study considered the impact of activating performance prototypes by giving raters prototypical trait adjectives of effective and ineffective performers, and found that such priming minimally affected ratings of videotaped performance, regardless of whether they were made immediately or after a certain delay. The priming effect was observed using pencil-and-paper vignettes, as opposed to more richly embedded stimuli in videotape methods. Still another investigation compared the accuracy of performance ratings in an assessment center context when performance was observed directly and on videotape, and found no difference between the two modalities. However, using in-basket and videotape methods to present stimulus information about ratees, it has been demonstrated that ratings are more accurate when assessors are made to feel accountable by having to justify their evaluations.

Murphy and Cleveland (1995) consider the impact of an assessee's previous ratings on subsequent performance appraisal in terms of 'contrast effects' (inappropriate high or low ratings because of prior evaluations). The findings they report reveal that individuals who reviewed, but did not rate, the previous performance demonstrated an assimilation effect, giving a second rating in the direction of the earlier performance. On the other hand, those who both reviewed and rated previous performance displayed a contrast effect, rating the second performance *away* from the direction of the previous one. Admittedly, however, the effect sizes for the main and interaction effects were low. An earlier investigation of contrast effects using checklists and diaries showed that not only did these cognitive aids not reduce potential contrast effects, but they may even have strengthened them.

In a similar vein, an examination of the impact of prior evaluations that varied in terms of performance level and ratee gender on the subsequent evaluations and recall of male and female assessees of average performance revealed that both the performance level and the gender of the ratees in the prior evaluation influenced the later rating. Moreover, relatively low performance for the prior ratee affected subsequent evaluations differentially for male and female assessees, with males receiving relatively higher evaluations than females.

Affective Concomitants

In addition to 'pure' cognitive processes, raters' feelings and attitudes – and even their moods and temperament – may affect the meaning assigned to appraisees' behavior. In addition, the significance attached to ratees' actions is generally based on their external manifestations, rather than on any awareness of the workers' hidden or internal motivations (which are probably better indications of their intent). Moreover, observers generally make inferences based on their own beliefs and proclivities, which in turn influence the meaning they attribute to the behavior observed. Thus an infinite variety of impressions may be derived from different forms of behavior. What is more, this kind of perceptive ability varies from one individual to another (Schneier, 1979).

Several studies on the role of affect in performance appraisal have focused on the potential biases that may emerge when a supervisor likes or dislikes a subordinate. One such study proposes a model in which supervisors' affect toward subordinates is a major factor in rated performance. The model was tested on a sample of 95 staff nurses and 28 nurse supervisors, and found a good fit; supervisors' affect toward subordinates correlated .74 with performance ratings. The conclusions to be drawn from these findings, however, are not clear-cut. Even one well-designed laboratory study that found support for these results, admits that affect may very likely be a function of how well or poorly a person performs on the job, and that affect is more apt to represent a valid piece of information than an irrelevant source of bias. A subsequent field study found evidence consistent with this argument.

With respect to an observer's need to interpret assessees' personalities, it is important to note the tendency to attribute causality to what is actually observed, rather than to other external or internal factors that may have influenced the perceived behavior. It follows that if observers attribute the causation of a certain behavior to external factors, they may assume that other ratees would behave similarly in the same circumstances. If, however, the cause of the behavior is attributed to internal factors, it can then be assumed that the response is unique to the individual being evaluated (Kelley, 1973).

Another factor related to affect and observer efficiency concerns the hierarchical gap between the raters and the subordinates they are rating, since members of each hierarchical level perceive and analyze the state and performance of the organization from their own unique point of view. Furthermore, as Tziner (1990) notes, the wider this hierarchical gap, the greater the likelihood of there being a difference in the way each perceives the organization, the less chance there is that mutual acquaintance is based on daily contact, and the less familiar the raters are with the job and work routine of the ratees. In such cases, judgments are apt to be based on general impressions alone and on small samplings of behavior.

Purposes and Context of Observation

As noted above, the purpose of the observation and the context in which it is performed also influence both its outcomes and the raters' cognitive style (Zedeck and Cascio, 1982). The purpose of the exercise directs observers to attend to the particular stimuli that appear relevant and will help them later in forming the impression they are being asked for. The environment affects the relative salience of each stimulus. For instance, if appraisals are carried out for the purpose of promotion decisions, then appraisers will tend to seek cues specifically related to differences in potential revealed by the behavior of those being appraised, and will focus particularly on a comparison of the various assessees' achievements. Farr and Werbel (1986) demonstrate how observers tend to be more lenient when they know that the results of their appraisals are to be used in making administrative decisions of this kind. We shall return to these issues below.

Errors in the Recording of Appraisals

Tziner (1990) notes that even at the final stage of the appraisal process, when evaluations are recorded on forms, there may be errors that interfere with 'true' assessments. These errors often occur unconsciously. Three of them, touched on briefly in the preceding sections, have received extensive treatment in the literature and therefore warrant greater elaboration.

1 *Halo effect* The halo effect appears to derive from the natural human tendency to form general impressions of other people. Indeed, it is an error that occurs at the stage when the first impression of the ratee is being formed. As a result of this overall impression, the rater may find it difficult

to distinguish between the various levels of the ratee's performance, as indicated by the different dimensions on the performance appraisal form. He or she therefore tends to evaluate the ratee as either generally high or generally low on all counts.

2   *Central tendency* The central tendency is the propensity of a rater to avoid extreme evaluations. Hence, his or her assessments tend to cluster around the midpoint of the scale and consequently do not allow for clear distinctions between different ratees. One possible underlying reason for this error may be the raters' attempt to 'insure' themselves against having to elaborate on and justify their evaluations at a later time.

3   *Negative and positive leniency* In contrast to the central tendency, the leniency error manifests itself as an inclination to make excessive use of below- or above-average values when assigning scores to the various dimensions.

Murphy et al.'s reservations about the halo effect have already been noted in the discussion of cognitive errors. In a later discussion, Murphy and Cleveland (1995) add that multiple operational definitions exist for each of the various types of rating errors; yet, the definitions of the same error are not equivalent. The arguments presented by Murphy et al. appear to be very cogent, and indeed more recent literature on performance appraisal tends to play down the concept of rating errors.

Toward an Evaluation of the Use of the Appraisal Process

Efficient construction of the system of worker performance appraisal, with its various components and methods, is meant to ensure that the control and management of manpower are based essentially on the quality of worker performance. On that basis alone the promotion, training, and development of workers should be determined. We have noted that rater errors, poor design, and even the lack of inter-rater agreement on many aspects of performance appraisal, mitigate against the achievement of this goal. Indeed, the poor psychometric qualities of appraisal systems reported in the literature are so normative (Prince, Lawler and Mohrman, 1991) that some researchers have despaired of achieving high validity on performance ratings.

Attempts have been made to overcome some of these drawbacks. We have noted various suggestions for the elimination or reduction of distortions, including the use of rating scales impermeable to cognitive rating biases

(Tziner, 1990), and the adaptation of methods and formats of performance appraisal to the requirements of the organization. In addition, Tziner (1990) cites the creation of built-in mechanisms to protect the outcomes from specific drawbacks, such as standardization procedures to neutralize distorted evaluations.

Nevertheless, the themes running through Tziner's (1990) review and the consequent series of investigations of the three major appraisal formats make it clear that the procedures for implementing appraisal systems should focus on something beyond the immediacy of a one-off evaluation of a particular worker in the organization. Proper procedures essentially presuppose periodic evaluations that attempt to integrate three objectives: (1) review of the effectiveness of workers' performance during the period between appraisals; (2) appropriate goal-setting for the future; and (3) attainment of the workers' commitment to perform more efficiently.

Put succinctly, the PA system should incorporate an array of variables that connect the organizational level with the individual level, the host of daily interpersonal relationships between superiors and their subordinates, as well as between peers in the workplace. At its best, efficient use of the system of appraisal can be expected to aid in the establishment of interpersonal relations on trust, honesty, and mutual respect. Even when circumstances are less than ideal, the system should at least counterbalance those subjective personal variables that adversely affect relationships between people who, although they may differ from each other, are thrown into close association within an obligatory organizational environment with its own rules of play.

Clearly, then, the proper use of rating systems depends on factors that extend beyond the cognitive processes of rating, rater training, the psychometric qualities of rating scales (Murphy and Cleveland, 1995), and the degree to which various stages of the rating system are employed correctly. Tziner (in press) argues that the high frequency of reported rating inaccuracies may not be exclusively due to raters' inadvertent cognitive errors (see: Landy and Farr, 1980; Cleveland and Murphy, 1992), or what Bernardin and Villanova (1986) label 'non-deliberate rating distortions'. In fact, there is increasing evidence that human, organizational, and contextual aspects indeed play a major role in the misrepresentation of PA results. As Tziner (1990) notes, these factors include the organizational climate created around the performance appraisal, the mutual trust between employee and supervisor, the uses to which PA is put, and the degree of importance conferred on it by different parties involved in the process. It is to a more detailed discussion of these somewhat intangible political dimensions that we now turn.

Performance Appraisal and Political Considerations in the Workplace

The evidence that rating inaccuracy has more to do with the deliberate, volitional distortion of performance ratings than was previously recognized has been growing in recent years (Bernardin and Beatty, 1984; Bernardin and Villanova, 1986; Longenecker, Sims and Gioia, 1987; Kane and Kane, 1992; Murphy and Cleveland, 1995). This notion is also supported by anecdotal evidence. For example, a survey of raters, ratees, and administrators of performance appraisal systems revealed that the majority of respondents in all these groups felt that rating inaccuracy stemmed much more from deliberate distortions than from raters' inadvertent, cognitive errors (Bernardin and Villanova, 1986). The empirical data indicates that these deliberate rating distortions occur because of supervisors' feelings of discomfort with the appraisal system and its outcomes, and reflect their conscious efforts to produce ratings that will achieve personal goals. Such manipulative behaviors can be subsumed under the heading of organizational politics.

Organizational politics would appear to be an integral part of organizational life that relates to power, authority, and influence, where power is defined as an attempt to influence others (Pfeffer, 1981; Cobb, 1984) and the ability to mobilize resources, energy, and information in order to further a preferred goal or strategy (Tushman, 1977). Tziner et al. (1996) propose that the intent of organizational politics is either to protect and/or enhance an individual's self-interests, or to further the interests or goals of another person or group, using both legitimate and non-sanctioned means (Altman, Valenzi, and Hodgetts, 1985). It has, in fact, been suggested that some form of irregularity is always associated with organizational politics. Whatever its definition, Pfeffer (1981) claims that political behavior and the use of power affect almost every important decision in organizations.

According to Cleveland and Murphy (1992), the goals of supervisors' political behavior include: (1) projecting a favorable image of their units in terms of effectiveness and efficiency; (2) procuring for themselves valuable organizational 'goodies' (such as access to central networks of information and bonuses); (3) portraying the image of a caring boss; (4) avoiding negative consequences and confrontations with employees; and (5) avoiding disapproval from peers. Raters first establish these personal goals and then intentionally distort performance ratings (e.g., give lenient scores, fail to discriminate stronger from weaker employees) in order to realize them.

Although considerable attention has been paid to the broader aspects of organizational politics (Pfeffer, 1981), only a small number of sporadic investigations have looked at the connection between political behavior and appraisal. These studies indicate that managers (Longenecker, Sims and Gioia, 1987; Longenecker and Gioia, 1988) or naval officers (Bjerke, Cleveland, Morrison and Wilson, 1987) manipulate ratings deliberately in order to: (1) obtain rewards for subordinates; (2) maintain a positive work group climate; (3) avoid negative outcomes for their ratees; or (4) favor those with whom they have close working relationships or social ties (Mohrman and Lawler, 1983; Prince et al., 1991). Some of the supervisors in these investigations had such poor perceptions of PA that they viewed it as no more than a discretionary tool for motivating and rewarding subordinates. Under such circumstances, the question of accuracy becomes irrelevant.

Until recently, the issue of distorted (or negligent) rating as a political tool was not pursued within any systematic framework or by means of any quantitative methodology. The reports were largely impressionistic and anecdotal, and the few studies of how organizational politics influence performance appraisal generally used open-ended interviews with executives as the basis for their empirical data.

In order to correct these faults, Tziner and various associates have conducted a number of investigations over the past decade. These studies of political influences in the workplace had two independent objectives: (1) to incorporate organizational political influences into investigations of the effects of rater beliefs on ratee and rater behaviors; and (2) to design and provide a psychometric assessment of a structured instrument capable of measuring quantitatively the extent to which particular political considerations are manifest in performance appraisal.

Raters' Attitudes Toward Performance Appraisal Systems and the Organizational Context

As we have seen, current models of performance appraisal now point to both the intrinsic nature of the appraisal system and its organizational context as critical dimensions for a clear understanding of the rating process (e.g., Cleveland and Murphy, 1992; Murphy and Cleveland, 1995). Following Murphy and Cleveland (1995), the contextual influences on raters' performance can be broken down into two major categories: raters' attitudes and beliefs relevant to the immediate task of appraising subordinates' performance ('proximal influences'), and their attitudes and beliefs about their organization ('distal influences'). To these 'influences', Tziner, Murphy, and Cleveland (in press) have recently added an additional dimension, defined as 'comfort with performance appraisal'. In order to comprehend their resulting research design, let us first familiarize ourselves with these concepts.

Proximal influences Proximal influences represent the various beliefs that raters have about the actual process of performance appraisal. They may reflect concerns about their motivation or ability to appraise subordinates accurately, or their perceptions of the ways that organizations use PA information and the organizational consequences that ensue from it.

1 *Self-efficacy* Raters differ in self-efficacy, that is, the extent to which they believe they have the information, tools, and skills necessary to appraise subordinates' performance accurately. Self-efficacy, as perceived by the individual, is likely to play a motivational role and to influence behavioral choices, affecting the mobilization of efforts and the perseverance with which goals are pursued. Thus, raters with low self-efficacy might lack sufficient motivation to provide well-documented, solidly grounded, reliable and accurate evaluations (Frayne and Latham, 1987), and they may even consider the appraisal to be an exercise in futility (Napier and Latham, 1986). Also, invoking Bandura's (1977, 1982) social learning theory, low efficacy raters are likely to distort their ratings, usually in those directions that will achieve political goals (Napier and Latham, 1986). Conversely, a rater with a high level of self-efficacy can be expected to perform the appraising task more conscientiously.

Not surprisingly, correlations between self-esteem (one dimension of self-efficacy) and confidence in appraisal have consistently been found. Higher levels of self-efficacy may also be induced by participative climates (Chiles and Zorn, 1995), and may be related to strong feelings of organizational commitment (Coladarci, 1992), although the causal direction of the latter relationship is uncertain.

2 *Uses of performance appraisal* A substantial body of research indicates differences in raters' behaviors when they believe that appraisals are to be used for achieving administrative rewards, such as promotion or salary raises, rather than for feedback and development purposes. In the former situation, raters are more likely to be motivated (Cleveland and Murphy, 1992), lenient (for reviews, see: Landy and Farr, 1983; Murphy and Cleveland, 1991), and attentive (Steers and Lee, 1983). One possible explanation for this is that a strong link between ratings and rewards increases the rater's belief that performance ratings matter, and that the organization values performance appraisal. It is interesting to note, however,

that heightened attention to appraisal is no guarantee of increased accuracy (Murphy and Cleveland, 1995).

On the other hand, the separation of performance appraisal from important administrative rewards does not necessarily guarantee improved rater performance either. On the contrary, it has been shown that in appraisal for purposes of feedback and development, supervisors may consciously discriminate against subordinates, especially those with little job experience or who are known to demonstrate low confidence levels in the supervisor and/or in the appraisal system (Fried, Tiegs, and Bellamy, 1992). In the extreme instance, which occasionally reflects an unfortunate reality, raters may have so little faith in the ultimate uses of the PA system in their organization that they view their rating performance as futile and have little or no motivation to produce an accurate appraisal.

Distal influences   Distal influences are those rater concerns that relate to organizational context characteristics. These characteristics include a heterogeneous mix of factors, such as organizational climate and attitudes towards the organization, which affect the rater indirectly (i.e., determine norms for evaluating performance).

1   *Attitudes toward the organization*   Rater commitment to the organization is generally reflected in a strong belief in, and acceptance of, its goals and values. Several researchers distinguish between attitudinal and instrumental commitment (Becker, 1960; Kelman, 1961; Salancik, 1977; Staw, 1977; Gould, 1979). Meyer and Allen (1984) describe attitudinal commitment as the desire to remain part of an organization, whereas instrumental commitment is a function of the perceived costs and benefits of remaining in an organization (Becker, 1960), as when more lucrative alternative employment opportunities are limited. In general, committed employees exhibit the desire to expend efforts to promote the organization's success, and are eager to stay in the organization because this fulfills an intrinsic need related to personal goals and values. Both attitudinal and instrumental commitment are likely to affect rater behaviors, although the former generally exerts a stronger influence.

It will be recalled that performance appraisal requires raters to invest considerable effort and to take substantial risks, since low ratings, for example, may harm interpersonal relationships within workgroups and lead to resentment and complaints. Thus, it is reasonable to assume that supervisors' willingness to engage in the rating process is a reflection of positive attitudes toward the organization. And insofar as raters identify strongly with their organization, there is a greater likelihood that they will make the effort to develop the skills and tools needed to evaluate their subordinates' performance effectively. This strong relationship between commitment and efforts to master the professional role is a phenomenon that has been demonstrated in several other contexts (e.g., Locke, Frederick, Lee and Bobko, 1984; Mathieu and Zajac, 1990; Tannenbaum, Mathieu, Salas and Cannon-Bowers, 1991; Riggs, Warka, Babasa, Betancourt and Hooker, 1994), and there is no reason to believe that it does not apply equally to performance appraisal.

Steers and Lee (1983) suggest that commitment to the organization might also influence perceptions of the performance appraisal system. However, this influence may be reciprocal, or the causal flow may be in the opposite direction (Meyer, Allen, and Gellatly, 1990). Nonetheless, in general, there seems to be good reason to believe that commitment to the organization and confidence in important decision-making systems (such as PA) will tend to be positively correlated.

2 *Organizational climate* Organizational climate refers to the relationship between rater and ratee. In an organizational climate characterized by high work performance, ambitious goals, workers who accept high levels of responsibility, and cooperative relationships (Litwin and Stringer, 1968; Tziner and Dolan, 1984), raters might be reluctant to assign low ratings to subordinates because of the fear of destroying strong interpersonal relationships and thereby perhaps lowering team productivity. Thus, in such circumstances, there is a likelihood that supervisors will manifest lower levels of discrimination and inflate their subordinates' overall ratings.

On the other hand, a substantial body of research demonstrates the positive influences of such participatory climates on the attitudes, behavior, and performance of individuals in organizations (Kaczka and Kirk, 1968; Litwin and Stringer, 1968; Pritchard and Karasick, 1973). According to these investigations, a participative climate characterized by cooperative relationships, individual responsibility, trust, and communication is conducive to both high levels of performance and effective performance appraisals (Likert, 1961; Litwin and Stringer, 1968; Tziner and Dolan, 1984). In such conditions, raters can be expected to display confidence and loyalty, effective communication, and positive attitudes to fellow workers (Likert, 1961). Moreover, a cooperative atmosphere should induce lower levels of supervisor-subordinate conflict and political manipulation of performance ratings, as well as motivating raters to give (and ratees to receive) accurate and helpful performance feedback (Litwin and Stringer, 1968). The added possibility of the enhanced levels of commitment to the organization induced by a participatory climate (Tziner, 1987; Allen and Meyer, 1990; Barling, Wade and Fullagar, 1990; Mathieu and Zajac, 1990; Tyagi and Wotruba, 1993) also suggests that both raters and ratees would approach performance appraisal in a more positive light.

Orientation to appraisal systems   As noted above, Tziner et al. (in press) identified a further attitudinal factor that impinges on PA raters' performance and that can be labeled in general terms 'comfort and confidence in the performance appraisal'. It seems clear that while some raters place considerable trust in, and feel comfortable with, the appraisal system, others are more cynical and less comfortable with it. It is a reasonable assumption that raters who have confidence in the results of the appraisal will provide different ratings from those whose orientation toward it is more negative or pessimistic. One source of irritation to some raters is their awareness that other raters in the organization are biasing their assessments. For instance, as already suggested, if raters believe that others are lenient and are inflating their ratings to increase the benefits accruing to their subordinates, they might be induced to do likewise, especially when performance appraisals are used for administrative purposes.

Raters frequently report discomfort with having to monitor subordinates' performance, evaluate that performance, and provide subordinates with performance feedback (Murphy and Cleveland, 1991; 1995). Villanova, Bernardin, Dahmus, and Sims (1993) note that raters who show high levels of appraisal discomfort are more likely to provide inflated ratings and less likely to distinguish among subordinates. By giving uniformly high ratings, it appears they can avoid the potentially unpleasant consequences of assigning high scores to some subordinates and low scores to others.

Rater frustration with the appraisal system is less likely to be induced in participatory climates, since the positive atmosphere encourages openness. Raters are thus more likely to feel comfortable providing honest feedback, and will probably be less prone to engage in political manipulation of the system. Moreover, following Steers and Lee (1983), it is reasonable to assume that employee acceptance and support of the PA process will increase to the extent that they collaborate in its actual design and implementation. This, in turn, should enhance the confidence of both raters and ratees in the appraisal system as a whole; by the same token, confidence in the appraisal system should strengthen perceptions of a supportive organizational climate. Thus, generally speaking, raters with a high level of trust are likely to feel comfortable giving their ratees feedback, to be more discerning, and to be better able to distinguish stronger from weaker performers (Murphy and Cleveland, 1995).

Rating Behaviors Affected by Proximal and Distal Influences: A Preliminary Empirical Test

Despite the difficulty of obtaining adequate measures of the psychometric quality and accuracy of performance ratings collected in field settings (Murphy and Cleveland, 1995), Tziner et al. (1998) identify three quantifiable rating behaviors which they argue can be logically and empirically related to the attitudes and beliefs described above. These are: (1) the extent to which raters discriminate among ratees; (2) the extent to which raters discriminate among different aspects of performance; and (3) the extent to which raters assign high vs. low ratings to their subordinates.

In a preliminary empirical test of Murphy and Cleveland's ideas, Tziner et al. conducted a study in Montreal, Canada to examine the relationships between political attitudes and beliefs and these rating behaviors. The study measured the rating performance of two samples of raters: Sample I, consisting of 121 university students who evaluated their professors; and Sample II, 37 managers randomly chosen from two professional organizations. In Sample I, measures of trust in the PA system were obtained, as were raters' self-evaluations regarding self-efficacy, perceptions of organizational climate, and organizational commitment. In Sample II, the researchers recorded managers' discomfort giving feedback, as well as their beliefs about the outcomes of performance appraisal, their perceptions of the organizational climate, and the quality of supervisor-subordinate relationships. These variables were correlated with several measures of rating quality.

Based on the previous findings outlined above, the following hypotheses were formulated:

1 raters with higher levels of trust in the PA system are more likely to discriminate among ratees and dimensions, and more likely to assign low ratings than raters with lower levels of trust;
2 raters with higher levels of self-efficacy are more likely to discriminate among ratees and dimensions, and more likely to assign low ratings than raters with lower levels of self-efficacy;
3 raters who are highly committed are more likely to discriminate among ratees and dimensions, and more likely to assign low ratings than raters with lower levels of commitment;

4   raters who perceive the climate of the organization as more positive and participative are more likely to discriminate among dimensions than raters who perceive the climate to be less participative;

4a raters who perceive the climate of the organization as more positive and participative are less likely to discriminate among ratees or to assign low ratings than raters who perceive the climate as less positive and participative;

5   raters who experience higher levels of discomfort giving feedback are less likely to discriminate among ratees and dimensions, and less likely to assign low ratings than raters with lower levels of feedback discomfort;

6   raters who believe that ratings have substantial impact on organizational outcomes are more likely to discriminate among dimensions than raters who report lower outcome expectancies;

6a raters who believe that ratings have substantial impact on organizational outcomes are less likely to discriminate among ratees or to assign low ratings than raters who report lower outcome expectancies;

7   raters who perceive the climate of the organization as more positive and participative are more likely to discriminate among dimensions than raters who perceive the climate to be less participative;

7a raters who perceive the climate of the organization as more positive and participative are less likely to discriminate among ratees or to assign low ratings than raters who perceive the climate as less positive and participative;

8   raters who report high quality relationships with their subordinates are more likely to discriminate among dimensions than raters who report lower-quality relationships;

8a raters who report high-quality relationships with their subordinates are less likely to discriminate among ratees or to assign low ratings than raters who report lower-quality relationships.

In order not to overburden raters in Sample I with questionnaires, they were divided into two groups. For 58 of the raters, the confidence in the system of evaluation and organizational commitment were measured; for the remaining 63, perceptions of organizational climate and feelings of self-efficacy were measured.

A number of different measures were employed to assess proximal and distal influences, namely: trust in the PA system, self-efficacy, organizational commitment, climate perception, outcome expectancies, organizational climate, discomfort in displaying feedback, and supervisor-subordinate relationships. Rating behavior measures were obtained in the first sample from items on a teacher evaluation questionnaire used at the University of Montreal, and in the second sample from a 10-item Behavior Observation Scale. Three rating measures: rating level, discrimination among ratees, and discrimination among dimensions, were obtained for each rater (Tziner et al., 1998, pp. 461–3).

The means, standard deviations, scale reliabilities, and correlations among the measures for both samples can be found in Tables 6.2 and 6.3. All significant tests were one-tailed, and significance was established using an alpha level of .10 because of the small size of the samples. Support was found for 18 of the 24 directional predictions (p<.005), although many of the individual relationships were weak to moderate in strength, largely due to the combination of relatively weak relationships and relatively small samples. The authors duly note the consequent difficulty of ascertaining the degree of meaningfulness that can be attached to all the confirmed predictions. Nevertheless, they argue that the pattern of results is consistent with the overall hypothesis that attitudes toward performance appraisal and organizational context provide useful information for understanding rating behavior.

A Comprehensive Multi-national Study of Performance Appraisal

Following this initial test of the notions put forward by Murphy and Cleveland, Tziner, Murphy and Cleveland (in press) conducted a comprehensive multi-national study of performance appraisal in which data were collected in seven separate samples in three nations (US, Canada, and Israel). In their introduction to this integrative review, Tziner et al. reiterate that the underlying reason for so-called rater errors in the appraisal process is actually a conscious decision on the part of raters to distort performance ratings: supervisors' rating behavior reflects their beliefs about the organization and the appraisal system, and the distortions are an expression of their personal or organizational goals. Indeed, the authors argue that unless one considers the organizational contexts in which performance ratings are assigned, the appraisals cannot be adequately understood.

The data collected were now expanded to incorporate the three broad categories of attitudes and beliefs identified in the research literature (and discussed above) as central for an understanding of performance appraisal: (1) perceptions of the organization (climate, commitment); (2) beliefs about appraisal systems (self-efficacy, uses of appraisal); and (3) raters' orientations to appraisal systems (confidence and comfort), including their relationship to

Table 6.2   Correlations among proximal influences, distal influences, and rating behavior measures – Sample I

	Mean	SD	1	2	3	4	5	6
Proximal influences								
1 Trust in system	2.30	.83	(.81)[a]					
2 Self-efficacy	4.33	.92	–	(.78)				
Distal influences								
3 Org. commitment	3.65	1.07	.11	–	(.89)			
4 Org. climate	3.77	.72	–	.07	–	(.92)		
Rating behavior								
5 Level	4.59	.66	-.34**	-.16	.18*	.20*		
6 Discrimination (Ratees)	.87	.48	.16	-.15	-.32*	-.18*	-.28*	
7 Discrimination (Dims.)	.48	.21	.03	-.22**	.08	-.03	.02	-.53

Notes

[a] coefficient alpha listed in parentheses. 90% confidence intervals for the correlations in this table range in width from .21 to .22 points.
*   p<.10   **   p<.05.

Table 6.3   Correlations among proximal influences, distal influences, and rating behavior measures – Sample II

	Mean	SD	1	2	3	4	5	6
Proximal influences								
1 Trust in system	2.15	.94	(.97)[a]					
2 Self-efficacy	3.31	.99	.15	(.66)				
Distal influences								
3 Org. commitment	13.36	2.56	.05	-.18	(.89)			
4 Org. climate	3.57	.94	.18	.36*	-.05	(.92)		
Rating behavior								
5 Level	4.83	.42	-.01	.38**	-.01*	.25*		
6 Discrimination (Ratees)	.57	.22	.08	-.30	.02	.03	-.21	
7 Discrimination (Dims.)	.65	.14	.33**	.17	.02	.10	-.32**	-.10

Notes

[a] coefficient alpha listed in parentheses. 90% confidence intervals for the correlations in this table range in width from .21 to .22 points.
*   p<.10   **   p<.05.

specific rating behaviors. As we have seen, these attitudes and beliefs are likely to affect a number of aspects of the appraisal process (e.g., how ratings are performed, how feedback is handled), and ultimately to have a bearing on the accuracy and usefulness of performance ratings as reflected in the extent to which raters discriminate among ratees, the extent to which they discriminate among different aspects of performance, and the extent to which they assign high vs. low ratings to their subordinates.

Two major features distinguished this study from the preliminary investigation described above. The first was the broad scope of the research. Not only were different cultures surveyed, but the choice of organizations also represented a wide range of professions and organizational contexts. Data were obtained from English-speaking samples in the US (military cadets), French-speaking samples in Canada (an academic, a managerial, and a manufacturing sample), and from two samples in Israel (Jewish managers and Arab managers), both presented with measures in Hebrew.

Secondly, the study employed meta-analytic methods to combine the results from multiple samples (rather than primary analyses coupled with significance tests), as no single sample was large enough to provide an accurate estimate of the relationships under investigation. The study also focused on effect sizes rather than p values. Following a frequently used convention in statistical power analysis, Tziner et al. employed R^2 values of .01, .10, and .25, respectively, to describe small, medium, and large effects. The researchers hypothesized that measures of the three areas of attitudes and beliefs would have at least small to moderate effects (i.e., account for at least 5–10 per cent of the variance) in the three respective measures of rating behavior.

Measures of attitudes towards performance appraisal were collected in all the organizations examined in the three countries, and operational performance ratings were obtained from several of the samples, enabling an empirical assessment of the relationships between attitudes and rating behavior. Specifically, each of the individual studies included measures of one or more of the following: (1) organizational climate; (2) organizational commitment; (3) self-efficacy as a rater; (4) confidence in the appraisal system; (5) raters' beliefs about the use of appraisal in the organization; and (6) raters' comfort with performance appraisal.

As indicated, the actual performance appraisal ratings acquired from several of the samples were used to calculate the raters' tendencies to give high vs. low ratings, to discriminate among ratees, and to discriminate among rating dimensions when rating their subordinates. For each rater, the overall mean of his or her evaluations was calculated, and represented the measure of overall level of rating. Discrimination among ratees was measured by calculating the variability of the ratings assigned to the different ratees by each assessor (the number of ratees evaluated ranged from 2 to 12 in the different samples). That is, the standard deviation of the ratee means was calculated for each rater and was used as a measure of discrimination among ratees. Finally, discrimination among dimensions was defined in terms of the variability of the mean scores assigned to each performance dimension by each rater (the number of dimensions evaluated ranged from 2 to 21 in the different samples). To remove overall differences between dimensions, scores were first standardized (z scores) across all raters, and then the standard deviation of the mean ratings on the dimensions was calculated for each rater.

In each sample, correlations were obtained between attitudes, beliefs, and rater behavior measures. Meta-analytic methods were employed to combine these results into a composite correlation matrix, which was then used to obtain estimates of the proportion of variance in rater behavior measures explained by each of the three behavioral performance measures.

The results of the various investigations represent pooled estimates (weighted by sample size) of the correlations obtained (in most cases) from the multiple samples. The correlations yielded by each study were corrected for the unreliability of the measures used in that particular examination.

Table 6.4 presents the meta-analytic estimates of the correlations among the seven attitude and belief measures.

Confirmatory factor analysis (LISREL VIII) was used to test the reasonableness of a three-factor model grouping the sub-measures into combined factors, as follows: (1) climate and commitment into a factor of 'attitudes toward the organization'; (2) measures of self-efficacy as a rater and belief about the extent to which ratings are used to make distinctions within and between individuals into a factor of 'beliefs about how appraisal systems work'; and (3) measures of confidence in, and comfort with, performance appraisal into a factor of 'orientation toward performance appraisal'. The result of the 'fit' for this three-factor model (GFI=.884, RMSR=.09) demonstrates the credibility of this particular grouping of variables.

Table 6.5 presents the squared multiple correlations between the attitude and belief measures and the three rater behavior measures. Contrary to Tziner et al.'s original hypothesis, attitudes toward the organization accounted for relatively small portions of the variance in the behavior measures ($R2$ values were .02, .02, and .01 for rating level, ratee discrimination, and dimension discrimination, respectively, whereas R^2 values of .05 to .10 or higher were predicted).

Table 6.4   Average correlations among attitude and belief measures

	1	2	3	4	5	6	7	8	9
Attitudes toward org.									
1 Participative climate									
2 Affective commitment	.40[a] [.35][b] (198)[c]								
Beliefs about appraisal system									
3 Self-efficacy	.26 [.23] (261)	.31 [.22] (198)							
4 Use of PA – between	.20 [.12] (198)	.32 [.24] (198)	.62 [.40] (198)						
5 Use of PA – within	.50 [.27] (198)	.38 [.26] (198)	.57 [.40] (198)	.72 [.49] (198)					
Orientation to performance appraisal system									
6 Comfort with PA	-.06 [-.05] (189)	.26 [.16] (198)	.21 [.18] (228)	.44 [.41] (198)	.47 [.37] (198)				
7 Confidence in PA	.28 [.23] (198)	.20 [.16] (198)	.06 [.04] (228)	.22 [.20] (198)	.60 [.50] (198)	.37 [.28] (228)			
Rating behavior measures									
8 Rating level	.06 [.05] (179)	.13 [.11] (146)	.11 [.10] (181)	.25 [.15] (88)	.49 [.44] (88)	.00 [.00] (154)	.35 [.28] (176)		
9 Discrimination: Ratees	-.15 [-.13] (179)	-.05 [-.04] (146)	.18 [.16] (181)	.39 [.18] (88)	.25 [.22] (88)	.03 [.02] (154)	.01 [.01] (176)	-.34 [-.29] (275)	
10 Discrimination: Dims.[.11]	.12 [.09] (179)	.10 [-.11] (146)	-.12 [.11] (181)	.13 [.11] (88)	.14 [-.01] (88)	-.01 [.18] (154)	.21 [-.06] (176)	-.08 [-.33] (275)	-.39 (275)

Notes

a   Correlations are corrected for unreliability
b   Uncorrected correlations are shown in brackets
c   Total *N* for each correlation is shown in parentheses

Table 6.5   Structural coefficients linking attitudes, beliefs and rating behavior

	Rating level	Discrimination: Ratees	Discrimination: Dimensions
Attitudes toward the organization	.16	-.31	.15
Beliefs about the appraisal system	.20	.46	-.40
Orientation to performance appraisal system	-.27	-.21	.59
R^2 for the structural model	.07	.12	.22

However, the authors report additional results which are far more in accord with the expectations drawn from the theoretical discussion. Beliefs about performance appraisal systems accounted for considerably larger portions of the variance in rater behavior (R^2 values of .29, .13, and .10 for rating level, ratee discrimination, and dimension discrimination, respectively). These values correspond roughly with conventional definitions of large and medium effects (R^2 values of .10 and .25 are often used to describe moderate and large effects, respectively). They indicate, therefore, that beliefs about performance appraisal systems are substantially linked to raters' tendencies to give high vs. low ratings, to discriminate among ratees, and to discriminate among rating dimensions. Moreover, as hypothesized, orientations to performance appraisal systems accounted for substantial variance in rating level measures ($R^2=.14$), and were also linked to raters' tendencies to discriminate among rating dimensions ($R^2=.06$). However, they were essentially unrelated to raters' tendencies to discriminate among ratees.

Although most of the correlations between specific attitudes and beliefs and rating behavior measures shown in Table 6.4 are small, several are sufficiently large to represent at least small to moderate effects (i.e., R^2 values of .05, or r values of .25 or larger). In particular, Tziner et al. note that raters' beliefs about the uses of ratings had clear implications for the ratings they gave. Raters who believed that their organizations would use performance ratings to make administrative decisions about ratees, or to distinguish ratee strengths from weaknesses, were more likely to give high ratings (correlations of .25 and .49, respectively), and tended to distinguish better among ratees (correlations of .39 and .25, respectively). They were also more likely to distinguish among rating dimensions, although here the correlations were at a level commonly interpreted as representing small effects (correlations of .13 and .14, respectively, where a correlation of .10 is conventionally used to represent small effects). Another correlation between beliefs and rating behavior that is large enough to meet the operational definition of a moderate effect is associated with raters who believed that other managers inflated their subordinates' ratings. They, too, were more likely to give high ratings to their own subordinates ($r=.35$).

The observed variance in corrected correlation coefficients across samples was compared with the variance expected on the basis of sampling error. In virtually all cases, the empirical variation in correlation coefficients was equal to or smaller than what could be attributed to sampling error. In fact, none of the correlations between attitude and belief measures and rating behavior measures showed more variability across samples than would be expected solely on the basis of sampling error.

Tziner et al. point out that the samples in their investigation did not sufficiently cover all strata of organizations or cultures, as would be needed to determine exactly what factors moderate the relationships between attitudes, beliefs, and rating behaviors. Moreover, they note that the small sample sizes severely limit the statistical power necessary to detect the consistency of results across samples. Although the combined samples provide reasonable numbers of observations for most of the correlations reported, they are not sufficiently large to determine whether the apparent consistency in results is itself meaningful, or whether it simply reflects the limited ability to detect meaningful differences across samples.

Despite these reservations, the researchers suggest that the relatively stable correlations obtained from samples in very different industries, countries, and languages indicate that the results are not specific to particular contexts or cultures. In their view, the findings of this extended research program provide at least partial support for the central premise that attitudes and beliefs about organizations and performance appraisal systems affect supervisors' appraisal ratings. As hypothesized, beliefs about the PA system and orientations toward performance appraisal accounted for substantial variance in raters' tendencies to give high vs. low ratings, to discriminate among ratees, and to discriminate among rating dimensions when evaluating their subordinates.

Contrary to their predictions, however, the authors conclude that general attitudes toward the organization (i.e., climate perception and commitment to the organization) account for very little variance in rater behavior. Nevertheless, they suggest that while the findings call into question the hypothesis that general attitudes toward organizations translate directly into rater tendencies such as assigning high ratings and discriminating among ratees, the generally weak correlations here do not necessarily mean that attitudes toward the organization are irrelevant to understanding performance appraisal. They argue that such perceptions might influence a number of aspects of PA without directly affecting variables such as mean rating or variability in ratings, as a function of the ratees or the dimensions being evaluated, respectively.

Despite the fact that their hypotheses were only confirmed in part, as well as the limitations on interpretation imposed by the small sample sizes, Tziner et al. propose that two preliminary conclusions can be drawn from the findings presented in Table 6.4. First, they reiterate the importance of raters' perceptions of the use of performance appraisal in organizations both formally (to discriminate between employees) and informally (supervisors' tendency to assign high ratings in order to motivate and placate subordinates). In view of their results, these perceptions appear to be related to several rater behavior measures, a finding that reinforces Cleveland and Murphy's (1992) contention that 'rater errors' are somewhat adaptive behaviors intended to match rater performance evaluation strategies to the realities of their organizations. Secondly, the authors note that confidence in appraisal systems seems to be the single most important predictor of rating level measures. Raters who believe that others distort and inflate their ratings are likely to do the same.

Extensive cross-cultural literature suggests that cultural differences might affect the operation and use of a number of human resource systems (Hofstede, 1980; Arvey, Bhagat and Salas, 1991; Erez, 1994; Triandis, 1994). It might be assumed that this phenomenon would apply equally to the relationships between attitudes, beliefs, and rating behavior. Yet the results of both these studies (Tziner et al., 1998; Tziner et al., in press) suggest that these particular relationships may be universally stable. On the other hand, Tziner et al. (in press) stress the preliminary nature of these findings across types of organizations, languages, and national borders, and concede that more data and larger samples are needed before confident conclusions regarding the consistency of outcomes can be drawn.

In looking forward to future research in this field, they indicate four principal strengths of the current approach. First, unlike previous studies linking attitudes and beliefs to rating behavior, all their samples involved experienced raters. Secondly, many of the studies used actual performance ratings to derive dependent measures. Thirdly, the investigations incorporated a range of different countries, scales, languages, organizations, and rating systems. And finally, the results in the samples were reasonably consistent, suggesting that the links obtained between attitudes, beliefs, and rating behaviors are not mere artifacts of some specific setting. In their view, the studies provide clear evidence that attitudes and beliefs about organizations and performance appraisal systems can be linked to rating behaviors, and that the tendency to assign high or low ratings can be predicted with some confidence on the basis of these measures. Future research, they suggest, should determine whether broad cultural differences moderate some or all of the relationships they examined.

Developing a Structured Instrument to Measure the Extent of Political Considerations in Performance Appraisal

Stage One: Preliminary Design and Test of Psychometric Qualities (Tziner, Latham, Prince and Haccoun, 1996)

Tziner, Latham, Prince and Haccoun (1996) emphasize two factors to be considered when designing an instrument to measure raters' perceptions of the political considerations manifest in performance appraisal. The first, as noted above, is the need for a quantitative tool. The second is that the instrument should make it possible to identify which particular political consideration is exerting an operative influence on the rater's PA performance.

With these aims in mind, the researchers devised the Political Considerations in Performance Appraisal Questionnaire (PCPAQ), a pool of items based on: (1) the literature regarding political considerations likely to operate on raters during PA (e.g., Longenecker et al., 1987; Murphy and Cleveland, 1991); (2) empirical research on the motivations for distorting performance ratings (Kane and Kane, 1992); (3) personal observations of factors contributing to the intentional biasing of ratings (based on the authors' professional experience); and (4) the general literature on organizational power, politics, and decision-making processes.

Thirty items were generated for the initial pool that was to be tested with respect to clarity, appropriateness, and content validity. They included considerations such as raters' attempts to enhance their organizational status, to avoid conflicts with employees, to conform with social pressures, to settle personal disputes, and to attain personal benefits (see Table 6.6).

Phase I: Preliminary Analysis

1 *Pretesting* Using the procedure of back-translation, an equivalent French

Table 6.6   Means, standard deviations, item-total correlation, and correlation with the social desirability score for the political considerations in Performance Appraisal Questionnaire (PCPAQ)

Item	M	SD	Item–total r	Correlation with social desirability
1 Supervisors avoid giving performance ratings that may antagonize employees (e.g., a low rating) [PC1]	2.84 (3.25)	1.39 (1.43)	0.71 (0.51)	0.02
2 Supervisors are giving low performance ratings because they fear that their employees will try to be transferred to another boss [PC2]	2.90 (2.90)	1.49 (1.38)	0.66 (0.51)	0.01
3 Supervisors avoid giving a low performance rating because they fear violent behavior on the part of their employees[a]	2.00	1.13	0.49	0.03
4 Supervisors inflate performance ratings of those employees who are able to procure them special services, favors, or benefits [PC3](0.73)	2.55 (2.67)	1.47 (1.43)	0.64	0.04
5 Supervisors inflate performance ratings of employees who have access to valuable sources of information [PC4]	3.16 (3.35)	1.45 (1.45)	0.66 (0.74)	0.06
6 Supervisors' performance ratings reflect in part their personal liking or disliking of the employees [PC5]	2.20 (2.68)	1.30 (1.33)	0.77 (0.78)	0.20
7 Supervisors' performance ratings are affected by the extent to which employees are perceived as sharing the same basic values as they do [PC6]	2.08 (2.52)	1.16 (1.33)	0.73 (0.78)	0.20
8 The performance ratings of employees are affected by their ability to inspire the enthusiasm of the supervisor who rates their performance [PC7]	3.29 (3.30)	1.66 (1.54)	0.56 (0.64)	0.11
9 Supervisors give performance ratings that will make them look good to their supervisors [PC8]	2.76 (2.78)	1.56 (1.36)	0.63 (0.52)	0.0003
10 The quality of the supervisor-employee personal relationship throughout the rating period (e.g., tense-relaxed, trusting-distrusting, friendly-hostile) affects the performance rating [PC9]	3.25 (3.17)	1.49 (1.40)	(1.40) (0.69)	0.09
11 Supervisors are likely to give an inflated performance rating in order to avoid negative/uncomfortable feedback sessions with their employees [PC10]	3.83 (3.28)	1.39 (1.44)	0.68 (0.67)	0.04

Table 6.6 cont'd

Item	M	SD	Item – total r	Correlation with social desirability
12 Supervisors avoid giving performance ratings which may have negative consequences for the employee (e.g., demotion, lay-off, no bonus, salary freeze, etc.) [PC11]	3.22 (3.03)	1.66 (1.43)	0.61 (0.74)	0.08
13 Supervisors inflate performance ratings in order to maximize rewards offered to their employees (e.g., salary increases, promotions, prestigious assignments, etc.) [PC12]	2.20 (2.39)	1.20 (1.21)	0.74 (0.70)	0.08
14 Supervisors inflate performance ratings in order to maintain a positive image of their department or organization[a] to others	1.73	0.80	0.50	0.04
15 Supervisors produce accurate performance ratings only to the extent that they perceive that they may be rewarded for doing so or penalized for failing to do so [PC13]	2.47 (2.75)	1.36 (1.38)	0.72 (0.84)	0.07
16 Supervisors produce accurate performance ratings only to the extent that they perceive that this is the norm in the organization [PC14]	2.04 (2.42)	1.22 (1.36)	0.80 (0.78)	0.06
17 Employees holding a high status-position in their organization will get a higher performance rating than is deserved (i.e., regardless of their real performance, employees' ratings are affected by their status in the organization [PC15]	2.43 (2.72)	1.33 (1.43)	0.78 (0.83)	0.07
18 Supervisors give high performance ratings because they believe that their employees have already passed through many organizational hurdles and therefore are highly competent [PC16]	3.06 (2.90)	1.33 (1.35)	0.61 (0.83)	0.01
19 In assigning ratings, supervisors conform to what they believe is the norm ('acceptable') in their organization so as to avoid disapproval by their peers [PC17]	2.39 (2.52)	1.27 (1.33)	0.81 (0.83)	0.07
20 Supervisors give low performance ratings to teach rebellious employee a lesson [PC18]	2.76 (3.16)	1.54 (1.47)	0.80 (0.78)	0.02
21 Supervisors give low performance ratings to encourage an employee to leave the organization[a]	3.06	1.49	0.20	0.04
22 Supervisors use performance ratings to send a message to their employees (e.g., encourage risk-taking, creativity, etc.) [PC19]	2.69 (2.50)	1.50 (1.30)	0.68 (0.62)	0.22

Table 6.6 cont'd

Item	M	SD	Item – total r	Correlation with social desirability
23 Supervisors give accurate performance ratings only to the extent that they think they will be rewarded for doing so[a]	4.04	1.44	0.52	0.05
24 Supervisors inflate performance ratings of those employees who possess special characteristics (e.g., high popularity, compliancy, etc.) [PC20]	2.55 (2.71)	1.32 (1.33)	0.80 (0.85)	0.05
25 The fear that performance ratings may threaten the self-esteem of employees discourage supervisors from giving negative – though accurate – ratings [PC21]	2.41 (2.72)	1.10 (1.34)	0.69 (0.79)	0.04
26 Supervisors give higher performance ratings than is deserved in order to gain support/cooperation from their employees [PC22]	2.50 (2.76)	1.25 (1.40)	0.78 (0.84)	0.04
27 Supervisors give higher performance ratings than is deserved in order to repay favors to their employees [PC23]	2.20 (2.63)	1.10 (1.40)	0.64 (073)	0.19
28 Supervisors give equivalent performance ratings to all their employees in order to avoid resentment and rivalries among them [PC24]	2.59 (2.68)	1.70 (1.32)	0.72 (0.83)	0.08
29 Supervisors give higher performance ratings than is deserved to those employees who control valuable organizational resources [PC25]	2.63 (2.86)	1.17 (1.42)	0.55 (0.75)	0.04
30 Supervisors' performance ratings are determined in part by the power of the employees (i.e., control of decisions, expertise in certain areas, indispensability, centrality in the information network, etc.)[a]	2.06	1.25	0.54	0.13
Total	78.90 (70.61)	26.33 (26.51)		

Notes

1   The figures in brackets derive from Phase 2 respondents (N=157), whereas the remainder come from the Phase 1 subjects (N=51). Response to each of the items ranged from '1' (very atypical) to '6' (very typical of the reality in the respondents organization).

2   The items marked (a) are those that were dropped after Phase 1.

version of the 30-item instrument was designed and administered to a randomly selected sample of employees (N=51) holding managerial positions in a French-speaking institution in Montreal. The subjects were to indicate the extent to which they perceived each of the 30 items to be descriptive of considerations that come to bear on raters in their organization when they appraise the performance of their employees. Responses were recorded on a six point Likert-type scale ranging from '1' (very atypical) to '6' (very typical). The managers were also administered the French version of the Social Desirability Scale in order to determine whether their responses to the PCPAQ were affected by considerations of social desirability.

2 *Item selection* The results of the pretesting were then analyzed in order to identify the items that most accurately represent the perceived political considerations prevailing in the PA process. Items were retained if: (1) an item-total correlation was at least 0.55; and (2) there was a lack of significant correlation with the Social Desirability Scale (Crown and Marlowe's Social Desirability Scale). Five items were eliminated, leaving 25 whose item-total correlations ranged from 0.55 to 0.81 and whose correlations with the Social Desirability Scale (alpha=0.79) were non-significant, varying from 0.01 to 0.20 (p>0.05). The means, standard deviations, item-total correlations, and the correlations with the total score on the Social Desirability Scale for the 30-item PCPAQ are displayed in Table 6.6.

Phase 2: Structure, Reliability and Validity Analyses

The psychometric properties of the PCPAQ were ascertained by its administration to managers in the same organization who had not participated in Phase 1. To determine convergent and discriminant validities (see below), this second sample was also asked to respond to four additional questionnaires, the French versions of the Need for Power, Machiavellianism, State-Trait Anxiety, and Organizational Commitment inventories. The sequence of the items on each questionnaire was alternated so as to prevent a possible order effect. A total of 157 questionnaires (i.e., 60 per cent) were completed and returned.

Of the respondents, 56 per cent were men and 44 per cent women, all were employed full-time, the average age was 46.6 years (SD=7.3 years), 56 per cent held an academic degree, and 28 per cent had completed partial academic studies. Their average years of experience as raters was 10 (SD=8.89 years), average seniority in managerial positions 13.09 years (SD=8.84 years), and they were responsible for an average of 15 subordinates each.

Factor analysis   To determine whether the structure of the PCPAQ was homogeneous/unidimensional or multidimensional, a principal component analysis rotated to a varimax solution was performed. Table 6.7 presents the results of this analysis, from which Tziner et al. concluded that the structure of the questionnaire could be reasonably interpreted in terms of a single general factor. This conclusion was supported by: (1) the level of internal consistency of the entire scale (Cronbach's alpha = 0.97) which, although it might be explained by the number of items, suggests that the items represent the same construct domain; and (2) the dramatic scree plot produced by the eigenvalues. The authors note that in the context of performance appraisal, this empirical finding confirms the coherent structure of the general concept of organizational politics (Pfeffer, 1981).

Reliability   The reliability of the instrument was determined by examining internal consistency and stability over time (an interval of two weeks between the two administrations). Internal consistencies were alpha=0.97 and 0.98 for first and second administrations, respectively, and stability over time, as measured by the correlation between the two administrations, was r=0.86. These results indicate that the instrument is highly reliable.

Convergent validity   The total score of the PCPAQ was compared with those obtained on the Need for Power Scale (adapted from the Manifest Needs Questionnaire) and the Machiavellianism (Mach IV) scale, both judged to be capable of measuring concepts related to the researchers' notion of political considerations in performance appraisal (for details, see: Tziner et al., 1996, p. 187.) The PCPAQ score correlated 0.23 (p<0.01) with the Need for Power score (M=4.46, SD=0.76, alpha=0.57), and produced a reasonably high correlation (r=0.33) with the Machiavellianism score (M=5.07, SD=0.63, alpha=0.69).

Discriminant validity   The Organizational Commitment Questionnaire and State-Trait Anxiety Inventory were judged to measure concepts that are in no way theoretically related to that which underlies the PCPAQ (Tziner et al., 1996, pp. 187–8). The Organizational Commitment Questionnaire (OCQ) assesses the degree of worker loyalty, satisfaction, and pride in the organization, as well as the intention to leave. The score derived from the French version of the OCQ was M=5.08 (SD=0.93, alpha=0.86), and correlated only moderately, and negatively, with the PCPAQ score, r = -.27 (p<0.01). The implication of this finding is that raters who score high on organizational commitment are

Table 6.7 **Factor analysis of the 25-item political considerations in Performance Appraisal Questionnaire**

Item	Communality	Factor loadings		
		Factor I (manipulation to acquire benefits)	Factor II Attaining and exercising control	Factor III Social/ interpersonal
PC1	0.68	0.60	0.55	0.09
PC2	0.65	0.69	0.39	0.12
PC3	0.74	0.75	0.14	0.38
PC4	0.65	0.76	0.06	0.26
PC5	0.73	0.80	0.03	0.31
PC6	0.77	0.82	0.18	0.24
PC7	0.45	0.66	0.01	0.09
PC8	0.63	0.55	0.58	0.06
PC9	0.60	0.71	0.29	0.11
PC10	0.57	0.69	0.29	0.07
PC11	0.66	0.76	0.24	0.12
PC12	0.74	0.81	0.20	0.20
PC13	0.77	0.86	0.16	0.09
PC14	0.65	0.80	0.03	0.11
PC15	0.74	0.85	0.06	0.09
PC16	0.74	0.85	0.15	0.06
PC17	0.75	0.85	0.04	0.13
PC18	0.72	0.80	0.06	0.27
PC19	0.55	0.65	0.35	0.08
PC20	0.77	0.87	0.11	0.08
PC21	0.73	0.81	0.09	0.26
PC22	0.80	0.85	0.10	0.21
PC23	0.71	0.76	0.16	0.33
PC24	0.82	0.85	0.05	0.32
PC25	0.77	0.77	0.02	0.41
Eigenvalue		14.91	1.35	1.10
% of variance explained		59.7%	5.4%	4.4%

perceived as being less inclined to invoke political considerations when formulating performance ratings, and therefore this result could not be considered a supportive index of the PCPAQ's discriminant validity. However, correlating the PCPAQ score with an index score of anxiety (State-Trait Anxiety Inventory) produced a non-significant correlation of 0.14 (M=1.57, SD=0.35, alpha=0.86), which is sufficiently solid to confirm the discriminant validity of the PCPAQ.

Overall, these results, obtained in a Francophone culture, clearly demonstrate the PCPAQ's reliability with regard to both internal consistency and stability over time, a finding reinforced by the high degree of similarity between the means, standard deviations, and item-total correlations of the items yielded by Phases 1 and 2. The empirical data also sustains both the convergent and discriminant validities, albeit in a much less spectacular way. Tziner et al. concede that additional concepts should be used in future investigations for the purpose of revalidation (e.g., for convergent validity, the propensity to behave politically, and for discriminant validity, an unrelated concept such as spatial ability, rather than organizational commitment).

Stage Two: Further Evidence of the Psychometric Qualities of the PCPAQ (Tziner, Prince and Murphy, 1997)

With respect to the generalization of the conclusions of their preliminary study of the PCPAQ, Tziner et al. (1996) note the importance of testing the instrument further using a wider range of respondents, an English-speaking milieu, and different types of organizations. Larger samples would also make it feasible to conduct a more complex corroborative analysis (i.e., LISREL) of the underlying structure of organizational political considerations. To this end, Tziner, Prince, and Murphy (1997) replicated the initial test of the PCPAQ in an Anglophone work environment, employing the original English version of the questionnaire. As suggested in the first study, a number of alternative variables were used to test the convergent and discriminant validities of the instrument.

The rationale behind the cultural shift stems from the fact that the differences between the Francophone and Anglophone cultural milieus are particularly in evidence in Canada. Supervisors (i.e., raters) also belong to a specific environment, and are no less subject to the same cultural divide than anyone else in their social grouping (Kanungo, Corn and Dauderis, 1976). Moreover, the Francophone organizational milieu is characterized by an open, participative climate and a consultative management process, whereas in the Anglophone milieu (at least in Canada), the management style is more reserved, less consultative, and less likely to reveal genuine feelings.

Validation Procedures

1 *Discriminant validity* The original measures of state-trait anxiety were

again employed, but this time together with an additional indicator, family involvement (instead of organizational commitment), in line with Tziner et al'.s (1996) recommendation. Both concepts were believed to have no theoretical relationship to the concept underlying the PCPAQ (for details, see: Tziner et al., 1997, p.193).

2 *Convergent validity* 'Self-monitoring' was added to organizational commitment as a second variable, in line with finding that individuals high on self-monitoring will scan the environment for social cues and modify their behavior accordingly, a phenomenon that would certainly apply to PA (for details, see Tziner et al., 1997, pp. 193–4).

Procedure

Questionnaires were distributed by mail to some 600 MBA graduates of an English-speaking university in Montreal who were known to be responsible for a number of subordinates. The participants were asked to complete the PCPAQ and the four other questionnaires used for validation. The covering letter explained that the purpose of the survey was to explore organization-related and performance appraisal-related attitudes. No personal identification was requested in order to guarantee total anonymity, deemed essential to ensure that the participants would respond frankly to the sensitive matters contained in the questionnaire.

This is an important point in light of Kane's (1994) suggestion that the paucity of research on volitional distortions of rating may be attributable to the difficulty of obtaining reliable data. In his view, this is especially true in respect to the extent to which raters can be expected to report honestly on their motivations to falsify or misrepresent evaluations. Although Kane believes the attempt to acquire this type of data is a futile exercise, the response rate in Tziner et al.'s study was 50 per cent.

Results

Analysis of common method bias Harman's one-factor test (Podsakoff and Organ, 1986) was used to assess the degree to which intercorrelations among the five scales might be an artifact of common method variance. No general factor emerged. Rather, at least three factors were necessary to account for the major part of the explained variance. The authors note that while these results do not completely rule out the possibility of same-source bias, it is an unlikely explanation of the findings.

Distribution of responses on the instrument   From the mean (M=3.47) and standard deviation (SD=.56) of the instrument scores, Tziner et al. were able to conclude that the responses across the 25 items were normally distributed over the 6-point range (with the theoretical mean of a 6-point scale being 3.5). This conclusion is reinforced by the distribution of the response frequency to each of the 25 items on the questionnaire (Table 6.8).

Reliability   The reliability of the PCPAQ was established by calculating the coefficient of internal consistency, which yielded a Cronbach's alpha of .93. This is a high level of internal consistency, indicating the reliability of the questionnaire. It will be remembered that alpha coefficients measure the extent to which the items of an instrument have high communalities, and not their undimensionality or homogeneity. Accordingly, confirmatory factor analysis was conducted on the responses using LISREL 8, and confirmed that the structure of the PCPAQ is virtually homogeneous/unidimensional. Indeed, a one-factor model fitted the data very well [Comparative Fit Index (CFI)=.89, $C^2 (289)=50.76$].

Discriminant validity   As predicted, non-significant correlations were found between the PCPAQ score and the scores on the State-Trait Anxiety Inventory and the index of involvement with family life (r=-.05, p>.40, and r=.04, p>.54, respectively). These results are convincing evidence of the discriminant validity of the instrument.

Convergent validity   As expected, a significant relationship was found between PCPAQ scores and the measures of self-monitoring (r=.11; p<.04) and organizational commitment (r=-.20, p<.001). The results confirm the relationship between self-monitoring as a tool used by the supervisor for the purposes of impression management, and the degree to which political considerations manifested in performance appraisal are aimed at gaining control over organizational behavior and resources. The communality of the two variables may reside in the rater's attempt to gain control in order to enhance personal goals/interests. The negative correlation for organizational commitment reflects the anticipated notion that during performance appraisal, loyal raters high on organizational commitment are less inclined to invoke political considerations that may jeopardize organizational goals.

This second investigation clearly demonstrates that the structure of the English version of the PCPAQ, designed to measure political considerations in performance rating, is unidimensional, and that the instrument is highly

Table 6.8   Means and standard deviations for the Political Considerations in Performance Appraisal Questionnaire

Item	M	SD
1 Supervisors avoid giving performance appraisals that may antagonize employees (e.g., a low rating)	3.64	1.29
2 Supervisors avoid giving a low performance appraisal because they fear that the employee will try to transfer to another boss	2.17	1.07
3 Supervisors inflate performance appraisals of those people who are able to procure for them special services, favors, or benefits	3.24	1.07
4 Supervisors inflate the performance appraisal of employees who have access to valuable sources of information	3.31	1.43
5 Supervisors' performance appraisals reflect in part their personal liking or disliking of employees	4.49	1.13
6 Supervisors/ appraisal are affected b the extent to which employees are perceived as sharing the same basic values as they do	4.42	1.13
7 The performance ratings of employees are affected by their ability to inspire enthusiasm in the supervisor who appraises their performance	4.34	1.05
8 Supervisors give performance appraisals that will make them look good to their supervisors	3.70	1.33
9 The quality of the supervisor-subordinate personal relationship throughout the appraisal period (e.g., tense-relaxed; trusting-distrusting; friendly-hostile) affects the performance rating	4.23	1.31
10 Supervisors are likely to give an inflated performance appraisal in order to avoid negative/uncomfortable feedback sessions with a subordinate	3.55	1.33
11 Supervisors avoid giving performance appraisals which may have negative consequences for the employee (e.g., demotion, layoff, no bonus, salary freeze, etc.)	3.27	1.38
12 Supervisors inflate performance appraisals in order to maximize rewards for their subordinates (e.g., salary increases, promotions, prestigious assignments)	3.10	1.32
13 Supervisors produce accurate performance appraisals on to the extent that they may be rewarded for doing so or penalized for failing to do so	3.21	1.43
14 Supervisors produce accurate performance appraisals only to the extent that they perceive that this is the norm in their organization	3.73	1.40

Item	M	SD
15 Employees holding a high status position in their organization will get a higher performance appraisal than is deserved (i.e., regardless of their real performance, employee appraisals are affected by the organizational status of the positions they hold)	3.73	1.48
16 Supervisors give high performance ratings because they believe that their subordinates have already passed through many organizational hurdles and therefore are highly competent	2.84	1.28
17 In assigning ratings, supervisors conform to what they believe is normative ('acceptable') in their organization so as to avoid disapproval by their peers	3.80	1.40
18 Supervisors give low performance appraisals to teach a rebellious employee a lesson	3.40	1.39
19 Supervisors use performance appraisals to send a message to their employees (e.g., encourage risk-taking, creativity, etc.)	4.41	1.28
20 Supervisors inflate performance appraisals of those employees who possess special characteristics (e.g., a high popularity, compliancy, etc.)	3.83	1.23
21 The fear that performance appraisals may threaten the self-esteem of subordinates discourages supervisors from giving negative – though accurate – appraisals	3.07	1.24
22 Supervisors give higher performance ratings than is deserved in order to gain support or cooperation from their employees	3.42	1.23
23 Supervisors give higher performance appraisals than is deserved in order to repay favors to their employees	3.11	1.42
24 Supervisors give equivalent performance ratings to all their subordinates in order to avoid resentment and rivalries among them	2.95	1.43
25 Supervisors give higher performance appraisals than is deserved to those employees who control valuable organizational resources	3.38	1.39

Note

Responses to each of the items ranged from '1' (very atypical) to '6' (very typical) of raters' behavior in the studied organization.

reliable. It also provides clear evidence of its convergent and discriminant validities. These findings, which are consistent with those produced by the examination of the psychometric qualities of the French version, lend substantial support to the soundness of the instrument and the possibility of establishing generalizable qualities from investigations of different linguistic/ cultural milieus.

The new instrument has opened the door to the systematic and quantitative investigation of the way in which perceived political considerations affect the psychometric properties of performance ratings, as well as to the study of the distal and proximal factors which predispose raters to invoke political considerations when appraising performance. Considering the somewhat speculative nature of previous research in this area, this constitutes a major advance that should spur further interest.

The results of these two investigations (Tziner et al., 1996; Tziner et al., 1997) also refute Kane's contention that respondents will not be prepared to answer such questionnaires honestly. The PCPAQ has proved its potential for meaningful exploration of the painful area of volitional distortion of ratings in the workplace. It demonstrably succeeded in uncovering both the personal motivations and political considerations that particularly affect the outcomes of the PA process and job satisfaction.

Rater Training

One approach to improving efficiency in the evaluation process is the attempt to modify performance appraisal through methodological improvements in the tools of evaluation, as described above. Other approaches center primarily on the characteristics, powers of observation, and evaluation skills of the raters. As we have seen, the accrued empirical evidence indicates that the major part of variation in appraisal errors (insofar as they can be said to exist) is accounted for by the various abilities displayed by assessors. How, then, can the raters be assisted to perform more efficiently, thus also minimizing the effects of political considerations?

Wexley, Singh and Yukl (1973) claim that: (1) it is possible to train raters so that typical errors in evaluation are virtually eliminated; (2) the most appropriate training method for this purpose involves workshops that allow for active learning and feedback for raters on the quality of their performance appraisal; and (3) the effect of what is learned by raters in an active, sustained framework is likely to last a relatively long time. In line with this conviction,

Goldstein and Sorcher (1974) designed a training program model containing four elements: modeling, practice, group support, and repetition (where appropriate).

A rater training program must also deal with raters' perceptions of the parameters of performance, both good and bad, and mold these views in a way that accurately reflects the elements of successful performance within the organization. This can be done not only by creating a clear frame of reference that includes defined work norms and requirements, but also by honing the ability to sort these behaviors into categories. Clearly, information alone, conveyed through lectures or assigned reading, is not sufficient to change rater behavior; only active learning, through experience and feedback, contains this potential. Trainees must be introduced to the various tools that aid accuracy in judgment, such as deciding what to observe, how to classify and interpret data, and how to use the scale on which the performance appraisal form is based. Moreover, they must be presented with examples of perceptual illusions and distortions, as well as errors of interpersonal judgment.

Research indicates that effective training programs must also emphasize (through discussion) the great complexity of the evaluation process, the importance of recording the facts in an objective manner, the development of examples of effective and ineffective worker behaviors, and the context in which the appraisal process takes place (Carroll and Schneier, 1982; Bernardin and Beatty, 1984). Bernardin and Beatty also stress the importance of discussing with potential appraisers the possible relations between different dimensions of performance and their influence on the general impression formed by the rater.

Methods and Contents of Training

Relying on Borman's (1978) Evaluation Model, D.E. Smith (1986) surveys no less than 24 studies aimed at testing the effectiveness of rater training programs. He concludes that training programs differ from one another both in the manner in which the contents of the program are presented and in the actual content itself.

Manner of presentation Generally speaking, the three most popular methods for presenting content in rater training courses are lectures, group discussion, and practice with feedback.

1 *Lecture* This is the traditional approach of class and teacher, whereby

material is transmitted from the lecturer to the student with no group discussion and without ensuring that the student has comprehended the material. For ease of classification, the assignment of written material is included in this category.

2 *Group discussion* This approach assumes that the active participation of trainees is important to ensure that the course contents are fully understood by every student. Through discussion, trainees may be required to raise problems, find solutions, suggest alternatives, and so on.

3 *Practice and feedback* Here trainee raters are given the opportunity to gain experience of the appraisal system and compare their evaluations with those of a professional in the field. In this way, they are given the chance to identify and correct any appraisal errors they may be making.

In general, the more the raters themselves are involved in the training process, the better the results, especially with respect to accuracy of evaluation and reduction of leniency errors. However, all three methods have been shown to be effective in decreasing evaluation errors. Thus, notwithstanding all the advantages to be gained from trainee involvement, economic considerations favor the use of the lecture.

Content D.E. Smith (1986), identifies three main foci of instruction:

1 *Rating error training* This refers to a direct attempt to reduce rating errors, usually by demonstrating actual errors and examples of routine mistakes. This is the most popular topic of training programs, as it saves the instructor time.

2 *Performance dimension training* Here training focuses on improving the effectiveness of evaluation by helping raters to better understand the dimensions of job performance which they are being asked to evaluate.

3 *Performance standards training* Trainees here are given a framework within which to proceed with their evaluations, the objective being to arrive at a normative situation in which all raters share and agree on common standards for effective performance.

According to Borman's (1978) model, training must include three specific stages in order for the validity and eventual precision of the evaluations to be enhanced. The raters must be taught: (1) to examine relevant behaviors for efficient work performance; (2) to rate each behavior independently and, concurrently, be aware of misconceptions resulting from interpersonal perceptions and the specific rating situation; and (3) to weight each behavior in accordance with the accepted standards of the organization. The rater is thus required to internalize the normative standards of the organization, and, on that basis alone, evaluate the behavior of the worker. With respect to organizational standards, Borman (1979) adds that raters need to be taught a common or standard terminology ('frame of reference') for defining the importance of each relevant behavior component.

The majority of training programs, whether they focus on performance dimensions or rating errors, tend to concentrate on the second stage, training the rater to evaluate independently each behavior found relevant to efficient functioning. Rating-error training is too often limited to teaching raters what *not* to do in the assessment process, rather than providing clear instructions as to what they should do. Consequently, although fewer errors are made and a wider divergence on the rating scales is achieved, this kind of training does not necessarily improve the accuracy of evaluation.

Bernardin and Beatty (1984) note that making raters aware of rating errors themselves essentially ignores the sources of cognitive distortion which they hold are the cause of errors in the first place. They claim that rater training should first assist raters to look at the relevant behaviors (performance dimensions), and then help them internalize the accepted standards of the organization (content stages 1 and 3 in Borman's model). The combination of these aptitudes and training in the observation and identification of specific behaviors has been found to be most effective.

Rater training is intended to assist in determining the weight of each unit of behavior and its unique contribution to the total evaluation in the given dimension. By providing raters with the standards of performance, they are able to develop a frame of reference with which the efficiency of performance rating can be calibrated. The raters then need to be helped to find a balance between observation and recording, and to develop the awareness that the observation of workers' behavior is central to the evaluation process, and even more important than recording the final rating. Conversely, they must be trained to focus the process of recording specifically on the performance behaviors of the ratees, ignoring task- irrelevant behaviors. A series of recent studies has produced significant empirical evidence indicating that this 'frames of reference' approach to rater training notably improves rater accuracy.

As noted above, another technique for improving the accuracy of evaluation is to train raters to keep a diary of observations (Bernardin and Beatty, 1984). This is based on Bernardin's (1981) finding that such a collection of nonjudgmental events throughout the entire period of the evaluation tends to decrease cognitive errors. Thus, a major purpose of the diary is to standardize the observation of behavior and to promote a functional connection between observation and performance appraisal.

Management by Objectives

Finally, one of the best-known techniques for improving rater efficiency can be subsumed under the notion of management by objectives (MBO). Essentially, this system requires that goals be set for each employee, so that the subsequent appraisal process determines how the actual level of attainment compares with the set goals. MBO capitalizes on goal-setting theory (Locke, 1968), which is based on the assumption that the most immediate, direct motivational determinant of task performance is the individual's goal or intention, defined as what the individual is consciously trying to achieve.

In essence, very simple forms of goal-setting are recognized, either implicitly or explicitly, by nearly every theory of work motivation. While the technique itself was largely ignored in early versions of human relations and expectancy theories, it is now more expressly acknowledged and invoked by the proponents of scientific management and management by objectives. In contrast, researchers of the cognitive growth and behavioral modification schools have tended to deny the significance of goal-setting, although even they have used MBO when putting their theories into practice (Locke, 1977).

In the context of performance appraisal, the use of MBO can be broken down into four steps. In the first, goals are set for each ratee. In the second step, a time frame within which the ratee must accomplish the set goals is established. In the third stage, the actual level of attainment is compared with the set goals. Finally, a decision is reached concerning new goals, and strategies are set for achieving those not yet achieved.

The results of numerous experimental investigations in both laboratory and field settings support the conclusion that specific and/or challenging goals do, in fact, lead to higher levels of performance than do vague or easy ones (Latham and Yukl, 1975; Ivancevich, 1977; Dossett, Latham and Mitchell, 1979; Locke et al., 1981). Furthermore, Tziner and Latham (1989) document the significantly positive and substantial effects on organizational commitment, perceived fairness of evaluation, and work satisfaction when MBO is utilized in conjunction with a BOS-based performance appraisal. Indeed, in a recent investigation, the MBO approach was a component of the performance appraisal systems in 31.8 per cent of the companies examined.

Performance Appraisal Toward the Future

Performance appraisal has made considerable strides over the last decade. Clearly, we have seen that ultimately the extent and significance of the effects of PA go beyond the immediacy of the results of the appraisal process on the ratees to considerations of their future job performance. As human resource personnel become more aware of this potential, they can be expected to gain a greater appreciation of the importance of training supervisors to use PA tools effectively in order to give timely and specific feedback to their subordinates. The payoff will be not only in short-term gains, but also in the long-term enhancement of worker motivation, loyalty, and goal processing that urge employees toward improved job performance and diminished withholding behaviors.

The choice of the appropriate rating format will, of course, remain the key decision. The choice will be made on the basis of the internal qualities of the rating scales, the purposes for which they are to be used, their likely affects on political attitudes, and their financial utility. In time, performance appraisal processes are likely to be operationalized so that they can be factored into a cost-effectiveness analysis. The ultimate objective is for performance appraisals to highlight those effective workers in whom it is worthwhile for the organization to invest, for, when all is said and done, satisfied and loyal workers make for productive and profit-making organizations.

References

Abbott, J.R. and Bernardin, J.H. (1983). 'The Development of a Scale of Self-Efficacy for Giving Performance Feedback'. Unpublished manuscript, Florida Atlantic University.

Allen, N.J. and Meyer, J.P. (1990). 'The Measurement and Antecedents of Affective, Continuance, and Normative Commitment to the Organization'. *Journal of Occupational Psychology*, 6, pp. 1-18.

Altman, S., Valenzi, E. and Hodgetts, R.M. (1985). *Organizational Behavior: Theory and Practice*. Orlando, FL: Academic Press.

Arpin, R. (1994). 'Evaluer sans Tricher'. *Gestion* (Sept.), pp. 8–9.

Arvey, R.D., Bhagat, R.S. and Salas, E. (1991). 'Cross-cultural and Cross-national Issues in Personnel and Human Resources Management: Where Do We Go From Here?' In G. Ferris and K. Rowland, *Personnel and Human Resources Management,* Vol. 9, Greenwich, CT: JAI Press, pp. 367-407.

Bandura, A. (1977). *Social Learning Theory*. Englewood Cliffs, NJ: Prentice Hall.

Bandura, A. (1982). 'Self-Efficacy Mechanisms in Human Agency'. *American Psychologist*, 37, pp. 127–47.

Barling, J., Wade, B. and Fullagar, C. (1990). 'Predicting Employee Commitment to Company and Union: Divergent Models'. *Journal of Occupational Psychology*, 63, pp. 49–61.

Becker, H. (1960). 'Notes on the Concept of Commitment'. *American Journal of Sociology*, 66, pp. 32-42.

Bernardin, H.J. (1981). 'Rater Training Strategies: An Integrative Model'. Paper presented at the Annual Meeting of the American Psychological Association, San Diego.

Bernardin, H.J. and Beatty, R.W. (1984). *Performance Appraisal: Assessing Human Behavior at Work*. Boston: Kent.

Bernardin, H.J. and Buckley, R.M. (1981). 'A Consideration of Strategies in Rater Training'. *Academy of Management Review*, 6, pp. 205–12.

Bernardin, H.J. and Carlyle, J.J. (1979). 'The Effects of Forced Choice Methodology on Psychometric Characteristics of Resultant Scales'. Paper presented at the Annual Meeting of the Southern Society of Philosophy and Psychology, Atlanta, GA.

Bernardin, H.J. and Pence, E.C. (1980). 'Rater Training: Creating New Response Sets and Decreasing Accuracy'. *Journal of Applied Psychology*, 65, pp. 60–66.

Bernardin, H.J. and Smith, P.C. (1981). 'A Clarification of Some Issues Regarding the Development and Use of Behaviorally Anchored Rating Scales'. *Journal of Applied Psychology*, 66, pp. 458–63.

Bernardin, H.J. and Villanova, P. (1986). 'Performance Appraisal'. In E. Locke (ed.), *Generalizing from Laboratory to Field Settings*. Lexington, MA: Lexington Books.

Bjerke, D.G, Cleveland, J.N., Morrison, R.R. and Wilson, W.C. (1987). 'Officer Fitness Report Evaluation Study'. Navy Personnel Research and Development Center Report, TR 88–4.

Blanz, F. (1965). *A New Merit Rating Method*. Unpublished doctoral dissertation. Stockholm: University of Stockholm.

Blanz, F. and Ghiselli, E.E. (1972). 'The Mixed Standard Scale: A New Rating System'. *Personnel Psychology*, 25, pp. 185–99.

Borman, W.C. (1974). 'The Rating of Individuals in Organizations: An Alternative Approach'. *Organizational Behavior and Human Performance*, 12, pp. 105–24.

Borman, W.C. (1978). 'Exploring Upper Limits of Reliability and Validity in Performance Ratings'. *Journal of Applied Psychology*, 63, pp. 135–44.

Borman, W.C. (1979). 'Format and Training Effects on Rating Accuracy and Rater Errors'. *Journal of Applied Psychology*, 64, pp. 410–21.

Borman, W.C. (1986). 'Behavior-Based Rating Scale'. In R.A. Berk (ed.), *Performance Assessment: Method and Application*. Baltimore, MD: John Hopkins University Press.

Burke, R.S., Weitzel, W. and Weir, T. (1978). 'Characteristics of Effective Employee Performance Review and Development Interviews: Replication and Extension'. *Personnel Psychology*, 31, pp. 903–19.

Campbel, D.J. and Lee, C. (1988). 'Self-appraisal in Performance Evaluation: Development Versus Evaluation'. *Academy of Management Review*, 13, pp. 302–14.

Campbel, D.J., and Pritchard, R.D. (1976). 'Motivation Theory in Industrial and Organizational Psychology'. In M.D. Dunnette (ed.), *Handbook of Industrial and Organizational Psychology*. Chicago: Rand McNally.

Carroll, R.S. and Schneier, C.E. (1982*). Performance Appraisal and Review Systems*. Glenview, IL: Scott, Foresman and Co.

Cawley, B.D., Keeping, L.M. and Levy, P.E. (1998). 'Participation in the Performance Appraisal Process and Employee Reactions: A Meta-Analytic Review of Field Investigations'. *Journal of Applied Psychology*, 83, pp. 615–33.

Chiles, A.M. and Zorn, T.E. (1995). 'Empowerment in Organizations: Employees' Perceptions of the Influence of Empowerment'. *Journal of Communication Research*, 23, pp. 1–25.

Cleveland, J.N. and Murphy, K. (1992). 'Analyzing Performance Appraisal as Goal-Directed Behavior'. *Research in Personnel and Human Resources Management*, 10, pp. 121–85.

Cobb, A.T. (1984). 'An Episodic Model of Power: Toward an Integration of Theory and Research'. *Academy of Management Review*, 9, pp. 482–93.

Coladarci, T. (1992). 'Teachers' Sense of Efficacy and Commitment to Teaching'. *Journal of Experimental Education*, 60, pp. 323–37.

Dawis, R.V. and Lofquist, L.H. (1984). *A Psychological Theory of Work Adjustment*. Minneapolis: University of Minnesota.

DeNisi, A.S., Cafferty, T. and Meglino, B. (1984). 'A Cognitive View of the Performance Appraisal Process: A Model and Research Proposition'. *Organizational Behavior and Human Performance*, 33, pp. 360–90.

Dolan, S. and Schuler, R. (1987). *Personnel and Human Resource Management in Canada*. St Paul, MN: West.

Dorfman, P.W., Stephan, W.G. and Loveland, J. (1986). 'Performance Appraisal Behaviors: Supervisor Perception and Subordinate Reactions'. *Personnel Psychology*, 39, pp. 579–97.

Dosset, D.L., Latham, G.P. and Mitchell, T.R. (1979). 'The Effects of Assigned versus Participatively Set Goals'. *Journal of Applied Psychology*, 64, pp. 291–8.

Dunnette, M.D. (1963). 'A Modified Model for Test Validation and Selection Research'. *Journal of Applied Psychology*, 47, pp. 317–23.

Early, P.C. and Kanfer, P. (1985). 'The Influence of Component Participation, Goal Satisfaction, and Performance'. *Organizational Behavior and Human Decision Processes*, 36, pp. 378–90.

Erez, M. (1977). 'Feedback: A Necessary Condition for the Goal-Setting Performance Relationship'. *Journal of Applied Psychology*, 62, pp. 624–7.

Erez, M. (1994). 'Toward a Model of Cross-cultural Industrial and Organizational Psychology'. In H.C. Triandis, M.D. Dunnette and L.M. Hough (eds), *Handbook of Industrial and Organizational Psychology*, 2nd edn, Vol. 4. Palo Alto, CA: Consulting Psychologists Press, pp. 560–607.

Farr, J.L. and Werbel, J.D. (1986). 'Effects of Purpose of the Appraisal and Expectation of Validation on Self-Appraisal Leniency'. *Journal of Applied Psychology*, 71, pp. 527–9.

Fay, C.H. and Latham, G.P. (1982). 'Effects of Training and Rating Scales on Errors'. *Personnel Psychology*, 35, pp. 105–16.

Feldman, J.M. (1981). 'Beyond Attribution Theory: Cognitive Processes in Performance Appraisal'. *Journal of Applied Psychology*, 66, pp. 127–48.

Fisher, C.D. (1979). 'Transmission of Positive and Negative Feedback to Subordinates: A Laboratory Investigation'. *Journal of Applied Psychology*, 64, pp. 533–40.

Frayne, C.A. and Latham, G.P. (1987). 'Application of Social Training Theory to Employer Self-Management of Attendance'. *Journal of Applied Psychology*, 72, pp. 387–92.

Fried, Y., Tiegs, R.B. and Bellamy, A.R. (1992). 'Personal and Interpersonal Predictors of Supervisors' Avoidance of Evaluating Subordinates'. *Journal of Applied Psychology*, 77, pp. 462–8.

Ghiselli, E.E. (1956). 'Dimensional Problems of Criteria'. *Journal of Applied Psychology*, 40, pp. 1–4.

Goldstein, A.P. and Sorcher, M. (1974). *Changing Supervisor Behavior*. New York: Pergamon.

Gosselin, A. and Murphy, K.R. (1994). 'L'Echec de l'evaluation de la Performance'. *Gestion* (Sept.), pp. 17–26.

Gosselin, A., Werner, J. and Halle, N. (1994). 'So Why Don't We Just Ask Them?: A Survey of Ratee Preferences Concerning Performance Appraisal and Management'. Unpublished Manuscript. Montreal: University of Montreal.

Gould, S. (1979). 'An Equity-Exchange Model of Organizational Involvement'. *Academy of Management Review*, 4, pp. 53–62.

Guion, R.M. (1961). 'Criterion Measurement and Personnel Judgment'. *Personnel Psychology*, 14, pp. 141–9.

Hedge, J.W. and Borman, W.C. (1995). 'Changing Conceptions and Practices in Performance Appraisal'. In A. Howard (ed.), *The Changing Nature of Work*. San Francisco CA: Jossey-Bass, pp. 451–81.

Hofstede, G. (1980). *Culture's Consequences: International Differences in Work-related Values*. Newbury Park, CA: Sage.

Huber, L.L. (1985). 'Effects of Task Difficulty, Goal Setting, and Strategy on Performance of A Heuristic Task'. 70, pp. 492–504.

Ilgen, D.R., Fisher, C.D. and Taylor, M.S. (1979). 'Consequences of Individual Feedback on Behavior in Organizations'. *Journal of Applied Psychology*, 64, pp. 349–71.

Ivancevich, J.M. (1977). 'Different Goal Setting Treatments and Their Effects on Performance and Job Satisfaction'. *Academy of Management Journal*, 3, pp. 406–17.

Ivancevich, J.M. (1979). 'An Analysis of Participation in Decision Making among Project Engineers'. *Academy of Management Journal*, 22, pp. 253–69.

Ivancevich, J.M. (1980). 'A Longitudinal Study of Behavioral Expectation Scales: Attitude and Performance'. *Journal of Applied Psychology*, 65, pp. 139–40.

Kaczka, E. and Kirk, R. (1968). 'Managerial Climate, Work Groups and Organizational Performance'. *Administrative Science Quarterly*, 12, pp. 253–72.

Kane, J.S. (1994). 'A Model of Volitional Rating Behavior'. *Human Resource Management Review*, 4, pp. 283–310.

Kane, J.S. and Freeman, K.K. (1987). 'MBO and Performance Appraisal: A Mixture That's not a Solution'. *Personnel*, Dec., pp. 26–37.

Kane, J.S. and Kane, K.F. (1992). *Extension and Validation of a Model for Motivated Rating Error*. Unpublished Manuscript. Greensboro: University of North Carolina.

Kane, J.S. and Lawler, E.E. (1979). 'Performance Appraisal Effectiveness: Its Assessment and Determinants'. *Research in Organizational Behavior*, 1, pp. 425–78.

Kanungo, R.N., Gorn, G.J. and Dauderis, H.J. (1976). 'A Motivational Orientation of Canadian Anglophone and Francophone Hospital Employees'. *Canadian Journal of Behavioral Science*, 8, pp. 160–63.

Kelley, H.H. (1973). 'The Process of Causal Attribution'. *American Psychologist*, 28, pp. 107–28.

Kelman, H. (1961). 'Process of Opinion Change'. *Public Opinion Quarterly*, 25, pp. 57–78.

Kingstrom, P.O. and Bass, A.R. (1981). 'A Critical Analysis Comparing Behaviorally Anchored Rating Scales (BARS) and other Formats'. *Personnel Psychology*, 34, pp. 263–89.

Knauft, E.B. (1948). 'Construction and Use of Weighted Checklist Rating Scales for Two Industrial Situations'. *Journal of Applied Psychology*, 32, pp. 63–70.

Kopelman, R.E. (1986). *Managing Productivity in Organizations: A Practical, People-Oriented Perspective*. New York: McGraw Hill.

Landy, F.J. and Farr, J.L. (1980). 'Performance Rating'. *Psychological Bulletin*, 87, pp. 72–107.

316   *Human Resource Management*

Landy, F.J and Farr, J.L. (1983). *The Measurement of Work Performance*. New York: Academic Press.

Latham, G.P., Fay, C.H. and Saari, L.M. (1979). 'The Development of Behavioral Observation Scales for Appraising the Performance of Foremen'. *Personnel Psychology*, 32, pp. 299–311.

Latham, G.P. and Wexley, K.N. (1981). *Increasing Productivity through Performance Appraisal*. Reading, MA: Addison-Wesley.

Latham, G.P., Wexley, K.N. and Pursell, E.D. (1975). 'Training Managers to Minimize Rating Errors in the Observation of Behavior'. *Journal of Applied Psychology*, 60, pp. 550–55.

Latham, G.P. and Yukl, G.A. (1975). 'A Review of Research on the Application of Goal Setting in Organizations'. *Academy of Management Journal*, 18, pp. 824–45.

Likert, R. (1961). *New Patterns of Management*. New York: McGraw Hill.

Litwin, G.H. and Stringer, R.A. (1968). *Motivation and Organizational Climate*. Boston: Harvard University Press.

Locke, E.A. (1968). 'Toward a Theory of Task Motivation and Incentives'. *Organizational Behavior and Human Performance*, 3, pp. 157–89.

Locke, E.A. (1977). 'The Myths of Behavior Mod. In Organizations'. *Academy of Management Review*, 2, pp. 543–53.

Locke, E.A., Frederick, E., Lee, C. and Bobko, P. (1984). 'Effect of Self-efficacy, Goals, and Task Strategies on Task Performance'. *Journal of Applied Psychology*, 69, pp. 241–51.

Locke, E.A., Latham, G.P. and Erez, M. (1988). 'The Determinant of Goal Commitment'. *Academy of Management Review*, 13, pp. 23–9.

Locke, E.A., Shaw, K.N., Saari, L.M. and Latham, G.P. (1981). 'Goal Setting and Task Performance: 1969–1980', *Psychological Bulletin*, 90, pp. 125–52.

Lofquist, L.H. and Dawis, R.V. (1969). *Adjustment to Work*. Minneapolis: University of Minnesota.

Longenecker, C.O. and Gioia, D.A. (1988). 'Neglected at the Top: Executives Talk About Executive Appraisal'. *Sloan Management Review*, Winter, pp. 41–7.

Longenecker, C.O., Sims, H.P. and Gioia, D.A. (1987). 'Behind the Mask: The Politics of Employee Appraisal'. *Academy of Management Executive*, 1, pp. 183–93.

Love, K.G. (1981). 'Comparison of Peer Assessment Methods: Reliability, Validity, Friendship Bias, and Users Reaction'. *Journal of Applied Psychology*, 66, pp. 451–7.

Maier, N.R.F. (1976). *The Appraisal Interview: Three Basic Approaches*. La Jolla, CA: University Associates.

Mathieu, J.E. and Zajac, D.M. (1990). 'A Review and Meta-analysis of the Antecedents, Correlates, and Consequences of Organizational Commitment'. *Psychological Bulletin*, 108, pp. 171–94.

McGregor, D. (1957). 'An Uneasy Look at Performance Appraisal'. *Harvard Business Review*, 35, pp. 89–94.

Meyer, J.P. and Allen, N.J. (1984). 'Testing the 'Side-Bet' Theory of Organizational Commitment: Some Methodological Considerations'. *Journal of Applied Psychology*, 69, pp. 372–8.

Meyer, J.P., Allen, N.J. and Gellatly, I.R. (1990). 'Affective and Continuance Commitment to the Organization: Evaluation of Measures and Analysis of Concurrent and Time-Lagged Relations'. *Journal of Applied Psychology*, 75, pp. 710–20.

Mohrman, A.M. and Lawler, E.E. (1983). 'Motivation and Appraisal Performance Behavior'. In F. Landry, S. Zedeck and J. Cleveland (eds), *Performance Measurement and Theory*. Hillsdale, NJ: Erlbaum, pp. 173–89.

Mount, M.K. (1983). 'Comparison of Managerial and Employee Satisfaction with Performance Appraisal System'. *Personnel Psychology*, 36, pp. 99–110.

Murphy, K.R. and Cleveland, J. (1991). *Performance Appraisal: An Organizational Perspective*. Boston: Allyn and Bacon.

Murphy, K.R. and Cleveland, J. (1995). *Understanding Performance Appraisal: Social, Organizational, and Goal-Based Perspectives*. Thousand Oaks, CA: Sage.

Napier, N. and Latham, G.P. (1986). 'Outcome Expectancies of People Who Conduct Performance Appraisals', *Personnel Psychology*, 39, pp. 827–37.

Nathan, B.R., Morhrman, A.M. and Milliman, J. (1991). 'Interpersonal Relations as a Context for the Effects of Appraisal Interview on Performance and Satisfaction – A Longitudinal Study', *Academy of Management Journal*, 30, pp. 352–69.

Petit, A. and Haines, V. (1994). 'Trois Instruments D'evaluation du Rendement', *Gestion*, Sep., pp. 59–68.

Pfeffer, J. (1981). *Power in Organizations*. Marshfield, MA: Pittman Publishing Co.

Podsakoff, P.M. and Organ, D.W. (1986). 'Self-Reports in Organizational Research: Problems and Prospects'. *Journal of Management*, 12, pp. 531–44.

Prince, J.B., Lawler, E.E. and Mohrman, A.M. (1991). 'Manager-Subordinate Divergence in Performance'. Unpublished manuscript, Concordia University.

Pritchard, R.D. and Karasick, B.W. (1973). 'The Effect of Organizational Climate on Managerial Job Perceptions and Job Satisfaction'. *Organizational Behavior and Human Performance*, 9, pp. 126–46.

Riggs, M.L., Warka, J., Babasa, B., Betancourt, R. and Hooker, S. (1994). 'Development and Validation of Self-efficacy and Outcome Expectancy Scales for Job-related Applications'. *Educational and Psychological Measurement*, 54, pp. 793–802.

Salancik, G.R. (1977). 'Commitment and the Control of Organizational Behavior and Belief'. In B. Staw and G. Salancik (eds), *New Directions in Organizational Behavior*. Chicago: St-Clair Press.

Shneier, C.E. (1979). 'Measuring Cognitive Complexity: Developing Reliability, Validity and Norm Tables for a Personality Instrument'. *Educational and Psychological Measurement*, 39, pp. 599–611.

Shneier, C.E., Shaw, D.G. and Beatty, R.W. (1991). 'Performance Measurement and Management: A Tool for Strategy and Execution'. *Human Resource*, 30, pp. 279–301.

Smith, D.E. (1986). 'Training Programs for Performance Appraisal: A Review'. *The Academy of Management Review*, 11, pp. 22–40.

Smith, P.C. (1976). 'Behaviors, Results, and Organizational Effectiveness: The Problem of Criteria'. In M.D. Dunnette (ed.), *Handbook of Industrial and Organizational Psychology*. Chicago: Rand McNally.

Staw, B. (1977). 'Two Sides of Commitment'. Paper presented at the Annual Convention of the Academy of Management, Orlando, FL.

Steers, R.M. (1975). 'Task-Goal Attributes, Achievement, and Supervisory Performance'. *Organizational Behavior and Human Performance*, 13, pp. 392–403.

Steers, R.M. and Lee, T.W. (1983). 'Facilitating Effective Performance Appraisals: The Role of Employee Commitment and Organizational Climate'. In F. Landry, S. Zedeck and J. Cleveland (eds), *Performance Measurement and Theory*. Hillsdale, NJ: Lawrence Erlbaum Associates, pp. 75–88.

Steers, R.M. and Wotruba, T.R. (1993). 'An Exploratory Study of Reverse Causality Relationships Among Sales Turnover Variables'. *Journal of the Academy of Marketing Science*, 21, pp. 143–53.

Steiner, D.D., Rain, J.S. and Smalley, M.M. (1993). 'Distributional Rating of Performance Further Examination of a New Rating Format'. *Journal of Applied Psychology*, 78, pp. 438–42.

Tannenbaum, S.I., Mathieu, J.E., Salas, E. and Cannon-Bowers, J.A. (1991). 'Meeting Trainees' Expectations: The Influence of Training Fulfillment on the Development of Commitment, Self-efficacy, and Motivation'. *Journal of Applied Psychology*, 76, pp. 759–69.

Teel, K.S. (1980). 'Performance Appraisal: Current Trends, Persistent Progress', *Personnel Journal*, 59, pp. 296–301, 316.

Tharenou, P. (1995). 'The Impact of a Developmental Performance Appraisal Program on Employee Perceptions in an Australian Federal Agency'. *Group and Organization Management*, 20, pp. 245–71.

Thornton, G.C. III (1980). 'Psychometric Properties of Self-Appraisals of Job Performance'. *Personnel Psychology*, 33, pp. 263–71.

Triandis, H.C. (1994). 'Cross-cultural Industrial and Organizational Psychology'. In H.C. Triandis, M.D. Dunnette and L.M. Hough (eds), *Handbook of Industrial and Organizational Psychology*, 2nd edn, Vol. 4. Palo-Alto, CA: Consulting Psychology Press, pp. 103–72.

Tsvi, A.S. and Barry, B. (1986). 'Interpersonal Affect and Rating Errors'. *Academy of Management Journal*, 29, pp. 586–98.

Tushman, M.L. (1977). 'A Political Approach to Organizations: A Review and Rationale'. *Academy of Management Review*, 2, pp. 206–16.

Tyagi, P.K. and Wotruba, T.R. (1993). 'An Exploratory Study of Reverse Causality Relationship Among Sales Turnover Variables'. *Journal of Academy of Marketing Science*, 21, pp. 143–53.

Tziner, A. (1984a). 'A Fairer Examination of Rating Scales When Used for Performance Appraisal in a Real Organizational Setting'. *Journal of Occupational Behavior*, 5, pp. 103–12.

Tziner, A. (1984b). 'Prediction of Peer Rating in a Military Assessment Center: A Longitudinal Follow-up'. *Canadian Journal of Administrative Science*, 1, pp. 146–60.

Tziner, A. (1987). 'The Relationship of Some Distal and Proximal Factors with the Extent of Use of Political Considerations in Performance Appraisal'. Paper presented at the Annual Conference of the Academy of Management, Vancouver, Canada.

Tziner, A. (1990). *Organization Staffing and Work Adjustment*. New York: Praeger.

Tziner, A. and Dolan, S. (1984). 'The Relationship of Two Sociodemographic Variables and Perceived Climate Dimensions to Performance'. *The Canadian Journal of Administrative Sciences*, 1, pp. 272–87.

Tziner, A., Joanis, C. and Murphy, K. (2000). 'A Comparison of Three Methods of Performance Appraisal with Regard to Goal Properties, Goal Perception, and Ratee Satisfaction'. *Group and Organizational Management*, 25, pp. 175–90.

Tziner, A., Kopelman, R.E. and Joanis, C. (1997). 'Investigation of Raters' and Ratees' Reactions to Three Methods of Performance Appraisal: BOS, BARS, and GRS'. *Canadian Journal of Administrative Sciences*, 14, pp. 396–404.

Tziner, A., Kopelman, R.E. and Livneh, N. (1993). 'Effects of Performance Appraisal Format on Perceived Goal Characteristics, Appraisal Process Satisfaction, and Changes in Rated Job Performance: A Field Experiment', *Journal of Psychology*, 127, pp. 281–92.

Tziner, A. and Latham, G.P. (1989). 'The Effects of Appraisal Instrument, Feedback and Goal-Setting on Worker Satisfaction and Commitment'. *Journal of Organizational Behavior*, 10, pp. 145–53.

Tziner, A., Latham, G.P., Prince, B.S. and Haccoun, R. (1996). 'Development and Validation of a Questionnaire for Measuring Political Considerations in Performance Appraisal'. *Journal of Organizational Behavior*, 17, pp. 179–90.

Tziner, A., Murphy, K. and Cleveland, J.N. (in press). 'Relationship Between Attitudes Toward Organizations and Performance Appraisal Systems and Rating Behavior'. *International Journal of Selection and Assessment*.

Tziner, A., Murphy, K., Cleveland, J., Beaudin, G. and Marchand, S. (1998). 'Impact of Rater Beliefs Regarding Performance Appraisal and its Organizational Contexts on Appraisal Quality'. *Journal of Business and Psychology*, 12, pp. 457–67.

Tziner, A, Prince, B.S. and Murphy, K.R. (1997), 'PCPAQ: The Questionnaire for Measuring Perceived Political Considerations in Performance Appraisal: some New Evidence Regarding its Psychometric Qualities'. *Journal of Social Behavior and Personality*, pp. 189–99.

Villanova, P., Bernardin, H.J., Dahmus, S.A. and Sims, R.L. (1993). 'Rater Leniency and Performance Appraisal Discomfort'. *Educational and Psychological Measurement*, 53, pp. 789–99.

Wallace, S.R. (1965). 'Criteria for What?'. *American Psychologist*, 20, pp. 411–17.

Wexley, K.N., Singh, J.P. and Yukl, G.A. (1973). 'Subordinate Personality as a Moderator of the Effects of Participation in Three Types of Appraisal Interview'. *Journal of Applied Psychology*, 58, pp. 54–9.

Wiersma, V.C. and Latham, G.P. (1986). 'The Practicality of Behavioral Observation Scales, Behavioral Observation, Behavioral Expectation and Trait Scales'. *Group and Organization Management*, 20, pp. 297–309.

Wiersma, V.C., Van Den Berg, P.T. and Latham, G.P. (1995). 'Dutch Reactions to Behavioral Observation, Behavioral Expectation, and Trait Scales'. *Group and Organization Management*, 20, pp. 297–309.

Zavala, A. (1965). 'Development of the Forced Choice Rating Scale Technique'. *Psychological Bulletin*, 63, pp. 117–24.

Zedeck, S.A. and Cascio, W. (1982). 'Performance Appraisal Decisions as a Function of Rater Training and Purpose of the Appraisal'. *Journal of Applied Psychology*, 67, pp. 752–8.

7 Assessing the Financial Value of Worker Organizational Behaviors and Human Resource Management Programs and Interventions

AHARON TZINER AND ASSA BIRATI

The Need to Assess Financial Value

On the conceptual level, human resource research has advanced remarkably in recent decades. In regard to employee behavior in the workplace, it has focused on patterns that are both functional and dysfunctional, where the former refers to positive employee dispositions and actions that contribute to the work climate and to the efficiency of production, such as work satisfaction, organizational commitment, high motivation, and superior performance (Gupta and Jenkins, 1982; Meyer and Allen, 1991).

In respect to human resource management programs and interventions, there is similarly a wealth of solid literature on how to conduct activities such as recruitment, staffing, orientation and training, performance appraisal, career management, restructuring, and relocation. Since the outcomes of these strategies are so crucial to the economic viability of the companies planning to utilize them, it is not surprising that much of the research has focused on the extensive analysis of their effectiveness. Yet while this area of research has been treated intensely and has recorded considerable progress, the results are by no means clear cut.

The efficacy of the different methods is left in even greater doubt when an attempt is made to compute their cost effectiveness as part of the analytical model adopted by the decision makers in an organization. In fact, much less attention has been devoted to the assessment of the net real post-tax financial benefits of these intervention strategies than to the investigation of their operational validity. This is especially surprising in view of the fact that cost-benefit analysis is routinely employed to assess the economic utility of streamlining in other areas of company activity. Indeed, neglect of this issue may very well be the reason for the restricted use of human resource management programs in the market place.

Since saving money is an important goal, cost-benefit analysis can often prove to be a critical tool in enabling employers to estimate the economic utility of any organizational intervention method, or any combination of them, as a means of improving the firm's performance. Moreover, the outcome of a financial feasibility investigation may reinforce, or alternatively call into question, the implementation of the classical procedures in human resource management, where the sole criteria of success has been the question of operational validity. A good case in point is assessment centers. Despite evidence of their high predictive validity, the considerable cost involved has cast doubt on the merits of using their services.

This chapter serves to highlight some of the recent, innovative work in the field of the economic assessment of worker organizational behaviors and human resource management strategies. The basic thrust of this effort is to enable the use of quantitative models that allow decision makers to generate all the factors needed to estimate real financial gains and/or losses before any intervention strategy is implemented in the workplace.

As we have seen, it clearly makes sense for organizations interested in adopting human resource management strategies to make the effort to pinpoint the criteria that represent efficient reliability and validity. By the same token, such organizations cannot afford to ignore the payoff factor when using these criteria as predictors of efficacy. Unless the estimated economic real gain resulting from the implementation of a method can be seen to exceed the estimated real cost of administering it, the validity of the criteria is of little or no consequence.

Obvious benefits derive from calculating the financial value of worker organizational behaviors and the economic utility of human resource management programs and interventions. Senior managers can use economic estimates, where appropriate, to limit the deleterious effects of negative behavior, to plan and implement organizational interventions, and to assist company planners within the context of an overall business strategy. Indeed, the estimation of the future potential rate of return of a particular human resource management program can (and should) be weighed against other options for improving the company's overall financial status (e.g., Cronshaw and Alexander, 1991).

Below we review the application of the payoff factor in organizational planning for human resources in a number of areas in which the joint authors have collaborated in recent years. In respect to employee behavior, these include withdrawal behaviors and voluntary turnover. In the realm of organizational intervention and programs, the topics relate to staffing procedures, assessment centers, early retirement, training, and organizational downsizing. In all of these studies, the underlying rationale has been that the use of quantitative models to estimate the value of certain types of worker behavior, or the net financial gains of using a particular intervention strategy, can save companies from making gross tactical errors and, more positively, can assist management in promoting the organization's long-term economic goals.

Historical Review

Earlier attempts to assess the financial value of worker organizational behaviors and the economic utility of human resource management programs and interventions can be traced to a handful of seminal studies that introduced the notion of the economic value of human behavior in the organizational or commercial context. In these classic investigations, the estimation of the value of an employee's contribution was based on his or her productivity, and the cost of an intervention program was computed as a function of the direct outlays made to cover the expense of the project. In most of the research, the direct costs associated with human behaviors or organizational interventions was computed by means of an additive formula. For example, Brogden (1949) and Brogden and Taylor (1950) proposed a formula designed to assist organizations in choosing an efficient staffing method. Tziner (1990) notes that the rationale behind the model was that 'the cost of using a specific staffing method should be evaluated in terms of the relative value to the organization of an excellent employee as opposed to a mediocre employee'. Thus, unless the value of one candidate over another exceeds the cost of administering a staffing method, the predictor generated by the method 'is of no benefit to the organization, regardless of its validity' (Tziner, 1990, p. 101).

This cost was expressed by Brogden (1949) in terms of the mean gain productivity in dollars per applicant (ΔU) as follows:

$$\Delta U = r_{xy} \, SD_y \, Z_{xy} - C/p \qquad (1)$$

where:

rxy = the predictive validity of the staffing method (i.e., the correlation coefficient among prescreened applicants) between predictor score (x) and dollar-value payoff (y)

SDy = the standard deviation of performance in dollars among employees of the type selected

Z = the mean standard score on the staffing method for those selected

C = the cost of the staffing method per applicant

P = the selection ratio

This mathematical expression is basically a linear function with four variables: predictive ability, the cost of the method, the criterion variance (a reflection of the selectee's value to the firm), and the mean predictor score (the score on the staffing method). According to the formula, the utility gain – the increase in average dollar payoff that results from using a staff method – grows linearly when the following conditions pertain: there is an increase in the standard deviation of performance in dollars (SDy), in the mean predictor scores of those selected (Zxy), and in the validity coefficient (rxy), and there is a decrease in cost per applicant of running the staffing method (C).

As the research evolved, however, it became clear that there was a need to reexamine the criteria associated with earlier financial estimations of this nature (with respect to the above example, see: Cronbach and Glezer, 1965; Boudreau, 1983; Tziner, 1990). This reappraisal engendered revised formulae in which variables impinging on the financial payoff were adjusted, or added, in order to increase the precision of the estimate of cost effectiveness.

This is better understood when we realize that performance, for example, is a function of the work attitudes and work conduct of the employee, no less than of his or her knowledge and skills. Further elements contributing to workers' worth to a company might include the degree to which their organizational expectations are compatible with the unique features of the organizational culture, and the extent to which they identify with the organization's goals and are receptive to continued upgrading of knowledge and skills. The variables contributing to the value of a worker are thus both direct (salaries, benefits, etc.) and indirect (concomitants of personality, knowledge, attitude, and skills).

One example of this modified approach appears in a recent study of withdrawal behavior (Birati and Tziner, 1996). In examining the loss of probability to the firm as a result of withdrawal behavior and withholding efforts at work, the authors adopt a quantitative approach that incorporates the added value of foregone revenue (an indirect result of behavior), rather than merely the cost of payments to the absentees, as in earlier quantifications (Cascio, 1991).

Moreover, employees do not work in a vacuum. The company in which a worker is employed will continually be reacting to market trends, competition, newfound opportunities to improve efficiency, and the like. Thus, from time to time the firm will initiate human resource management interventions, such as recruitment, staffing and training, or the revamping of organizational structures, which are designed to enhance its competitive edge and improve profitability.

Staff recruitment is another instance of an organizational intervention which involves a number of expenses to the company that go beyond the direct costs of the program. For instance, new workers need time to adjust to the work environment and to shore up their skills until their normal level of productivity is achieved. Until this happens, their performance is under par. The consequent loss of earnings to the firm from lower productivity is therefore another example of an indirect expense to be considered in factoring the potential gains of hiring new staff, especially when they are replacing others who are being fired.

A major contribution of the later studies into the financial aspects of human resource management was the emerging realization that the computation of the expenses of any intervention program should incorporate the indirect costs associated with both the immediate outlays and the long-term outcomes. Birati and Tziner (1999), for example, note that in figuring the financial gains from an upcoming training program designed to enhance the output returns to the company, the first requirement is that the long-range real post-tax rate of return on the investment must exceed the real post-tax cost of capital to the firm in order for the organizational strategy be considered seriously. (This calculation should take place at the advanced stage of investment planning.) Later formulae thus incorporated concepts that reflect this notion of delayed financial returns on investment, such as the present vs. future value of an item, clear vs. amortized costs, and the real post-tax rate of return vs. real post-tax cost of capital. We shall return to these concepts below.

One of the more recent developments in this field of research has been the shift away from the revision of earlier models of utility assessment (Cascio and Ramos, 1986; Steffy and Maurer, 1988) to the application of the principle of cost effectiveness to totally new areas in human resource management. Accordingly, whereas studies of the financial cost of withdrawal behavior (Birati and Tziner, 1996) and turnover costs (Tziner and Birati, 1996) modified earlier contributions to the field, the same authors' more recent papers break new ground. Here they utilize the quantitative approach to assist decision makers to assess the costs of the successful promotion of early retirement (Birati and Tziner, 1995) and to estimate the financial benefits to a firm from a downsizing operation (Birati and Tziner, 1998).

All in all, the authors have modified or developed mathematical utility models and demonstrated their instrumentality in seven domains related to human organizational behaviors and human resource management programs and interventions. In respect to worker behavior, they have related to withdrawal and withholding efforts at work (Birati and Tziner, 1996) and employee turnover (Tziner and Birati, 1996), and in respect to human resource management programs and organizational interventions, to staff selection (Birati and Tziner, 1990), assessment centers (Tziner, Meir, Dahan and Birati, 1994), the promotion of early retirement (Birati and Tziner, 1995), training procedures (Birati and Tziner, 1999), and downsizing/restructuring (Birati and Tziner, 1998).

The Economic Approach to Human Resource Management

For a better understanding of the underlying mathematical process at work in the utility formulae employed in the quantitative approach to human resource management, it is useful to begin with certain basic concepts.

First, just as standard financial procedures are used by a firm in other areas of its activities, so should they be employed wherever feasible with respect to all the human resource management factors related to an organizational intervention being proposed, or to an employee behavior being evaluated. In other words, the utility analysis of personnel programs is unlikely to be accurate if the same economic considerations applied to any traditional management decision are not applied to those associated with human resource management.

Secondly, as indicated above, the elements of the formulae used in a cost-benefit analysis should generally include components that reflect both: (1) fixed costs, that is, the historical cost of the asset or investment in real value; and (2) an estimate of the post-tax real rate of return on the investment. This return may be affected by the consequent behavior patterns of employees (absenteeism, turnover, etc.) or by objective factors relating to tax considerations, elapsed time before productivity benefits are achieved, additional costs, and so on.

With respect to fixed costs, it is worth noting Boudreau's (1983) caveat, which reflects the basic thinking underlying utility analysis: 'Fixed costs are irrelevant to utility.' From the point of view of economic and decision theory, the utility of any decision or action (e.g., the use of a selection device) reflects the changes that action brings to various outcomes. Thus, in the case of staff selection, for example, it is the change in payoff (ΔU) resulting from choosing a particular selection procedure over the random selection of new staff 'that is the phenomenon of interest'. In Boudreau's view, costs or benefits which do not change as a result of a program 'have no role in defining the utility of that program' (Boudreau, 1983, p. 556).

Thirdly, each behavioral element to which a cost can be assigned needs to be identified, and these elements must be separate and mutually exclusive of one another. As already noted, the costs associated with human resource management are both direct and indirect, and they may also include extraordinary payments to workers where circumstances, such as early retirement, demand. The firm needs to distinguish between costs that are controllable and those which are not (costs resulting from spouse transfer, death, etc.). For benefit costing methodology to be applied properly, all these factors must be considered (Cascio, 1989). However, it is precisely the identification and clear operational definition of these variables that have generated many of the revisions in the field in recent years.

Finally, the formulae generally incorporate the notion that the costs and benefits accrued through human resource management processes are to be measured at two separate time intervals: (1) prior to the organizational intervention; and (2) after the intervention has taken place. One concomitant of this effect of time on utility estimates is the need for decision-makers to adjust their calculations to the inflationary factors operating within the time period in which the effects of the employee behaviors or organizational interventions are likely to be felt. Another important variable to be considered here is the tax arrangement impinging on an organization's operation. Tax rates and the conditions under which taxes are paid may differ over time, as well as from place to place and from firm to firm. In general, costs and benefits should be calculated on an after-tax basis, which is a better reflection of the true relationship between the financial inflow and outflow of a company.

As the field of human resource management has progressed, there has been a growing trend to treat this area of a firm's operation with the same budgetary scrutiny as any other fiscal item in the organization's functioning. Recent studies have clearly demonstrated that organizations that fail to adopt such an approach, relying merely on a descriptive and additive assessment of interventions and their effects, are likely to generate distorted analytical data (usually upwardly biased utility estimates), with all the negative consequences this entails for the firms and their investors. Quantitative utility research has also established that by looking ahead, as it were, to the financial consequences and indirect costs associated with a human resource management activity, the firm can better assess whether or not the program or intervention will produce a worthwhile real economic payoff, with all the obvious economic advantages to workers, management, and stockholders alike. It must be remembered, however, that even a favorable utility result does not mean that a given program should be adopted automatically, without the careful weighing of the financial payoff against the potential gains of other possible strategies within the framework of the financial priorities set by the company.

Incorporating Economic Theory – Boudreau (1983)

To illustrate the development of some of these ideas, let us return to Brogden's (1946) general utility equation for assessing the economic utility of selection programs in terms of mean gain productivity in dollars per selectee (ΔU) (see Equation 1 above). Here the gross dollar payoff is seen as a combination of the validity of the selection method, the variability of job performance in dollars, and the average predictor score of the hired staff. The payoff is greatest when the validity is high, few applicants are selected, and variability in job performance is large. In light of the comments above, however, it is now clear that to determine the net dollar payoff of implementing a particular selection procedure, we need to consider, and consequently detract, the *total* estimated cost of the project from the estimated financial saving or benefits it may produce.

In the context of considering all the costs involved, Boudreau (1983), elaborates on various refinements to Brogden's model (e.g., Cronbach and Glezer, 1965; Cascio and Silbey, 1979), specifically on that presented by Schmidt et al. (1979; 1982), to propose a formula that goes beyond the integration of decision theory and industrial psychology concepts to incorporate economic theory and its implications (see: Boudreau, 1983, p. 53).

The extension of the selection utility model suggested by Schmidt et al. (1979) was:

$$\Delta U = (N) \, (T) \, (r_{xy}) \, (\bar{Z}x) - C \tag{2}$$

where:

ΔU = the increase in dollar value payoff that results from selecting N employees using a test or procedure (x) instead of selecting them randomly

N = the number of employees selected

T = the expected tenure of the selected group

r_{xy} = the correlation coefficient (among prescreened applicants) between predictor score (x) and the dollar-value payoff (y)

$\bar{Z}_x$ = the average standard predictor score of the selected group

C = the total selection cost for all the applicants

Schmidt et al. (1982) further extended the utility model of Equation 2 (for selection utility) to apply to any personnel program designed to increase the job performance of those treated by the program, and demonstrated that the product of r_{xy} and $\bar{Z}_x$ in Equation 2 may be replaced by the 'true difference in job performance' between the treated and untreated group in the standard deviation units. The revised utility formula was now:

$$\Delta U = (N)(T)(d_t)(SD_y) - C \qquad (3)$$

where:

ΔU = the increase in utility resulting from the program

N = the number treated

T = the expected duration of benefits in the treated group

d_t = the true difference in job performance between the treated and untreated groups in the standard deviation units

SD_y = the standard deviation of dollar-valued job performance among the incumbent employees

C = the cost of treating N employees

Boudreau (1983) noted that the utility model in Equation 3 paved the way for the extension of the model to other kinds of personnel programs (e.g., Landy et al., 1982), but held that the existing utility models did not go far enough in incorporating 'the same economic considerations applied to traditional management decisions' (p. 553). He expressed criticism of what were, in his view, the deficient definitions of the payoff function (y) of the earlier researchers, such as 'the value of products and services' (Schmidt et al., 1979) or 'output as sold' (Hunter and Schmidt, 1982, pp. 268–9). Instead of referring to the value of an article 'as sold', Boudreau renamed it the 'sales value of productivity'. Furthermore, he argued that these earlier payoff definitions did not adequately reflect the 'institutional benefit' (after Cronbach and Glezer, 1965, p. 8) of treating a group of applicants or employees, that is, they failed to reflect *'certain economic concepts which are basic to organizational decisions'* (Boudreau, 1983, p. 553; emphasis ours).

Accordingly, Boudreau incorporated three major economic constructs into the existing theoretical models in order to demonstrate their effect on previous utility estimates of a chosen staff selection device. Both alone and in combination, these concepts identified deficiencies in the existing utility definitions, which were shown to lead to upwardly biased estimates. The three new concepts, presented briefly below, are variable costs, tax rate, and discount rate. (For a full discussion of these terms, see Boudreau, 1983.)

Variable Costs

Since the decision to increase productivity can alter variable costs associated with the productivity, this change should be subtracted from the increased value generated by the increased activity. For example, better-selected sales people may perform better by selling more units and generating more revenue. However, not all of this increased margin from revenue accrues to the firm, since higher producing salespeople often receive higher pay in the form of a bonus or commission. Similarly, higher sales levels may require larger inventories and increased unit material and production costs (such as overtime pay), making the benefits of the increased productivity less than the increase in the margin from sales revenue. In general, variable costs which vary positively with productivity offset some of the sales value of increased productivity, while variable costs which vary inversely with productivity augment the sales value of the increased productivity.

To translate this into quantitative terms, Boudreau (1983, pp. 554–5) addressed the question of the payoff function (y) in Equation 1, and distinguished between 'sales value' (sv), and 'cost of productivity' (sc). He then derived the term 'net benefit' (nb), which is the difference between (sv), the present and future benefits (e.g., sales revenue) generated by the selectee as he moves through the various stages of absorption during his tenure in the company, and (sc), the present and future company sacrifices (e.g., wages, benefits, and materials required to maintain, support, and induce those functions). These three constructs represent random variables over the population of prescreened applicants. Net benefit (nb) appears to be a more logically correct definition of the payoff (y in Equation 1) than either sales value or service costs alone (or any combination of them). While in Boudreau's model, a selection device (x) is seen to correlate with sales value and/or services costs, the correlations need not be identical. For example, whereas sales value may reflect the value of the increased production speed of selectees, some service costs may vary positively with production speed (e.g., materials, piece-rate wages), and others may vary inversely (e.g., per unit of supervision required). The refined equation (Equation 4) reflects these factors:

$$\Delta U = (N)\,(T)\,(rx, sv)\,(\bar{Z}x)\,(SDsv) - (rx, sc)\,(\bar{Z}x)\,(SDsc)] - C \qquad (4)$$

For the sake of simplicity, Boudreau posited a situation in which service costs are perfectly correlated with sales values, so that (sc) is treated as a proportion of (sv) (e.g., where commissions equal a percent of sales revenue, or variable cost of materials comprises a percent of the selling price). Equation 4 then becomes:

$$DU = (N)\,(T)\,(rx, sv)\,(\bar{Z}x)\,(SDsv)\,(1 + V) - C \qquad (5)$$

where (V) equals the proportion of (sv) represented by (sc) (i.e., sc/sv = V). (V) will be negative when a higher proportion of costs varies positively with sales value, and positive when a higher proportion of costs varies negatively with sales value (Boudreau, 1983, p. 555).

In reference to wages, Boudreau argued that previous research largely ignored potential variable compensation effects, such as increased bonuses and benefits linked to output. Also, with respect to the assumption made by previous researchers that 'wages equal sales value' (Cascio, 1982, pp. 163-173), Boudreau asserted that 'for analyzing utility to the organization ... the appropriate 'economic value' is not the wage (fixed by the labor market), adjusted for variable costs (and other factors)' (Boudreau, 1983, p. 558). When wages vary positively with sales value, they are a cost which reduces the value of (SDnb).

Similarly, Boudreau proposed that when non-compensation variable costs vary positively with sales value, the standard deviation of sales value (SDsv) will overestimate the standard deviation of net benefits (SDnb) and vice versa (1983, pp. 558–9). The major such non-compensation cost is probably raw materials. Thus, when the non-compensation costs which vary positively are larger, (V) is smaller (or more negative), the value (SDnb) is smaller, and (ΔU) is reduced. Non-compensation costs which vary negatively with (sv) would further reduce (V), as may happen in some unlikely cases where, as

Boudreau notes, costs such as damage or scrap vary inversely, rather than positively, with the increase in sales value generated by personnel programs.

The combination of all these factors implies a situation in which (V) could range from -.50 to +1.33. In relation to Equation 5, Boudreau states that the expression 1 + V would then range from .50 to 1.33. The actual value of (V) in any application would be the difference between the proportion of sales value represented by costs varying negatively with sales value increases, and the proportion represented by costs varying positively with these increases.

Using an empirical example based on Cascio and Silbey (1979, p. 111) that focuses on the selection of sales managers (a job in which 'variable costs are likely to be … substantial'), Boudreau (1983) demonstrates that the refined estimated utility to a particular company of an improved internal selection process (over an interview with an assessment center) is in the region of 57 per cent of the previous estimate, where variable costs were assumed to be around 40 per cent (Boudreau, 1983, p. 560).

Tax Rate

As stated above, it is a basic principle of capital budgeting analysis that the appropriate basis for decisions are after-tax costs and benefits, because taxes affect both the flow of net costs and the benefits from investments. Since organizations may vary in their tax rates, inter-organizational utility comparisons require adjusting utility values to account for different tax consequences (Boudreau, 1983, pp. 560–61). Boudreau adds that since existing utility definitions express the effects of personnel programs on productivity 'as sold' (see above) and on costs, both of which usually affect reported profits directly, the appropriate adjustment is the marginal tax rate (TAX), i.e., the tax rate applicable to changes in reported profits generated by a given decision.

After-tax benefits may be denoted as (1- TAX) (nb), where, as we have seen, (nb) is defined as the random variable representing sales value minus service costs. As (nb) is defined earlier as (1 + V) (sv), Equation 5 can now be rewritten as:

$$\Delta U = (N)\ (T)\ (r_x, sv)\ (\bar{Z}_x)\ (SD_{sv})\ (1+V)\ (1 - TAX) - (C)\ (1 - TAX) \quad (6)$$

Taxes produce a proportional decrease in (SD$_{nb}$) and (C). Because (SD$_{nb}$) is usually greater than (C), this will usually reduce (ΔU). In general, Boudreau asserts that all else being equal, the higher the organization's marginal tax rate, the lower the utility. Again citing Cascio and Silbey's (1979) study of selection utility (and other studies), Boudreau figures a 45 per cent tax rate to which the assumed private-sector organization is subject, and demonstrates how the utility gains, now readjusted, are reduced by from 57 per cent to 31 per cent of the previous estimate reported by Cascio and Silbey (1979).

Discount Rate

The third factor cited by Boudreau (1983) as impinging on the estimation of the utility factor relates to the notion that future monetary values cannot be directly equated with present monetary values, because benefits received in the present, or costs delayed into the future, would be invested to earn returns. Stated in slightly different terms, this principle of discounting is relevant because personnel program utility involves benefits and costs which accrue over time. In general, the formula for the present value (PV) of an amount (a) received or paid out over (t) periods in the future, at a rate of a return (i) may be expressed as:

$$PV(a) = [1/(1+i)^t(a)] \tag{7}$$

The formula for net benefits can then be readjusted to include the accrual of benefits and costs at their present value. Thus total net benefits for individual *j*, (nb (sum)j), may be expressed as the sum of the net benefits occurring over (T) future periods:

$$nb(sum)_j = \sum_{t=1}^{T} nb_{jt} \tag{8}$$

where (t) signifies the time period in which the net benefits occur. Thus, [nb (sum)] is actually a random variable over individuals defined by the sum of period-to-period net benefits for each individual. Accounting for a discount rate (i), the pre-tax payoff function can now be expressed in light of the economic concept of discounted present value as:

$$PV[nb(sum)] = \sum_{t=1}^{T} (nbt)[1/1+i)^t] \tag{9}$$

Defining net benefits in this way, Equation 6 now becomes:

$$\Delta U = (N)\{\sum_{t=1}^{T} [1/(1+i)^t (SDnb_t)(1\text{-}TAXt)(rx, nb_t)(\overline{Z}x)\} - (C)(1\text{-}TAX) \tag{10}$$

Adjusting for the effects of variable costs (see above), by expressing (SDnb) as the product of (SDsv) and $1 + V$, we get:

$$\Delta U = (N)\{\sum_{t=1}^{T} [1/(1+i)^t (SDsv_t)(1+Vt)(1\text{-}TAXt)(rx, sv_t)(\overline{Z}x)\} -$$

$$(C)(1\text{-}TAXt) \tag{11}$$

It is important to stress Boudreau's comment that this equation 'indicates that the analytically correct expression for the utility accruing from applying a personnel program to a group of employees involves not one constant payoff level [i.e., (rxy) (SDy) (Zx), in Equation 2], but a series of discounted yearly payoffs which may vary over time' (Boudreau, 1983, p. 564).

In general, Boudreau posits that, all else being equal, the larger the discount rate (i), the lower the utility of a personnel program. In reference to Cascio and Silbey's (1979) study of selection utility, Boudreau assumes a discount rate of 10 per cent. The resulting discounted after-cost, after-tax utility estimate for replacing an interview with an assessment center would now be 27 per cent of the sum previously reported.

Toward a Revised General Utility Formula

For the purposes of analytical development, Boudreau (p. 565) then proceeded to isolate the effects of the discount rate by ignoring variability in (rx), (sv), and (SDsv) over time, and treating them as constants, while also assuming that the variable cost level (Vt) and tax rate (TAXt) similarly remain constant over time. Equation 11 was then reformulated as:

$$\Delta U = (N)\{\sum_{t=1}^{T} [1/(1+i)^t (SDsv)(1+V)(1\text{-}TAX)(PxTy)(\overline{Z}x)\} -$$

$$(C)(1\text{-}TAX) \tag{12}$$

where:

ΔU = the increase in average dollar-value payoff (i.e., utility gain) that results from using a personnel program after variable costs, taxes and discounting

N   = the number of employees selected by the program

t   = the average time period an employee selected by the program is expected to work for the organization

i   = the organization's discount rate

SDsv = the standard deviation of dollar-valued job performance among employees of the type treated by the program

V   = the proportion of SDy represented by variable costs

TAX = the organization's applicable tax

PxTy = the true operational validity

Z̄x   = the mean standard score on the personnel program of those selected

C   = the total selection cost for all applicants

According to Boudreau, Equation 12 assumes that the costs of a program (C) are incurred only at the beginning (t = 0), and thus are not subject to discounting (when t = 0, PV(a) = a). This is usually true for selection programs, where all testing occurs prior to hiring, although Boudreau concedes that some programs (e.g., sensitivity training) may require continuing intervention in every period. In that case, he proposes multiplying the cost term by the discount factor:

$$\sum_{t=1}^{T} \left[1/(1+i)^t\right] \tag{13}$$

This procedure takes into account the fact that program costs, as well as payoffs, are subject to 'opportunity costs of time. Costs which occur later affect the present value of utility less strongly than more immediate costs' (Boudreau, 1983, p. 565).

Boudreau also notes that the actual levels of the three variables discussed above differ across various situations. Yet, both individually and in combination, these economic considerations are critical in order to prevent the upward biases of earlier utility estimates, which did not reflect the effects of variable costs, taxes, and discounting on personnel program utility. In view of the variability and magnitude of such effects, Boudreau suggests that Equation 12 'provides a more complete utility formula than those previously used'. Significantly, he stresses that this general utility formula can apply to any type of personnel program, including selection, training, and organizational interventions.

An Extension of Boudreau – Birati and Tziner (1990)

Birati and Tziner (1990) question some of the assumptions underlying Boudreau's (1983) general utility formula (Equation 12), including its overall applicability and, more specifically, its treatment of the cost of the personnel program and the concept of deferred charges. The authors then recommend an extension to Equation 12, based on the following arguments.

The Cost of the Human Resource Management Intervention

Birati and Tziner note that Boudreau assumes that the budget related to a personnel program is allocated at the same time that the benefits accrue. However, the authors argue that in most instances, the effective cost involved in a program (C) is actually cleared prior to the flow of the gains. Consequently, the money spent on the program should be increased to include the additional cost of financing the project, so that the effective cost to be taken into account is $C(1 + i)^n$, where (n) is the number of periods that will elapse between the investment and the first period of the benefit. For example, if the cost of a personnel selection program is $1,000 and the firm's post-tax cost of capital (i) is 10 per cent, and the money is invested one year before the benefits, then the total accountable costs should increase to $1,000 $(1 + 0.10)^1 = \$1,100$.

Deferred Charges

Birati and Tziner further assert that the resources spent on the program produce benefits that may last for several years, reflecting the average length of time individuals remain in positions attained after successfully passing through the staffing program. For instance, one could assume that individuals promoted to the position of first-level management as the result of a selection procedure will remain in their jobs for an average of four years. It follows that the benefit accruing from the use of the program equals the added value of the new manager's performance (if at all) over this entire period. Thus the costs associated with the operation of the selection program would be regarded as deferred charges, which should be amortized over the effective life span of the project, since they conform to the common definition of this concept as an 'expenditure for a service that will contribute to the generation of future economic benefits' (Welsch, Newman and Zlatkovich, 1986, p. 724).

Following this line of reasoning, the authors concur with Welsch et al. (1986) that costs associated with any personnel program constitute deferred charges that should be capitalized and amortized throughout the useful life of the program. For example, assuming that the length of time of the benefits is four years (i.e., $t = 4$), and that the firm will receive the tax refund for the cost (C) in four future annual installments – i.e., C/4 (TAX) after the first year, C/4 (TAX) after the second year, and so on to the fourth year – then the present value of the nominal tax rebate would net only:

$$\sum_{t=1}^{T} \frac{C\,(TAX)}{T} \cdot \frac{1}{(1+i)^t} \qquad (14)$$

where:

T   = the average time that a new employee selected by the program works for the firm

TAX = the organization's tax rate

i   = the firm's discount rate

Birati and Tziner suggest that part of these costs could be cleared prior to the flow of the gains. Accordingly, (C) should be decomposed into two elements: $(C = C_1 + C_2)$, where only (C_1) is amortized over the life of the program, and (C_2) is deducted in the period when it is paid. As a result, the present real net value of the tax refund (Q) to be deducted from the real costs would be:

$$Q = C_2\,(TAX) + \sum_{t=1}^{T} \frac{C_1\,(TAX)}{T} \; \frac{1}{(1+i)^t} \qquad (15)$$

and the present real net value of tax costs (A) would total:

$$A = C\,(1+i)^n - Q \qquad (16)$$

A Modified Utility Formula

On the basis of the above arguments, Birati and Tziner (1990) revised the utility formula (Equation 12), to read:

$$\Delta U = Ns \left[\sum_{t=1}^{T} \frac{1}{3(1+i)^t (1+II)^4} (SDv)(1+V)(1-TAX)(PxTx)\bar{Z}s \right] - A \tag{17}$$

where (Ns) is the number of employees successfully completing the program. (For further discussion, see: Birati and Tziner, 1990.)

In addition, following Mathieu and Leonard (1987), if senior managers wish to assess the effectiveness of a certain increment (change) in performance/ behavior instead of calculating either the operational validity (PxTx), or the change in operational validity (Px1Tx1 - Px2Tx2), associated with the use of an HRM intervention program (e.g., a training program or performance appraisal system), then the following adjusted formula should be used:

$$\Delta U = N_s \left[\sum_{t=1}^{T} \frac{1}{3(1+i)^t (1+II)^t_{4}} (SDv)(1+V)(1-TAX)(dt) \right] - A \tag{17a}$$

In order to produce Formula 17a, the terms PxTx (operational validity) or Px1Tx1 - Px2Tx2 (change in operational validity following implementation of a new HRM procedure), and (Zs), the mean standard score on the HRM program procedure of those who successfully complete it, are replaced with the term (dt) the appropriate effect size estimate of the HRM intervention program.

The modifications introduced into Equation 17 may, in some cases, actually reduce the estimated utility gain derived from the use of a personnel selection program. The degree to which the estimated gain matches the figure obtained from Boudreau's (1983) original utility formula (Equation 2) depends on the sizes of (C), (T), (i), and the tax rate (TAX).

To demonstrate the empirical effects of this modified utility formula (Equation 17) numerically, we can refer to a calculation originally provided by Burke and Frederick (1986) for the utility analysis of an assessment center. In the following illustration, Equation 17 is similar in all components to Equation 12, with the exception of the tax variable.

In Burke and Frederick's analysis, the estimated cost of selecting a district manager was assumed to be $1,741 and the corporate tax rate to be 49 per cent (0.49), from which it followed that the net tax cost of selecting one district manager was:

$$C (1-TAX) = \$1,741 (1-0.49) \sim \$888 \tag{18}$$

If, however, the modified component is used, and it is assumed that one year will elapse between the point at which the cost of selection is incurred and the time period when benefit will begin, the effective costs should be:

$$C (1+i)^n = \$1,741 (1-0.10)^1 \sim \$1,915 \tag{19}$$

where 0.10 stands for the nominal corporate cost of capital after tax (i.e., 10 per cent), as in Burke and Frederick's case. Moreover, assuming that the period of the selection program's effect is four years, that only 50 per cent of the cost is amortized over four years (i.e., $C_1 = \$870.5$), and that the product of (i), the post-tax cost of money, is equal to 0.10, then the present value of the total tax shelters (B) from (C_1) and (C_2) that might be accepted by the tax authorities would be:

$$B = 870.50 (0.49) + \left[\frac{870.5}{4}\right] \left[\frac{(0.49)}{(1+0.10)^1}\right] + \left[\frac{870.5}{4}\right] \left[\frac{(0.49)}{(1+0.10)^2}\right] +$$

$$\left[\frac{870.5}{4}\right] \left[\frac{(0.49)}{(1+0.10)^3}\right] + \left[\frac{870.5}{4}\right] \left[\frac{(0.49)}{(1+0.10)^4}\right] \approx \$765 \tag{20}$$

Combining the results of Equations 19 and 20 indicates that the value of the net tax cost of selecting one district sales manager would approximate $1,915 - $765 = $1,150, which is nearly 1.3 times the cost ($888) estimated by the unamended utility formula. Consequently, Equation 17 substantially reduces the post-tax utility gain of the assessment center as a personnel selection device.

Tziner, Meir, Dahan and Birati (1994) employed Birati and Tziner's (1990) amended formula (Equation 17) in a further study of the economic utility of the assessment center, and concluded that despite the high cost of the operation (Cascio and Ramos, 1986), and the relatively small validity coefficients, the assessment center proved to be cost-effective. Moreover, the refined utility model helped to obtain a more accurate estimate of effectiveness than the earlier formula employed by Cascio and Silbey (1978).

Birati and Tziner note that their modified formula further attenuates the upward bias in financial payoff estimations (see: Boudreau, 1983), thus reducing the post-tax estimation of the per-individual utility gain. Given the high cost of assessment centers as a personnel selection program, and the inconclusive advantages they hold over ordinary selection programs employing biographical data, tests, and interviews (see Chapter 5), the authors conclude that their revised utility formula (Equation 17) offers a significant and timely contribution to the refined estimation of the cost effectiveness of this method. Indeed, they assert that, in general, the formula may be a critical tool in all aspects of human resource management, thus further stressing the efficacy of the quantitative approach to utility estimates in this field.

Below are examples of additional studies that illustrate the quantitative approach to human resource management research, that is, assessing the financial value of worker behavior and HRM programs and interventions. These studies illustrate the versatility of this approach, as well as the rationale and methodology employed in research of this type. The first two studies relate to the economic effects of organizational behaviors, investigating employee withdrawal behavior (Birati and Tziner, 1996) and staff turnover (Tziner and Birati, 1996). The following three studies explore the estimation of the payoffs related to early retirement projects (Birati and Tziner, 1995), downsizing (Birati and Tziner, 1998), and training programs (Birati and Tziner, 1999), thus reflecting research into the economic utility of organizational interventions designed to improve the financial efficacy of a firm. On the whole, they represent adaptations of earlier attempts to employ quantitative approaches to assess the efficacy of human resource management methods and/or to demonstrate new applications of this methodology.

Withdrawal Behavior and Withholding Efforts at Work (WBWEW) – Birati and Tziner, 1996

In an increasingly competitive commercial world, it is not unusual to find managers fretting over employees who shirk their duties by taking unnecessary and unscheduled leaves of absence, disappearing during working hours, wasting time socializing with associates in the office, or simply daydreaming at their workstations. Such negative withdrawal behavior is of concern to all managers who operate in profit-oriented companies, where the primary goal is to maximize the wealth of the owners. Absenteeism and the propensity to withhold work (WBWEW) inevitably reduce profits, and are also likely to have some sort of effect on the total risk of the entity. Exactly what does such errant behavior cost a company? Although theoretical perspectives and empirical research into the underlying causes of withdrawal behavior is available (see, for example: Tziner and Vardi, 1984; Koslowsky, Sagie, Krauz and Dolman-Singer, 1987), in practice, they do little to help companies reduce its probability. The quantitative approach, however, makes it possible to estimate the monetary costs of the negative outcomes of absenteeism and withdrawal behavior. Building on the earlier efforts of Cascio (1991), whose study was restricted to physical absenteeism alone (and only on the hourly remuneration of the absentee), Birati and Tziner (1996) offer a general framework for evaluating the potential cost of WBWEW.

The real loss to the company (P) stems from two sources: direct costs, related to the individual employee; and indirect costs, which generally reflect the cost of the distorted flow of operation.

Direct Costs

Direct costs include the 'added value' of revenues foregone as a result of the inability to provide goods and services on time which, under certain circumstances, can be very high. For example, in the high-tech industry, most of the cost of producing a given product is incurred in the initial development stage. The absence of a key senior employee at this stage may lead to delays and cancellations, and ultimately to the loss of customers. In extreme cases, these may be major clients. If this happens, the ratio of loss in gross profit resulting form WBWEW to expenses paid to the employee may become disproportionately high.

Direct costs also incorporate the increased expenses related to catching up with the backlog, whether this involves overtime pay, bonuses to other employees who have to shoulder an additional burden, higher payments to outside contractors to help take up the slack, or any other additional expenditures that may be required to enable the company to meet its business commitments. Lastly, estimates of direct costs include a WBWEW multiplier factor which expresses the relation of the deleterious effects that a physically or mentally absent worker may have on other employees, for example, the likely reduced output of workers when a supervisor is not around, and the economic consequences thereof.

The direct cost of WBWEW (Pd) may therefore include the following factors:

Loss of revenues (R) The added value of revenue lost (if any) as a result of WBWEW may range from zero (whereby the existing work force makes up for the missing employees without any additional pay) to a very substantial sum (whereby loyal customers are lost). (R) should therefore include estimates of the present value of the total loss from the decline in present and future revenues from transactions missed and customers lost as a result of WBWEW.

Extra payments (E) These are the sum of the additional expenditures that may be required to meet commitments. Overtime pay and additional monetary compensation to outside contractors (above and beyond normal costs) can be gleaned from accounting records. In many cases, there is a negative correlation between (R) and (E). If co-workers or contractors can offset the loss of production, (R) will decline or diminish, while (E) will be positive. Likewise, if co-workers or contractors cannot close the production gap, (E) will decline and (R) will increase.

WBWEW multipliers (M_{ar} and M_{ae}) The total direct cost of WBWEW is the total losses related to reduced revenue (R) and additional outlays (E) as a result of one worker's withdrawal behavior. The multiplier effect (M_a) relates to the additional lost output of the absentee's co-workers (M_{ar}) and the loss of customers (M_{ae}), and thus designates an increase in the cost of absenteeism. The direct cost (Pd) should thus increase by these two factors.

The total direct loss (Pd) is therefore:

$$(Pd) = R\,(1 + M_{ar}) + E\,(1 + M_{ae}) \tag{21}$$

Indirect Costs

The indirect future consequences of WBWEW that need to be considered may include the high price tag associated with an increased propensity for turnover (see: Mirta, Jenkins and Gupta, 1992; Tziner and Birati, 1996), as well as financial losses stemming from a decline in morale and efforts resulting from workers' feelings of exploitation and victimization (see: Kerr, 1983; Kindwell and Bennett, 1993).

Thus, the indirect costs of WBWEW (Pi) are composed of the following factors:

Cost due to an increased propensity for turnover (T) The upward trend in turnover likely to result from WBWEW imposes even further additional costs on the corporation. It has even been suggested that turnover itself may affect WBWEW behavior negatively. Thus a vicious circle is created, the negative outcomes of which may exert an indirect influence on profits. The magnitude of the turnover attributable to WBWEW can be based on the correlation coefficient r = 0.33, reported in a recent meta-analysis (Mirta, Jenkins and Gupta, 1992). A procedure suggested by Tziner and Birati (1996) can then be used to estimate the additional cost related to the change in turnover as a result of WBWEW.

Loss due to decline in morale (M) Although not easy to measure, (M) should be estimated and included in the calculations because of its potential magnitude. This may be achieved by means of the following steps:

1   periodically administering a morale survey to the employees of the firm;
2   deriving an overall morale score;
3   concurrently assessing the standard deviation of the dollar-valued job performance (SDy) among the employees of the firm at time points coinciding with the morale assessment;
4   drawing on the overall morale score and respective SDy to calculate the drop in SDy corresponding to the drop of one unit of morale that may be attributed to the employee's WBWEW.

The total indirect loss (Pi) is therefore:

$$(Pi) = T + M \tag{22}$$

and the total loss (P) due to WBWEW is:

$$P = Pd + Pi = (R)\,(1 + M_{ar}) + (E)\,(1 + M_{ae}) + T + M \tag{23}$$

Using hypothetical numerical values, Birati and Tziner (1996) compute the estimated daily before-tax cost of a physically or mentally absent employee as follows:

$$P = (\$200)\,(1 + 0.1) + (\$100)(1 + 0.1) + 50 + 50 = \$430 \tag{24}$$

In conclusion, the authors note that this advanced and improved behavior costing approach, which stresses the overall estimated direct and indirect losses to a firm as a result of withdrawal and withholding efforts from work, provides crucial data to a company seeking to estimate the cost effectiveness of preventive programs aimed at curbing the adverse effects of WBWEW. The emphasis here is on a quantitative approach that incorporates the added value of foregone revenue, rather than merely the cost of payments to the absentees, as previously suggested.

Assessing Employee Turnover Costs – Tziner and Birati (1996)

In this study, the researchers amended Cascio's (1991) computational formula as applied to dysfunctional turnover in organizations, that is, when good workers choose to quit of their own volition or their jobs are terminated due to downsizing. The effects may be negative, or dysfunctional, because of the potential by-products of the departure of these workers, such as: impaired performance among the 'remaining' employees (due to role overload and stress, among other factors); the high cost of recruiting, socializing, and supervising new workers; lost customers due to the inability to provide goods and services on time; excess overtime compensation to remaining employees making up for the loss of superior performers who have left; and disturbances in the normal functioning of the entire organization.

In reference to Cascio's (1991) demonstration of the extent to which turnover costs are significant, Tziner and Birati (1996) note the need to amend Cascio's formula to take into account some of these negative consequences, as well as the need to express immediate expenses generated by an employee's departure (e.g., separation costs) in the same financial terms as future expenditures (e.g., replacement costs). In other words, all future potential costs must be translated into their present value, as explained in the review of basic concepts above.

The cost components incorporated into the revised conceptual and computational framework were grouped into the following categories: (1) direct outlays to the firm incurred by the replacement process – recruiting, hiring, training, and socializing new employees, and the extra effort required of supervisors and coworkers to integrate them into the company; (2) indirect costs and potential losses that relate to interruptions in production, sales, and the delivery of goods and services to customers; and (3) the financial value of the estimated effect on performance as a result of the possible drop in morale of the remaining work force following dysfunctional turnover.

Direct Cost (D)

The direct cost to the firm of replacing a departing employee may include any or all of the following components:

- The difference between the total cost of employing a new worker, R(m), and the total sum that would have been paid to the veteran worker who left, R(o). This item can be estimated by means of the following equation:

$$C = \sum_{z=i}^{t} \frac{R(m) - R(o)}{(1 + i)^z} \tag{25}$$

where:

C = the present value of the cost differentials for the entire period
t = the period (in years) in which the departing employee was expected to perform efficiently if he or she did not leave
i = the rate of the cost of money to the employer
z = the period (in years) of the change in salaries.

Thus C will be positive (loss to the firm) if R(m) - R(o) > 0, and negative (gain to the firm) if R(m) - R(o) < 0.

- The total cost related to acquiring the new employee, including advertising and the selection process (S).
- The direct expenditures required to train the new employee (T).
- The cost generated by the socialization of the newcomer until that worker becomes operational, including the cost related to the extra efforts of supervisors and co-workers to integrate the new employee into the firm (U).

The direct cost (D) therefore totals:

$$D = C + S + T + U \tag{26}$$

Indirect Cost (I)

The indirect cost to the firm includes: (1) the excess overtime pay to current employees and/or excess monetary compensation to outside substitute employees (O); (2) the financial value of loss of production and/or customers to competition (F), if any, until a replacement is found and produces at the level of the departing employee; and (3) the 'turnover effect' on morale (M). Despite the difficulty of measuring the dysfunctional effects of the departure of a worker on remaining staff, we have seen that Tziner and Birati suggest an approach for estimating a computed morale factor based on a survey of company workers and the standard deviation of the dollar-valued job performance (SDy - s). Using this method, it should be possible to calculate the drop in SDy which corresponds to the downfall of 'one unit of morale' which is probably attributable to dysfunctional turnover.

The indirect cost (I) will thus total:

$$I = \quad O + F + M \tag{27}$$

Turnover Rate Multiplier (f)

This expense is a function of the increased likelihood that a new worker will stay in the new job for less time than the worker he or she is replacing. The amended formula for the total turnover costs is thus multiplied by f, making the total before-tax turnover cost (L):

$$L = (D + I)(1 + f) = (C + S + T + U + O + F + M)(1 + f) \tag{28}$$

To illustrate the use of this formula, Tziner and Birati (1996) compute the turnover cost of a single employee, using probable numerical figures, some of which are derived from an earlier example, but are increased to adjust approximately for changes in the American economy in the intervening years. The rest of the figures in the illustration have their source in the authors' experience as consultants.

Let:

t	= total number of years that the departing employees was expected to work:	10
i	= interest rate paid by the employer on borrowing money (discount value):	10%
R(o)	= annual total remuneration to the person leaving the organization:	$64,380
R(m)	= annual total remuneration to the new employee:	$60,380
S	= cost of acquiring the new employee:	$ 3,150
T	= cost of training the new employee:	$10,000
U	= socialization cost of the new employee:	$48,600
O	= excess over-time payment and/or compensation to outsiders:	$ 1,000
F	= loss of production and/or customers resulting from the turnover of	

one employee: $55,440

M   = the estimated monetary value (loss) from the turnover effect on
the morale of remaining employees: $ 3,000

f   = newcomer-to-organization turnover rate factor: 0.1

According to Equations 28 and 25, the total before-tax outlay to the employer
is:

$$L = (C + S + T + U + O + F + M)(1 + f)$$

when

$$C = \sum_{z=i}^{t} \frac{R(m) - R(o)}{(1 + i)^z}$$

Thus, in our example:

$$C = \sum_{z=i}^{10} \frac{\$60,380 - \$64,800}{(1.1)^z}$$

and:

$$L = [-\$27,169 + \$3,150 + 10,000 + \$48,600 + 1,000 + \$55,440 + \$3,000]$$
$$(1 + 0.1) = \$103,434$$

Hence, the overall before-tax cost of the dysfunctional turnover of a single
employee would be US$103,434.

The high potential cost of dysfunctional turnover underscores the value
of the amended formula in providing firms with an effective instrument for
monitoring its financial consequences on a constant basis. By doing so, the
company can then attempt to keep the phenomenon under control by initiating
preventive measures aimed at strong performers (especially in essential
positions) within the context of a tight employment market in which
downsizing options are also being contemplated.

Successful Promotion of Early Retirement – Birati and Tziner (1995)

In a study of the value of encouraging workers to retire early as a means of
consolidating the work force and invigorating an organization's financial

standing, Birati and Tziner (1995) discuss the possible incentives that might spur employees to agree to quit their jobs earlier than proscribed by pension laws, regulations, and collective work agreements. Besides coping with the psychological concomitants of such a decision, potential early retirees inevitably consider the size of the financial package offered them as well. For their part, firms need to examine the payoff factor associated with the dismissal of a portion of their work force. The size of the package offered to potential laid-off workers generally has to exceed the accumulated pension benefits, and the computation of the compensation offered to the dismissed employees must include a factor that expresses the degree to which early retirement is valued by the worker.

From the employer's perspective, the greater the subjective value placed by an employee on the prospect of early retirement, the lower the additional financial incentives the employee needs to be offered to leave prematurely. This factor, of course, varies from employee to employee. Over and above a consideration of all the psycho-social factors to be weighed here, a mathematical formula that derives an assessment of the potential maximum cost of laying off one (or more) employees through early retirement is a useful device for the employer. It can serve both as an effective facilitating tool in the negotiating process, and as an instrument for weighing the financial advantages of early retirement programs.

In computing this assessment, the first assumption is that the maximum expenditures should approximate the total present value of the estimated losses to the employees incurred by leaving their jobs prior to the normal retirement age. These losses include: (1) the present value of their net salaries less the current value of any net income that would be earned (including unemployment compensation) during the 'idle periods' between the year of actual retirement and normal retirement; (2) the present value of the potential accumulated loss in pension funds, resulting from the lack of contributions during the idle periods; (3) the present value of the future decline in social security earnings (if any); and (4) the subjective value of quitting the present job, expressed by the employee in quantitative, financial terms (for a discussion of this concept, see: Tziner and Birati, 1996, pp. 54–6).

These variables can be expressed mathematically, as follows:

(1) The present value of the net salaries foregone during the 'idle years' (q) is equal to the gross annual earning (Q) minus the yearly deduction rate (Te), consisting of taxes, social security, etc., computed as follows:

$$\Sigma = \frac{Q_1(1\text{-}T_e)}{(1+i)^1} + \frac{Q_2(1\text{-}T_e)}{(1+i)^2} + ... + \frac{Q_{t\text{-}n}(1\text{-}T_e)}{(1+i)^{t\text{-}n}} = Q(1\text{-}T_e) \sum_{z=1}^{t\text{-}n} \frac{1}{(1+I)^z}$$

(29)

where:

t = the total number of years the worker will have been employed if he or she retires at the normal retirement age

n = the total number of years the retiree actually worked

t - n = the idle years

i = the appropriate discount rate

(2) Future savings lost in the pension fund (R) during the idle years (t − n) is expressed as follows :

$$R = \frac{q.}{(1+i)^1} + \frac{q.}{(1+i)^2} + ... + \frac{q.}{(1+i)^{t\text{-}n}} = q.\sum_{z=1}^{t\text{-}n} \frac{1}{(1+i)^z}$$

(30)

where α is the fraction of the annual salary contributed to the pension fund, including the employers' contribution (For simplicity, the model assumes that the annual contributions and salaries are the same for all periods and are paid at the end of each period.)

(3) Social security losses after normal retirement age (S) are assumed to be zero. However, if as a result of early retirement, the retiree will be able to generate alternative income during the unemployment period, including revenue from unemployment compensation, the losses will be reduced by U dollars, where U equals the present value of all these net potential sources of income at the date of actual retirement.

(4) The current value of quitting the present job (B) may have a positive or negative numerical value (see: Tziner and Birati, 1996, pp. 54–6): the greater the desire to leave the job, the more likely that B will be low or negative.

The sum of all these potential expenses to the employee are equivalent to the maximum losses to the employer and incorporated into one equation, such that:

$$\text{Loss} = q + R + S - U - B \tag{31}$$

where $S \leq 0$, and $B \geq 0$.

The maximum after tax costs to the employer (L_1), should then total:

$$L = \text{Loss} (1\text{-}T_{em}) = (q + R + S - U - B)(1\text{-}T_{em}) \tag{32}$$

where T_{em} is the employer's marginal tax rate.

Birati and Tziner (1995) illustrate these constructs with a numerical example, as follows:

Let

t	= the total number of years until normal retirement	20
n	= the number of years actually worked	18
i	= the discount rate	10%
α	= the fraction of gross salary contributed to pension	10%
Te	= the total deduction rate from the employee's salary	20%
T_{em}	= the marginal tax rate for the employer	50%
Q	= the mean annual salary over the years of employment	$30,000
S	= the present value of losses from reduced social security receipts from normal retirement date onwards	$0
U	= the present value of alternative income during idle years	$10,000
B	= the present subjective value of quitting the present job	$2,000

According to Equation 31, the total post-tax maximum outlay to the employer is:

$$L = (q + R + S - U - B)(1 - T_{em})$$

Based on the above figures:

$$q = \frac{\$30,000 \, (1 - 0.2)}{(1 + 0.1)} + \frac{\$30,000 \, (1 - 0.2)}{(1 + 0.1)^2} = \$41,653$$

and the loss in pension fund is:

$$R = \frac{\$30,000 \ (0.1)}{(1 + 0.1)} + \frac{\$30,000 \ (0.1)}{(1 + 0.1)^2} = \$5,207$$

Therefore, the maximum after-tax cost to the employer is:

$$L = \$ \ (41,653 + 5,207 + 0 - 10,000 - 2,000) \ (1 - 0.5) = \$17,430$$

Birati and Tziner (1995) point out that the outlay of $17,430 in the above example may be considered a worthwhile expenditure if there is a high probability that a younger, more efficient worker will be found to fill the job freed by the early retiree, as the improved performance is likely to more than compensate the company in increased output. The deal is also attractive to the laid-off employee, who gains an attractive package that makes early retirement more palatable. Finally, the authors note the value of the quantitative approach to early retirement in circumstances where organizations are engaged in operations of downsizing or restructuring.

The Case for Downsizing/Restructuring – Birati and Tziner, 1998

Downsizing is designed to better the financial standing of a firm primarily by reducing and changing the structure of the work force in order to improve operational results. More recently, this strategy has also been adopted by companies that wish to be more flexible, less bureaucratic, and more efficient in the realms of decision making, communication, and entrepreneurship (Bruton, Keels and Shook, 1996; Mroczkowski and Hanaoka, 1997). Since downsizing often entails the massive transfer of employees, this painful and costly procedure should be undertaken (if at all) only after all the factors involved in the layoffs have been thoroughly analyzed, and only if the process can be shown to advance the long-term goals of the company (Feldman, 1995).

While job cuts are likely to produce savings in the short term, few studies have attempted to demonstrate their potential medium- and long-term effects. Furthermore, unilateral downsizing procedures do not necessarily guarantee long-range financial returns: higher profitability is much more likely when downsizing is conducted in tandem with asset restructuring (Cascio, Young and Morris, 1997). It must be remembered that job elimination involves not only direct costs, but also extraordinary expenses, such as severance pay, remuneration for early retirement programs, outplacement services, and the like. Moreover, as we have seen above, there may also be additional costs related to the dysfunctional effects on the remaining employees in terms of lost production, the adjustment of the 'surviving' employees to the new conditions prevailing in the firm, and the hiring of ancillary staff to make up for production shortfalls.

Here, too, the quantitative approach may be helpful, assisting decision makers to determine whether to adopt (or discard) a proposed downsizing procedure by enabling assessment of the potential net post-tax real gains. Management can thereby evaluate the financial advisability of the downsizing option by calculating its expected financial benefits and costs. Since the wealth of the existing shareholders, as measured mainly by the market value of the company's shares, may be affected by downsizing, the analysis must include an investigation of the effects of the operation on variables that may influence the firm's share value, such as profitability, financial stability, and expected growth in earnings (see, for example: Hastings, 1996).

If downsizing is to be treated as a potential investment and thus subjected to the normal procedures of capital budgeting, the first requirement is that the post-tax real rate of return from the project (R) be greater than the real, after-tax cost of capital to the firm (K); i. e., $R > K$. Thus the following calculations are required.

Rate of Return on Downsizing (R)

Initially, the evaluation of R, the rate of return on the downsizing procedure, requires the concurrent estimation of the values and timing of the net cash inflows of the plan (V) and the projected net cash outflows (F). These variables should then be adjusted to inflation-adjusted post-tax cash flows.

Cash Inflow or Gross Savings (V)

From the firm's perspective, an important source of benefits from the downsizing operation derives from the reduction in future payroll. The gross savings are comprised of: (1) the annual sum (net of inflation) of payroll savings associated with the dismissed employees (A) for the expected time frame; and (2) savings resulting from the elimination of services and facilities to the dismissed workers (B).

Thus, the total gross savings for the period (t) is:

$$V_t = A_t + B_t. \tag{33}$$

The reduction in the number of employees is not necessarily a permanent act in the life of the firm. In certain cases, the re-employment of employees with similar skills can be expected at a later stage. Thus, the estimation of savings must be reduced to account for the net effective cuts. In general, however, the dismissals will reduce payroll costs in future periods, so that the timing of each reduction in payroll should be entered into the calculation of the project's rate of return, as indicated above. Moreover, all figures must be stated in real inflation-adjusted values.

Cash Outflows (F)

Cash outflows from downsizing projects (F) include direct (C_d) and indirect (C_i) payments that may affect additional cash movement in the future. Direct expenses can be divided into initial (Cd_1) and additional (Cd_2) cash outflows.

Initial direct cash outflows (Cd₁) The most important immediate outflows are likely to include: (1) severance pay to fired employees (S); (2) extra payments for early retirement plans (E); and (3) all other expenses related to the layoffs, such as outplacement services, extended health coverage, and retraining (O). The estimation of these cash outflows must also include the timing of each payment.

Thus the estimated direct cash outflow before tax, at the initial stage of the project, is:

$$Cd_1 = S + E + O \tag{34}$$

Cd_1 is, in effect, the investment in the downsizing process, and as such we shall refer to it again in the following discussion.

Additional direct cash outflows (Cd₂) Additional direct costs may include: (1) losses from reduced production or services (L), which may range from a minimal sum, whereby the remaining employees compensate adequately for the missing staff without additional pay, to a very substantial figure if it results in the loss of loyal customers; and (2) overtime or additional pay (Q) to members of the remaining staff who take on extra work, or to outsourcers who do the same work at higher cost. These extra costs must be estimated on a periodic basis and deducted from the periodic gross savings.

The total of these additional direct costs (or outflows) in period (t) is thus:

$$Cd_{2t} = L_t + Q_t \qquad (35)$$

Indirect costs (C_{il}) The following indirect expenses related to the downsizing process, although difficult to estimate, also need to be deducted from the projected cash inflows:

1 *Disability claims* (P): Job elimination has been found to contribute to an increase in disability claims (Peak, 1977), especially immediately following dismissal.
2 *Decline in morale* (M): Layoffs may have the effect of creating insecurity among the remaining workers who have to ask themselves if they are next in line for dismissal. In addition, the 'surviving' work force may also have to cope with the stress of shouldering the added workload of absent colleagues. As a result, employees may begin to feel less valued or respected, while at the same time developing a growing sense of mistrust toward their employer. In such an environment, organizational commitment and morale are apt to plummet (Evans, Gunz and Jalland, 1996; Franks and Mayer, 1996; Mroczkowski and Hanaoka, 1997). During the first year after downsizing, a decline in morale among remaining workers is far more probable than an increase in morale (Balutis, 1996), although this trend is likely to decline as time passes. Low morale may reduce efficiency significantly, thereby negatively affecting productivity and consequent income, and ultimately defeating the very purpose of the downsizing operation. This shortfall must also be quantified and incorporated into the analytical assessment.
3 *Cost of increased turnover* (N): The decline in employee morale that often follows the dismissal of workers is probably one of the major contributing factors to the increased staff turnover that typically occurs after downsizing. One year or more after job cuts have been implemented, employee turnover is more likely to increase than decrease, with the corresponding costs this is apt to engender (Evans, Gunz and Jalland, 1996; Tziner and Birati, 1996).

The total indirect cost of downsizing will thus be:

$$C_{il} = P_t + M_t + N_t \qquad (36)$$

Therefore, direct and indirect costs before-tax for a given period will total:

$$F_t = Cd_{2t} + C_{il} = L_t + Q_t + P_t + M_t + N_t \qquad (37)$$

Net of Tax Real Saving

In order to calculate the net of tax real saving to the company, the correct anticipated effective tax rate (T_t) must first be added to the formula. This variable may have a critical bearing on the desirability of the downsizing project. It must also be remembered that the tax rate may differ from one firm to another, and even from one year to another for the same firm.

The net of tax real saving in a given period (W_t), as related to the estimated cash flow, can then be calculated as follows:

$$W_t = (V_t - F_t)(1 - T_t) \tag{38}$$

Assuming that all the above variables have been calculated on an after-tax basis and in real inflation-adjusted terms, the value of the real post-tax rate of return on the downsizing project (R) can be calculated using the following equation:

$$Cd_1 - \sum_{z=0}^{n} \frac{W_t}{(1+R)^t} = 0 \tag{39}$$

where Cd_1 and W_t are derived from equations 34 and 38, respectively.

Once the estimated post-tax inflation-adjusted rate of return on the downsizing project (R) has been calculated, it can be compared with the known post-tax inflation-adjusted cost of capital to the firm (K). If $R > K$, then the rate of return on the downsizing project is greater than the cost of capital to the firm, that is, it will result in a positive return to the company.

Nevertheless, determining that $R > K$ does not necessarily mean that the project should be launched blindly without examining all the risks involved and carefully comparing this strategy with other investment options. Given a limited annual budget for capital investment, if $R > K$, the downsizing plan should be ranked according to its relative financial contribution to the firm, and should have to compete with other investment opportunities. Needless to say, if $K > R$, that is, the cost of capital exceeds the rate to return from the plan, the idea of downsizing should be abandoned.

Economic Utility of Training Programs – Birati and Tziner (1999)

Global competition, technological advances, demographic shifts, and diversity in the work place are all exerting increasing pressure on organizations to improve the skills of their work force. In economic terms, training represents a major outlay for American organizations (Noe, 1986; Carnevale, Gainer and Villet, 1990; Cascio, 1989, 1992), with an estimated annual cost of 100 billion dollars in 1996 (Saks, Haccoun and Laxer, 1996). However, only few studies have attempted to evaluate the effectiveness of training (i.e., the level of success of a training program) in a rigorous scientific manner (Tziner, Haccoun and Kadish, 1991; Tracey, Tannenbaum and Kavanagh, 1995).

Surprisingly enough, the investigations that do seek to determine training effectiveness rely heavily on employee responses (e.g., Tannenbaum and Yukl, 1992). However, as Tannenbaum and Yukl (1992) state, reactions can not serve as the sole criterion of effectiveness. Instead, as Kraiger, Ford and Salas (1993) suggest, learning may be evidenced by changes in cognitive, affective, and skill capacities, so that an examination of training effectiveness should target changes in all these areas.

Cognitive-based outcomes of the training process involve a meaningful change in: (1) the level of declarative knowledge; (2) the acquisition of meaningful structures for organizing knowledge; and (3) the development of superior cognitive strategies. Affect-based learning outcomes refer to changes in stated attitudes and motivation in the desired direction, such as the trainee recognizing the value of the acquired knowledge/skills, attraction toward the object of learning, increased self-efficacy, and/or willingness to exert effort in order to implement the acquired knowledge/skills (assuming these outcomes are attributable to the training process). Skill-based outcomes relate to the extent and automaticity with which trained skills, attitudes, and behaviors are exhibited after training. Thus, an evaluation conducted with respect to cognitive, affective, and skill-based outcomes is more likely to produce an accurate estimate of whether training objectives have been achieved (i.e., whether the training program has proved effective).

Instrumental as this approach may be to assessing the effectiveness of training, it still does not tackle the issue of their cost-effectiveness. Although there is a growing awareness of the importance of this consideration in promoting sound management of human resources, systematic cost-benefit studies of training programs are hard to find. This may very well be attributable to the lack of a sound conceptual and computational framework.

Although Cohen (1985) addresses this problem, his conceptual model and ensuing computational formula are, unfortunately, deficient. In fact, the model contains an incomplete measure of training cost-effectiveness, incorporating solely: (1) the productive value of employee training less earnings paid after training; (2) the cost of training; and (3) the length of time the trainee will continue working for the company after training is completed.

In addition, Cohen also ignores the following important considerations:

1 relative profitability, i.e., the return on the training project as compared with the cost of capital (money) to the employers. As the cost of resources may differ substantially from one firm to the next, the relative desirability of each training program must be matched with the cost of money to the investing firm. Thus, only projects whose rate of return exceeds the cost of money can be considered profitable, and should be further evaluated;
2 the tangible investment in training on the part of the employer, including the following potential inflows that may reduce the actual cost to the firm:
   i participation in the training costs by employees, not reflected in their future (reduced) remunerations;
   ii participation in the training costs by an external authority (local or federal government, unions, etc.);
   iii income tax considerations; while training costs are usually a tax deductible item, tax exempt firms, such as not-for-profit organizations or firms with accumulated tax losses, will not enjoy this benefit.

Furthermore, in terms of the employer's benefit, Cohen's formula ignores the following non-tangible variables which should also be analyzed, estimated, and quantified:

1 the *improvement* in the cognitive, affective and skill capacities of the trained employees after training, less the increase in the workers' remuneration resulting from training; Cohen merely equates benefit with the 'productive value of the worker after training';
2 the fact that employers known to invest in training may be more attractive to future potential recruitees than non-training employers;
3 the probable rise in morale in a training-oriented firm, as employees perceive such an employer to be committed to their career enhancement.

Another attempt to evaluate the cost-effectiveness of training programs was made by Mathieu and Leonard Jr (1987), who offer an advanced approach to the estimation of gains from training. However, while their study capitalizes the expected future cash flows from training, it does not compare the internal rate of return from training with the cost of capital to the firm. Likewise, as indicated below, it does not take into consideration the relative profitability of the investment in training as compared with the firm's other investment opportunities. These drawbacks are addressed by Birati and Tziner (1999). Before elaborating on their approach, let us first consider the principle behind it, that is, the notion of the capital budgeting procedure and its bearing on training cost-effectiveness.

The Application of Capital Budgeting to Training Programs

As mentioned above, training has long been recognized as a major cost factor for many firms, requiring substantial resources. This being the case, we might expect training to be treated like other investment plans and be incorporated into the capital budgeting process of the company. (Although admittedly the adoption of the capital budgeting procedure for the evaluation of investment in training should apply to most economic entities, including not-for profit organizations, Birati and Tziner deal only with profit-seeking firms.) Moreover, the evaluation of training projects should consider the special features related to investment in human capital, and include an in-depth investigation into the specific risk of investing in employees, as compared to other types of investments. For example, investment in other assets (whether tangible on non-tangible) involves the transfer of ownership to the acquiring firm with a relatively high degree of certainty that the firm will be able to utilize these assets for a predetermined number of years. A trained employee, on the other hand, might quit, so that the firm may lose some or all of its investment in his or her training. This sort of uncertainty must be carefully evaluated, and, insofar as possible, the expected loss should be deducted from the projected benefits of the training program.

In addition, the first requirement from any given potential investment according to capital budgeting procedures is that it produce a real post-tax rate of return that will exceed the real post-tax cost of capital to the firm at the time of the advanced stage of investment planning. Assuming that the firm is able to estimate its real post-tax cost of capital, measurement of the real post-tax rate of return on training programs is therefore the first step in evaluating their desirability.

To put this in the same formal terms we have used above, the principal requirement that must be satisfied before considering any investment decision (training included) is not merely the estimated post-tax real rate of return on the potential investment (R), but rather a comparison between the size of (R) and the estimated real post-tax cost of capital (K). The result should also satisfy the condition that R - K > 0, and not only in absolute terms, but also relative to the firm's other investment options.

Assuming that the firm knows the value of K, Birati and Tziner (1999) start their model with the estimation of (R).

Rate of Return on Training Programs

In order to evaluate the rate of return on training investments, it is advisable to estimate the cash outflows (for the investment) and cash inflows (benefits provided by the investment) associated with the potential projects.

Cash outflows (C) Cohen (1985) includes the following in employers' tangible cost of training:

1   training costs;
2   earning paid during training, less positive production during training (Table 1, p. 328).

Birati and Tziner denote Cohen's total factor (i.e., 1 + 2) by the letter (H). They then suggest that the computation also include the following deductions (where relevant):

1   any cash participation by employees that is not reflected in their reduced future wages (P);
2   training subsidies offered to the employers by local or central government and/or unions (E).

The authors further contend that another factor that should be considered in evaluating both the costs and benefits of training is the tax standing of the entity. This may have a crucial impact on the desirability of the planned investment. Effective income tax rates may differ by type of firm, by country, and by specific location (as the income tax rates of different states and cities in the U.S. are not identical). Furthermore, the tax standing for start-up firms and entities with accumulated tax losses will most certainly be lower than the rates imposed on profitable organizations. This factor may indeed be critical for the final decision of whether or not to implement a given project. Thus, assuming that the effective tax-rates may differ among firms, or even for the same firm in different years, (Tt) represents the effective income-tax rate for any particular firm in period (t).

It is also assumed that the net training costs (C), are made in cash at the initial stage of the program.

The after-tax cash outflow for the cost of training is therefore:

$$C = (H - P - E)(1 - Tt) \tag{40}$$

Cash inflows (B) Again referring to Cohen's (1985) formula, the following benefits accrue to the employer from training:

1 the productive value of the worker after training, less earnings paid after training;
2 the higher retention of workers in the company (Table 1, p. 328).

Birati and Tziner suggest that Cohen's 'productive value of the worker after training' does not represent the true benefit from training. For this variable, they suggest instead the economic value of the improvement in cognitive, affective, and skill-based capacities (Kraiger et al., 1993) as a result of training, less the increased salary in the future of the worker as a result of the newly-acquired capacities. Therefore, to estimate the potential future cash inflow from training (brought to present values), they propose including the following benefits:

1 the estimated economic value of the improvement in workers' capacities attributable to training, less the increased remuneration to the worker in each future period resulting from the training process (S_t);
2 as in Cohen's approach, the estimated cash savings from 'higher retention' (or lower voluntary turnover) of workers in firms that provide training programs (N_t);
3 the estimated cash saving from improved performance by non-trained employees resulting from improved morale in a training-oriented entity (M_t).

Thus the calculation of benefits from training procedures (B_t), that is, the estimated total annual real cash inflows resulting from a training program, would be:

$$B_t = (S_t + N_t + M_t)(1 - T_t) \tag{41}$$

where B_t is the present value of the cash inflow from the benefits in period t, and S_t, N_t, and M_t are the estimated future cash inflows resulting from improved performance, higher retention rate, and improved morale in period t, respectively.

Calculating the internal rate of return on training investments To arrive at the estimated rate of return on training investment, the authors start with the assumption that all the estimated variables were converted to their present value and are in real inflation-adjusted terms. (R) can then be calculated as follows:

$$Cd_1 - \sum_{t=0}^{n} \frac{B_t}{(1+R)^t} = 0 \tag{42}$$

where C and Bt are derived from equations (40) and (41), respectively, and t is the period of the benefits.

When to Approve a Training Program

Once the estimated internal rate of return on a proposed training program (R) is calculated, it can be compared to the known estimate of the cost of capital to the firm (K) to determine whether the project is profitable. If R > K, then the real post-tax return on the investment exceeds the real post-tax cost of capital, resulting in a net real profit to the entity.

If this requirement is met, the relative profitability of the training project should also be compared with all of the firm's other investment options, an important requirement in the capital budgeting process in general. As a matter of course, in any given period of time the total resources available to the firm for investment are limited. Thus, even profitable investment opportunities must be ranked according to their relative potential contribution to the goals of the entity. Only the highest ranked projects with acceptable operational risks should be approved, and this goes for training as well.

Conclusions and Avenues of Future Research

Human resource management research in organizations has advanced remarkably in recent decades. On the conceptual level, a wealth of well-grounded notions of how to effectively conduct activities such as recruitment, staffing, orientation and training, performance appraisal, and career management are now available. Conspicuously less, however, has been achieved with respect to conceiving economic approaches to account for the potential costs and benefits of human resource management activities and employee organizational behavior. The seminal works of researchers such as Boudreau and Cascio have laid the foundations for the developments that serve as the basis of this chapter.

The examples provided here of the use of the payoff utility approach in human resource management underscore the importance that companies should attach to quantitative approaches to decision making in this significant area of financial endeavor and corporate management. The economic success of a firm is contingent on careful planning, not only in the realms of production and marketing, but also in the selection (Cronshaw, 1986; Cronshaw and Alexander, 1991), maintenance, and training (Mathieu and Leonard, 1987) of a highly loyal and skilled work force whose size and performance ratings are compatible with the firm's short- and long-term financial strategies. The indiscriminate laying-off of workers, as we have seen, could lead to considerable direct and indirect dysfunctional consequences that may negatively affect production, incur losses in investment, and lead to substantial financial havoc. On the other hand, careful selection, development, and treatment of employees can result in enhanced efficiency, increased production, and consequent savings of a significant nature. These notions are particularly pertinent with respect to the core of highly placed specialists within the organization, whose loss or replacement may cause ripples far beyond the immediacy of their departure.

General accounting notions, approaches, and methods can be applied successfully to the assessment of economic consequences of this kind, as well as to a variety of additional organizational interventions and programs for the management of employee behaviors in the workplace, thus adding new perspectives and applications to traditional concepts, both theoretical and practical. The ability to evaluate estimated cash outflows and inflows provides planners with improved diagnostic tools with which to make decisions regarding the utility of their staffing projects, as well as enabling decision makers to choose sensibly from a number of available options. The careful application of accounting notions in the areas described above enhance the calculation of utility payoffs, in most cases attenuating previously inflated and biased estimations made on the basis of earlier versions of utility formulae. Moreover, it has repeatedly been stressed here that these revised utility estimates, computed using the latest quantitative procedures, must be considered within the context of a company's overall budgetary planning, in common with all other critical areas of a firm's functioning.

In relating to specific areas in the field of human management research, we have particularly emphasized the need to reexamine and revise many of the individual constructs used in earlier mathematical models designed to compute estimates of the utility of organizational interventions or the financial value of various employee behaviors in the workplace (e.g., organizational commitment, absenteeism, tardiness, turnover, job satisfaction, and organizational citizenship behavior). By incorporating economic variables into the earlier quantitative models and extending them to a variety of personnel programs, the amended versions of the utility formulae are, to cite Boudreau (1983), 'arguably more consistent with the economic nature of most organizations and more compatible with typical investment analyses' (p. 574). In particular, we have noted the importance of taking into consideration inflationary processes over time and of computing the current real value of the future activities that are incorporated into these equations.

Furthermore, in line with Boudreau (1983), we have cautioned managers employing quantitative formulae to also give due consideration to tax rates operating within the company's accounting systems in order to ensure that the calculations reflect an honest and unbiased estimate of current and future financial costs and monetary inflow. Ultimately, these intricate calculations promote the efforts of those whose job it is to determine the steps to be taken to enhance efficacy in a profit-seeking entity. In other words, human resource management decisions play a contributory and critical role in advancing the wealth of the shareholders, without whom the firm could not function.

The 'economic nature' of organizations in today's competitive global environment is no longer the exclusive province of the chief executive officer. As a result of the growing financial pressures on firms, it is becoming increasingly important for human resource managers, who are usually more comfortable with people than with balance sheets, to understand and focus upon key business imperatives as well. To cite Berra and Whitford (1995): 'Today's human resource managers must speak the language of their firm's line managers. ... They must understand the key concepts that security analysts focus upon, the factors that will determine value enhancement in security markets' (p. 83).

The CEO's priority is the firm's shareholders. CEOs are interested in the public perception of the company's management team as reflected in an evaluation of stock prices (where relevant) and daily trading volumes. They are concerned with the state of the firm's cash flow today, and how the stockholders can be rewarded and persuaded to invest further in the company tomorrow. Strategic success thus imposes on every member of the management team the need to appreciate various organizational duties and responsibilities, and their impact on corporate cash flow and long-run economic viability (Berra and Whitford, 1995, p. 90). Moreover, CEOs increasingly want their HR managers to contribute significantly to the firm's strategic decisions. However, for HR executives to achieve this goal and impact their organizations in a significant manner, 'they must understand what drives the business and therefore dominates the focus of the CEO' (Overman, 1991).

The significance of this new understanding cannot be underestimated. Berra and Whitford (1995) note that a company that recently released 4,000 workers was willing to pay out $369.6 million in order to 'acquire' an early-out restructuring (downsizing operation) that had an attractive after-tax net financial value. The authors show that the aggregate value of this firm's stock could have been expected to increase by slightly over $2 billion. In practice, the actual change in market value was $1.024 billion, reflecting a 'rational' reaction that manifested itself in a 7 percent increase in the firm's stock price (Berra and Whitford, 1995, pp. 96–8).

Improved utility models provide a more precise definition of economic utility which can facilitate the closer liaison between psychologists and cost accountants (Cascio and Silbey, 1979; Boudreau, 1983). Future research will no doubt elicit more areas in which this meeting of disciplines can take place. Further matching of accounting procedures to the decision-making processes involved in human resource management will almost certainly lead to additional refinement of the mathematical constructs and formulae, as new and uncharted variables are explored and found to impinge on various employee behaviors or managerial interventions. These include direct and indirect costs that reflect a diverse range of consequences and constraints among companies whose economic circumstances, investment strategies, and tax status vary in time and place.

One of the refinements of the revised quantitative models that we can, hopefully, look forward to relates to the nature of the variables which measure the behavior of employees in the workplace. In general, for the moment these tend to be instrumental in character, that is, the behavioral concomitants are directly measurable, allowing their financial value to be quantified relatively easily in financial terms. For example, the financial loss to a company of a particular worker's absence over a given period of time can be estimated with reasonable accuracy. However, cognitive or affective variables (e.g., attitudes

364 Human Resource Management

to the workplace, feelings of insecurity, lowered self-esteem), which essentially underlie a host of employee behaviors, have an indirect relationship with these instrumental variables, the causal nature of which is often unclear. These underlying aspects of worker behavior need to be defined more carefully, operationalized, and incorporated into the quantitative utility models for human resource management. An initial step in this direction would be their mathematical 'quantification' based on a sound theoretical analysis of the specific behaviors in the workplace, as can be found in the literature.

While the research and quantitative approaches outlined in this chapter illustrate the benefits of applying mathematical approaches to the assessment of the financial value of organizational behaviors and HRM programs and interventions, there is clearly a need for more research in the field to provide empirical support for the notions advanced here. To this end, research in all seven areas investigated by the authors should be accelerated, while data from corporations that have employed these techniques should be collected and analyzed. In other words, the research needs to move from the purely theoretical level to the realm of industry, which stands to reap substantial rewards from adopting this utility approach to their HRM endeavors.

Moreover, a comprehensive review of the field of human resource management (see, for example: Cascio, 1989) indicates that research in this area is still in its infancy. There remain many untapped areas of HRM, pertaining to management style, supervision, work environments, quality of life in the workplace, incentives, and labor relations, to name just a few. These issues await the fruits of research and the application of utility methods, along with the financial benefits to be gained from the link between HRM theory and economics.

Utility estimates of the economic worth of employee organizational behavior and of human resource management intervention methods and procedures is an accounting approach whose time has come. The quantitative model reflects a more complete and realistic description of the effect of personnel programs and employee behavior in companies, which are increasingly fighting for survival as global competition intensifies. As theoretical definitions of utility are extended, new areas of application are explored, and the general utility model is revised and extended, there can be no doubt that utility estimates of human resource management procedures will become an accepted and conventional tool in corporate management, and this is likely to happen in the foreseeable future.

References

Balutis, A.P. (1996). 'Getting Thin the Healthy Way'. *Government Executive*, 28, pp. 45–48.

Berra, R.L. and Whitford, D.T. (1995). 'Analytical Financial Tools and Human Resource Management'. In G.R. Ferris, S.D. Rosen and D.T. Barnum (eds), *Handbook of Human Resource Management,* Oxford : Blackwell, pp. 83–99.

Birati, A. and Tziner, A. (1990). 'A Note on the Estimation of Economic Utility of Personnel Programs'. *Man and Work*, 22, pp. 44–52.

Birati, A. and Tziner, A. (1995). 'Successful Promotion of Early Retirement: A Quantitative Approach'. *Human Resource Management Review*, 5, pp. 53–62.

Birati, A. and Tziner, A. (1996). 'Withdrawal Behavior and Withholding Efforts at Work (WBWEW): Assessing the Financial Cost'. *Human Resource Management Review*, 6, pp. 305–14.

Birati, A. and Tziner, A. (1999). 'Economic Utility of Training Programs'. *Journal of Business and Psychology*, 14, pp. 155–64.

Boudreau, J.W. (1983). 'Economic Considerations in Estimating the Utility of Human Resource Productivity Improvement Programs'. *Personnel Psychology*, 36, pp. 551–76.

Brogden, H.E. (1946). 'On the Interpretation of the Correlation Coefficient as Measure of Predictive Validity'. *Journal of Educational Psychology*, 37, pp. 64–76.

Brogden, H.E. and Taylor, E.K. (1950). 'The Dollar Criterion: Applying the Cost Accounting Concept to Criterion Construction'. *Personnel Psychology*, 3, pp. 133–54.

Bruton, G.D., Keels, K.J. and Shook, C.L. (1996). 'Downsizing the Firm: Answering the Strategic Questions'. *The Academy of Management Executive*, 10, pp. 38–45.

Burke, M.J. and Frederick, J.T. (1986). 'A Comparison of Economic Utility Estimates for SDy Estimation Procedures'. *Journal of Applied Psychology*, 71, pp. 334–9.

Caplan, G. and Teese, M. (1997). *Survivors: How to Keep Your Best People on Board After Downsizing.* Palo Alto, CA.: Davies-Black.

Carnevale, A.P., Gainer, L.J. and Villet, J. (1990). *Training in America: The Organization and Strategic Role of Training.* San Francisco: Jossey-Bass.

Cascio, W. F. (1982). *Applied Psychology in Personnel Management,* 2nd edn, Reston, VA: Reston.

Cascio, W.F. (1989). 'Using Utility Analysis to Assess Training Outcomes'. In I.L. Goldstein (ed.), *Training and Development in Organizations*, San Francisco: Jossey-Bass, pp. 63–88.

Cascio, W.F. (1991). *Costing Human Resources: The Financial Impact of Behavior in Organizations*, 3rd edn, Boston, MA: Kent.

Cascio, W.F. (1993). 'Downsizing : What Do We Know? What Have We Learned?' *The Executive*, 7, pp. 95–104.

Cascio, W.F. and Ramos, R.A. (1986). 'Development and Application of a New Method for Assessing Job Performance in Behavioral/Economic Terms'. *Journal of Applied Psychology*, 71, pp. 20–28.

Cascio, W.F. and Silbey, V. (1979). 'Utility of the Assessment Center as a Selection Device'. *Journal of Applied Psychology*, 64, pp. 107–18.

Cascio, W.F., Young, E.Y. and Morris, J.R. (1997). 'Financial Consequences of Employment-change Decisions in Major U. S. Corporations'. *The Academy of Management Journal*, 40, pp. 1175–89.

Cohen, S.I. (1985). 'A Cost-Benefit Analysis of Industrial Training'. *Economics of Education Review*, 4, pp. 327–39.

Cronbach, L.J. and Glezer, G.C. (1965). *Psychological Testing and Personnel Decisions*, 2nd edn, Urbana: University of Illinois Press.

Cronshaw, S.F. (1986). 'The Utility of Employment Testing for Clerical/Administrative Trades in the Canadian Military'. *Canadian Journal of Administrative Sciences*, 3, pp. 376–85.

Cronshaw, S.F. and Alexander, R.A. (1991). 'Why Capital Budgeting Techniques are Suited for Assessing the Utility of Personnel Programs: A Reply to Hunter, Schmidt, and Coggin (1988)'. *Journal of Management Studies*, 19, pp. 395–412.

Evans, M., Gunz, H.P. and Jalland, R.M. (1997). 'Implications of Organizational Downsizing for Managerial Careers'. *Canadian Journal of Administrative Sciences*, 14, pp. 359–71.

Feldman, D.C. (1995). 'The Impact of Downsizing on Organizational Career Development Opportunities'. *Human Resource Management Review*, 5, pp. 189–222.

Franks, J.G. and Mayer, C. (1996). 'Hostile Takeovers and the Correction of Managerial Failure'. *Journal of Financial Economics*, 40, pp. 163–81.

Gupta, N. and Jenkins, G.D. Jr (1982). 'Absenteeism and Turnover: Is there a progression?'. *Journal of Management Studies*, 19, pp. 395–412.

Hastings, D.F. (1996). 'Guaranteed Employment: A Practical Solution for Today's Corporations'. *Vital Speeches of the Day (VSP)*, 12, pp. 691–3.

Hunter, J.E. and Schmidt, F.L. (1982). 'Fitting people to jobs: The Impact of Personnel Selection on National Productivity'. In M.D. Dunnette and E.O. Fleishman (eds), *Human Performance and Productivity*, Vol. 1, Hillsdale, NJ: Erlbaum.

Kerr, A.L. (1983). 'Motivation Losses in Small Groups: A Social Dilemma Analysis'. *Journal of Personality and Social Psychology*, 45, pp. 819–828.

Kindwell, R.E. and Bennett, N. (1993). 'Employee Propensity to Withhold Efforts: A Conceptual Model to Intersect Three Avenues of Research'. *Academy of Management Review*, 18, pp. 429–56.

Koslowsky, M., Sagie, A., Krauz, M. and Dolman, A. (1997). 'Correlates of Employee Lateness: Some Theoretical Considerations'. *Journal of Applied Psychology*, 17, pp. 81–91.

Kraiger, K., Ford, J.K. and Salas, E. (1993). 'Application of Cognitive, Skill-based and Affective Theories of Learning Outcomes to New Methods of Training Evaluation'. *Journal of Applied Psychology*, 78, pp. 311–28.

Landy, F.J., Farr, J.L. and Jacobs, R.R. (1982). 'Utility Concepts in Performance Measurement'. *Organizational Behavior and Human Performance*, 30, pp. 15–40.

Lascio, W.F. (1992). *Managing Human Resources: Productivity, Quality of Work and Profits*. New York: McGraw-Hill.

Mathieu, J.E. and Leonard, R.L. Jr (1987). 'Applying Utility Concepts to a Training Program in Supervisory Skills: A Time-based Approach'. *Academy of Management Journal*, 30, pp. 316–335.

Meisenheimer, J.R. II (1990). 'Employee Absences in 1989: A New Look at Data From CPS'. *Monthly Labor Review*, August, pp. 28–33.

Meyer, J.P. and Allen, N.J. (1991). 'A Three-component Conceptualization of Organizational Commitment'. *Human Resource Management Review*, 1, pp. 61–89.

Mirta, A., Jenkins, G.D. and Gupta, N. (1992). 'A Meta-analytic Review of the Relationship Between Absences and Turnover'. *Journal of Applied Psychology*, 77, pp. 879–89.

Mroczkowski, T. and Hanaoka, M. (1997). 'Effective Rightsizing Strategies in Japan and America: Is There a Convergence of Employment Practices?'. *The Academy of Management Executive*, 11, pp. 57–67.

Nadler, D.A. and Tushman, M.L. (1997). *Competing by Design*. New York: Oxford University.

Noe, R.A. (1986). 'Trainees' Attributes: Neglected Influences on Training Effectiveness'. *Academy of Management Review*, 11, pp. 736–49.

Overman, S. (1991). 'What Does the CEO Want?'. *Human Resource Magazine*, 36, pp. 41–3.

Peak, M.H. (1997). 'Cutting Jobs? Watch Your Disability Expenses Grow'. *Management Review*, 86, p. 9.

Saks, A.M., Haccoun, R. and Laxer, D. (1996). 'Transfer Training: A Comparison of Self-management and Relapse Prevention/Interventions'. *Administrative Science Association of Canada (ASAC) Proceedings*.

Schmidt, F.L., Hunter, J.E., McKenzie, R.C. and Muldrow, T.W. (1979). 'Impact of Valid Selection Procedures on Workforce Productivity'. *Journal of Applied Psychology*, 64, pp. 609–26.

Schmidt, F.L., Hunter, J.E. and Pearlman, K. (1982). 'Assessing the Economic Impact of Personnel Programs in Workforce Productivity'. *Personnel Psychology*, 35, pp. 333–47.

Steffy, B.D. and Maurer, S.D. (1988). 'Conceptualizing and Measuring the Economic Effectiveness of Human Resource Activities'. *The Academy of Management Review*, 13, pp. 271–86.

Tannenbaum, S.I. and Yukl, G. (1992). 'Training and Development in Work Organizations'. *Annual Review of Psychology*, 43, pp. 399–441.

Tracey, J.B., Tannenbaum, S.I. and Kavanagh, M.J. (1995). 'Applying Trained Skills on the Job: The Importance of the Work Environment'. *Journal of Applied Psychology*, 80, pp. 239–52.

Tziner, A. (1990). *Organization Staffing and Word Adjustment*. New York: Praeger.

Tziner, A. and Birati, A. (1996). 'Assessing Employee Turnover Costs: A Revised Approach'. *Human Resource Management Review*, 6, pp. 113–22.

Tziner, A., Haccoun, R.R. and Kadish, A. (1991). 'Personal and Situational Characteristics Influencing the Effectiveness of Transfer of Training Improvement Strategies'. *Journal of Occupational Psychology*, 64, pp. 167–77.

Tziner, A. and Meir, E.I. (1997). 'Work Adjustment: Extension of the Theoretical Framework'. *International Review of Industrial and Organizational Psychology*, 12, pp. 95–114.

Tziner, A., Meir, E.I., Dahan, M. and Birati, A. (1994). 'An Investigation of the Predictive and Economic Utility of the Assessment Center for High-management Level'. *Canadian Journal for Behavioral Sciences*, 26, pp. 228–45.

Tziner, A. and Vardi, Y. (1984). 'Work Satisfaction and Absenteeism Among Social Workers'. *Work and Occupations*, 11, pp. 461–70.

Welsch, C.A., Newman, D.P. and Zlatkovich, C.T. (1986). *Intermediate Accounting*, 7th edn, Urbana, IL.: Irwin.

Final Remarks: Toward a Synthesis of HRM and OBM

We have seen repeatedly throughout this volume that numerous researchers maintain that considerable economic returns can be obtained through effective human resource management practices. This is particularly true at a time when organizations must operate in an extremely competitive global market. Most recently, a striking empirical demonstration of this contention reported that for each standard deviation of improvement in the practices of employee management in 706 companies, there was a concomitant increase of 14 per cent in the company's market value premium! Another study found an impressive decrease in turnover rate, as well as an increase in profitability, which could be attributed to the implementation of management practices that ascribe central importance to employees. These and similar investigations discussed in the preceding chapters strongly suggest that management practices which foster positive work attitudes, such as high organizational commitment and organizational citizenship behavior, contribute to the enhanced financial performance of a firm.

Seven themes have been treated here, most of them related to employee behaviors. The main conclusion to be drawn is that organizations serious about obtaining financial advantages through their employees should expand their human resource efforts in several areas concurrently. To ensure that they hire the right people and achieve long-term optimal gains from these employees for the overall benefit of the company, human resource personnel need to tackle a number of issues that together constitute an entire process. This process commences with the assessment of potential candidates, and culminates with the assessment of employee attitudes and performance and the decision-making process at the managerial level that emerges from this evaluation. Improvements in any one area of human resource functioning alone will be insufficient to maximize the gains that can be derived from this area of organizational activity. Only an approach which incorporates and applies the range of conclusions that can be drawn from theoretical and empirical research in the areas of both Human Resource Management and Organizational Behavior Management can lead to the optimization of the search for increased productivity at the human resource level.

Each of the seven areas discussed in the preceding chapters therefore represents part of an overall endeavor. To recap, the issues addressed were as follows.

Chapter 1 contains an updated critical review of the most frequently used tools and methods for hiring the best-suited individuals. 'Best-suited' here implies that they have the skills, aptitudes, and personality attributes essential to perform the job successfully, and also possess work values and attitudes congruent with the company's culture and values. A great deal of research reveals that both functional congruence (adequacy to job performance requirements) and contextual factors (e.g., values/culture) account for adjustment to work in organizations. Following the theoretical discussion, this chapter also recommends procedures to help in reaping the maximal benefits from these staffing tools and methodologies.

Chapter 2 demonstrates that work interests also play a decisive role in determining successful adjustment to work. Indeed, congruency between individual work interests and organization-job rewards and reinforcements has repeatedly been shown to affect behavior, attitudes, and performance on the job. The chapter offers the reader both an innovative conceptualization of interests, and a recommendation for how to assess applicants' work interests accurately that is well-grounded in empirical research.

No matter how effective the staffing process is in targeting potential workers whose initial adjustment and well-being in the workplace is optimal, the employee's state of mind may change over time. Both individuals and organizations fluctuate: different factors may affect work adjustment at different stages in an employee's career; an individual's work interests may shift; competencies may decay as work demands change; and there may be modifications in the organizational structure and culture. Chapter 3, devoted to the essence and outcomes of work adjustment, is novel in conceiving a broad theoretical framework of successful adjustment that reflects these fluctuations in the workplace. The synthesis of Holland's Congruence theory and Lofquist and Dawis' Work Adjustment theory, described in this chapter, makes it possible to conceptualize work adjustment dynamically and comprehensively. It is now clear that the degree of well-being felt by an individual in the workplace may be reflected in a wide array of outcomes, such as work satisfaction, absenteeism, psychological strains, organizational citizenship, and job performance. The chapter also identifies the various mediating factors at work in the process (e.g. organizational commitment, job involvement, withdrawal cognitions), thereby contributing to a clearer understanding of the nature of work adjustment. The resulting integrated model offers a conceptual framework with a greater potential for predicting and detecting changes in work adjustment, as well as indicating possible means for reinstating it.

With an increasing number of organizations structuring their workload by teams, adequate fit into a work team also contributes to successful adjustment to work. Chapter 4 discusses several attributes of work team composition, such as the effect of members' personalities and abilities on outcomes including intragroup processes, team effectiveness, and productivity. The main contribution of this chapter is in elaborating how an entire gamut of individual task-related attributes combine to influence intragroup processes, which in turn affect team effectiveness. An understanding of these dynamics allows organizations to design teams in such a way as to maximize the benefits that can be derived from them.

It is a well-known fact that monetary payment acts as a forceful inducement for the enhancement of job performance. However, salary scales must be designed so that compensation is perceived as both just and competitive. Chapter 5 presents a critical review of various methods of devising remuneration scales to ensure that employees receive comparable monetary compensation for work of comparable worth. This is where job evaluation comes into play, as it is the *only* impartial device for maximizing the fairness of payroll policy. The chapter recommends several amendments to existing methods of job evaluation, and advances a relatively new model based on the facet approach.

Nevertheless, individuals are not motivated solely by the regular salary they receive for fulfilling normal work requirements. Other incentives for excelling at work may also be available. One of the major tools that enable supervisors and managers to allocate these incentives properly is the performance appraisal (PA) process. Chapter 6 is devoted to a discussion of this dynamic process and its effects on work behavior. The advantages and disadvantages of the various methods of PA are outlined here, and theoretical and practical amendments are suggested, along with strategies for overcoming the impediments to accurate performance ratings. Of particular interest in this chapter is a detailed discussion of a cumulative series of recent studies conducted by the author regarding the proximal and distal factors impinging on raters, which account for their deliberate manipulation of performance ratings.

Finally, Chapter 7 tackles a very timely issue. With organizations operating in an era of fierce rivalry and global competition, cost effectiveness has become the magic word. This concern cannot be ignored in the context of the management of human behavior in organizations. Chapter 7 illustrates the benefits of applying mathematical approaches to estimation of the financial value of a number of worker behaviors (e.g., absenteeism, turnover, withdrawing efforts at work) and human resource-related programs (e.g., training, staffing, downsizing).

In short, then, seven major areas related to the human aspect of organizational functioning are addressed in this book in an attempt to create a coherent framework which combines elements from the two disciplines of Human Resource Management and Organizational Behavior Management. The chapters relating to each of these areas offer critical reviews of existing research and practice, revisions of theoretical paradigms, suggestions for practical strategies, and directions for future research.

While this volume describes research spanning half a century, it also primarily reflects the work of one individual whose studies in the field in various cultural settings have contributed to a comprehensive view of human behavior and human resource management in the workplace. By sharing my insights, I trust that I have not only stimulated interest, but will also have stirred current and potential practitioners of human resource management to adopt a discerning, optimistic, and integrative view of the field as a whole. As we enter a new millennium, it is fitting to wish that the benefits of this book reach beyond the immediacy of the individual reader. One can but hope that the conclusions drawn will be internalized by those who occupy the board rooms of national corporations, and who are striving to improve workers' well-being and productivity in a fast-moving, technology-based, and competitive marketplace.

Index